Shakespearean Tragedy and Its Double

Shakespearean

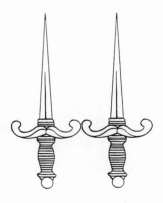

Tragedy and Its Double:

The Rhythms
of Audience Response

Kent Cartwright

The Pennsylvania State University Press
University Park, Pennsylvania

Library of Congress Cataloging-in-Publication Data

Cartwright, Kent, 1943–
    Shakespearean tragedy and its double: the rhythms of audience
response / by Kent Cartwright.
        p.   cm.
    Includes bibliographical references and index.
    ISBN 0-271-00738-9
    1. Shakespeare, William, 1564–1616—Tragedies. 2. Shakespeare,
William, 1564–1616—Dramatic production. 3. Theater audiences.
4. Tragedy. I. Title.
PR2983.C37 1991
822.3'3—dc20   90-45895
                                                                   CIP

It is the policy of The Pennsylvania State University Press to use acid-free paper for the
first printing of all clothbound books. Publications on uncoated stock satisfy the minimum
requirements of American National Standard for Information Sciences—Permanence of Paper
for Printed Library Materials, ANSI Z39.48-1984.

To
Robert Ornstein

Contents

Preface

Shakespearean Tragedy and Its Double applies the concept of spectatorial (or "aesthetic") distance to Shakespearean tragedy. I hope my title might suggest both a Bradleyan attention to the details of the tragic world and an Artaudian concern for the effect of performance upon an audience. The book examines how plays invite a rhythm of "engaged" and "detached" responses from the audience: how, for example, tragedy makes use of the spectators' detachment from character or action and their engagement with acting or theatricality. I view "engagement" as the audience's surrender of self-awareness through empathy, sympathy, or identification; detachment as the audience's sense of its autonomy, experienced as doubt, evaluation, mediated emotion. If the essence of dramatic action is conflict, then the essence of the audience's experience may be the conflict or tension between its various engagements and detachments.

Throughout, I am interested not so much in the development of tragic protagonists as the development of the audience. My approach is phenomeno-logical and modernist. I argue that the audience's sense of fiction and illusion, of blatant and even joyous theatricality, helps shape the effect of the dramatic action. Hence, my discussion will often attend to instances of detachment from character or events, that, surprisingly, may forward the unfolding of the play. A tragedy's overall movement in spectatorial distance—generally, from engagement through detachment to a heightened balancing of the two—confers upon spectators an empowering sense of openness and possibility (wonder) in the tragic moment. The workings of "distance" may thus provide a structure or paradigm for a spectatorial poetics of Shakespearean tragedy.

In the first chapter, I suggest that the audience's distance in *Romeo and Juliet* works as a caution against the tragedy's overt insistence upon the inevitability or necessity of its action. In the second chapter, dealing with *Hamlet,* I describe the audience's movement through a groundplan of positional identification, decontextualization, and finally wonder, offering a model for the spectator's engagements and detachments toward a tragic hero. Chapter 3 treats the divided spirit of *Othello* —the quality that yields both heroic (engaged) and antiheroic (detached) views of its protagonist—as expressed in the alternating rhythms of several key scenes. In chapter 4, I explore how *King Lear's* secondary characters constitute "response regulators," releasing, altering, and complicating the spectator's intense and painful emotional development. Chapter 5, on *Antony and Cleopatra,* concludes the book by arguing that spectatorship, reciprocally with acting, constitutes the unifying action of the tragedy. In such ways, I examine how a tragedy marshals the audience's engagement and detachment: in relation to theatricality itself, protagonist, scenic structure, secondary characters, and action. Through all these discussions, I attend variously to the problems of acting and the kinesthetics of spectatorship. As I shall argue, rhythms of spectatorial distance inhere in Shakespeare's tragedies, helping to create their meaning and significance.

I am indebted to a vast number of my colleagues for advice and encouragement. Through these individuals *Shakespearean Tragedy and Its Double* became real and authentic to me. In the early period of writing this book I was privileged to participate in a 1987 summer seminar, offered by the Folger Shakespeare Library—that Platonic dream of a library—and led by Michael Goldman. The seminar stimulated enormously my thinking about a performance-oriented criticism of Shakespeare, and my debt to Professor Goldman and his brilliant seminarians vastly exceeds my meager thanks, which I offer now. John Fuegi read my first, inchoate mutterings on this project and encouraged me anyway. A number of colleagues reviewed my prospectus and offered helpful comments, among them Leeds Barroll, Lars Engle, Michael Goldman, Margaret Knapp, and Barbara Mowat. Others have generously provided suggestions on individual chapters, including Howard Dobin, James Siemon, Jeanne Roberts, Susan Snyder, Brenda Szittya, Theodore Leinwand, and Laurie Osborne. My Shakespeare colleagues at the University of Maryland reviewed my introduction, and I have profited from their suggestions. Several other individuals have contributed heroically to this book. Kathleen Campbell has read many of its chapters, and her frequent conversations with me have been an inexhaustible source of stimulation. Ralph Alan Cohen has likewise commented helpfully on several of these chapters and has shared his ideas about staging Shakespeare with me again and again. Bernice Kliman offered detailed suggestions for various chapters, with a humbling energy and commitment. Nancy Maguire's tenacious stand for clarity has brought light to many a dark paragraph over several chapters. Maynard Mack, Jr., read the entire manuscript (some of it more than once) and improved the book with his acute good sense; my debt there almost matches my debt for his moral support. Likewise, Gary Taylor generously read the complete manuscript and offered helpful comments page after page. To all these, my heartfelt thanks. Authorship is indeed a communal phenomenon! The Folger Shakespeare Library has provided the hospitable environment for inspiration and research in which most of this book was written. I am indebted beyond measure to its resources and excellent staff. The University of Maryland also allowed me the leave time that enabled me to draft a large share of the book. Lastly I extend my appreciation to several others outside my profession whose support brought this book to reality: Linda Dusman, Thomas Moore, Caryn Rosenberg, and most of all my wife, Pam.

A section of Chapter 3: Scenic Rhythms in *Othello* appears in altered form as "Audience Response and the Denouement of *Othello*" in Othello: *New Perspectives,* edited by Virginia Mason Vaughan and Kent Cartwright (Rutherford, N.J.: Fairleigh Dickinson University Press, 1991).

Introduction:
Spectatorial Distance
in Shakespearean Tragedy

Audience members at a play will often, for a moment, shift their attention from character to performer. Shakespearean tragedy can systematically appropriate this detachment from the fictional persona and engagement with the actor so as to heighten the emotional power and complicate the meaning of the play. The tragedies, for example, sometimes showcase "playing dead" as an acting problem, one reshaping the mix of engagement and detachment, sympathy and judgment, that audiences feel toward the finale. The death of Desdemona, as one fascinating instance, achieves part of its harrowing effect from the spectator's unexpected doubt about distinguishing the fictional persona from the actor. What we know about the limitations of acting confuses what we think we know about the character.

Following his murder of Desdemona, Othello's focus darts away from and then back to her body four distinct times, wrenching the spectator's gaze and feelings with him. The breaks in the audience's attention intensify its anxiety for her: Is she or is she not dead? First, as Othello "smothers" or "stifles" her[1]—traditionally with a pillow—Emilia interrupts him (and us), pounding at the door. Othello reconnects the audience's gaze to Desdemona, scrutinizing

1. These alternate stage directions are from the First Folio (1623) and First Quarto (1622) texts, respectively.

her for signs of life, "Not dead? not yet quite dead?" (*Othello,* V.ii.86)[2] —possibly she has moved—and he kills her a second time, "So, so" (89). Then once more our attention flashes back to the door as Emilia calls and knocks again and yet again (89–90). But Othello's chopped responses pull us back to Desdemona's body: "Yes.— 'Tis Emilia.—By and by.—She's dead" (91). For a third time his mind returns to Emilia.—"'Tis like she comes to speak of Cassio's death; / The noise was high" (92–93)—but swings again to Desdemona as he suddenly thinks he sees something: "Hah, no more moving? / Still as the grave" (93–94). That question invites the Othello-actor to pause at the endline while he studies her body for signs of life, or perhaps makes a gesture like Olivier's when he rolls Desdemona's limp head from side to side. Finally, for the fourth time, Othello's attention reverts to Emilia (likely still pounding), but breaks focus sharply back to the body, with the same doubt and pause for observation: "Shall she come in? Were't good? / I think she stirs again. No. What's best to do?" (94–95). His delayed reaction, because of this suspended indecision, drives home the shocking realization: "I have no wife. / O insupportable! O heavy hour!" (97–98).

The text calls the spectator's attention to the Desdemona-performer's *acting* of death as a crucial part of the scene. Even without Othello's focus, spectators would scrutinize Desdemona, as they do any actor playing dead, for signs of life, the rhythm of breath, the barely perceptible movement. But the scene's structure (Emilia's interruptions, Othello's repeated doubts) insists, to the spectator, on the possibility that Desdemona lives, an agonizing uncertainty. That possibility mounts with the local problems of playing dead. Should the boy-actor or actress stir each time Othello thinks Desdemona moves and then lie still as he investigates? Should the performer try throughout to remain as impassive as stone, suggesting that Othello's mind hallucinates? Should Desdemona move the first or second of the four times he doubts but not thereafter? If the performer shifts or twitches, then the audience will become deeply engaged with the possibility that the character survives, exacerbating the fear and hope for Desdemona that the murder scene has notoriously prompted in audiences. Yet if the Desdemona-performer does not stir, the audience will still hang in doubt, for most actors or actresses will betray some signs of life, of breath, no matter how faint. In either case, conceivably, the audience will be left *unable* to tell the acting from the narrative, the truth of

2. References to Shakespeare's plays, except where otherwise noted, are to G. Blakemore Evans, ed., *The Riverside Shakespeare* (Boston: Houghton Mifflin, 1974). For ease of reading and for avoiding some confusions, I have eliminated the brackets Evans uses to note deviations from the copy text.

the performer from the truth of the character. Acting will have become indistinguishable from action.

That spectatorial tension, the insolvable unknowingness forced upon the audience, explains part of the power of the murder. The playgoer continues unresolved toward Desdemona's death, unable to feel the relief of sorrow or the satisfaction that comes from completing a long anticipated action. And despite Othello's self-assurances, of course, Desdemona has not died yet. Moments later she will call out, utterly confirming our anxiety. That pattern might offer one explanation for why audiences to *Othello* have historically made "extra-theatrical" responses to the play: anger, outrage, shouting, the desire to interrupt. The play itself provokes such responses. When an audience engages with acting, it (typically) detaches to some degree from an identification with character; in such ways, audiences maintain their equanimity in a tragedy, their certainty that the play is only a play, and their pleasure in its execution. Desdemona's murder briefly destabilizes, terrorizes, our normal habits of engagement and detachment. That Desdemona really might have lived hints, indeed, at a vast aleatory randomness at the heart of this tragedy.

I

Shakespeare's tragedies shape meaning by orchestrating spectatorial engagement and detachment, as when playgoers lose themselves in unfolding events, or withdraw their identification with a character, or become charmed by a piece of acting, or recognize with particular keenness the theatrical event itself. The theatrics of "playing dead" illustrate in miniature the rhythm of engagement and detachment that characterizes spectatorship in the tragedies. While the development of the hero culminates in death at the play's end, witnessing the acting of death marks a transition in the development of the playgoer. Playing dead constitutes one of the few challenges in acting (fainting and madness are two others) where the performer must always pretend and not "be." As beholders, we watch with fascination how actors present death: Will we see them breathing? Will they go completely limp? Will they hold still? (No performer can create full verisimilitude; a living body, for example, cannot physically collapse so rapidly or so completely as an inert body, no matter how well trained the actor.) Rather than diverting our focus from this difficult imitating, Shakespeare can fasten the audience's attention, sometimes repeatedly, on acting dead: He forces spectators to wonder if a character really is dead; he brings the presumed dead back to life; he points at the death-likeness, or lack of it, in an actor's representation. Shakespeare, typical to his genius, makes the actor's difficulty in playing dead serve the spectatorial experience of the narrative.[3] The exposure of artificiality actually confirms the drama.

Hamlet shows death in its violence and suddenness, like so many changes of mood, tempo, and condition in that tragedy. Actors die on stage by collapsing from a standing position: stabbed, poisoned, or both. Death is the last of the "thousand natural shocks / That flesh is heir to" (III.i.61–62). Hamlet will "lug" Polonius's "guts" away (III.iv.212), emphasizing death's grotesque reductiveness. Ironically, audiences will often confront a partially or wholly revealed Polonius-actor forced to play dead through almost 200 lines of the closet scene. The clumsy and indecorous maneuvering of the body implied in "lug" graphs Hamlet's own forgetting of the dead, whose remembrance has been his sorrow. An elegy to Burbage (1619) hints at the spectatorial electricity of death in *Hamlet* as it recalls how the great tragedian could deceive the play's audience and even his fellow actors with his "lifelike" acting dead: "oft have I seene him, play this part in jeast, / soe livly, that Spectators, and the rest / of his sad Crew, whilst he but seem'd to bleed, / amazed, thought even then hee dyed in deed."[4] (The memorability of that moment suggests how much the audience needs, simultaneously, the pleasure of realistic acting of death and the awareness of stage illusion.) In one theatrical tradition, Hamlet falls dead into Claudius's chair as if sitting down (as with Richard Burton's Prince), allowing the hero's body to look royally put on and uncannily alive—a haunting stage icon in this play of memory. Our conditioning to the violent, dehumanizing finality of death makes Hamlet's life-imitating expiration the moment of poignant "recognition" of all the lost, fair expectancy of Denmark. Rather different, the Coriolanus-actor, in a violent death with a less heartrending effect, must demonstrate as much physical strength in playing dead as the Coriolanus-character has in brutalizing others, pursuant to the Folio's curious stage direction: "Draw the Conspirators, and kills Martius, who falls; Aufidius stands on him" (*Coriolanus,* at V.vi.130). Coriolanus's armour (if he wears it) would help hold up Aufidius, but the latter's "standing" must disconcert the spectator (even if Aufidius places only one foot on Coriolanus),

3. John Bayley discusses compellingly how the nature of a tragic character's death serves to confirm his or her particular existence, "The Natures of Death," in *Shakespeare and Tragedy* (London: Routledge and Kegan Paul, 1981), 49–73.

4. Cited in Andrew Gurr, *Playgoing in Shakespeare's London* (Cambridge: Cambridge University Press, 1987), 233.

introducing a grotesque and perhaps comic air, that is, a shift toward detachment.

Such clear-cut deaths are by no means the rule in Shakespeare's tragedies. A play often teases the audience with doubt about whether the apparently dead really died, as with Desdemona. In *Othello*, Roderigo prematurely calls himself "slain" after his first wound, and Iago calls him "quite dead" after his second (V.i.26,114), yet the irrepressible Roderigo revives offstage. Later, Othello stabs Iago with a sword, but, like Roderigo, the ancient only bleeds, "not kill'd" (V.ii.288). *Othello* plays with delayed deaths, drawing our doubt to the wounded body and unsettling expectations. The tomb scene in *Romeo and Juliet* provides three degrees of deadness: Tybalt (likely a dummy) long dead, rigid, and wrapped in a bloody sheet off to the side; Paris freshly killed and bleeding heavily (V.iii.145); and Juliet, deathlike enough not to betray Romeo's misconception yet live enough to excite him sexually. While Tybalt's dummy may only make Juliet more alone, the Paris-actor imitating death (real death) takes a physical exception to the exclusivity the lovers seek. *Romeo and Juliet* plays visually, as thematically, on the cusp of love and death.

Shakespeare's confusion of looking dead with looking alive increases with the later tragedies. Death comes seamlessly in *Antony and Cleopatra* (as opposed, for example, to *Macbeth*): Enobarbus dies imperceptibly of feeling or thought, Iras of a kiss; Cleopatra faints like death and then dies like sleep; likewise, Charmian expires like fainting. Antony dies vaguely enough that modern editors sometimes insert the stage direction for his demise at a different textual line from that in the Folio. Cordelia in *King Lear* offers one of Shakespeare's most striking examples of playing dead, engaging the watcher's doubt intently and lingeringly. Lear's agonistic uncertainty creates a spectatorial conundrum: Is Cordelia alive or dead? The king's emblematic entrance with Cordelia in his arms (a reverse pietà) concentrates the audience's attention on her acting: the limpness of her limbs, her complete physical surrender. Lear studies her breath with, or at least calls for, a looking glass; he sees a feather stir about her; he thinks he hears her speak; her lips seem to move. The Cordelia-performer here must represent death with tremendous concentration and muscular release, especially if Lear raises or grasps her. But the very inability of any actor to look completely dead will tease the spectator's doubts or desires about Cordelia, our vain emotional hopes flickering in the shadow of Lear's greater agony.

By means of "playing dead," Shakespearean tragedy can slide auditorial attention and engagement from the character to the actor. We take pleasure in a death well performed, a pleasure that actually contributes to our respect for the heroism of the protagonist. The actor's skillful mastery of playing dead, that rising to a challenge accentuated by the playwright, can confer a certain largeness on the figure portrayed.[5] A character such as Macbeth, who is not given one of the great onstage deaths, forfeits some dramatic presence, an effect that Shakespeare must have sought for the usurper and tyrant who appears to his enemies as too small for his clothes. Engagement with acting translates into exactly enough detachment from the hero at the end to afford the spectator a contemplative and valorizing distance, with the blemishes of the hero's personality submerged in the virtuosic portrayal. The audience needs this transference, for it must loosen its emotional ties to the dying hero enough to leave the play and the theater psychologically whole and at rest. Playing dead illustrates the stitching between dramatic illusion and nonillusion, drawing electricity from the ambivalence. We desire in playing dead both the triumph of realism and the certainty of just-pretending (for we always assure ourselves that the actor really breathes, lives). What appears as a moment where we hold contradictory desires for character and performer becomes a consummate affirmation of each. Involvement with acting works a needed removal from character. Tragic closure depends for its full power on, unexpectedly, the audience's consciousness of theatricality.

II

While Shakespearean tragic heroes find their destinies increasingly cabined and chosen, the audience to tragedy receives, instead, a powerful enfranchisement. Critics often describe this tragic pleasure as calmness, reconciliation, and the access of energy reflecting the playgoer's enlarged vision.[6] Such expansiveness arises not just from the playing of pity and fear to extinction; rather it expresses, I would argue, a rhythm of spectatorial engagement and detachment evolving through the play. While the study of spectatorial distance can illuminate comedy as well as tragedy, I am particularly interested in the latter. For

5. Bert O. States discusses a similar reciprocity in the traces of characterization that the tragic actor might retain in gesture or facial expression during the curtain call, in *Great Reckonings in Little Rooms: On the Phenomenology of Theater* (Berkeley: University of California Press, 1985), 197–206.

6. As one of innumerable examples, Dorothea Krook writes of catharsis, "We feel . . . not depressed or oppressed, but in a curious way exhilarated; not angry and bitter but somehow reconciled; our faith in man and the human condition not destroyed or undermined but restored, fortified, reaffirmed," in her *Elements of Tragedy* (New Haven: Yale University Press, 1969), 14.

tragedy builds its effects upon a special identification and an active tension between audience and character not typical of comedy.[7] Marjorie Garber argues that tragedy denies its audience the clarification and release of comedy, and that the tragic audience experiences a confrontation and sense of suffering and survival unique to the genre.[8] Though audiences do identify with tragic heroes, the reactions of spectators often diverge from the reactions of protagonists: Enobarbus's betrayal may anger the audience more than it does Antony; Seleucus's betrayal outrages Cleopatra more than it does the audience. Spectators, moreover, typically attempt to guess ahead, to predict the outcome within the possibilities of genre, a domain of action peculiar to the audience which Michael Goldman distinguishes as *theoria*.[9] We delight in the anticipation, satisfaction, and sometimes deferral of formal expectations quite beyond our sympathy for characters: Playgoers require, at some level, that Juliet die. Criticism has frequently studied the "development" of the hero; conversely, we might examine a tragedy's affective engagements and detachments to assess the "development" of the audience.

My focus on a tragedy's development of the audience takes its place within the growth of performance-oriented criticism in Shakespearean studies.[10]

7. In tragedy, "It is mainly through the hero's thoughts and feelings that we judge the truth of the world which the dramatist asks us to accept, its 'values.' . . . [W]e identify ourselves, and go, with him," Roy Morrell, "The Psychology of Tragic Pleasure," *Essays in Criticism* 6 (January 1956): 27. Maynard Mack argues that a visionary engagement constitutes the very greatness of the tragic hero; see his "Engagement and Detachment in Shakespeare's Plays," in *Essays on Shakespeare and Elizabethan Drama in Honor of Hardin Craig,* ed. Richard Hosley (Columbia: University of Missouri Press, 1962), 275-96. Exemplifying a different, historically oriented perspective, Martha Tuck Rozett connects the audience's special engagement with and detachment from the Elizabethan tragic protagonist to Puritan views of divine election and the tactics of Puritan sermonizing; see *The Doctrine of Election and the Emergence of Elizabethan Tragedy* (Princeton: Princeton University Press, 1984).

8. Marjorie Garber, " 'Vassal Actors': The Role of the Audience in Shakespearean Tragedy," *Renaissance Drama,* n.s. 9, ed. Leonard Barkan (Evanston, Ill.: Northwestern University Press, 1978), 71-89.

9. Michael Goldman, *Acting and Action in Shakespearean Tragedy* (Princeton: Princeton University Press, 1985, 12; see Introduction, 3-16.

10. The article by Michael Shapiro cited in note 11 contains a useful overview of performance-oriented criticism. Recent book-length studies not mentioned by Shapiro's overview or in my comments in this chapter include Ralph Berry, *Shakespeare and the Awareness of the Audience* (London: Macmillan, 1985); David Bevington, *Action Is Eloquence: Shakespeare's Language of Gesture* (Cambridge: Harvard University Press, 1984); Philip C. McGuire, *Speechless Dialect: Shakespeare's Open Silences* (Berkeley: University of California Press, 1985); and Ann Pasternak Slater, *Shakespeare the Director* (Sussex: Harvester, 1982). Descriptive comments on criticism interested in "metadrama," "dramatic reflexivity," and response, appear in Ekbert Faas, *Shakespeare's Poetics* (Cambridge: Cambridge University Press, 1986), ix-xi. For an argument that performance excludes intellectual response, and hence that performance-oriented criticism cannot comprehend

Surveying such criticism, Michael Shapiro contrasts a Johnsonian view of the "spectators' constant awareness 'that the stage is only a stage, and that the players are only players'" with a Coleridgean "ideal response" involving the spectator's "rapt absorption in the work of art, as in a dream."[11] Modern critics, by admitting a Johnsonian "awareness of theatrical and dramatic artifice into critical discourse," have challenged "the naturalistic reduction of drama to mimesis" (147). While theatrically conscious criticism has sometimes argued for a thematic "reflexivity" that discovers the "idea of the theater" as one of the ideas of the play, recent, more phenomenological studies have investigated the complexity of theatrical effect and meaning that emerges from questioning mimetic assumptions.

Performance-oriented criticism assumes that dramatic language is to be performed, that it takes on different valences and nuances in spoken dialogue than in reading, that the challenges of performance define and animate the experience of the play, that signals to performative choices and to spectatorial responses inhere in the text itself, and that the transaction between audience and actor-as-character develops its own special and intense "energies." Performance-oriented criticism focuses on process, the "how" often displacing or subsuming the "why." Maynard Mack first introduced into Shakespearean criticism the terms "engagement" and "detachment" to distinguish the "built-in balances" of Elizabethan theater, engagement "reminding us of the real world whose image the playhouse is," and detachment emphasizing "the playhouse itself and the artifice we are taking part in."[12] That awareness of artifice begins to distinguish a special domain of spectatorial response. E. A. J. Honigmann details techniques (many of them effecting detachment) by which "Shakespeare gave

---

the social and contextual focus of structuralism, feminism, and new historicism, see, among his several articles, Harry Berger, Jr., "Text Against Performance in Shakespeare: The Example of *Macbeth,*" *Genre,* 15 (Spring–Summer 1982), ed. Stephen Greenblatt: 49–79.

11. Michael Shapiro, "Role-Playing, Reflexivity, and Metadrama in Recent Shakespearean Criticism," *Renaissance Drama,* n.s. 12, ed. Alan C. Dessen (Evanston, Ill.: Northwestern University Press, 1981), 146.

12. "Engagement and Detachment in Shakespeare's Plays," 277, 281. Eugene Paul Nasser treats such "balance" as the characterizing "tone" of Shakespeare: "a familiarity with his audience that allows him to create a core situation or action and then to feel free to move back and forth from the dramatic illusion to a rather choric posture with his audience toward it"; through detachment, then, the audience gains a "bracing" and "temporary confidence that we have the same control and understanding of experience that our author has," "Shakespeare's Games with His Audience," in *The Rape of Cinderella: Essays in Literary Continuity* (Bloomington: Indiana University Press, 1970), 101, 108.

his unremitting attention to audience-response in each of the tragedies."[13] Such Shakespearean "standard devices" for directing spectators include, among others, blurred or contradictory impressions given to the audience, actions by characters that overtly "regulate" response, scenes arranged serially so as to create prospective or retrospective effects, and controlled access to the protagonist's mind. Jean E. Howard has suggested that a pattern of "aural, visual, and kinesthetic effects" inheres in each of Shakespeare's plays and that, likewise, as he "orchestrated the play, he was indirectly orchestrating the experience of the viewer."[14] In a recent study, Robert Hapgood investigates the audience's "role" and the range of responses Shakespeare sought from his spectator, favoring the term "guidance" over "orchestration" or "regulation."[15] Hapgood focuses primarily on the audience's response to action and argues that "[a]bove all, responsive members of Shakespeare's audience, like his major characters, will *develop* in the course of the play" (223).

Performance-oriented perspectives on Shakespeare and theater take a concern for engagement and detachment into new avenues of philosophical understanding of tragedy. Stanley Cavell's essay "The Avoidance of Love" explores the countervailing pulls of "radical contingency" and "radical necessity," qualities fundamental to Shakespearean tragedy.[16] The "radical contingency" of tragedy is its sense that each death is "inflicted" and therefore need not have happened. Yet no one knows how to have prevented it; so a "radical necessity" haunts tragedy, as well. That "enveloping of contingency and necessity by one another . . . is why the death that ends a tragedy strikes one as *inexplicable,* necessary, but we do not know why; avoidable, but we do not know how; wrapped in meaning, but the meaning has come out, and so wrapped in mystery" (341). For Shakespearean tragedy, I associate "engagement" with the audience's experience of "radical necessity" and "detachment" with its experience of "radical contingency." Cavell's analysis suggests a sense of irrepressible possibility and openness in the spectatorship of tragedy. Bruce Wilshire discusses theater phenomenologically as an attitude or perspective from the audience that privileges the event; drama is an art of detachment that illuminates our

13. E. A. J. Honigmann, *Shakespeare: Seven Tragedies: The Dramatist's Manipulation of Response* (London: Macmillan, 1976), 192.

14. Jean E. Howard, *Shakespeare's Art of Orchestration: Stage Technique and Audience Response* (Urbana: University of Illinois Press, 1984), 2, 6.

15. Robert Hapgood, *Shakespeare the Theatre-Poet* (Oxford: Clarendon, 1988).

16. Stanley Cavell, "The Avoidance of Love: A Reading of *King Lear,*" in *Must We Mean What We Say?: A Book of Essays* (New York: Charles Scribner's Sons, 1969), 267–353.

engagements.[17] The objects, characters, and events of the theater do not simply absorb us, Wilshire argues. We also perceive them in a way that reveals their meaning or, rather, reveals them as possessing meaning. Wilshire's study displays the complexity of spectatorial consciousness, a heightened engagement and detachment both, defining theatrical meaning. Perhaps more than any other writer, Michael Goldman has demonstrated the rewards of a performance-oriented criticism of Shakespeare.[18] Goldman, arguing that in the theater we are principally aware of the actor's presence, has explored Shakespearean tragedy so as to discover the particular acting challenges contained in the major roles. Such challenges call forth the actor's virtuosity, a virtuosity that illuminates the special greatness of the character represented and makes possible the theatrical exhilaration of the audience. Drama, Goldman maintains in *The Actor's Freedom,* "exists to satisfy a profound and largely unexplored human appetite, the appetite for acting" (3). Acting constitutes more than imitation or representation, for the actor remains not quite the character and yet other than himself. Theater's special electricity, a power both "awesome and fearful," both "exciting and terrifying," derives from the audience's ambivalent awareness of the power and process of the actor, toward whom we are both attracted and repelled (7). Such thinkers suggest that Shakespearean tragedy arises out of a special transaction—a push and pull, an intimacy and removal—between audience and actor, and between audience and play, inherent in the theatrical event. Drama's special transaction defines, we might argue, the very meaning of the play: As Goldman remarks, to consider what happens in *Hamlet* is to consider "what happens *to us* in *Hamlet*" (4).

The shifting pattern of spectatorial engagement and detachment—sometimes called "aesthetic distance"—constitutes dramatic response.[19] Engagement can invite the spectator's participation in completing a tragedy's form, just as detachment invites consciousness of the open moment of a protagonist's choice;[20] a mutual heightening of engagement and detachment may inspire

17. Bruce Wilshire, *Role Playing and Identity: The Limits of Theatre as a Metaphor* (Bloomington: Indiana University Press, 1982). See also Bert O. States, *Great Reckonings in Little Rooms.*

18. Michael Goldman, *Shakespeare and the Energies of the Drama* (Princeton: Princeton University Press, 1972); *The Actor's Freedom: Toward a Theory of Drama* (New York: Viking, 1975); *Acting and Action in Shakespearean Tragedy.*

19. "These principles [engagement and detachment] underlie to some extent our experience of any art, and the drama notably," Maynard Mack, "Engagement and Detachment in Shakespeare's Plays," 275.

20. Cf. Honigmann: "Indeed, the 'mix' and quality of our response changes in every play from

"wonder." Issues of distance impinge particularly on drama, for not only do playgoers perceive "imaginative life as if it were physical presence,"[21] but also the very liveness of that "physical presence" makes it dangerous, threatening. Aesthetic distance has interested twentieth-century theorists: Edward Bullough, who first developed a concept of "Psychical Distance" as fundamental to art; Sartre, who saw distance in the theater as the activity of "imaging" and the paradoxical source of our emotional connectedness with characters; Brecht, who sought to counter the overempathic nineteenth-century theater with an alienation-effect promoting historical consciousness in the viewer; Artaud, who wished to use the theater's resources to obliterate the distinction between life and drama.[22] Distance determines spectatorial experience—and ultimately tragic meaning. That play of engagement and detachment opens a vista onto the underlying question of the essays that follow: Why do we, even we moderns, attend tragedies? Surely not for information, or for history, or for "the message," or even for vicarious experience, though all those may come. Rather, tragedy leaves us (individually and collectively) in a certain state of consciousness, of being, a paradoxical state of deepened responsiveness and heightened autonomy. (The political effects of tragedy depend upon that state.) Tragedy empowers its audience through distance.

III

By "engagement" I mean the spectator's surrender of self-awareness. Drama usually (though not always) posits the playgoers' freeing assumption that actions in the theater are not directly related to them, what Bullough describes

---

scene to scene. Even in one as centrally concerned with character as *Othello* . . . we find that after a time our interest partially disengages itself from character. Here, and in all of the tragedies, our response becomes detached and intellectual towards the end . . . and the intellectual interest interferes with our capacity for sympathetic 'identification,' " *Shakespeare: Seven Tragedies,* 193.

21. David Cole, *The Theatrical Event* (Middletown, Conn.: Wesleyan University Press, 1975), x.

22. For a study of philosophical views regarding aesthetic distance, see Daphna Ben Chaim, *Distance in the Theatre: The Aesthetics of Audience Response* (Ann Arbor, Mich.: UMI Research Press, 1984).

in his landmark essay as "Psychical Distance."[23] "Distance," for Bullough, "is obtained by separating the object and its appeal from one's own self" (96). It "describes a *personal* relation" between artifact and audience, "often highly emotionally colored," but "filtered . . . cleared of the practical, concrete" basis of appeal (97). Of course, distance varies for different individuals and with different artworks. With drama, distance will also fluctuate over a play's temporal duration. In such oscillations, engagement would designate those moments of the spectator's emotional assimilation into a work of art, free of his or her individual worldly concerns. Engagement connotes that immediate, sympathetic response, physical and emotional, that we make to character, acting, language, or action, the experience of being absorbed, lost in the event, "rapt out of" ourselves.[24] More so than other aesthetic forms, theater is quintessentially an "art of *involvement.*"[25] Yet engagement has its degrees, building from interestedness (the kind of limited attraction toward knaves, for example, that Robert Jones discusses) to sympathy to identification and empathy.[26] The term embraces a continuum of responses, and my use of "engagement" resembles Honigmann's use of "sympathy" to indicate a "community of feeling."[27] Whatever its degree, engagement implies imitation, the audience "taking the part" imaginatively and kinesthetically of a character's expression or action.

In engagement with immediate action—a guard sees a ghost, strikes at it with a partisan—audience attention focuses simply on what comes next; such action impresses through speed, suspense, and surprise. Dramatic irony, by detaching the audience from a character's presumptions and expectations, exposes a correlative engagement with events as they become imminent structure.

23. " 'Psychical Distance' as a Factor in Art and an Aesthetic Principle," in Edward Bullough, *Aesthetics: Lectures and Essays,* ed. Elizabeth M. Wilkinson (Westport, Conn.: Greenwood, 1977), 91–130; orig. pub. *British Journal of Psychology,* 5 (1912): 87–118. For different uses of the phrase "aesthetic distance," see Barbara A. Mowat, "Aesthetic Distance and Dramatic Illusion," *The Dramaturgy of Shakespeare's Romances* (Athens: University of Georgia Press, 1976), 121–28.

24. Mack, "Engagement and Detachment in Shakespeare's Plays," 276.

25. Wilshire, *Role Playing and Identity,* 13.

26. Robert C. Jones contends that engagement is not necessarily "identification": "And to argue . . . that we are engaged into Richard [III]'s point of view is not the least to suggest that we identify with him. His monstrous appearance . . . naturally works to preclude such identification. . . . We can share a knave's enjoyment of his own sport at a foolish victim's expense without likening ourselves to him," *Engagement With Knavery: Point of View in* Richard III, The Jew of Malta, Volpone, *and* The Revenger's Tragedy (Durham, N.C.: Duke University Press, 1986), 5–6.

27. Honigmann, *Shakespeare: Seven Tragedies,* 195 n.12; for a discussion of spectatorial sympathy, particularly in relation to moral approval, see 16–23, also Jones, *Engagement With Knavery,* 1–25.

That playgoers feel instinctively suspicious toward Lady Macbeth's remark, "A little water clears us of this deed; / How easy it is then!" (*Macbeth,* II.ii.64-65), for example, arises as they invest themselves, for the moment, less with the character's confidence than with action as it promises predictability, form. Such engagement can work as fusion, our expectations justifying action. Paris at Juliet's tomb, for example, takes needless precautions against discovery, instructing his page explicitly about listening to the hollow churchyard ground (*Romeo and Juliet,* V.iii.2-8). The audience unconsciously accepts his caution because it already knows that Romeo hurries hither: We explain Paris's action by reasons inaccessible to him.

With character, engagement can range from simply identifying to identifying-with or empathizing. As "identifying," engagement involves the recognition—a basic form of theatrical pleasure—of character in characteristics, such as how the Porter's inebriation and wit expose his "humor." Empathy closes the gap. Though we may not identify with Iago, we may with Macbeth; indeed, the latter's power arises from the audience's ability to take on a temporary kinship with him in the face of his murders. Such identifying-with amounts to heightened mimicry, for theatrical audiences echo with their musculature and their emotions the experiences of characters: recoiling, advancing, laughing, weeping. The audience will experience, like Macbeth, the jumpiness, speed, fracturing of thought, and rushing hope and fear in his soliloquy, "If it were done, when 'tis done" (I.vii.1-28). Shakespeare often indicates intense engagement by invoking the image of "taking another's part": Edgar's empathy for Lear's madness, for example, overwhelms his playacting: "My tears begin to take his part so much, / They mar my counterfeiting" (*King Lear,* III.vi.60-61).

Audiences engage not just with character but with the virtuosity of acting. In the rhythm of aesthetic distance, engagement with the actor can alter the spectator's engagement with the character. Sometimes our attention simply moves toward the acting itself; at other moments the audience's consciousness of acting can heighten its experience of the character, as, for example, the playgoers' delight in Sarah Bernhardt's acting apparently created their assent for the character she played.[28] The actor's success, as it infuses and illumi-

---

28. Robert Garis quotes G. B. Shaw on "the childishly egoistical character of her acting, which is not the art of making you think more highly or feel more deeply, but the art of making you admire her, pity her, champion her, weep with her, laugh at her jokes, follow her fortunes breathlessly, and applaud her wildly when the curtain fall," *The Dickens Theater* (London: Oxford University Press, 1965), 23, cited in Linda Bamber, *Comic Women, Tragic Men: A Study of Gender and Genre in Shakespeare* (Stanford: Stanford University Press, 1982), 68.

nates character, has much to do with "wonder" in the theater. Shakespeare's major tragic roles may offer acting challenges that demand rising admiration from their audiences, as Goldman has persuasively argued. We watch acting with a double intention: first to "get" the character, that is to construe the signals of histrionic technique into a portrait, and second, to test the "fit" of the acting itself to what it impersonates. This second intention concerns credibility, "Can I imagine those words spoken like that?" The audience verifies acting with its imagination, but not necessarily according to standards of objective behavior in the quotidian world. Audiences for live drama (far more than for film) recognize acting and test it emotionally and kinesthetically. Virtuosic acting can compel our engagement with the performer: In the economics of dramatic distance, one compensation for the audience's gradual detachment from the dying hero is its engagement with the triumphs of the performance.

By detachment I mean the spectator's heightened self-consciousness. Detachment includes our interpretations aroused from moment to moment, our sense of removal from the point of view of any single character, our contrasting of events and attitudes, our awareness of illusion, our moral or intellectual judgments as invited by the dramatic context, and even our hypotheses about "facts." New historicism, with its interest in whether or not Renaissance drama subverts dominant structures of social power, makes the investigation of detachment particularly timely. If, as Louis Montrose argues, Shakespearean theater critiques the Elizabethans' "dramatistic conception of human life," so that plays become "provocations to thought and patterns for action," we need a systematic understanding of such "provocations."[29] At the heart of detachment lies doubt. Shakespeare, particularly, advertises what we do not know, "endlessly referring the spectators to events, objects, situations, landscapes that cannot be shown them."[30] Obliged to "infer a fictional world elsewhere, offstage," the playgoer must periodically stand back, judge, conjecture: "The art of spectatorship is an art of diagnosis" (Maus, 575). Theater conditions itself on our uncertainty, doubt. John Styan observes that "[t]o empathize is the natural human impulse, but in alienation lies the drama."[31] Detachment is not a failure of emotional response so much as recognized or deliberated

29. Louis A. Montrose, "The Purpose of Playing: Reflections on a Shakespearean Anthropology," *Helios* n.s. 7 (1979–80): 53, 68.

30. Katherine Eisaman Maus, "Horns of Dilemma: Jealousy, Gender, and Spectatorship in English Renaissance Drama," *ELH* 54 (Fall 1987): 575–76.

31. John Styan, *Drama, Stage and Audience* (Cambridge: Cambridge University Press, 1975), 228.

emotion; it is conception as well as perception. Detachment resembles Brecht's *Verfremdungseffekt*.[32] It might arise from moments in a play that compare characters or action, that look back, that offer moral commentary, or that set the verbal against the visual. Friar Lawrence's lines, "Virtue itself turns vice, being misapplied, / And vice sometimes by action dignified" (*Romeo and Juliet,* II.iii.21–22), for example, distance the audience from the entering, Juliet-enamored Romeo to whom the lines may apply contextually. Prologues, choruses, animals on stage, reflective soliloquies, apostrophes, sententiae, long speeches, doubled actions, repeated imagery, actors reappearing in different roles, juxtaposed scenes, betrayed expectations—all may prompt self-consciousness, detachment. Breaks in stage illusion or realism account for much detachment and may arise from plays-within-the-play, onstage audiences, diction turned ornate or naturalistic, or any of the variants of audience address (what we might call "audience contact")[33] in Elizabethan drama. "Discrepant awareness," the spectator's knowledge of Iago's secret intentions in the "temptation scene," for example, spells detachment.[34] In the tragedies, we often feel some remove exactly when characters choose or decide, such as when Romeo weighs fighting Tybalt. Scenes of great passion for a character may be ones of detachment for an audience. Such "fission" creates a special kind of energy in the audience that can heighten its consciousness and sharpen its responses. Detachment liberates: As Wilshire suggests, "One is not just a being in the world but becomes aware *that* one is a being in the world. One becomes aware of oneself as aware, interpreting, and free" (xii).

Detachment involves "conception": insights and ideas. But how much does the detached audience actually make evaluative judgments in the theatrical instant? Bradley confines the performative experience to emotions such as attraction, repulsion, pity, wonder, and horror and dismisses any notion of the spectator judging the justice of events or of characters' deserts,[35] though

32. See, for example, *A Short Organum for the Theatre* (1949) in *Brecht on Theatre: The Development of an Aesthetic,* ed. John Willet (New York: Hill and Wang, 1964), 179–205. For a discussion of the relationship between the alienation effect and Elizabethan theater, see John Fuegi, *The Essential Brecht* (Los Angeles, Calif.: Hennessey and Ingalls, 1972), 25–48.

33. I borrow "audience contact" from discussion with Ralph Alan Cohen (January 1988) who, in stage-directing Shakespeare, applies the term to physical and verbal interaction between player and audience beyond asides and soliloquies.

34. I take the term "discrepant awareness" from Bertrand Evans, *Shakespeare's Tragic Practice* (New York: Clarendon, 1979).

35. A. C. Bradley, *Shakespearean Tragedy: Lectures on* Hamlet, Othello, King Lear, Macbeth (London: Macmillan, 1904), 32–33.

more recent critics accept "judgment" as part of spectatorship.[36] Bernard Beckerman calls the process of dramatic response "empathic parallelism," the spectators resonating to "the shifts of tension either between characters or between ourselves and the performers";[37] it involves cognition as well as emotion and motivation. Yet "participational" responses, those during performance, differ from postperformance or memorial ones.[38] We might consider participational "conceptions" as comparative and contextual, involving, for example, an ongoing balancing or weighing of spectatorial impressions, attitudes, and evaluations. Spectators discover Iago or Shylock, that is, through an accretion of details that sets successive bits of information at odds with those preceding, forcing at each step a comparative reevaluation. Postperformance conceptions, on the other hand, imply abstract meanings (Beckerman, 166), the kind of lesson we might draw from *Othello,* for example, about male-female relations or the objectivity of evil. Yet spectators in the theater surely make moral judgments, Bradley and Wilson Knight notwithstanding,[39] and a play may depend upon the moral assumptions that the audience brings—such as the revulsion toward regicide that *Macbeth* makes also fascinating—or may construct its own moral system, as Othello enunciates a set of moral attitudes toward Desdemona that he violates to our frustration. Detachment provides the space for such moral awareness. Spectatorial detachment differs from postperformance evaluation in being provisional, comparative, contextual, and concrete; postperformance evaluation differs from spectatorial detachment in being conclusive, generalized, selective, and abstract.

Engagement and detachment dance together. Shakespeare may shift the weight of auditorial response from one to the other, but the two effects always

36. For a comment on Bradley's view, in the example of *Othello,* see Robert Hapgood, "The Trials of Othello," in *Pacific Coast Studies in Shakespeare,* ed. Waldo F. McNeir and Thelma N. Greenfield (Eugene: University of Oregon Press, 1966), 146. Mack envisions the detached moment as causing the spectator to "reflect on meaning," "Engagement and Detachment in Shakespeare's Plays," 295.

37. *Dynamics of Drama: Theory and Method of Analysis* (1970; repr. New York: Drama Book Specialists, 1979), 149; see 145–56 for a full discussion of empathic parallelism.

38. For a discussion of the differences, see Beckerman, 129–67, especially 157–67.

39. G. Wilson Knight argues, as do others, that the playgoer tends to check his or her everyday moral responses at the theater door; see G. Wilson Knight, *The Wheel of Fire: Interpretations of Shakespearean Tragedy with Three New Essays* (1930; repr. London: Methuen, 1961), 1–16. While a play might create a structure of value that overrides our quotidian morality, drama can surely activate our societal responses: *The Diary of Anne Frank,* as Beckerman argues, for example, depends upon a moral revulsion already available in the spectator and only obliquely present in the play.

occur simultaneously, for to be engaged, and engaged only, might have us rushing the stage to prevent Othello from killing Desdemona, and to be detached only would leave us indifferent to him. In the symbiotic rhythm of distance, engagement participates ("What's next?") while detachment stands chorus ("Why that?"). Mack associates engagement with the psychological moment, detachment with the emblematic (294–96). Engagement with one character, Ophelia anguished at the end of the nunnery scene, often creates detachment toward others, Polonius and Claudius, blind to her, huddled conspiratorially. Engagement and detachment can work simultaneously yet paradoxically, as, to take an example from Chekhov, Vanya's attempted suicide inspires audience members to both laugh and cry, or Gloucester's attempted suicide can appear both courageous and embarrassing. Formal expectations can create engagement; delay may heighten it; denial may swing us into detachment. If Aristotelean pity and fear might apply to the audience for tragedy, then pity for a character suggests engagement, fear for ourselves detachment. Engagement and detachment together stimulate an expansive sense of choice, the "development," one might argue, that tragedy induces in its audience. The doubting and then the mental and emotional connecting performed by the dramatic audience generate ultimately a freeing energy, as when we realize that Macbeth's pursuit of the "be-all and the end-all—here" (*Macbeth,* I.vii.5) has become merely the repetitive gesture of a lifetime. Detachment toward the illusion, we might even say, becomes participation in illusion-making. Wilshire observes that "As art, theatre involves artistic detachment, but as theatre it is a detachment which reveals our involvements" (14). Mack recalls exactly that idea from James Shirley's preface to the first folio of Beaumont and Fletcher: You the spectator "stand admiring the subtile Trackes of your engagement."[40] Tragedy invites the audience to discover consciously and powerfully the very way—in drama, in life—that distance creates meaning.

---

40. James Shirley writes, "You may here find passions raised to that excellent pitch and by such insinuating degrees that you shalt not chuse but consent, & go along with them, finding your self at last grown insensibly the very same person you read, and then stand admiring the subtile Trackes of your engagement," Francis Beaumont and John Fletcher, *Comedies and Tragedies* (1647), sig. A3v. For Mack, "The essential condition of dramatic experience, and in fact the Renaissance view of art generally, has rarely been put better" (276); see also Honigmann, *Shakespeare: Seven Tragedies,* 16–23.

IV

Shakespeare's use of the word "behold" suggests that he imagined the proximate working of engagement and detachment in the immediate theatrical response.[41] "Behold" can even cue exactly those effects in the audience. Shakespeare applies "behold" and its variants to distinguish the special experience of dramatic spectatorship: "A kingdom for a stage, princes to act, / And monarchs to behold the swelling scene!" (*Henry V,* Prologue.3–4); "And the beholders of this frantic play" (*Richard III,* IV.iv.68). "Behold" describes an action originating in the senses but also imaginative and intellectual, and connotes an impression retained or lingering. It suggests a paradoxical "contemplation with the eyes." Likewise, Thomas Heywood speaks of beholders "wrapt in contemplation," mental recognition infusing spectatorial bewitchment.[42] Typically, "behold" in the tragedies arises for divergent purposes: on the one hand, to confirm a deeply affecting spectacle and, on the other hand, to suggest symbolic or proleptic meaning. "Behold," then, announces a mix of inherent psychological and emblematic possibilities, and in practice the deeply affecting spectacle (engagement) calls forth the reflexive intellectual meditation (detachment).

"Behold" may announce that some empathic revelation is at hand. It might invite extreme pity before an unnatural sight: Mark Antony, for example, uses "behold" when he calls citizens to weep over Caesar's wounds (*Julius Caesar,* III.ii.195–96). So also does Richard's Queen for her deposed husband: "yet look up, behold, / That you in pity may dissolve to dew" (*Richard II,* V.i.8–9).[43] If "behold" sometimes calls for spectatorial pity, it might also call for spectatorial fear and wonder. Macbeth calls out "Behold!" to marshall the thanes' attention to Banquo's ghost; he then stands shocked that they "can behold such sights, / And keep the natural ruby" of their cheeks (*Macbeth,* III.iv.68, 113–14). "Beholding" need not always terrify, of course, as Capulet's invitation for Paris's awe indicates: "At my poor house look to behold this night / Earth-

---

41. Andrew Gurr discusses the Elizabethans' search for an appropriate term for theatergoers, noting the visual bent of "spectators" and the aural bent of "audience," the first emphasizing visual stimulation, the second emphasizing sense. According to Gurr, Sidney first introduced "spectator," which gradually took hold; Puttenham, a linguist, favored "hearer" or "beholder": *Playgoing in Shakespeare's London,* 85–97.

42. Thomas Heywood, *An Apology for Actors* (1612), sig. B4r.

43. For an example in the comedies, see Le Beau's depiction of Charles's wrestling victims in *As You Like It:* "Yonder they lie, the poor old man, their father, making such pitiful dole over them that all the beholders take his part with weeping" (I.ii.129–32).

treading stars that make dark heaven light" (*Romeo and Juliet*, I.ii.24-25).
Capulet uses "behold" dualistically, for he invites Paris's sensual imagination,
as much as his actual perspicacity, to the ball. Along those lines, "behold" can
signal not only engagement but also detached, emblematic meaning, demonstrated precisely in Kent's "recognition" of the blasted Lear: "If Fortune brag of
two she lov'd and hated, / One of them we behold" (*King Lear*, V.iii.281-82).
Macduff cries out, "Hail, King! for so thou art," to Malcolm, "Behold where
stands / Th' usurper's cursed head: the time is free" (*Macbeth*, V.ix.20-21).
Here "beholding" the shocking, pitiful, theatrically wondrous, physical image
completes the past emotionally and morally and promises a future of renewal:
Malcolm's own fulfillment stands for the release and freedom of the tragic
spectator.[44] More prosaically, Iago associates "behold" with just that capacity
for judgment which Bradley excludes from the auditorial experience when the
ensign attempts to convince Lodovico and Gratiano of Bianca's guilt: "Behold
her well; I pray you look on her. / Do you see, gentlemen? Nay, guiltiness will
speak" (*Othello*, V.i.108-9). While the two Venetians "behold" Bianca
unconvinced, the offstage audience may "behold" Iago, recognizing the ironic
application of his theatrical maxim to its very speaker. Such a call to "behold"
subtly interprets the shape of Iago's career, pushing the audience back momentarily from the narrative business.

Likewise "behold" may hint disengagingly at the likenesses or revealing
differences between characters and spectators. Coriolanus uses "behold" to
catch at such reflections of the audience inside his play: "For the mutable,
rank-scented meiny, let them / Regard me as I do not flatter, and / Therein
behold themselves" (*Coriolanus*, III.i.66-68). "From my manners extrapolate,"
he says: Here "behold" summons its hearers to an interpretive action of
self-awareness, detachment. In a scene (III.iii) from *Troilus and Cressida*
crowded with theatrical references, Achilles and Ulysses use "behold" to
explore the reflected self.[45] Ulysses moves beyond the Renaissance commonplace metaphor, that the eye cannot see itself, to argue that "no man is lord of
any thing," even though, paradoxically, he might possess much in objects or
virtues, "Till he communicate his parts to others; / Nor doth he of himself
know them for aught, / Till he behold them formed in th' applause / Where th'

44. This interpretation emphasizes the benign. One could imagine, however, a production in
which the grotesque pole-hoisted head of Macbeth might threaten emotionally, creating an
undertow of irony toward the future. In either case, Macduff's invitation to "behold" will be cause
for reflection.

45. The scene works through various comparisons and contrasts: Achilles-Ajax, Achilles-
Hector, Ulysses-Thersites; Achilles will long to "behold" Hector (240), his double, and later in
the play, when the two meet, Hector will indeed invite Achilles to "Behold thy fill" (IV.v.236).

are extended" (III.iii.117–20). Ulysses suggests that the self creates its self-hood as the reflex to public approval, the public's taking our part, as we then take the public's in receiving approval. "Beholding" one's own personal value depends upon the volition, the choice to approve, of others; that process does not discover a preexisting worth so much as call worth into existence. I stress Ulysses's complicated context for "behold" here because it exposes the active, volitional interdependency at the heart of theatrical spectatorship, between characters and between characters and auditors, in Shakespeare's tragedies.[46] The theatrical use of "behold" can cue that taking-of-another's-part so special to the activity of actor and theatergoer. Worth arrives not as a property inherent in objects but as an expression of "distance," engagement and detachment.[47]

V

I have spoken innocently of audiences and spectatorship. Yet theoretical discussions of audience response risk ignoring the cultural differences within any single audience, let alone the differences in audiences from night to night, production to production, age to age. Interpreting the audience influences interpreting the play: After all, the democratic, liberal humanist view that the Elizabethan theater was "the one common meeting ground of literary genius and the mass audience"[48] inspired a generation of Shakespearean scholarship in America. Portraits of the Elizabethan audience have verged from Harbage's middle- and working-class spectators to Cook's "privileged playgoer," with Andrew Gurr now demarcating a middle position that views the audience as representative of Elizabethan social classes—gentry, gallants, Inns of Court students, merchant-citizens and wives, workers and artisans—yet also as dividing and converging among old and new venues in shifting patterns and tastes

46. For a stimulating discussion of Shakespeare in this regard, see Robert Hapgood, "Shakespeare and the Included Spectator," in *Reinterpretations of Elizabethan Drama: Selected Papers from the English Institute,* ed. Norman Rabkin (New York: Columbia University Press, 1969), 117–36.

47. The Prologue to *Troilus and Cressida* captures the symbiotic doubleness between actors and spectators wonderfully when he likens the warfare of Troy to the warfare of spectatorship, inviting his "fair beholders" to "Like or find fault, do as your pleasures are, / Now good or bad, 'tis but the chance of war" (Prologue. 20–31).

48. Robert Ornstein, *The Moral Vision of Jacobean Tragedy* (Madison: University of Wisconsin Press, 1965), 9.

from year to year.[49] Gurr characterizes the Elizabethan audience as exhibitionistic, noisy, physically and verbally responsive, significantly female, potentially disruptive, composed of the literate but substantially of the illiterate (particularly women), yet with a capacity for aural memory quite beyond modern expectations.[50] Social groups followed their tastes. According to Gurr, for example, in the half decade after 1599, citizens and lower members of society favored the playhouses north of the city, while the Globe and the boy companies drew the gentry and Inns of Court students. Of interest for this study, Gurr notes from 1599 to 1609, among the boy players but also in Shakespeare's company, a newly emerging "anti-mimetic" theatrical mode "making the audience self-conscious, flaunting the artificiality of stage pretence and insisting that audiences became not spell-bound believers but sceptical judges" (153). In the next decade, the Globe seems to have broadened its appeal once again to "all tastes" and "all social ranks" (158), a representativeness that characterizes Shakespeare's playhouse more persistently than it does any other.[51]

If social and aesthetic patterns shifted in the decades of Elizabethan and Jacobean theater, they have varied even more drastically since.[52] The Restoration, of course, introduced female actors, movable scenery, and a new stage: the proscenium, a deep hall with painted backdrop and side entrances, though action often took place on an apron fronting, and thus outside, the localized setting—an effect that tended to generalize meaning in the direction of cynicism.[53] The audience was dominated by the court: small (barely supporting two theaters), fashionable, gossipy, restless, often struggling through drama with the recollection and aftermath of revolution and regicide. Wickham notes that Restoration drama pointed spectators toward moral and argumentative, as opposed to narrative, content (163)—an aesthetic emphasizing detachment.

49. Alfred Harbage, *Shakespeare's Audience* (New York: Columbia University Press, 1941); Ann Jennalie Cook, *The Privileged Playgoers of Shakespeare's London: 1576–1642* (Princeton: Princeton University Press, 1981); Andrew Gurr, *Playgoing in Shakespeare's London.*

50. Gurr, *Playgoing,* 72–85; see also Cook, *Privileged Playgoers,* 152–67, 249–71.

51. See Gurr, *Playgoing,* 149–53, 156–58.

52. Histories of the theater and Shakespearean production abound. Among many choices, one might consult George C. D. Odell, *Shakespeare from Betterton to Irving,* 2 vols. (New York: Charles Scribner's Sons, 1920); Arthur Colby Spague, *Shakespearian Players and Performances* (Cambridge: Harvard University Press, 1953); Robert Speaight, *Shakespeare on the Stage: An Illustrated History of Shakespearean Performance* (London: William Collins, 1973); Cesare Molinari, *Theatre Through the Ages,* trans. Colin Hamer (London: Cassell, 1975); T. W. Craik, Clifford Leech, and Lois Potter, gen. eds., *The Revels History of Drama in English,* 8 vols. (London: Methuen, 1975–83); and Glynne Wickham, *A History of the Theatre* (Cambridge: Cambridge University Press, 1985).

53. Molinari, *Theatre Through the Ages,* 222.

Shakespearean tragedy fell subject to heroic tastes, French neoclassical poetics, cuttings and alterations for the sake of refinement, decorous acting—and happy endings. Shakespeare, that is, succeeded on spectatorial grounds more distanced than those of the Elizabethan playgoer.

Audiences broadened once again in the eighteenth century to include the rising middle class, accompanied by a shift in tragedy toward pathetic engagement: the age of sensibility. After 1740, Garrick brought a new psychological realism to acting, and thus to the experience of the playgoer, startling audiences as he altered the emphasis, pacing, and rhythm of lines according to the emotions and thoughts of his character. While in the early part of the nineteenth century, the apotheosis of the poetical, read Shakespeare discouraged theatrical productions, the later nineteenth century imbued stage treatments with all the "fourth wall" effects of wavering gas lighting and lavish scenic verisimilitude, creating not so much realism as a distanced fantasticality safely separating the passionately aroused audience. Victorian productions still truncated Shakespeare's text, in favor of enobled heroes (with fewer complicating perspectives from secondary characters) and vast scenery (with lengthy changes); it appealed both to sophisticated, even antiquarian, spectatorial tastes and to those of the new, less refined middle class. Visual splendor and melodramatic acting created an intensely empathic theater for Shakespearean tragedy, exactly the kind of emotional underdistancing against which Brecht reacted. Overall, stage history shows Shakespearean tragedy yielding successfully to opposing styles, contradictory interpretations, baroquely detailed sets or minimalist boxes, and varying extremes of emotion and reflection. Audiences can narrow to the court circle or expand for the lower classes, and those different audiences can be moved with idealistic sentiment, emotional empathy, and historical estrangement—by the same plays. If nothing else, extremes of engagement and detachment oscillate through these periods as persistently available auditorial effects of Shakespearean tragedy. What Bert States says of theatrical history applies paradigmatically to Shakespearean drama: "In one way or another, . . . [it] can be viewed as a history of flirtation with the psychical distance between stage and audience."[54]

Can one really speak of "auditorial effects," moreover, as if they registered equally throughout an audience, regardless of its disparities in social class, age, gender, education, and economic status? Might responses of various groups within an audience differ categorically? In a play such as *Othello,* touched with sexual politics and class distinctions, for example, Shakespeare's female and plebeian playgoers might have responded to Emilia's contemptuous exposure of

54. Bert O. States, *Great Reckonings in Little Rooms,* 96.

Othello with much different pleasures than did their "privileged" male compatriots. Women spectators help illustrate the question of divided or coalescent audience responses. Feminist scholarship over the last decade has spotlighted female subservience or resistance to patriarchy as an arena of Elizabethan social conflict with implications for drama.[55] Howard poses the question: "Did the theatre . . . form part of the cultural apparatus for policing gender boundaries, or did it serve as a site for their further disturbance?" (428). Did Elizabethan bourgeois wives, whose very presence at a playhouse had political implications, respond to gender issues in drama differently than did men (439–40)? Beyond sexual themes or matters of costume, moreover, could the theatrical or tragic experience, by its very nature, divide spectatorial responses along lines of gender? Katharine Maus interestingly parallels the engaged spectator in Renaissance drama with the jealous, cuckolded male (so often the subject of such drama), both aroused and rendered impotent by the scene of female sexuality.[56] On the other hand, Marianne Novy suggests that in Shakespeare's tragedies women, often sympathetically mediating the travails of the male hero for the spectator, "are like the tragic audience in their sense of powerlessness and separateness."[57] Novy adds that women share characteristics with the actor, too, for both are perceived as "other," associated with sexuality, physicality, diversion, role-playing, and emotional variety (92–98). Linda Bamber explores such female "otherness" as a structural principle of most Shakespearean tragedy, where "the satisfactions of the genre depend upon the alienation of both the tragic universe and the feminine Other from the tragic hero, the masculine Self."[58]

Bamber argues that the male self forms the perspective that will dominate the audience's experience of a tragedy—without necessarily estranging female spectators.[59] In a recent discussion, Richard Levin notes that Shakespeare

55. See, for example, Lisa Jardine, *Still Harping on Daughters: Women and Drama in the Age of Shakespeare* (Totowa, N.J.: Barnes and Noble, 1983) and Catherine Belsey, *The Subject of Tragedy: Identity and Difference in Renaissance Drama* (London: Methuen, 1985). For a recent view of the problem in terms of cross-dressing, see Jean E. Howard, "Crossdressing, The Theatre, and Gender Struggle in Early Modern England," *Shakespeare Quarterly* 39 (Winter 1988): 418–40.

56. Katharine Eisaman Maus, "Horns of Dilemma: Jealousy, Gender, and Spectatorship in Renaissance Drama."

57. Marianne Novy, "Tragic Women as Actors and Audience," in *Love's Argument: Gender Relations in Shakespeare* (Chapel Hill: University of North Carolina Press, 1984), 84; first published in slightly different form as "Shakespeare's Female Characters as Actors and Audience," in *The Women's Part: Feminist Criticism of Shakespeare,* ed. Carolyn Ruth Swift Lenz, Gayle Greene, and Carol Thomas Neely (Urbana: University of Illinois Press, 1980), 256–70.

58. Linda Bamber, *Comic Women, Tragic Men,* 24.

59. See Bamber, *Comic Women, Tragic Men,* 1–27.

usually employs collective and gender-neutral terms to his audience ("fair beholders," "gentle hearers").[60] Yet his three epilogues that do address ladies suggest to Levin that "the author regarded women spectators as more charitable than the men" (168), a notion that coincides with evidence that Renaissance playwrights may have seen women as possessing "a special sensitivity to . . . pathetic plots and situations" (171).[61] But even such modest distinctions seem more of degree than of kind.[62] The Shakespearean epilogues that distinguish women's responses from men's, moreover, all undertake to evaporate differences and harmonize views: As the Epilogue to 2 Henry IV puts it, "All the gentlewomen here have forgiven me; if the gentlemen will not, then the gentlemen do not agree with the gentlewomen, which was never seen in such an assembly" (Epilogue.22–25).[63] Overall, Andrew Gurr concludes that Shakespeare viewed the audience as a collective: While Jonson railed against the many brainless spectators, as opposed to those few judicious hearers of his poetry, or Beaumont in The Knight of the Burning Pestle may have set the gentry in his audience against his citizen-playgoers, Shakespeare practiced no such polarizing.[64] Ann Cook observes, too, that Renaissance playwrights generally depicted the audience as a unity.[65] Likewise, reviewing playwrights' actual statements about their spectators, Levin rejects the fashionable split audience theory in which the ignorant Elizabethan "uncapable multitude" would derive a false, superficial meaning from a play and the judicious "wiser sort" the "real" ironic meaning. Rather, he argues, playwrights distinguish audience members by their taste, not by their interpretations,[66] an argument that would seem to bear on distinctions of gender as well as of class or training.

60. Richard Levin, "Women in the Renaissance Theatre Audience," Shakespeare Quarterly 40 (Summer 1989): 168.

61. Timothy Murray discusses interestingly the fear of Elizabethan antitheatricalists that women were more susceptible (underdistancing) to dramatic impressions than were men, "Othello's Foul Generic Thoughts and Methods," in Persons in Groups: Social Behavior as Identity Formation in Medieval and Renaissance Europe, ed. Richard C. Trexler (Binghamton, N.Y.: Medieval and Renaissance Texts and Studies, 1985), 70–71.

62. As Levin notes, "There are also references to men crying in the theatre (which they apparently did much more easily than do men today) and to entire audiences crying" (171).

63. Juliet Dusinberre views the "feminist" sympathies of Shakespeare's plays as knitting together responses of socially disparate spectators around a common public concern for women, in Shakespeare and the Nature of Women (London: Macmillan, 1975), 1–19. Her sanguine view of the empowerment of women in Renaissance England has been challenged by some feminist critics, noticeably Lisa Jardine, Still Harping on Daughters and Catherine Belsey, The Subject of Tragedy.

64. See Gurr, Playgoing, 75–104.

65. Cook, Privileged Playgoers, 267.

66. Richard Levin, "The Two-Audience Theory of English Renaissance Drama," Shakespeare

Thus, while Elizabethan responses may have varied in intensity and possibly by gender (or other considerations), Shakespeare largely appears to have sought a coalescent audience. Robert Hapgood offers a particularly useful view of audience receptivity: Though audience members need not move in lockstep, they often tend to move in the same direction.[67] Hapgood observes of *Richard II*, for example, that different members of an audience might shift sympathetically toward Richard at different points in the text, but all will shift by a certain point, a strategy that acknowledges both collective response and individual idiosyncracies (217–19). Yet Hapgood emphasizes (as do many others) that part of theater's distinctive power is to seek at key moments a single audience response. Here the differences between reading and attending the theater can instruct us. Gary Taylor characterizes reader-response critics as presupposing "anonymity, absence, isolation, and silence" in the reading experience; a theatrical criticism, on the other hand, must presuppose "presence, recognition, community, and sound."[68] With dramatic performance, auditors are present to each other, recognize their own and others' reactions, respond univocally as a community, and make noises that express and reinforce recognition and unanimity. Errant individual reactions modulate, in a community, toward a shared ground, although the group response will also bend toward extremes, as in laughter or tears, from which the lone individual might shrink. Elizabethan commentators on audience experience also tend to emphasize extreme emotional reactions expressive of group rapport, as does Heywood when he says, in a famous passage, "so bewitching a thing is liuely and well spirited action, that it hath power to new mold the harts of spectators and fashion them to the shape of any noble and notable attempt."[69] Recent excavations of the Rose and Globe theaters suggest, furthermore, that the diameters of the theaters were smaller than previously estimated, with spectators standing or sitting surprisingly close together, a physical proximity likely to encourage communal response. In an earlier work, Taylor reports testing audience coalescence by interviewing spectators for a production of *Henry V* and finding no appreciable differences in their responses to the play.[70] We might conclude that, beyond different intensities and pacings in response or some reactions diverg-

---

67. Robert Hapgood, *Shakespeare the Theatre-Poet.*

68. Gary Taylor, *Reinventing Shakespeare: A Cultural History, from the Restoration to the Present* (New York: Weidenfeld and Nicolson, 1989), 323–24.

69. Thomas Heywood, *An Apology for Actors,* sig. B4r.

70. Gary Taylor, *To Analyze Delight: A Hedonist Criticism of Shakespeare* (Newark: University of Delaware Press, 1985), 117; for the valuable full discussion of audiences responding to an actual production, see 112–61.

ing at incidents involving particularly divisive issues, Shakespearean spectators tend towar comparable experiences.

A discussion of the "invitations" to spectatorial response embedded in Shakespeare's text would do well to consider its own subjectivity as well as that of the audience, for no study can fully avoid reinscribing its author's intellectual affections and blind spots, and those of his or her times, onto the playscript. Thus an extreme discretion might have moved me to substitute "I" for every "we," "the spectator," and "the audience" in this volume. Indeed, the ensuing chapters largely assume a modern spectatorial perspective, with some suggestions about how formal effects may strike a modern audience differently than its predecessors. Even new historicism and cultural materialism, those movements rejuvenating our sense of historical context and differences, face the same limitations in discussing "the audience" as do critics oriented toward performance theory. Stephen Greenblatt, for example, suggests as much in his recent book, *Shakespearean Negotiations,* when he acknowledges that his (or any) historical analysis of social energy in Shakespeare's theater still proceeds "under the terms of our own interests and pleasures and in the light of historical developments that cannot simply be stripped away."[71] New historicism itself, that is, takes color from the interests and sympathies of its author, his or her era, and that era's position in history. Historically oriented critics and theatrically oriented critics together must recognize the contingency of their readings.

The strategies employed by new historicists and cultural materialists, however, can illuminate the textual rhythms of engagement and detachment of a performance-oriented approach. Jonathan Dollimore's *Radical Tragedy,* perhaps the most influential cultural materialist study of Jacobean tragedy, reassesses tragedy's ideological content, particularly in light of the dramatic theories of Bertolt Brecht.[72] Aesthetically, Dollimore stresses "disjunction," "discontinuity," and "disconnectedness," breaks in dramatic structure and tone that induce critical reflection in the Jacobean audience, breaks that expose to the audience the differences between Christian and humanist (so-called essentialist) ideals, on the one hand, and materialist reality, on the other. Brechtian theater stands as the model for Dollimore's analysis, for such drama incorporates dynamic contradiction into its form, insists on differences between character

71. Stephen Greenblatt, *Shakespearean Negotiations: The Circulation of Social Energy in Renaissance England* (Berkeley: University of California Press, 1988), 20.

72. Jonathan Dollimore, *Radical Tragedy: Religion, Ideology and Power in the Drama of Shakespeare and his Contemporaries* (Chicago: University of Chicago Press, 1984); for the discussion of Brecht, see especially 63–69.

and actor, highlights the audience's consciousness of theater as illusion, and moves its spectators toward historical recognition through estrangement effects. Brechtian aesthetics can surely enrich the study of audience response, influenced as Brecht was by Renaissance drama. The very notion of a shifting rhythm of engagement and detachment and the emphasis of my study upon presentational effects, awareness of acting and theatricality, and, especially, detachment express concerns that Brecht made part of theatrical discourse. Indeed, the generating idea of tragedy's "radical contingency" (Cavell's term) accords with Walter Benjamin's description of Brechtian theater: "[I]t can happen this way, but it can also happen quite a different way."[73]

Both Greenblatt and Dollimore segue unavoidably into categorical statements about audience and theater beyond the pale of their historicism. Greenblatt asserts, for example, that "the practical usefulness of the theater depends largely on the illusion of its distance from ordinary social practice" (18). But would, say, the actors of the Living Theater in the 1960s or 1970s assent to such a proposition?[74] Would the audience agree, which rioted in favor of labor strikes after viewing the opening performance of *Waiting for Lefty?* Historicism fades as Dollimore and Greenblatt turn to the actual playtexts. Analyzing an incident in *The White Devil,* for example, Dollimore says, "that final touch, 'they depart laughing'— . . . makes for a lingering sense of the unnaturalness and *deliberate* inhumanity of court intrigue, an effect heightened by the subsequent pathos of Isabella's death in Giovanni's presence" (62). But just whose "lingering sense of unnaturalness" does Dollimore assert; the "effect heightened" upon whom? A few pages later, speaking of *The Duchess of Malfi,* Dollimore says, "Checked expectation, not enthralment or empathy, is the result and we are thereby provoked to dwell critically on, for example, the fate/chance disjunction . . . [running] throughout the play" (66). But who exactly is Dollimore's "we"? Did "the Jacobean spectator" really "dwell critically"? In what sense could that be proven historically? Or can Dollimore only be speaking of himself?

Greenblatt, interested in social power and its subversion in Renaissance drama, must resort to the same ahistoricalness. He would suggest, like Dollimore, that Shakespeare's plays open the dominant power structure to spectatorial

---

73. Cited in Dollimore, *Radical Tragedy,* 64.

74. Consider, for example, the following description of the Living Theater: "The search for uniqueness involved experiments with putting actuality on stage which led eventually to eliminating the separation between art and life, between dramatic action and social action, between living and acting, between spectator and performer, and between revolution and theatre," Theodore Shank, *American Alternative Theater* (New York: Grove, 1982), 9.

reconsideration and challenge: "Was it not possible inside the playhouse walls to question certain claims elsewhere unquestionable?" (61). Of *Henry V,* Greenblatt concludes, "Within this theatrical setting, there is a notable insistence upon the paradoxes, ambiguities, and tensions of authority" (65). But while his discussion of *Henry V,* for example, traffics heavily in issue of spectatorial effect, he can neither demonstrate nor insist that what is notable to him—the "apparent subversion of the monarch's glorification" (62)—would really have been noticed at all by an Elizabethan playgoer. Because of that dilemma, Greenblatt must return to Dollimoresque conjectures upon disjunctions: "Again and again in *1 Henry IV we are tantalized* by the possibility of an escape from theatricality. . . . The play operates in the manner of the central character, *charming us* with its visions of breadth and solidarity, 'redeeming' itself in the end by betraying *our hopes,* and earning with this betrayal *our slightly anxious admiration*" (46–47; emphasis mine). Greenblatt claims a historically fuzzy "we" for all this tantalization, charm, hope, and anxious admiration, perhaps because no textual analysis can guarantee the historical Elizabethan response.

I do not raise such examples simply to convict new historicism and cultural materialism of my own naïveté. Their generalizations about audience response, which can prove false in a particular time and place, point toward tendencies and problems in drama that recur enough over time to deserve notice. Such statements about "the audience," though essentially ahistorical, invoke a strategy necessary for illuminating structural elements that persist transhistorically in a playscript. Indeed, what a critic such as Dollimore treats as "disjunctions" of tone can hardly be extricated from considerations of auditorial effect, for a "disjunction" makes itself known by force of registering an effect (disengagement): We "dwell critically" or experience a "lingering sense of unnaturalness" or feel "slightly anxious admiration." "Disjunction" and "discontinuity" provide internal (formalist) terms for external (spectatorial) transactions.

Let me put the problem of "the audience" in a more theoretical context. M. M. Bakhtin has contributed profoundly to revealing the complicated social context qualifying all discourse.[75] Bakhtin discusses linguistic "audiences" in a way revealing for drama: "[E]very word is directed toward *an answer.* . . . [I]t provokes an answer, anticipates it and structures itself in the answer's direction" (280). Bakhtin rejects an older view of the "passive" listener in favor of a "responsive" listener "who actively answers and reacts. . . . Responsive under-

---

75. Among other works, see M. M. Bakhtin, "Discourse in the Novel," in *The Dialogic Imagination: Four Essays by M. M. Bakhtin,* ed. Michael Holquist, trans. Caryl Emerson and Michael Holquist (Austin: University of Texas Press, 1981), 259–422.

standing is a fundamental force, one that participates in the formulation of discourse, and it is moreover an *active* understanding, one that discourse senses as resistance or support enriching the discourse" (280–81). Resistance and support suggest exactly the kinds of activities I wish to discuss with detachment and engagement. In such a model of discourse, the speaker always attempts to refashion his listener: "The speaker breaks through the alien conceptual horizon of the listener, constructs his own utterance on alien territory, against his, the listener's apperceptive background" (282). Similarly, Walter J. Ong argues that all writers "fictionalize" their readers, re-creating them not as they are in their real-life occupations, but "in some sort of role—entertainment seekers, reflective sharers . . . , inhabitants of a lost and remembered world"—and "the audience must correspondingly fictionalize itself."[76]

Regarding drama, we can say that the playwright necessarily imagines "the audience" in the very gesture of writing, and that one activity of playwrights is to "fashion" their audience, to remodel it, to shape the actual listeners—by activating their support and even their resistance—into the respondents they intend. Recent sociological rhetoricians suggest that an audience will be significantly a "construction of the speaker," that because individuals adapt their opinions and responses radically to the role required within certain social institutions (such as theater), those responses can be "conditioned" by the speaker (or writer) and by devices of staging.[77] Studying Shakespeare with an interest in effect, then, draws us to the audience "implied" in the text, not a real audience but a fictional and abstract one, such as the audience imagined in the shifting rhythms of spectatorial distance. Thus, the theatrically oriented critic explores the text as a blueprint for performance (independent of any particular performances), viewing the audience as an entity the playwright sets out to construct with each play.[78] Here the idea of "the audience" becomes useful in defining the individuality of a play. Such a theory of spectatorship can

76. Walter J. Ong, "The Writer's Audience Is Always a Fiction," *PMLA* 90 (January 1975): 10–13.

77. Ch. Perelman and L. Olbrechts-Tyteca, *The New Rhetoric: A Treatise on Argumentation*, trans. John Wilkinson and Purcell Weaver (Notre Dame, Ind.: University of Notre Dame Press, 1969 [French edition, 1958]), 19–23.

78. See, for example, Howard, *Shakespeare's Art of Orchestration*, 3, 6–9; Hapgood, *Shakespeare the Theatre-Poet*; and Jones, *Engagement with Knavery*, 8. Gary Taylor argues that "every dramatist constructs a hypothetical audience, and . . . the success or failure of his intentions depends on the relation between his real and his hypothetical spectators," *To Analyze Delight*, 158. In a manner similar to Bakhtin's, Howard conceives of Shakespeare's implied audiences as actively participatory, latent with both "recalcitrance and suggestibility," *Shakespeare's Art of Orchestration*, 9.

pry open riches in the playtext that other analytical tools leave obscured. In a sense, a performance-oriented study can be viewed, as might Dollimore's and Greenblatt's, exactly as investigating what emerges from rehypothesizing the fiction of "the audience."

I wish, then, to investigate the invitations to certain communal responses embedded as formal properties in Shakespeare's text. Whatever use different productions and different generations might make of such invitations, they persist as latent structure. Such textual signals reside, for example, in the relationships between characters; the implied space between character and audience; the rhythms of attention or kinetics in a scene; the recalling of one character or action in another; and, frequently, the script's demands for virtuosic acting. The language of the play cues the choices of actors and their interaction with the audience and can signal the production values of staging, setting, lighting, and costume, though different epochal or ideological productions may make different uses of these possibilities. Though my discussion proceeds largely from the perspective of a modern theatergoer, we shall often consider the tragedies in terms of Elizabethan conditions of production—a fair concern for a century that has reexplored the bare stage and attempted a range of "minimalist" analogies for the Renaissance mise-en-scène. A modern audience, of course, lacks the Elizabethan's long familiarity with the popular stories and histories behind the tragedies, the fifteenth- and sixteenth-century retailings of Romeo and Juliet, for example, or the dozen-odd versions of King Lear. Yet we can also assume more Shakespearean sophistication than that of Tom Jones's Partridge before Garrick's Hamlet. Many modern theatergoers still arrive at a Shakespearean play having once studied, read, or seen it, or knowing the plot. Such familiarity, like the Renaissance groundling's with the stories behind the plays, will deepen the spectator's empathy and engagement, and deepen, as well, the resonant meanings the spectator will find in the detached moment.[79] The audience's participation makes Shakespearean tragedy perhaps always contemporary, "modern." Shakespeare's methods of involving the audience, as Ekbert Faas argues, draw the spectator into the action itself, into the co-creation of the dramatic progress, far more than does the work of any other dramatist.[80] In that sense, Shakespearean tragedy might resemble Mikhail Bakhtin's view of the novel, the

---

79. For a discussion of the effects on the spectator of seeing several productions of the same play in a brief time-span, see Stephen Booth, "On the Persistence of First Impressions," in King Lear, Macbeth, Indefinition, and Tragedy (New Haven: Yale University Press, 1983), 119–25.

80. Faas, Shakespeare's Poetics, 70.

collaborative openness of the very form making its meaning-as-experience relentlessly contingent, contemporary, evolving.[81]

VI

The ensuing chapters will investigate various elements of Shakespearean tragedy: form, particularly matters of causation and necessity; "positional" (as I term it) characterization; rhythms of action and scenes, particularly kinetic and choreographic; virtuosic acting and the demands for presentational and representational expression; and such direct audience contact in nonillusory theater as soliloquies spoken to the spectators. One could argue that this ordering of dramatic qualities approximates a continuum of audience involvement, from elements inviting unconscious spectatorial absorption (engagement) to more overt elements registering self-conscious involvement (detachment). We tend to be less aware of tragic form than of a soliloquy. Yet such schematics ultimately betray the schemer, for Shakespeare's art often revels in making the audience take notice of even its most casual dramatic assumptions.

For example, necessity. Studying the ship-in-the-bottle of Shakespeare's tragedies, Bradley perceived a complex, almost bureaucratic, "fate" as "the ultimate power in the tragic world."[82] Tragic heroes must discover that they participate in a mysterious teleology ordering their time and space, and obliging them to prove their integrity in an arena of fatal contradictions beyond their invention or remedy. Yet, particularly for the modern spectator, necessity may only emerge as necessity after the fact. As audience, we recognize inevitability by the long backward glance; in the dramatic "present" we experience the openness of a character's choice—in Shakespeare the frequent re-creation of deciding as an action—that makes integrity possible as a tragic attribute. For the playgoer, freedom is progressive, necessity retrogressive.

Like the ghost of Hamlet's father, the deterministic universe has vanished from contemporary sight. The grip of Coleridge's organic model of art, too, has loosened, so that the mechanics of the tragic world may strike us now as manipulations of the playwright's hand: The three witches in *Macbeth* are, for

---

81. M. M. Bakhtin, "Epic and Novel," in *The Dialogic Imagination,* 3–40.
82. A. C. Bradley, *Shakespearean Tragedy,* 21. Necessity may typically arise in the tragedies as medieval fate; the whirligig of fortune; historical, martial, or political urgency; communal and familial prejudice; passion and character.

many, no longer demonic or chaotic emblems, but merely (or wondrously) dramatic. Elizabethan tragedy rarely obeyed strict standards of unity anyway, refusing, unlike Prince Hal, to banish carnival, digression, irrelevance, mixed voices, generic miscegenation, or confusions of time, place, behavior, tone, and realism. Able to recognize the liberties of Renaissance drama, we can also recognize its strategies, such as repetition and foreshadowing, beneath the disguise of causation, fate, or fortune. Elizabethans may have, too; "analogical scenes," for example, can look different depending upon whether or not one's culture assumes that history repeats itself.[83] How do the tragedies play when we grasp the artistic conventions as conventions and reject the worldview?

Necessity in Shakespeare's tragic world might then sometimes resurface as a form of poetic consent between play and playgoer. Romeo, we might say, fights Tybalt in part because the play's poetic structure has promised that he will. It fits. Not bound in a work such as *Romeo and Juliet* by prior conceptions of fate, the modern spectator might begin to notice a tragedy's breaks in logic, its inconsistencies in character, its shifts in realism, effects inducing detachment.[84] Brecht, of course, favors viewing a catastrophe as tragic not because of its mysterious inevitability but because of its absence of inevitability—a detachment Brecht often finds in Shakespeare.[85] Brecht advocates that the actor use alienation-effects to uncover a character's choices as historical or provisional: "and now 'he did this' has got to become 'he did this, when he might have done

83. I take the term "analogical scene" from Joan Hartwig, *Shakespeare's Analogical Scene* (Lincoln: University of Nebraska Press, 1983).

84. Modern theater does not insist upon nineteenth-century linear plots, comprehensible characters, conversational dialogue, or pretenses of realism. Consider, for example, Theodore Shank's description of Robert Wilson's contemporary *Einstein on the Beach:* "The production incorporates techniques of repetition, extreme slow motion as well as fast repetitive dance movements, and non-discursive use of language. As in Wilson's other works there is no traditional dramatic narrative, but a visual and aural stream of images. The opera has a mathematical structure of nine scenes.... Each act is preceded and followed by a musical 'Knee Play' (that is, a joint) which serves as prelude, interlude, or postlude.... The spoken passages, like the music, are used for their aural rather than their discursive value," *American Alternative Theater,* 127–32. As a particularly stimulating modern aesthetic, John Cage's view of theater seems to endorse randomness (rather than teleology), simultaneity (rather than linearity), open-endedness (rather than closure), contingency (rather than necessity), and inseparability of observer from phenomenon (rather than objective mimesis): Natalie Crohn Schmitt, "John Cage, Nature, and Theater," *A John Cage Reader,* ed. Peter Gena and Jonathan Brent (New York: C. F. Peters, 1982), 17–37.

85. For a useful discussion, see Margot Heinemann, "How Brecht Read Shakespeare," in *Political Shakespeare: New Essays in Cultural Materialism,* ed. Jonathan Dollimore and Alan Sinfield (Ithaca, N.Y.: Cornell University Press, 1985), 202–30. Heinemann (206) quotes Brecht from a 1927 radio broadcast: "With Shakespeare the spectator does the construing. Shakespeare never bends the course of a human destiny in the second act to make a fifth act possible. With him everything takes its natural course. In the lack of connection between his acts we see the lack of connection in a human destiny."

something else.' "[86] Viewing necessity as provisional can make the wholeness or success of a play more fascinating, because it invites spectators to examine the source of their approval and the alternatives to the fatal vision that embroils the characters. Inflicted fate and free choice (or the character's sense of it)—Stanley Cavell's "radical necessity" and "radical contingency"—represent the double action of a tragic plot. Engagement and detachment, empathy and reflection, likewise comprehend the parallel double rhythm of audience experience, heightening feeling and self-awareness. The audience comes to know what it also comes to feel. The power of the tomb scene in *Romeo and Juliet,* for example, can gain from a modernist sense that the play describes the tragedy of a fatalist as much as a tragedy of fate; Romeo's story can terrify exactly because we recognize that on some deep level he chooses his doom as much as the stars cause it. Our detachment here gives weight to the "radical contingencies" of the plot and complicates tragic awe with ambivalence: wonder.

Tragedy's greater interest in complexity of character separates that genre from the comedies and even the histories. A. C. Bradley's *Shakespearean Tragedy* proceeds, of course, by studying character as something discrete and rounded, embodying destiny: "The center of the tragedy, therefore, may be said with equal truth to lie in action issuing from character, or in character issuing in action" (12). Writing several decades later, E. E. Stoll sets the opposing Aristotelian view by insisting that Shakespeare's tragedies hinge upon actions that can be psychologically impossible but that succeed by drama's internal conventions, those of circumstantial contrast and conflict.[87] In a contemporary, poststructuralist approach, René Girard views characters in terms of their "intersubjective strategies" in pursuit of desires; desire here constitutes a form of imitation, what Girard calls "imitative, or mimetic or mediated desire."[88] Characters tend to desire and value objects in imitation of the desires of others. Girard argues of *Troilus and Cressida,* for example, that "The enormous self-assurance of Achilles looks like . . . a permanent endowment that cannot be taken away from him. Literary critics would call it the 'character' of Achilles." But Ulysses manipulates Achilles by rejecting that " 'essentialist' conception." For him, Achilles's "formidable pride has no objec-

86. Bertolt Brecht, *A Short Organum for the Theatre,* 195.

87. See, for example, Elmer Edgar Stoll, *Art and Artifice in Shakespeare: A Study in Dramatic Contrast and Illusion* (Cambridge: Cambridge University Press, 1933).

88. René Girard, "The Politics of Desire in *Troilus and Cressida,*" in *Shakespeare and the Question of Theory,* ed. Patricia Parker and Geoffrey Hartman (New York: Methuen, 1985), 190, 198; see also René Girard, *Violence and the Sacred,* trans. Patrick Gregory (Baltimore, Md.: Johns Hopkins University Press, 1977).

tive basis; it is the result of universal worship, of the huge amount of admiration and desire directed toward Achilles" (204). With Girard, "character" becomes a function of "intersubjective," or social, dynamics. In a related manner, the spectatorial approach which I would advance might treat character as "positional." Our understanding of a character, that is, will arise out of his or her position in a drama, not only relative to other characters and the action but relative particularly to the audience's expectations, desires, needs, and awarenesses at any given moment.[89] *Antony and Cleopatra,* for example, demands that we understand Octavius in the context of Antony, inviting questions of Octavius's emotions that might not otherwise occur. Octavius's character becomes not so much intrinsic as extrinsic, a product of the spectator's thoughts and feelings about Antony. Likewise, psychological probability or improbability may constitute not tragic absolutes, but rather renderings of the audience's preferences and judgments of the moment. Othello's dive into jealousy in the "temptation" scene, for example, might be wholly probable if the audience were to see that action exclusively from Othello's eyes; our superior knowledge creates the dissonance in Othello's emotional credibility. An audience's awareness includes such "discrepancy," such superiority to what the character knows at the same moment (the basis of dramatic irony). Discrepant recognition, moreover, will heighten an audience's consciousness of the acting of character itself.

Peter Brook observes that "Acting begins with a tiny inner movement so slight that it is almost completely invisible."[90] Characterization requires motion, a distinction with implications. A novel may describe a character's impressions, emotions, and thoughts while the character sits motionless in a chair, physically static. In the performance of Shakespearean tragedy, however, thought is bodily action, revealing intention, conflict, contingency, resolution, or deepening irresolution: change. Dramatic character must always express its dramatic medium. In theater no such thing as character exists (as in Ulysses's argument) antecedent to a public, overt, social, directional, physical manifestation;

---

89. John Bayley suggests the importance of the audience's vantage point in defining character when he argues that " 'Character' in Shakespearean tragedy is mainly a matter of our discovering in what ways the individual and the action fail to get on," *Shakespeare and Tragedy,* 64. In an approach different in emphasis but not incompatible with my own, Thomas F. Van Laan stresses the theatrical and social creation of identity for Shakespeare's characters; Shakespeare's stage images "prompt the spectator . . . to perceive *as role-playing* the characters' fulfillment or violation, through their behaviour, of the roles they possess by virtue of their social situation or their dramatic function," *Role-playing in Shakespeare* (Toronto: University of Toronto Press, 1978), 8. For Van Laan, two categories of role-playing are dramatic role and mimetic social role, in which personal attributes might be viewed as improvisations within broadly scripted public roles (19–20).

90. Peter Brook, *The Empty Space* (1968; repr. New York: Atheneum, 1978), 109.

hence character does not reveal itself in dynamic relationship so much as it consists of the dynamic relationship revealed. And what we can say of character we can say of the audience's perception of character. To cite *Antony and Cleopatra* once more, the audience's understanding of Octavius derives essentially from our relationship (distance) to his relationship with Antony.[91] Because Shakespeare's tragic characters occur publicly, they can be opaque but never fixed, inscrutable, or unsusceptible to influence. Stressing characterization as "positional" illuminates the openness and possibility, even a certain "indeterminacy," that we often feel about dramatic personages. Our early impressions of Macbeth, for example, contradict each other; witnesses from battle report him as ferociously brave, while on entering he acts fearful and rapt. The possibilities of Macbeth's character embrace both extremes, and the audience will make up its characterization from its evolving engagement and detachment toward the thane. In *Antony and Cleopatra* Octavius's first speech is of Antony, whose errant spirit shapes Octavius's actions, so that the audience must assess Octavius's emotions, such as those toward his sister, in the shadow of emotions as Antony represents them. The playgoer's experience of Octavius, then, will be subtly but pervasively (to use Bakhtin's term) dialogic.

I mention Octavius in part to signal an interest in secondary characters as spectatorial filters to events, emotions, and attitudes in a tragedy (and an interest in their sometime absences as filters for the audience). The properties of secondary characters as transmitters may range from superconductivity to insulation, pure heat to a stopped furnace: Lear's pathos rises with Cordelia's tears; Lear's pathos diminishes before the Fool's laughter. The mere presence of secondary characters working as "response-regulators"[92] demonstrates the dialogics of positional characterization toward which my argument aims. That the Doctor and the Waiting-Gentlewoman, for example, overhear Lady Macbeth's sleepwalking speech isolates her in a stop-time more alienated from the simple honesty and human intercourse of workaday life than any such mutterings alone could reveal. A tragedy progresses, at least partially, in the audience's evolving proximity toward its mysterious heroes and heroines; hence my suggestion that the audience changes during a tragedy whether or not protagonists discover themselves or achieve a liberal education. The clear-cut stage responses of secondary characters entice us because heroes are so opaque (a

---

91. Obviously, then, if the audience's distance affects character, variants in the distance of individual playgoers will also produce differences in the same character as he or she is perceived from viewer to viewer. See Bullough, " 'Psychical Distance' as a Factor in Art and an Aesthetic Principle," 99–100.

92. I take this term from E. A. J. Honigmann, *Shakespeare: Seven Tragedies,* 28.

case of the more prosaic supporting player anchoring the more dramatically nuanced protagonist[93]). Secondary characters will be carefully listened to but cannot be fully trusted, for they translate, popularize, and censor, and Shakespeare will even loose them in batteries of two or three, all differing in response: "*Kent:* Is this the promis'd end? *Edgar:* Or image of that horror? *Albany:* Fall, and cease!" What captures us may not be the validity of any single reaction but the oscillating rhythm itself of reacting. Audience response is positional, relational. As Honigmann concludes, Shakespeare's onstage respondents demand from the offstage spectator exertion, perception, creativity, and "the very highest level of participation" (29).

Tragedy expresses itself in the kinesthetic rhythms of its episodes and scenes. Literary criticism has illuminated the visual and aural power of Shakespearean tragedy: the politics of the color red in *Macbeth;* group configurations in *Julius Caesar;* the sonnet-sounds of *Romeo and Juliet;* Lear's recidivism into bombast; Othello's music. To such a sensory vocabulary we may add kinesthetics, a tragedy's cuings of spectatorial muscular responses, notably contraction and release. John Martin, the first great critic of modern dance, observes that "Movement . . . in and of itself is a medium for the transference of an aesthetic and emotional concept from the consciousness of one individual to that of another."[94] Martin discusses "muscular sympathy" as the instantaneous muscular memory that associates an observed movement with its purpose (12). We recapitulate external physical movements and react even to inert objects with our muscles, as in the human tendency to shrink back when looking up at a skyscraper.[95] Martin describes "metakinesis" as the linkage between the physical and the psychical (13–16). To Martin, the actor is "a modified form of dancer," for "the business of both of them is to express internal feeling through the medium of the body" (96–97)—a view suggestive for the Elizabethan actor, who at the end of a play turned from "modified" to actual dancer. Similarly, Heywood located the actor's essential virtuosity in his "comely and elegant gesture, a gratious and a bewitching kinde of action, a naturall and a familiar motion of the head, the hand, the body, and a moderate and fit countenance sutable to all the rest."[96] Not only do actors communicate their emotions and thoughts kinetically, but Shakespeare's tragic scenes often develop structurally a rhythm of physical tension and relaxation in actors

---

93. Honigmann, *Shakespeare: Seven Tragedies,* 27; Honigmann cites A. C. Sprague on this point.

94. John Martin, *The Modern Dance* (1933; repr. New York: Dance Horizons, 1965), 13.

95. I am indebted to dance historian Larry Warren for valuable insights into these relationships.

96. Thomas Heywood, *An Apology for Actors,* sig. C4r.

and auditors. The opening scene of *Hamlet* achieves its famous power exactly through bodily contraction and release in relation to fear, stated and varied from the change of guard through the double confrontation of the ghost. Such rhythms express the larger emotions or ideas of the tragedy, as the first frightened rigidifying of muscles coincides with the play's social and epistemological paranoia: "Who's there?" The audience becomes rapt in this scene as much for its swings of extreme physical response as its mute poltergeist; such sudden pendular shifts of body and mood will also distinguish its hero. Rhythms of contraction and release, like muscular sympathy altogether, open another window upon the engagement and detachment of the tragedic audience, for tension, expectation, and engagement constitute a physical and conceptual and emotional chain, as do relaxation, resolution, and detachment.

In the theater, as Goldman argues, the art we primarily recognize is the art of acting. Because drama occurs live, we experience the actor working—making immediate physical choices potentially variable and even nuanced from performance to performance—at the same time that we experience the characterization so etched. The actor, then, is always both actor and character, "actor-as-character" (with the two elements often in equipoise but sometimes also seesawing for domination). Audiences will empathize with characters, but they will also engage with the actor's virtuosity, the flexibility, deftness, imagination, economy, and expressiveness that illustrate the art. An involvement with acting, and a complementary distancing from character, can excite a sense of freedom and possibility in the audience, particularly as engagement yields to the spectator's self-consciousness. Virtuosic acting demands that the audience experience the openness of characterization, and thus implicitly of character. Such a sense of openness, moreover, infuses Shakespeare's well-known motif of characters theatricalizing themselves. As Van Laan observes, Shakespeare's characters seldom "do" anything, instead they often "play" an abstract "part": That formula and "the many references to parts, scenes, acts, plays, pageants, and tragedies, helps to establish a world in which *action* equals *acting*" (4–5).

The actorly moment may swing from the passionate to the self-aware and acting styles from the "natural" to the "formal."[97] Tragedies can engage

---

97. I quote these terms from Bernard Beckerman, who summarizes the well-known debate over whether Elizabethan acting was objective, symbolic, obviously rhetorical, on the one hand, or subjective, personal, and realistic, on the other, or some middle or shifting ground between the two. Beckerman favors a view of conventionalized acting for certain character parts and situations, but more internalized acting for other demands, such as expressing significant passion. He demurs generally from the terms "formal" or "natural," and prefers the comprehensive "romantic": *Shakespeare at the Globe: 1599–1609* (1962; repr. New York: Collier Books, 1966), 109–56.

audiences in what Sir Philip Sidney terms "admiration" for their heroes, sometimes achieved by grand effects—such as tragic possession, that passionate overwhelming of body and psyche that, for example, Desdemona recognizes in Othello: "you're fatal then / When your eyes roll so" (*Othello,* V.ii.37–38) or "Alas, why gnaw you so your nether lip? / Some bloody passion shakes your very frame. / These are the portents" (43–45). At the other extreme, tragic performers can share a comparative intimacy with audience members, as when Iago or Hamlet or the Fool turns to them and speaks.[98] In the modern theater, some soliloquies will be performative beyond the already existing performance of the play: Every delivery of "To be" is a self-conscious recital, an action of quotation, aiming at the skill for which we acclaim Gielgud's or Olivier's or Burton's Hamlet. The passion or the self-consciousness that the text invites from its actors can create corresponding changes in spectatorial engagement and detachment. We might distinguish further between "presentational" and "representational" moments in acting style. By "presentational" I mean "formal" acting, the "large" style, but with an emphasis on gestures or actions that point at the fact of acting itself, that announce emotions rather than simply express them.[99] All of Shakespeare's tragic heroes have "presentational" moments, as Van Laan's approach stresses; one well-known example is Antony's "the nobleness of life / Is to do thus" (*Antony and Cleopatra,* I.i.36–37), whereat he presumably kisses or otherwise embraces Cleopatra. The "representational" expression tends toward the naturalistic, "doing" rather than stating or describing the emotion. Presentational passages will detach the audience, alienating it slightly from the action into recognition of theatricality. Such moments stud the protagonists' roles (Othello's last speech looms as an example) with definitive effects upon the audience's experience, if we are to judge by the famous reactions of Eliot and Leavis to Othello's "self-dramatizing."

Shakespearean acting inevitably prompts considerations of "audience contact." Shakespearean tragedy offers numerous opportunities for speaking directly to the audience: choruses, asides, soliloquies, apostrophes, even sententiae. Because such direct address accentuates the likelihood of a response (mental or even oral), an actor speaking to spectators places them "in a truly creative relationship with the actor . . . including the audience in narrative action or introspec-

---

98. Daniel Seltzer suggests that the soliloquies that employ direct audience address in the early and middle plays of Shakespeare yield to "half-soliloquies" and more ensemble scenes with shifting modulations of address in the later plays: "The Actors and Staging," in *A New Companion to Shakespeare Studies,* ed. Kenneth Muir and S. Schoenbaum (Cambridge: Cambridge University Press, 1971), 35–54.

99. Seltzer, "The Actors and Staging," 48.

tive thought."[100] Shakespeare's tragedies recognize audiences beyond direct address. Characters constitute important onstage spectators, and protagonists often become audience-surrogates, interpreting action for the playgoers in a way peculiar to the tragedies, where the hero's mind parallels the structure of the playworld. Tragedies reach out to audiences further through contemporaneous levels of realism: Sampson and Gregory in *Romeo and Juliet,* for example, draw Elizabethan slang and groundling sensibilities into fifteenth-century Verona. Blocking itself can bring the play into different zones of definition and possibility with the audience, as Robert Weimann argues with his distinction between *locus,* the geographically specific middle and rear region of the Elizabethan stage, and *platea,* the generalized no-man's-land proximate to, and shared psychically with, the audience.[101] These plays create their own carnivalesque gestures that can overflow the boundaries of the narrative and obscure the distance between artifact and witness.[102] That fluid interlacing of audience into play, that doubling, might ultimately contribute to the "reality" of the tragic world. Here the audience, at its farthest reaches, like the scientist observing the electron, conspires with the play to invent the facts and rules of the tragic universe. Volition and power expand: The knot of inevitability ("tragic necessity") slackens; protagonists increase in choices and unpredictability, that enlargement restated in the spectator's right to hesitate or embrace.

VII

The audience's relationship to Shakespearean tragedy emerges illustratively in *Romeo and Juliet, Hamlet, Othello, King Lear,* and *Antony and Cleopatra.* These plays collectively demonstrate the aspects of spectatorial distance that we have discussed: radical necessity and radical contingency; positional characterization; rhythms of action, kinetics, and choreography; virtuosic acting; and audience contact. Taken consecutively the plays represent the chronological sweep of Shakespeare's tragedies; as a group they touch on the major categories of previous criticism: the love plots, the Roman themes, the

100. Ibid., 49.

101. Robert Weimann, *Shakespeare and the Popular Tradition in the Theater: Studies in the Social Dimension of Dramatic Form and Function,* ed. Robert Schwartz (Baltimore, Md.: Johns Hopkins University Press, 1978), 73–85.

102. I take this view of the carnivalesque from Mikhail Bakhtin, *Rabelais and His World,* trans. Helene Iswolsky (Bloomington: Indiana University Press, 1984).

"mature" explorations of human consciousness and self-discovery, the ironic tone of the later tragedies. These plays reveal Shakespeare's consistent, varied interest in audience dynamics and audience-mediating devices shaping tragedy. They invite consideration of different aspects of engagement and detachment: detachment as an effect of tone and structure in *Romeo and Juliet,* shifts of distance as the groundplan of the audience's development in *Hamlet,* scenic rhythms creating engagement and detachment in *Othello,* secondary characters as elusive emotional shapers and transmitters in *King Lear,* and spectatorship as the spine of action in *Antony and Cleopatra.*

With *Romeo and Juliet* we can see the creative power of detachment, through structural and stylistic dissonances—including moments when theatrical spectacle undermines narrative argument—in a play that has deeply touched its audiences. *Romeo and Juliet* points to its own artificiality enough that it creates for the spectator a carnivalesque second life against official tragic necessity. From dissonance there, we turn to engagement, and ultimately dramatic memory, in *Hamlet,* whose hero initially behaves more like a spectator than an actor. *Hamlet* establishes a paradigm for the evolution of spectatorial distance from the tragic hero: from engagement, through a reflexive recoiling, to a wonder that the audience experiences in the last scene as both the intensity of the immediate and the uncanny remembering of the play's own past. With *Othello,* we will examine tragedy in its episodes, its rhythms of scenic structure, echoing for the audience the polarities of nobility and folly haunting its hero and the oscillations of auditorial engagement and detachment from moment to moment. In *Othello,* Shakespeare uses episodic structure rather than judgments of secondary characters to shape audience response. With *King Lear,* on the other hand, Shakespeare employs secondary characters, particularly Kent and Edgar, to mark and interpret emotionally and intellectually the features of Lear's progress. (My discussion emphasizes the First Quarto text, where secondary characters are more prominent than in the Folio.) The experience of the tragedy derives significantly from the way these and other characters become embroiled in what they presume to criticize, inducing in the spectator first reliance and then uncertainty. If in *Romeo and Juliet,* spectators share jokes with characters or the play, in *Antony and Cleopatra,* spectatorship becomes finally an internal, central, albeit subtextual, action of the tragedy itself. We come to understand Antony and Cleopatra and the characters who surround them as actors and audiences evolving in dynamic symbiosis. For each tragedy, our discussion will inevitably range among matters of necessity, character progression, secondary characters, acting, episodic rhythms, audience address, and action itself, but with varying emphasis from one play to another.

A performance-oriented study of distance in Shakespearean tragedy contains assumptions and preferences. It tends, for one, to focus on moment-by-moment happenings in a tragedy. An advantage of such detail is that the local events of a tragedy take on renewed multivalence. Though the chapters that follow will explore tragic openings and closings carefully, a performance-oriented criticism will perhaps decline to view the ending of a tragedy as the single great cathartic event capable of settling all that has happened. In the theater, however resonant an ending can be, the audience will never exactly sight backward down the whole corridor of the tragedy from that station. Endings are resting places, they enable us to go home; the finish can be electrifying, but the play in its progress will offer many small epiphanies, rather than waiting for one "big bang." Indeed, a tragedy could be viewed, within a spectatorial poetics, as evolving, capable of expressing emotions and values beyond those imaginable from its activating circumstances.

Spectatorial criticism emphasizes how audiences might be "moved" (physically as well as mentally) rather than the play's meaning expressed in the closed world of the artifact. A performative approach can bridge the gap between the critics' abstractions and what playgoers might actually experience. It subordinates thematic statements about tragedy—what *King Lear* concludes (if anything) about man's relationship with the gods, for example—to the cultural, social, and anthropological experience of the theatrical event. Distance anchors normative statements to contextual relationships within the tragedy and between it and the audience. "Metadramatic" critics have tended to examine tragedy from a thematic model of life-as-theater; I would distinguish the spectatorial approach here, however, as interested in how tragedy may illuminate certain crucial dynamics of human relationships (the "distance" between people) that already exist in social affairs and that structure (often unknowingly) cultural and personal values.

I close with a suggestion about the relational dynamics of tragic endings. We are accustomed in dramatic criticism to rejecting the point of view of any single character as standing fully for that of the play or the play's author. But Shakespearean tragedy contains moments when an action that the audience observes directly, and that beyond doubt occurs, becomes absolutely true only when affirmed by certain "outside" characters. The ghost in *Hamlet* may be fully real for us, for example, only when real to Hamlet; likewise, we are never certain about Macbeth's dagger or Banquo's ghost because no unincriminated character beholds them. Octavius's recognition of Cleopatra's death in *Antony and Cleopatra* offers a useful example. To Octavius, Cleopatra "looks like sleep, / As she would catch another Antony / In her strong toil of grace"

(V.ii.346–48). Yet Octavius reveals nothing to the spectator, only confirms redundantly what we have moments before observed precisely, richly, and elaborately, and that stage-respondents within the scene have confirmed by their own participation. Octavius verifies something that presumably needs no verification. We do not require Caesar only to feel superior to him (what he knows, we know better). Rather, our knowledge (I should say, our *feeling* about our knowledge) would lack something if Octavius did not pay Cleopatra tribute, too. He is an outsider who represents an alien, public point of view and demonstrates the audience's desire for a community of response. Without Caesar, Cleopatra's dream might dislimn like Bottom's dream. Octavius does not affirm our truth; rather he validates our engagement—our distance, the very ground of truth.

1

Theater and Narrative
in *Romeo and Juliet*

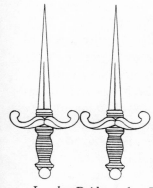

John Downes in his *Roscius Anglicanus, or an Historical Review of the Stage* (1708) tells two anecdotes about *Romeo and Juliet* in the early 1660s, after the reopening of the London theaters. In one Betterton performance, he notes, "There being a Fight and Scuffle in this Play, between the House of *Capulet,* and House of *Paris;* Mrs. *Holden* Acting his Wife, enter'd in a *Hurry,* Crying, O my Dear *Count!* She Inadvertently left out, O, in the pronuntiation of the Word *Count!* giving it a Vehement Accent, put the House into such a Laughter, that *London* Bridge at low Water was silence to it" (22). Downes follows Mrs. Holden's gaff with a second, though less titillating, turn to comedy: "This Tragedy of *Romeo* and *Juliet,* was made some time after into a TragiComedy, by Mr. *James Howard,* he preserving *Romeo* and *Juliet* alive; so that when the Tragedy was Reviv'd again 'twas Play'd Alternately, Tragical one Day, and Tragicomical another; for several Days together" (22). Would a comparable slip of the tongue by, say, Lady Macbeth bring down the house? Could Nahum Tate's *King Lear* play on alternating days with Shakespeare's to audience satisfaction? In Downes's anecdotes one hears the unusual relationship, an extranarrational conspiracy of the carnivalesque, that audiences share with *Romeo and Juliet.*

That *Romeo and Juliet* succeeds somehow derives from the fact that it ought not to. The wet blanket of malign fate, particularly in the claustrophobia of the play's second half, ought to douse the audience's good humor and sympathy. Yet Shakespeare manipulates the playgoer's distance to create the spectacular effectiveness of *Romeo and Juliet:* The audience's sense of the play's artificiality, our very awareness of attending a theatrical event, comes to serve the play itself. Oxymoron (a "pointedly foolish" trope) characterizes *Romeo and Juliet.*[1] The spectators' pleasure in the lovers—sometimes archetypes of doomed young love, other times ridiculous teenagers who talk wildly—depends upon our distance from them. Our engagement with the play's theatricality detaches us from the excesses of the lovers and provides the perspective for holding their passions sympathetically.[2] Detachment affords delight. The spectator's detachment will arise often from disruptions, dissonances in the dramatic moment. A character may violate the immediate narrative flow of action, or speak irrelevancies, or explain more than the context warrants (as with the talk of fate and necessity); theatrical manipulation may call attention to itself (as in the balcony scene), or physical energy and charm on stage may erode a scene's moralistic admonitions: In these cases, a question inserts itself between our engagement and the immediate narrative. Such dissonances are the triumph of *Romeo and Juliet.*

Critics have discussed brilliantly the interplay of comic and tragic expectations in *Romeo and Juliet.*[3] A related oxymoron emerges in the contrast between the determinism of its inner world and the carnivalesque of its theatricality. The carnivalesque, applied to literature by Mikhail Bakhtin, indicates parodic inversions of hierarchical values, which work to undermine the presumed borders of the artifact, such as those separating drama from spectator.[4] *Romeo and Juliet* engages spectators with theatrical play and comic perspectives that fall outside the narrative parabola. Dissonances of tone and texture offer the audience an experience alternate to that of the dead hand

1. Robert O. Evans, *The Osier Cage: Rhetorical Devices in* Romeo and Juliet (Lexington: University of Kentucky Press, 1966).

2. S. L. Bethell applies the term "multi-consciousness" to the Elizabethan audience's capacity to respond spontaneously and unconsciously on different dramatic planes at the same time, such as to conventionalism and naturalism. Suggestive for *Romeo and Juliet* is Bethell's example of Harold Lloyd: "The same incident demands attention from three different points of view simultaneously: as equilibristic performance, as farce, and as romance" (28), *Shakespeare and the Popular Dramatic Tradition* (London: Staples, 1944).

3. See, for example, Susan Snyder, *The Comic Matrix of Shakespeare's Tragedies* (Princeton: Princeton University Press, 1979), 56–70.

4. See Mikhail Bakhtin, *Rabelais and His World,* trans. Helene Iswolsky (Bloomington: Indiana University Press, 1984).

of fate: an open-endedness or freedom inherent in the bleakest moments of the tragedy—even Romeo's suicide. *Romeo and Juliet* is a play about star-crossed lovers that refuses, in the end, to claim the tyranny of its own laws. For the audience, the undertone of carnivalesque engagement can dispute the fatal necessity of the play's official voice. Spectatorial distance—engagement with the theatrical event detaching the audience from the narrative—creates the rebellious good humor by which we approve of the play's romantic passion.

I

Feminist critics have taught us to distinguish between Romeo and Juliet, for the pressures of social and sexual identity vary for each; although love transforms both, it transforms them differently.[5] *Romeo and Juliet* offers the audience two Romeos, distanced unequally from the spectator. The first Romeo charms us: lover and friend. Romeo loves Juliet with a naive earnestness that works to win the audience's heart as well as hers. But the spectator's pleasure (unlike Juliet's) rises from bemused equanimity as much as empathy, for the lovesick Romeo of the early scenes often induces laughter. The first, humorous Romeo also temporizes as one of the boys, Benvolio's and Mercutio's rival in the goose-chasing of wits. In that guise, which Mercutio considers the true Romeo (II.iv.89–90), Romeo charms the audience, too, but also at a distance. The sustained exchanges of wit between Mercutio and Romeo, for example, argue allegorically ("You are a lover, borrow Cupid's wings, / And soar with them above a common bound" [I.iv.17–18]), a humor that demands quick ratiocination and synthesis from the spectator. Such rhetoric will reinforce an audience's awareness of Romeo's habit of allegorizing fate.[6] That allegorist is the second Romeo, who finally swallows the lover and friend. The allegorizing

5. See, for example, Edward Snow, "Language and Sexual Difference in *Romeo and Juliet*," in *Shakespeare's "Rough Magic": Renaissance Essays in Honor of C. L. Barber*, ed. Peter Erickson and Coppélia Kahn (Newark: University of Delaware Press, 1985), 168–92; Irene G. Dash, *Wooing, Wedding, and Power: Women in Shakespeare's Plays* (New York: Columbia University Press, 1981), 67–100; and Coppélia Kahn, "Coming of Age in Verona," *Modern Language Studies* 8 (Winter 1977–78): 5–22.

6. For the phrase, "the allegorizing habit of mind," I am indebted to a conversation with Thomas Moisan (August 1988). Edward Snow notes also that Romeo's language "allegorizes instinctual promptings so that they become external to the self," in "Language and Sexual Difference in *Romeo and Juliet*," 175.

Romeo speaks and acts in ways suddenly disruptive of his dramatic context: He may respond disassociatively or excessively to the subject at hand, or his speeches may disengage the audience as in a set piece, or his energy level may jolt the pacing of a scene.[7] Collectively, such moments transform the audience's distance from Romeo into qualities of his character: Dramatic effect becomes personality. Romeo's dissonances, furthermore, anchor his character in the play's fatalism.[8] He evokes a sense of necessity, as Juliet evokes a more expansive possibility. Romeo does not fascinate the audience with any psycho-drama of grace against rude will or reason against passion.[9] What fascinates us is not so much Romeo's monocular vision of doomed life (viewers may instinctively favor Juliet)[10] as the binocular engagement and detachment by which Shakespeare reveals it. Dissonance will create an interest, a friction, beyond the charm of romance.

The events of *Romeo and Juliet* begin with a great, vigorous brawl, some-times two,[11] whose rushing energy, when Benvolio renarrates it, derails at Romeo's name: engagement and then detachment. As Benvolio tells of whirling "thrusts and blows" (I.i.104–15), Lady Montague switches horses, wondering where Romeo is today (116–17), and disrupts the pacing.[12] Although Lady Montague's fear for her son indirectly links Romeo to Tybalt, Romeo has no connection to the pell-mell. Various other expositional dead ends will haunt Romeo in this scene: The cause of his "Black and portendous" humor (141) is

7. Romeo's dissonances exceed the usual allowance that spectators make for figure against ground. For a consideration of figure–ground relationships in drama, see Bernard Beckerman, *Dynamics of Drama: Theory and Method of Analysis* (1970; repr. New York: Drama Book Specialists, 1979), 137–44.

8. Marilyn L. Williamson develops a similar view of Romeo in "Romeo and Death," *Shakespeare Studies,* vol. 14, ed. J. Leeds Barroll III (New York: Burt Franklin, 1981), 129–37. Williamson concludes that from the beginning Romeo suicidally pursues a "self-ordained destiny" (133) of early death, though she proposes, too, that the feud helps determine Romeo's self-destructive frame of mind. Similarly, Edward Snow observes that "there *is* a suggestion that Romeo is a 'carrier' of attitudes that are agents of tragedy in Shakespeare, and that Juliet's love only partially redeems him from them," in "Language and Sexual Difference in *Romeo and Juliet,*" 173.

9. On this subject, see Virgil K. Whitaker, *The Mirror Up to Nature* (San Marino, Calif.: Huntington Library, 1965), 113–19.

10. Discussing Romeo's "estrangement" even in the experience of love, Edward Snow remarks, "Always, it seems, there is a lack in Romeo that corresponds to an overflowing in Juliet," "Language and Sexual Difference in *Romeo and Juliet,*" 178.

11. The fight between the serving-men is frequently staged comically and as play, that launched by Tybalt's attack on Benvolio seriously and as a fencing display.

12. Nicholas Brooke notes a "radical change" in poetic tone here, parallel to the clash of poetry and prose (genre and effect) elsewhere in the play, in Brooke, *Shakespeare's Early Tragedies* (London: Methuen, 1968), 90.

first a great mystery "far from sounding and discovery" (150), yet Romeo discloses it to Benvolio in a twinkle: "Out of her favor where I am in love" (168). Similarly, Romeo withholds Rosaline's identity from Benevolio, yet a short scene later Benvolio speaks her name[13] (Mercutio will know it too). Why these red herrings? For such narrative false starts create auditorial suspense and then deflate it. Worse, Romeo's Petrarchan platitudes may suggest to the audience that he is not altogether present in mind or, more precariously, may induce our ennui after some initial amusement, especially coming behind the "whiz-bang exhilarating kinesthesia"[14] of the free-for-all. Why would a playwright leave an actor so vulnerable?

Romeo *is* interesting, even mysterious, but more as a melancholic than as a lover. Our interest arises from, first, the prophetic speeches that introduce him and, second, his contextual dissonances once he arrives. Before Romeo appears, Shakespeare paints a vision of him that will guide the audience's impressions. Benvolio and Montague describe together Romeo's pre-dawn peregrinations (118–55). These speeches, not "in character," "are primarily intended to make a direct emotional impression on the minds of the audience,"[15] so that spectators acquire unusual clarity about Romeo's character before he even shows up. Benvolio's and Montague's talk of Romeo becomes a verbal play-within-the-play that "bathes what we see before us in its quality."[16] The effect is to distance the audience from the physical event, two men talking on a platform, and to engage the audience with their imagery. The poetic washes over the corporeal (both the present occasion and Romeo's impending arrival), though later in *Romeo and Juliet* poetic language and the corporeal might dissociate. In a special theatrical sense, the poetry "motivates" Romeo's behavior in the viewer's consciousness. The father and kinsman define Romeo through the mise-en-scène of dew, grove, and chamber. Their language is uneconomical, spilling beyond explication: "the worshipp'd sun" peering through "the golden window of the east," for example; or "the all-cheering sun" "in the farthest east" drawing "The shady curtains from Aurora's bed." Such expansiveness irradiates the painted landscape: the "grove of sycamore" to the

13. On stage Benvolio is sometimes shown guessing that Rosaline is Romeo's love by the emphasis Romeo gives her name in reading over Capulet's invitation list.

14. Michael Goldman, *Shakespeare and the Energies of Drama* (Princeton: Princeton University Press, 1972), 33.

15. James Sutherland, "How Characters Talk," in *Shakespeare's World*, ed. James Sutherland and Joel Hurstfield (New York: St. Martin's, 1964), 122–23.

16. I borrow this language from Bert O. States, *Great Reckonings in Little Rooms: On the Phenomenology of Theater* (Berkeley: University of California Press, 1985), 57; see his discussion of the "tension between seeing and hearing" in Shakespeare, 54–57.

"westward" of the city; Benvolio, alone but "one too many by my weary self," glimpsing his melancholy double in the fleeing Romeo; "the fresh morning's dew" augmented with tears; and the clouds of sighs added to other clouds.

Description is prediction.[17] Montague takes up Benvolio's "stole" ("stole into the covert of the wood"), along with the image of darkness, and uses them to elaborate the lover's dolor five ways in four lines: "Away from light steals home my heavy son, / And private in his chamber pens himself, / Shuts up his windows, locks fair daylight out, / And makes himself an artificial night." Here repetition foretells, for the very reiteration of lugubrious darkness makes "Black and portendous" Romeo's melancholy. That portentousness derives from a poetic vision, an allegorizing habit of mind that will typify Romeo himself. Romeo acts in this language by verbs of closure—"pens," "shuts," "locks"—that he will later enact in life.[18] Benvolio and Montague announce Romeo's destiny. The description is so sustained, insistent, and underlined as to thump the audience into consciousness of its import. The moment is a set piece, one of several. Nor does the vision sound subjective; rather, its baroque amplitude of detail gives it anchorage; it is communal, precisely divided between two speakers who share words and connotations; it has the validation of "many other friends" and the Horatio-like sympathy of Benvolio, something of a lover himself (at least here). The voice of these voices is omniscient. For the audience, then, Romeo arrives psychologically determined.[19] Romeo's melancholy, as with Antonio's in *The Merchant of Venice,* is ontological; it may be puzzled over, but the play will never solve it. The prior description acts as a form of auditorial "discrepant awareness," detaching us from the entering figure, as if we already know him better than he knows himself. Accordingly, our sense of melancholy as his essence exceeds and encloses what we will learn here, the transient emotional weather named Rosaline.

Such knowledge poses an acting problem, for if Romeo's sonnetese offers him no more complexity than a sentimental lover's, he will eventually tire the

17. Sun, east, window, and bed brighten our imagination with a second life; later they will become Juliet.

18. Likewise, grove and chamber hint at sexuality, and the elaborate image of Romeo pursuing darkness will find its corollary in Juliet's tomb and his untimely death. For a discussion of this relationship, see Marjorie Garber, *Coming of Age in Shakespeare* (New York: Methuen, 1981), 163–70.

19. For a critique of the "slave of passion" view of Romeo and for the Thomist argument that Romeo's behavior demonstrates how "sin rises not from the appetite, but from the will" (63), see Stanley Stewart, "Romeo and Necessity," in *Pacific Coast Studies in Shakespeare,* ed. Waldo F. McNeir and Thelma N. Greenfield (Eugene: University of Oregon Press, 1966), 47–67.

audience. One solution offered the actor by the language is to reveal a strain of exasperation beneath the Petrarchan affectations.[20] Shakespeare erects *inside* Romeo's cataloging sonnetese a kind of impatient misery, a deep, restless fatalism. The role invests despair with youthful vigor, providing surprise for the audience against the locking of conventional end-rhymes. The Romeo-actor, assisted by emotions that shift like a signaling semaphore, can become sometimes unintentionally humorous, sometimes piqued, sometimes indecipherably formulaic. Take Romeo's second speech (161–62): It begins with an outburst sigh ("Ay me"—a phrase which Mercutio later parodies [II.i.10]), decelerates into dolefulness ("Sad hours seem long"), then breaks that drift with an errant interest in the passing scene ("Was that my father that went hence so fast?"—another red herring).[21] Romeo's fits and starts are cues by which the actor can reveal emotional paradoxes beneath or beyond the merely Petrarchan. He breaks off, "Where shall we dine?" (173)—bored? exasperated? Next he recognizes the world around him, "O me! what fray was here?" (173), but then informs us, remarkably, that he had already heard of the brawl (174)—and apparently forgotten it. He lapses into nonsense-that-sounds-like-sense: "Here's much to do with hate, but more with love. / Why then, O brawling love! O loving hate! / O any thing, of nothing first create" (175–77). This last formula carries a teasing suggestiveness that can detach the spectator. An editor might gloss the first line, for example, as "the combatants enjoyed their anger," yet in performance few audience members can make such a sophisticated leap from the abstract to the particular. Like many of Romeo's effusions here, the statement is inapplicable and unintelligible, essentially disengaging; it demands guesswork that the rush of speech forces us as quickly to abandon. Romeo's lines arrest us by their misdirections: "What is it else?" (193) hints at insincerity; "Farewell, my coz . . . I am not here" (195–97) fractured attention; "In sadness, cousin, I do love a woman" (204) oblivious humor. Such restless melancholy is the deepest engine we see in Romeo; the challenge—and opportunity—for the actor is to expose the personalized sadness under the prescriptive. Watching from the viewpoint of its prior initiation into Romeo's melancholy, the audience will become engaged with the mysterious, dissonant subtext developing underneath his Petrarchan imbecilities. Romeo's death-wish may be instanced as hopeless love, but it can reach the audience as

---

20. Nicholas Brooke observes in Romeo's witticisms about love a false detachment that reveals a "pressure from within him," *Shakespeare's Early Tragedies,* 91.

21. An even redder herring comes later in the scene: Says Romeo of Rosaline, "She will not . . . bide th' encounter of assailing eyes, / Nor ope her lap to saint-seducing gold" (212–14). If Romeo has winked at Rosaline, has he also offered her money?

more compelling than love.[22] Distanced from Romeo's feckless mooning over Rosaline, spectators will be able to sense a deeper ground of their curiosity about him. The way in which Romeo stands outside the action is really the way in which he stands inside his own fatal "humor."[23]

Romeo's ensuing scenes cue other moments of spectatorial detachment through disruptions of the narrative flow. To the servant's question, "can you read?" (I.ii.57), for example, Romeo extravagantly replies, "Ay, mine own fortune in my misery" (58). That Romeo's "story" will be sorrowful is a personal leap of despair: It sounds invented and pushes the spectator back from its claimant. Likewise, Shakespeare distances the viewer from Romeo in the scene before the ball (I.iv), where Romeo's allegorizing habit of mind conflicts with his friends' enticements to pleasure. Romeo completes his willful reading of his fortune in his misery with a sentence of doom, followed theatrically by marching drums:

> I fear, too early, for my mind misgives
> Some consequence yet hanging in the stars
> Shall bitterly begin his fearful date
> With this night's revels, and expire the term
> Of a despised life clos'd in my breast
> By some vile forfeit of untimely death.
>
> (106–11)

Such misgivings, uttered in a vacuum of proximate cause, leap out at the spectator. The sentimental allegorizing of "consequence" discourages complete auditorial empathy, and for some might invite disbelief. Romeo's fatalism may strike the modern mind as gratuitous more than it might have the Elizabethan. But maybe not: His remarks enforce the spectator's distanced sense of his dominating obsessions.[24] Romeo's speech calls attention to itself as prophecy and, dissonantly, as "presentation," for, with a heavy-handed staginess, it invites the actor to step out of the dramatic context (by facing or glancing at

22. Ruth Nevo argues that Romeo's self-awareness as a man doomed by "an external and inimical power" takes the place of villainy or division of the psyche. The lovers share misgivings that both fulfill the "Senecan formula" and are "their own imaginative creation"; see *Tragic Form in Shakespeare* (Princeton: Princeton University Press, 1972), 34.

23. Edward Snow observes that Romeo's "imaginative universe . . . is dominated by eyesight," tends to "assemble reality 'out there,'" and makes him an "onlooker rather than a participant," "Language and Sexual Difference in *Romeo and Juliet*," 170.

24. By contrast, Carlisle's prophecy in *Richard II* (IV.i.134–49) sounds omniscient partly because he speaks it about someone else, Bullingbroke; Romeo's prophecy sounds more fanciful, because he speaks it about himself.

the audience, even moving downstage), just as his despair exceeds that context. Various moments in the scene, moreover, hint at a reflexive theatrical humor, such as Romeo's and Mercutio's witty exchange on burning daylight (43–47), which sets, with comic effect, the darkness of the stage illusion against the actual daylight of the Elizabethan theater. Romeo's detachment from the reality around him encourages a corresponding spectatorial detachment from him.

Romeo's dissonance weighs down the play. *Romeo and Juliet's* language of heaviness and lightness provides the audience a visceral analogue for the experiences of its protagonists and a vertical complement to the play's explosive forward energy (early, swords "cut the winds" [I.i.111]; later, bodies fall). Approaching the masque, Romeo represents his lassitude as Petrarchan weightedness: "Being but heavy, I will bear the light" (I.iv.12); "I have a soul of lead / So stakes me to the ground I cannot move" (15–16); "Under love's heavy burthen do I sink" (22). This language is performative, not as speech-act, but as imagery that will demand a corresponding bodily carriage from the actor and a corresponding muscular response from the audience. Kinesthetically, the spectator may feel Romeo's heaviness. That physical engagement may lessen the distancing effect of Romeo's lugubrious allegorizing. His pre-masque manner of speech has changed, furthermore, from the earlier complaints of the textbook lover to a pain personalized and accessible to the audience. Romeo's style is plainer, more monosyllabic, more periodic; the dense parataxes, chiasmi, medial stops, and euphuisms of his first talk with Benvolio yield to a rhythm of the heart, investing the once-airy sonnetese with the new gravity of a "soul of lead."

Yet Romeo's leaden soul verges on the humorous. While Romeo might become transformed in loving Juliet, he still brings to the balcony scene, for example, his old formulaic conventions of bodily thought: injury ("He jests at scars that never felt a wound" [II.ii.1]), sickness ("the envious moon, / Who is already sick and pale with grief" [4–5]), and especially weight. True love confirms itself to the audience as antigravitational spectacle: the elevated body of Romeo, who has climbed the orchard wall—"With love's light wings" (66)—and then scales Juliet's balcony. Some productions will show Romeo dangling precariously and comically from the balusters of the Capulet facade, a visual pun on love and humor (both "lightness") as the defeat of "gravity"! Romeo loves Juliet in response to his weighted melancholy and unrequited love for Rosaline. In his kinetic imagery, Juliet stands wholly (and merely) as the redemptive angel to his sense of loss. Thus Romeo can both love Juliet and yet be driven by despair, and thus the audience can both engage with and detach itself from him. His "lightness" exhilarates the spectators, even as it ironically privileges his "heaviness." Romeo loves in the expectation of defeat; his fatalism fuses with his joy in Juliet to give his self-destructiveness a psychological compulsion beyond the conventions of romance. In the brief premarriage scene, Romeo declares, "but come what sorrow can, / It cannot countervail" the joy he feels in seeing Juliet (II.vi.3–4); so long as they will be married, "Then love-devouring death do what he dare" (7). Such formulations as "come what sorrow can" and "death do what he dare" locate oxymoronically a subjunctive mood within a third-person imperative. They are commands to a condition contrary to fact, invitations to disaster, the words of a man convinced that untimely death is already his fate. Likewise for Romeo, banishment is "the stroke that murders me" (III.iii.23), and, moments later, his sorrow literalizes the metaphor of weightedness as he falls to the ground, "Taking the measure of an unmade grave" (70). His statements are in the indicative mood, but one point in having Romeo make them is to indicate what is *not* happening. His imperative of doom exists largely in the nonexistent subjunctive. The drama of Romeo's fatalism thus offers the actor one characterological "through-line" for arousing the audience's interest.

The banishment scene (III.iii) constitutes perhaps the turning point in the play for the audience's view of Romeo: While the scene engages the audience with Romeo's passion, it fixes that sympathy inside a detachment (amused and serious in different respects) from his hyperbole. The scene structures an increasingly distanced view of Romeo. Friar Lawrence first tells Romeo of his banishment and tries to console him. Detachment and sympathy stalemate, with the Friar offering abstractly, "Adversity's sweet milk, philosophy," and Romeo retorting, to our immediate sympathy, "Hang up philosophy! / Unless philosophy can make a Juliet" (55, 57–58). The humor of Lawrence's repetitions of "banishment," however, works toward disengaging the spectator from Romeo. Then stock comedy takes the upper hand, as Romeo flails prone on the floor, and the Friar flutters between him and the door-knocking. At the Nurse's news, Romeo builds to an utterly melodramatic gesture: "O, tell me, friar, tell me, / In what vile part of this anatomy / Doth my name lodge?" (105–7), he cries, attempting to stab himself. Romeo, that is, stage-acts his suicide attempt; the gesture is presentational, and disengagingly funny, for it suggests that Romeo operates from a sense of spectatorial effect. The traditional stage direction from Q1, that the Nurse rather than Lawrence snatches away Romeo's dagger, underscores the comedy of his act. Romeo's attempted suicide provokes a fifty-line remonstrance from Friar Lawrence, the longest speech in the play. Though not without humor,[25] the speech rises to a new sobriety: "Thou hast amaz'd me! By my holy order, / I thought thy disposition better temper'd. . . . Wilt thou slay thyself, / And slay thy lady that in thy life lives, / By doing damned hate upon thyself?" (114–18). The subject of the scene becomes not Romeo's recent banishment but his present rashness, with the audience's sympathy for his sorrow couched inside a comically nuanced detachment from his impetuosity, the kind of framing that will typify the audience for the rest of the tragedy.

The audience notices Romeo's morbidity because it so frequently disrupts dramatic context, encouraging disengagement. Romeo's dramatic *position* moment by moment thus translates into spectatorial conclusions about his nature. *Romeo and Juliet* aims the audience's "development" toward a growing consciousness that Romeo's fatalism helps drive his fate. That recognition makes his speeches opening act V haunting, disturbing. Though Romeo tells us that his "dreams presage some joyful news," that his heart "sits lightly," and that "an unaccustom'd spirit / Lifts me above ground with cheerful thoughts" (2–5), not even the most innocent theatergoer will take this buoyancy at face value. For an audience can perceive in Romeo the loss of distinction between joy and final despair; one is the mirror of the other. We know, before Romeo promises it, that he will commit suicide, for only death will complete his allegory. What may disturb the spectator is that the surprised joy and the exultation of psychic release express the last station of melancholy (Shakespeare will return to this mood in *Macbeth*). "Then I defy you, stars!" (24) sounds like the achieved selfhood of Romeo's life, transmuting existence to a pure act of volition.[26] But the suspicion of delusion can unnerve and distance the audience. For Romeo surrenders a future to a past. His gesture of defiance is the last collapse into "artificial night," the image by which the audience has known Romeo first—and best.

Romeo is the most eminent of several characters (particularly the men: Mercutio, Tybalt, Paris) whose monocular vision betrays itself through spectatorial detachment. Mercutio's panegyric to Queen Mab (I.iv.53–95), the

25. The Friar's lines, "A pack of blessings light upon thy back, / Happiness courts thee in her best array" (141–42), for example, distance the audience by exaggeration. That will be the more true for audience members who hear in such lines a parody of Cicero's stoic definition of happiness, as in, for example, the *Tusculan Disputations,* a standard text in Tudor education. The distancing continues in the Nurse's comic praise and admiration for good counsel and learning (159–60).

26. For an interpretation of Romeo's defiance of the stars and his lightness before death as growth, see Gibbons, for example, who finds "Romeo's transformation of personality" expressed in the way his "images are felt as both spontaneous and inevitable products of the moment," Brian Gibbons, ed., *Romeo and Juliet* (New York: Methuen, 1980), 50–51.

ambassadress of wishful thinking, demonstrates that condition dramatically and emblematically, shifting the audience from charmed engagement to self-conscious distance in order to make the point. The speech is a set-piece that evolves wildly out of proportion to its motivation in present action; in that sense, it illustrates the dissonant excesses by which we mark Romeo. The Queen Mab speech functions by a superfluity of details—such as the agate-ring size of Queen Mab, her hazelnut chariot made by the joiner squirrel, her wagon spokes of spiders' legs, her collars of waterish moonshine—that retard its own narrative advance. A play-within-a-play, the Queen Mab speech invites its own improvisational hand-puppeteering before its inner audience of maskers (men-puppets). Mercutio's detailings of the bodily parts of Mab's victims, from knees to fingers to lips to noses to necks, constitute cues to the actor for mimicry, "showing." Mercutio's imagery and the sheer thespian virtuosity required of his talk intoxicate him; illustrative details lengthen into anecdotes (the soldier [82–88], the maids [92–95]); and Romeo must forcefully interrupt this careening. On stage the language surely runs away with Mercutio, absorbing, engrossing him. The Queen Mab speech dramatizes its own content; it both discusses and performs, before Romeo (who misses the point), the power of fantasy over reality, the inner allegory over the social fact.

For the audience, Mercutio's Queen Mab speech might be one of the most intense and disturbing, finally detaching, events in all of *Romeo and Juliet*. A whisper in the spectator's mind wonders momentarily about the episode's intention and relevance, as the speech is needless, self-contained. Yet we will engage initially more than we will doubt. The allegory's specificity of imagery, elaborateness of conceit, and witty strangeness seduce the audience as virtuosic poetry. Gradually, however, the speech's amplitude of detail weighs it down, raises spectatorial reservations. We connect with Mercutio, then recognize his loss of control, a pattern of spectatorial submersion followed by the jolt of self-awareness, a pattern that distinguishes *Romeo and Juliet* as a whole. Romeo's intervention—"Peace, peace, Mercutio, peace! / Thou talk'st of nothing" (95–96)—declares publicly what the audience has *already* come to feel. Mercutio's intoxication frightens, even threatens the spectator, necessitating Romeo's formal release. The moment, then, transforms into overt spectatorial recognition, and (if engagement favors the psychological and detachment the emblematic) the audience might experience directly the disturbing power of a "humor" that runs away with itself.

Much that is tragic arises from such self-puppetry, in a manner that calls to the spectator's consciousness. Tybalt offers a character noticeably wooden in speech and gesture,[27] yet strangely under everyone's skin—rebuked by Capulet, revered by Juliet, and reviled by Mercutio. At the play's outset, Tybalt rushes in "with his sword prepar'd" (I.i.109), convinced that Benvolio is quarreling with inferiors, despite Benvolio's straightforward explanation (66–70). Their exchange denotes Tybalt truly, informing the audience that Tybalt lives within his prior conception of events, despite reason or refutation. Tybalt, of course, will later assume that Romeo has invaded the Capulet feast only "to fleer and scorn at our solemnity" (I.v.57), a crucial misjudgment again emphasized in Capulet's demurral: " 'A bears him like a portly gentleman; / . . . a virtuous and well-govern'd youth" (66–68). Tybalt stands for Romeo's alter ego or double, alike in essence if not in manifestation, whose insistence on seeing the world solely in the light of his anger parallels the operation of Romeo's melancholy. That these two determinists should be in fatal opposition fits the real tragic nature (the opposition of likenesses) of the playworld.[28] Romeo's later decision to duel springs, at least partially, from his allegory of fate, exactly as Tybalt's from his allegory of feud: "This day's black fate on moe days doth depend" (III.i.119). When Benvolio remarks that he avoided Romeo in the early morning, "measuring his affections by my own" (I.i.126), he confesses a simple projection of subjective vision onto the world, a shared habit underlying the pathos so frustrating to the audience. In these respects, *Romeo and Juliet* embeds a morality inside its tragedy.

II

In terms of fate, *Romeo and Juliet* unveils its architecture by indulging and then exposing causation and necessity as essentially "poetic" manipulations. As *Titus Andronicus* parodies revenge, *Romeo and Juliet* parodies necessity. For if the play has anything, it has a herd of metaphysical and anthropological candidates for prime mover: hatred and anger, coincidence or accident,

27. Thomas Moisan notes that "Tybalt is a man of few words, and he tends to repeat the few he uses": "Rhetoric and the Rehearsal of Death: The 'Lamentations' Scene in *Romeo and Juliet*," *Shakespeare Quarterly* 34 (Winter 1983): 398.

28. Susan Snyder views Tybalt as a tragic type because the feud is his "inner law"; after his death, she argues, Tybalt's imperatives dominate the play, creating the turn from comic to tragic: *The Comic Matrix of Shakespeare's Tragedies*, 60–61.

misinterpretation, time, heaven, fate itself, and, of course, love.[29] For the spectator, the plot of *Romeo and Juliet* verges on an embarrassment of glitches, with the sheer profusion of explanations for disaster compromising each. Norman Rabkin points out that "the play is extraordinarily rich, even for Shakespeare, in poetic devices that call our attention to themselves" (167), a comment that applies well to the "devices" that suggest necessity.

The Capulets' discovery of Juliet's body (IV.v) can serve as a useful, if extreme, paradigm of the spectatorial mechanics of one such device, time as necessity. Time emerges as arguably the play's chief stalking-horse for fate or inevitability, particularly because the rush, protraction, and pressure of time operates as a theatrical experience as well as a concept. Scholars have noted the discovery scene's stilted, artificial language, "awakening in us more embarrassment than sympathy" (Rabkin, 173).[30] The cant phrases and rhymed *sententiae* in the scene can detach the audience critically from what the characters so busily talk themselves into, that they are victims of Time: "O day, O day, O day, O hateful day! / Never was seen so black a day as this" (52–53), cries the Nurse repeatedly; "Uncomfortable time, why cam'st thou now / To murther, murther our solemnity?," asks Capulet (60–61). The discovery scene follows the brisk, high-spirited wedding preparations (IV.iv). There the spectator feels the push of time: "the second cock hath crowed, / The curfew-bell hath rung, 'tis three a' clock" (3–4). Hours pass in minutes: "Good faith, 'tis day. /

29. Ruth Nevo, for example, stresses chance and fortune, *Tragic Form in Shakespeare*, 32–34. Norman Rabkin focuses on the lovers' passion as destructive yet wiser than the elders' words of caution, in *Shakespeare and the Common Understanding* (Chicago: University of Chicago Press, 1967), 181–83. Douglas L. Peterson emphasizes Providence (certain in ends though variable in means), in "*Romeo and Juliet* and The Art of Moral Navigation," in *Pacific Coast Studies in Shakespeare*, 33–46. On the other hand, Irving Ribner finds a prescriptive, merciful, and just Providence according to which, for the lovers, "there is no sin" (27), *Patterns in Shakespearean Tragedy* (1960; repr. London: Methuen, 1971), 25–35. Betrand Evans offers an extended treatment of the play as a tragedy of Fate in the form of "unawareness," *Shakespeare's Tragic Practice* (Oxford: Clarendon, 1979), 22–51. H. B. Charlton analyses the feud as the immediate and Fate as the ultimate inevitability, but finds neither convincing and argues that, even for the sixteenth-century spectator, "Fate was no longer a deity strong enough to carry the responsibility of a tragic universe" (61), *Shakespearean Tragedy* (Cambridge: Cambridge University Press, 1961), 49–63.

30. Rabkin discusses the style and rhetoric of the scene in detail, *Shakespeare and the Common Understanding*, 168–74. In an interesting deconstructive reading that emphasizes the distancing effect of "excessive" rhetoric, Thomas Moisan contends, further, that the mourners' "rhetorical response to, and retreat from, the issue of death in the 'lamentations' scene can only make us more—not less—wary in our response to that other confrontation with death, the one that Romeo and Juliet conceive and shape through the power of their rhetoric and enact in Juliet's tomb" (390), "Rhetoric and the Rehearsal of Death: The 'Lamentations' Scene in *Romeo and Juliet*": 389–404.

The County will be here with music straight" (21–22), and suddenly he arrives, "I hear him now" (23). Such speed halts in the discovery scene, where all the characters lengthen out, to our discomfort, their accusations of malignant time: "heavy day" (18), "miserable hour" (44), "woeful time" (30). These lamentings become embarrassing, suspect, and painful to the audience, given its "discrepant awareness" and the scene's exacerbated artificiality. They take up too much time![31] First, the spectators' unwanted complicity in the Capulets' deception will make them desire that the scene end quickly (particularly as the previous scene has just primed them for fast pacing)—the opposite of what happens. That dwelling upon the depredations of time, then, doubles the effect, calling our attention to our own discomfort. The repeated accusations against time can disengage audiences from the act of blaming time: Performance undercuts argument.

Second, the audience must watch the style of grief, its presentation, increasingly falsify the emotion of grief (Rabkin). The discovery scene, of course, offers a set-piece, a fixed dramatic protocol of keening that characters (and actors) simply fall into. Different characters will evoke different levels of realism and artificiality in grief. The Nurse will sound like a programmed chorus, even provoking reflexive laughter in the audience. Capulet, on the other hand, behaves at first much more realistically and sympathetically: testing Juliet's body ("she's cold . . . her joints are stiff" [25–26]), falling inarticulate in sorrow ("Death . . . / Ties up my tongue and will not let me speak" [31–32]). Yet their speeches become more and more rhetorically stilted, demanding from the actors an exaggeratedly presentational style and trapping the audience in an embarrassed knowledge compounded by aesthetic distaste. The audience, that is, starts uncomfortably and moves to more discomfort. We want out, and will need the formal release of Friar Lawrence's "Peace ho, for shame!" (65) as much as do the characters. As one emotional effect, then, the scene severely and progressively disengages the audience from the formulizing of fate. Such distancing characterizes *Romeo and Juliet*. Harry Levin notes, for example, the play's "mechanical and unnatural" architectonics, against which "the lovers stand out, the one organic relation amid an overplus of stylized expressions

31. My discussion assumes consecutive speaking of the characters' lamentations. Charles B. Lower argues to the contrary that the stage direction, "All at once cry out and wring their hand," from the "bad" quarto, Q1, expresses Shakespeare's "final intention," to create a "cacophony of four characters wailing simultaneously" that is unambiguously comic for the audience: "*Romeo and Juliet*, IV.v: A Stage Direction and Purposeful Comedy," *Shakespeare Studies*, vol. 8, ed. J. Leeds Barroll III (New York: Burt Franklin, 1975), 177–94. Such a staging makes the scene disengagingly comic, but eliminates the ironic stage rendering of time.

and attitudes."[32] The play, that is, develops an overarchingly presentational manner that forces the audience into detached recognition of its artificiality.

To explore "necessity" further in *Romeo and Juliet,* we might turn from an episode to a character, Friar Lawrence, whose appearance after the balcony scene illustrates the "stylized" in contrast to the "organic." The play's most ubiquitous and amiable prophet of the unseen hand, Friar Lawrence replaces the Chorus by internalizing its prophetic role into the action. Yet as Friar Lawrence changes from homilist to facilitator to strategist (becoming progressively less characterized, more mechanical, more embedded in events), the audience changes from a complex identification with him to a detachment from the "necessity" he unwittingly represents. Friar Lawrence's first appearance establishes the equivocal distance that the play will expand. His entrance lines (II.iii.1–30) are particularly stiff and formal; hereafter he inches toward the colloquial. The verses present a landmine for actors. Beyond the clichéd rhymes (night/light, tomb/womb), the metaphors verge on the strange, the syntax on the harrowing, and the moralism on the disembodied. Yet the Lawrence-actor can emerge winningly. The most important fact about Lawrence's speech is that it follows within a breath the balcony scene. Given the unreleased, supercharged sexual energy of that scene, Friar Lawrence's first dozen stilted lines might well be thrown away on an audience.[33] If the playgoer does listen, then the peculiar opening images will distance by their own effect. "And fleckled darkness like a drunkard reels" (2–3): Has anyone seen a lurching dawn? Or amuse with sing-song: "Now ere the sun advance his burning eye, / The day to cheer and night's dank dew to dry" (5–6). Or confuse with such reversed syntax as, "And from her womb children of divers kind / We sucking on her natural bosom find" (11–12). But the actor can turn these opening verses to entertainment through his own virtuosity. Their difficulty calls attention to their performance: The tricky plosives of day-dank-dew-dry (6), for example, call for a specific pacing and articulation, and "from her womb" can emerge as sense if well-parsed vocally. This theatrically problematic poetry makes its successful performance charming (an actor playing Lawrence will usually possess a comedian's

32. Harry Levin, "Form and Formality in *Romeo and Juliet,*" in *Shakespeare and the Revolution of the Times* (New York: Oxford University Press, 1976), 113–14.

33. George Walton Williams regards Lawrence's first four lines as textually "perhaps the most difficult of cruces in the play" (119). Q2 assigns almost identical lines to Romeo at the close of the balcony scene and to Lawrence at the opening of the next (other quartos and folios ascribe variously between these two). Williams leaves the lines with Romeo; most modern editors of the play assign them to Lawrence. See George Walton Williams, ed., *The Most Excellent and Lamentable Tragedie of Romeo and Juliet: A Critical Edition* (Durham, N.C.: Duke University Press, 1964), 119–21.

presentational skills). We detach from the character and engage with the acting. As this pattern foretells, Lawrence's moralisms and forebodings will lack the authority of a figure with whom spectators deeply engage.

The audience's distance from the Friar's homilies, moreover, can stimulate doubts about their application to Romeo. Lawrence culls his simples and totes up grace and rude will: "Virtue itself turns vice, being misapplied, / And vice sometime by action dignified"—here Romeo enters silently—"Within the infant rind of this weak flower / Poison hath residence and medicine power" (21-24). Although critics view these didactic lines as commentary upon Romeo, they succeed theatrically by their ambiguity. They might, for example, characterize Friar Lawrence himself (which later experience shall confirm), particularly if the spectator hears this "point" while watching the newly entered Romeo (instantly an audience-surrogate) watch an unsuspecting Lawrence. And if the lines aim at Romeo, they do not stick well. In the dramatic moment, we hardly grasp how virtue misapplied describes Romeo, nor does vice dignified by action capture our sense of him either. Instead, the audience might well experience the familiar friction between language and action. That effect will increase with Lawrence's couplet describing a flower's poison and medicine. The detail begins to hobble the comparison: Is not Romeo more substantial than "the infant rind of this weak flower" (23); are not "poison" and "medicine" (24) overmoralized for his dalliances? With the next couplet the Friar-actor may display and even pick apart the flower, pulling our attention to it: "For this, being smelt, with that part cheers each part, / Being tasted, stays all senses with the heart" (25-26). Is this still an analogy to Romeo? The elaboration of the metaphor can draw the audience's focus away from its application (something similar will happen with the Apothecary). In the study, we can tease an interpretation out of Lawrence's rhetoric; in the theater, his lines confuse our moral estimation of Romeo.[34] The Friar's opening speech, then, invites engagement with the actor's excellence but confronts the audience with the elusiveness of theatrical "meaning." His prophecies make a bad fit. Physical action and metaphysical speculation do not always complement each other in *Romeo and Juliet,* and their juxtaposition can produce an auditorial tension of heightened interest and doubt both—an unprivileging of any single conclusion. Throughout the ensuing interview, Friar Lawrence will chastise Romeo or react aghast, but always so as to make the audience sense his comic indulgence, as with "God pardon sin! Wast thou

---

34. For the view that Friar Lawrence's botany serves as a moral guide to the audience, see Whitaker, *The Mirror Up to Nature,* 117-18.

with Rosaline?" (44) or "Riddling confession finds but riddling shrift" (56). The Friar, who has had most of the words in the scene, gets the last ones: "Wisely and slow, they stumble that run fast" (94), as he exits contradictorily to abet Romeo's "sudden haste" (93). Our engagement with Lawrence's fellowship distances us from such dire warnings, just as his warmth of expression divides from his severe words. Phrases such as "Wisely and slow," of course, reach Romeo and Juliet as if from a far planet. These epigrams, essentially another of the play's stalking-horses for "necessity," remain so abstract (*Romeo and Juliet* offers no examples of "Wisely and slow") as themselves finally to disengage the audience.

Spectatorial engagement with the lovers consistently overpowers, and detaches the audience from, Lawrence's forebodings. As Romeo and Lawrence await Juliet for the marriage ceremony, the Friar takes occasion to chide Romeo in the familiar vein: "Therefore love moderately: long love doth so; / Too swift arrives as tardy as too slow" (II.vi.14–15). But the next arrival he sees is Juliet: "Here comes the lady. O, so light a foot / Will ne'er wear out the everlasting flint," and he proceeds to imagine lovers bestriding gossamers, "so light is vanity" (16–20). Conventional thoughts, but how auditorily dissonant in physical context! Lawrence wishes to score with Romeo and the audience a point about the vain lightness of youthful romance and its insubstantiality before life's "everlasting flint." Yet what actually touches him and what will turn the audience deaf to moralizing is the sylphlike grace and sheer physical presence of the lady. Beauty makes vanity beside the point, both in the theater and in the story. The tone of Lawrence's very lines will coerce the actor to speak them in admiration or wonder. Until we reach the lightness of vanity (20), the audience may easily miss the criticism in the acknowledgment of her soft tread, words that sound more like longing than regret. The Friar's proverbs become irrelevant in our viewing—and even in his voice.

Lawrence's sententiae, along with Romeo's despair, formulate the audience's sense of the laws of inevitability that the lovers presumably ignore to their peril. But the Friar, of course, manipulates the reality he presumes to describe; he is the observer whose presence contaminates what is observed.[35] Indeed, as "fate" apparently entangles the lovers more and more, Lawrence implicates himself increasingly as a shaper of the action, allowing spectators by the last

---

35. G. Blakemore Evans notes, as do others, that "the Friar's function as orthodox moral commentator . . . seems to be at odds with aspects of his character and actions as a man," in G. Blakemore Evans, ed., *Romeo and Juliet* (New York: Cambridge University Press, 1984), 25.

act to withdraw the privileges of commentary they have allowed him.[36] In that event, Friar Lawrence's providential etiology will reveal itself as merely another fragment in the evolving action, working just like Romeo's dooms-manship, so that "causation" for these characters may emerge as not so much fate but epigrams about fate.

Consider two species of dramatic "necessity." One, which we might call narrative necessity, advances with a cause-and-effect logic. Certain environments, certain characters, and certain stimuli produce certain results: That Tybalt, given his fiery and combative talk, would challenge Romeo is predictable from Romeo's intrusion upon the Capulet feast. In this species, drama works roughly like the mechanistic laws of nineteenth-century physics, so that causes appear to the viewer as "objective," internal to the plot, and external to the watcher. A different form of dramatic necessity, however, occurs not from such a chain-link logic. Its appropriateness derives from symmetry, decorum, analogy, repetition, prediction—the audience's poetic expectations. That Tybalt slays Mercutio "requires" as a matter of symmetry, whatever reasons else, that Romeo slay him. Shakespeare applies Chekhov's dictum that a loaded gun in the first act will go off in the third. Such "necessity" arises poetically. Indeed, the poetic features of a play create a field of possibilities, a tone, in which certain kinds of events can or cannot happen at a particular moment because they do or do not happen elsewhere. This causation demands our consent in a way that the first does not, for with narrative necessity, propriety arises from the events themselves, whereas poetic necessity works only if the spectator possesses a decorum parallel to that of the drama.

The audience comes to recognize (if not in these terms) that *Romeo and Juliet* works forcefully by poetic necessity, the loaded gun, as well as by narrative necessity. Recognizing this second, poetic necessity involves recogniz-ing the theatrics of the play, and *Romeo and Juliet* persistently calls attention to its own theater. Our theatrical awareness loosens the grip of narrative necessity, or, in this play, fatal inevitability. Narrative necessity constitutes merely a formal, structural version of Romeo's psychological determinism. The first exchange of the play, between Sampson and Gregory—where the argument progresses less by logic than by a "field" of puns[37]—establishes that poetic structure unconsciously in the audience's listening; it will emerge more consciously as the play progresses. The duels, particularly that between Mercutio

36. Levin observes that Lawrence contributes to the disaster by ignoring his own advice: "Wisely and slow," "Form and Formality in *Romeo and Juliet*," 114.

37. For a discussion of the effect of punning in *Romeo and Juliet*, see Michael Goldman, *Shakespeare and the Energies of Drama*, 33–44.

and Tybalt, demonstrate *Romeo and Juliet*'s poetic nexus of causation. The audience's engagement with Mercutio against Tybalt in III.i leads to a climactic moment of dissonance and detachment—"A plague a' both houses!" (III.i. 91)—illuminating the false necessities by which characters live and die. Tybalt's exit from and reentrance into the dueling scene suggest that deeper structure. Tybalt, upon wounding Mercutio, rushes offstage; after Mercutio's dying words, with the news of his passing freshly arrived, and with just enough time for Romeo to utter a handful of lines on his own dishonor, "comes the furious Tybalt back again" (121). Why does Tybalt rush away? Why does he return? The Tybalt-actor on stage will likely mime a motive for departure (maybe fear of apprehension or reflexive shock) and a motive for reentering (perhaps rejuvenated self-righteousness). But the actor's choices hardly matter; any reasonable pretenses will work; even that the actor makes clear choices hardly matters. The play offers no motives (no mechanical law), but the audience will not worry itself thereby. We shall grasp intuitively that Tybalt leaves so that Mercutio can curse both houses and Romeo can reflect; he returns so that Romeo can satisfy his "newly entertain'd revenge" (171). Essentially, the audience's poetic consent makes Tybalt's peregrination plausible; we want the play to hover over Mercutio's last words and Romeo's crisis of honor and love.[38]

Mercutio is a character who is, we might say, poetically or even theatrically constituted, as the Queen Mab speech may suggest. He never seems entirely *of* the play. Why, then, does the audience accept it as exactly appropriate that such a comic, long-winded gadfly as Mercutio should suddenly become Romeo's factor in a duel with Tybalt? The explanation lies not in the narrative plotline but in the structure of poetic possibilities: the play's conspiracy of consent with the audience. Waiting with Benvolio for Romeo in an early scene (II.iv), Mercutio displays annoyed fascination with the Prince of Cats's swordsmanship; the prospective fight begins to simmer.[39] Mercutio depicts Tybalt in two successive speeches (II.iv.19–26, 28–35) that virtually contradict each other. Tybalt's manner—the affected jargon of swordplay, the arithmetical fancy-dancing of his Spanish dueling style,[40] and, as Mercutio describes it more

38. "As much as we want the love of Romeo and Juliet to prosper, we also want the volatile enmity of Tybalt punished and the death of Mercutio, that spirit of vital gaiety, revenged, even at the cost of continuing the feud. Romeo's hard choice is also ours," Coppélia Kahn, "Coming of Age in Verona," 8.

39. Harry Levin suggests even that "In his repartee with Romeo, Mercutio looks forward to their fencing with Tybalt," "Form and Formality in *Romeo and Juliet,*" 113.

40. For an interesting discussion of dueling styles in the play and their implications for stage

excessively in the second speech, the lisping, antic aspect of such "phan-tasimes"[41] (a noun Holofernes uses twice of the Spaniard Don Armado)—all roil Mercutio's plain-speaking, xenophobic, proto-English blood. Yet the phantasime of Mercutio's mouth-frothing second speech does not sound like the grudgingly respected "butcher of a silk button" of his first cooler and more judicious speech. Typically, Mercutio's heated brain has carried him away: Tybalt, after all, can hardly be an Osric with a sword! Indeed, Mercutio's rhetorical darts may strike certain members of the Elizabethan audience, perhaps the very gallants sitting at the corners of the stage, as accurately as they do Tybalt.

Such talk (I term it *extranarrative* because it spills beyond the plot and points at the theater-house) makes the dueling scene possible poetically. There once again Mercutio and Benvolio enter without Romeo; "The day is hot, the Capels are abroad" (III.i.2). Mercutio's first speeches forecast the scene's action and the audience's reaction. He accuses Benvolio of outrageous quarrelsomeness (5–9, 11–13, 15–30), in excursions both absurdly false to their target and disproportionately long. Mercutio's Benvolio is so clearly not the spectators' Benvolio that they will enjoy his attack exactly as they reject it. The moment is a heightened balance of detachment and engagement. The audience will feel, too, the intensity of Mercutio's scorn and feel that it must be appropriate to something (Mercutio has before aimed past one target and toward another). Benvolio retorts by implying that Mercutio describes himself, a convincing (and distancing) charge for the audience. Mercutio's tirades may thinly dis-guise more carnivalesque social criticism, for his quarreler ("thou wilt quarrel with a man for cracking nuts") sounds much like the nut-cracking Elizabethan "privileged playgoer"[42] who might be the proud second son of gentry, study-ing law at the Inns of Court, trying the pleasures of the city, dining before the play, frequenting his tailor ("didst thou not fall out with a tailor"), and bearing arms ("claps his sword upon the table . . . and by the operation of the second cup draws him on the drawer"). Through a caricature of Benvolio, Mercutio may again be addressing the beaux around the arena. The surrounding specta-tors will serve triply as engaged audience, distanced interpreters, and half-

---

action, see Adolph L. Soens, "Tybalt's Spanish Fencing in *Romeo and Juliet*," *Shakespeare Quarterly* 20 (Spring 1969): 121–27.

41. "Phantasimes" is an editorial conjecture; Q1 prints "fantasticoes" and Q2, the standard copy text, "phantacies."

42. Ann Jenalie Cook, *The Privileged Playgoers of Shakespeare's London, 1576–1642* (Princeton: Princeton University Press, 1981).

aware targets, perhaps even eyed by Mercutio. His broadside is "liminoid,"[43] and Mercutio confirms himself as the curmudgeon of Elizabethan manners. Such addresses to the audience advance the poetic necessity of Mercutio's fight. He heightens the tension of engagement and detachment; he carries the audience's animosity toward Tybalt; he incites those spectators whom he satirizes: All these cry out for relief. Mercutio never remains anchored inside the narrative present; he works beyond the margins of the stage. He can say anything because he is the chorus of metaphysical conceits and of metamechanical —poetic—causes.

Mercutio describes Benvolio as if he were Tybalt. No wonder, then, that when the real Tybalt appears, Mercutio, true to Benvolio's prediction, baits him: "make it a word and a blow" (40; cf. 43–44), "Here's my fiddlestick" (48). Mercutio draws over some insult to honor ("O calm, dishonorable, vile submission!" [73]), but the play actually offers no "mechanical" explanation for why Mercutio makes the appropriate stand-in for Romeo. Mercutio has earlier traduced Tybalt, though not because of friendship to Romeo. Nor does Mercutio much affect the Montague cause. His name appears on Peter's guest list to Capulet's ball, along with that of his brother Valentine (I.ii.67). Mercutio "consorts" with Romeo, but more as a tyrant to romantic love (the counterpart of "Valentine") than as a tyrant to the Capulets. Mercutio's contempt for Tybalt, furthermore, is not entirely even contempt for Tybalt, since it works equally well as extranarrational social criticism. Neither does the play bother with reasons why Mercutio should be angrily fixated on quarrelsome phantasimes (other than that he is one himself). Nor are his reasons strongly psychological, as Mercutio's psyche is hardly developed. Yet the audience does accept Mercutio's duel with Tybalt, because it has been poetically motivated: Anticipation serves (and serves sufficiently) as causation. Mercutio's intercession works independent of any symbiosis he shares with Romeo (though the two are bound, particularly as Mercutio's sensualism is the ground privileging Romeo's sentimentality). Mercutio's special virtue as a character is that he is wholly theatrical, born to talk, to act, to gesture, to interpose his body. Mercutio fights Tybalt because he has subtextually predicted that he will and because he is ontologically suited.[44]

Fine. But a jolt—a sudden distancing of the audience—comes with Mer-

43. I take this term from the extensive work of anthropologist Victor Turner, who uses it to describe a threshold, betwixt-and-between condition, as when a young tribal male endures a formal rite of passage into manhood and warriorhood. See, for example, Victor Turner, *From Ritual to Theatre: The Human Seriousness of Play* (New York: Performing Arts Journal Publications, 1982).

44. Nicholas Brooke argues that Mercutio's death is the actual climax and the most moving

cutio's famous curse: "A plague a' both your houses!" (99–100; also 91, 106, 108).[45] This plague-rattling may in some sense "cause" the tragedy; it is the curse that hangs over the ensuing action. Though prophecies in tragedy generally detach the audience, Mercutio's curse may distance more than others. It is also only half-just. Mercutio is *not* a victim of the feud, even though the feud is the background of the encounter. Rather, Mercutio falls victim to his own hotheadedness and his scorn for Tybalt (Benvolio, with the phrases "all as hot," "martial scorn" [160, 161], even likens the two as combatants), but those qualities have nothing to do with the ancient grudge between Capulets and Montagues. The private and extranarrational beefs that qualify Mercutio to fight Tybalt actually disqualify him from plague-mongering. The curse is just the kind of disingenuous moral-drawing in which characters such as Romeo and Friar Lawrence engage. As a speech-act the curse has a performative power that captures the spectator's attention. But it ignites a slight spectatorial shock beyond such potency. The curse exceeds its circumstances; it leaps out in the awareness and the memory of the audience because it leaps away from its causes and context. Its theatrical power is actually of dissonance, and the effect is a momentary spectatorial distancing, a flash of wonder, decision.

With Mercutio's duel, "causation" occurs from the rich repetition of a dramatic detail, Mercutio's fixation on Tybalt, yet is tricked out as if it arose from events, the feud-as-plot. Shakespeare, that is, structures the conflict through poetic necessity, while Mercutio's dying curse pretends narrative necessity. Yet the two do not fit. That curse distances the spectator momentarily from the narrative, no matter whether or not the spectator immediately isolates the precise reason, by evoking the difference between plot and interpretation. Cumulatively such manipulation, like a second voice, invites the audience to hold in abeyance an easy, fatalistic parsing of victims and victimizers. *Romeo and Juliet* swims in allegorizing, didacticism, prediction, analogy, repetition, and other poetic devices publicizing doom. The theatrical dissonance of such devices ultimately calls the spectator's attention to them, so

---

scene of the play, and in it Romeo's (and the play's) undisturbed poeticizing stands "terribly reproved" by prose: "The whole play is challenged and redirected by this scene. The genre in which it is conceived is set sharply against a sense of actuality as Mercutio dies the way men do die—accidentally, irrelevantly, ridiculously; in a word, prosaically," *Shakespeare's Early Tragedies,* 82–83.

45. Joseph A. Porter, in *Shakespeare's Mercutio: His History and Drama* (Chapel Hill: University of North Carolina Press, 1988), suggests that the curse characterizes Mercutio's terrain: He is liminoid, of the public squares and marketplaces, betwixt-and-between official family positions signaled by the word "houses."

that we come to see them as art, not fate. Theatrical electricity, then, flickering beyond narrative logic, activates the playgoers' creative participation (their subtle detachment from the story) and ultimately their sense of freedom as a tragic response.

III

Romeo, moving reluctantly toward the ball, misgives "Some consequence yet hanging in the stars" (I.iv.107). That consequence is Juliet, who "hangs upon the cheek of night / As a rich jewel in an Ethiop's ear" (I.v.45–46). Romeo's fear and Juliet's appearance coalesce in the same image—something pendant in the heavens—yet how different the tone of these two moments! Is Juliet really the shape of Romeo's forebodings, or something else? She stands in exotic contrast to her environment, inspiring Romeo to imagine suddenly mysterious races ("an Ethiop's ear") beyond the playworld. Such contrasts invite the spectator's conscious pleasure and wonder for Juliet, a sense of something unpredictable and creative rather than Romeo's fatalism. That Shakespeare makes her perhaps the play's most engaging character argues a counterrotation to the Romeo–Lawrence axis of foreboding.

Feminist criticism has tended to elevate Juliet. Irene Dash, for example, considers her *Romeo and Juliet*'s "major tragic protagonist."[46] Applying Simone de Beauvoir's iconoclastic theory of female adolescence, Dash analyzes Juliet as a teenage girl in whom youth's independence, personal freedom, and sense of self as "essential" competes with the nascent adult female's sense of her self as dependent, "inessential," and "Other." Juliet's defiance confirms that "essential" self, encouraged by physical and sexual awakening (74). Linguistically, Edward Snow finds in Juliet the play's "locus of affirmative energies," for, unlike Romeo, she "manages to be both subject and object in love" and to generate "images of inwardness and depth rather than distance."[47] Theatrically, we can add, Juliet's love strengthens the play's second voice, the whisper of carnivalesque possibility that undermines the official voice of sepulchral necessity. If the audience takes its distance from Romeo according to the distance that he takes from love, imagining it "out there" ("O that I were a glove upon that hand" [II.ii.24]), the audience's engagement with Juliet, by

---

46. Irene G. Dash, *Wooing, Wedding, and Power,* 98.
47. Edward Snow, "Language and Sexual Difference in *Romeo and Juliet,*" 173.

contrast, will grow according to the intimacy and courage she displays in love.

But Juliet's naïveté contributes to the tragedy, even while she advances the play's carnivalesque possibility. As she realizes, in a sudden change of mood during the balcony scene, her contract with Romeo is "too rash, too unadvis'd, too sudden" (II.ii.118). While Juliet stands upon her affections, she has still to learn, in Coppélia Kahn's words, "the cost of such blithe individuality in the tradition-bound world of Verona."[48] Her innocence cannot measure the patriarchal weight of family and society opposing her love. Similarly, Juliet must move beyond using words for "a pretty refuge from hash reality" (Kahn, 16), as she does in the aubade scene. Yet those limitations notwithstanding, Juliet brings to the audience that "locus of affirmative energies" somehow greater than the play's "tragic frame of reference." Juliet's unexpected (unprophesiable) dynamism, moreover, aligns with various auditorially engaging, theatrical elements of the carnivalesque: plebeian figures such as Sampson and Gregory; the Musicians; the balcony scene. These disparate characters and moments share a way of appealing to audiences, first, by breaking the closed narrative world and, second, by inviting the spectator to help create the dramatic illusion—the erosion of boundaries between artifact and observer suggestive of the carnivalesque. Against Romeo's inevitability, this second voice speaks for open-endedness and human choice.

While the audience never sees Romeo within his family household, we almost never see Juliet outside of hers. When Romeo first appears his parents withdraw; the audience experiences Romeo through the medium of his witty, antiromantic, and high-spirited friends. Such a presentation gives him an immediate independence at the expense of a history: He is who we quickly grasp him to be. But the Capulet world of filial and domestic duty will serve initially to bury Juliet and then to display her new self moving against it.[49] She early impresses us as someone called, ordered, demanded. "Call her forth to me" (I.iii.1), says Lady Capulet, instigating Juliet's first arrival, the command's imperiousness underscored by the fussing of the Nurse: "I bade her come. What, lamb! What, ladybird! / God forbid! Where's this girl? What Juliet!" (3–4). But Juliet's first words—"How now, who calls? . . . Madam, I am here, / What is your will?" (5–6)—respond with filial alacrity. Is Juliet recalcitrant or obedient? The theatrical moment gives the audience interestingly different emotional effects. While Juliet acts the compliant daughter ("But no more will

---

48. Coppélia Kahn, "Coming of Age in Verona," 15.

49. For a discussion of Juliet in relation to the prevailing conception of femininity in the play, see Coppélia Kahn, "Coming of Age in Verona," 14–16.

I endart mine eye / Than your consent gives strength to make it fly" [98–99]), her seven lines in the scene leave us largely guessing about her deeper recesses. The audience will sympathize with Juliet partly because she is so interrupted and ordered-about. A servant treads the heels of Juliet's longest speech in this scene, for preparations are "in extremity" and "my young lady ask'd for" (101–2). At the ball, the Nurse interrupts Romeo and Juliet after their sonnet–pas de deux (I.v.111); similarly, the balcony scene founders upon that same voice calling Juliet three times from the house (at II.ii.135, 149, 151). Later, the Nurse disturbs Juliet's farewell to Romeo with news, painfully known to us, that "Your lady mother is coming to your chamber" (III.v.39), and Lady Capulet then breaks in with tidings of Paris (64). Ultimately the Nurse will call Juliet to her most definitive duty in the Capulet world—"I needs must wake her. Madam, madam, madam!" (IV.v.9)—and, at last, she will not answer. The audience empathizes with Juliet because, for one, disruptions to her life are disruptions to our parallel emotional pacing in a scene. The calling nightingale or the Nurse inside the balcony window drive the tension of these scenes, frustrating the audience's own desire to dwell in the moment and aligning it with the interrupted.[50]

Juliet's sensibilities appear constructed by domestic manipulators. We first meet her surrounded by her mother and nurse who joke about her childhood assent that she is destined to "fall backward" (I.iii.42). Old Capulet sees Juliet as essentially a weak, frail vessel whom he must betroth handsomely. Lady Capulet instructs Juliet in vacuity, in how she should think of herself as the beautiful bookcover to the spiritual content of Paris's "volume" (81–94), deriving her value from him. Whatever the Elizabethan representativeness of Lady Capulet's views of gender, her manner of presentation sounds precious and inapt: "The fish lives in the sea, and 'tis much pride / For fair without the fair within to hide" (89–90). The audience's detachment from the manipulation of Juliet by others exposes the thickheaded as well as zealously deterministic environment from which she proceeds.

The wonder of Juliet, however, is that she acts with more freedom, imagination, and courage than any character in the play.[51] The play marks sympathetically each step in Juliet's growing bravery.[52] Despite the patriarchal constraint of her environment, she heralds for the audience, like Portia, Viola, and Rosalind,

50. For a discussion of how the balcony scene creates the spectatorial impression of a "prolonged present," see Emrys Jones, *Scenic Form in Shakespeare* (Oxford: Clarendon, 1971), 33–37.

51. Cf. G. Blakemore Evans, ed., *Romeo and Juliet*, 26–27.

52. For a description of such movement, see, among others, Coppélia Kahn, "Coming of Age in Verona," 14–20.

an essentially comic possibility. Despite her sometimes humorous fits and starts, it is Juliet who propels the meeting with Romeo into immediate marriage (and makes the arrangements); Juliet who recalls herself from accusing Romeo after the death of Tybalt (unlike Romeo who knowingly forsakes Juliet after the death of Mercutio); Juliet who declares the blessings possible from Fortune, even as she loses Romeo to banishment (III.v.62–64); Juliet who seeks solutions to the forced nuptials before offering suicide (unlike Romeo who must be restrained from stabbing himself before he will listen); and Juliet who first defies the proposal of Paris and has the singular courage to surmount her alienation from parents and nurse, her own fear and melodramatic forebodings, and her momentary suspicion of the Friar as she swallows the potion.[53] The audience experiences Juliet alone in two soliloquies ("Gallop apace, you fiery-footed steeds" [III.ii.1–31] and "I have a faint cold fear thrills through my veins" [IV.iii.15–58]) that surpass its intimacies with Romeo and show her maturation into responsibility for love ("And learn me how to lose a winning match" [III.ii.12]) and, even more, her maturation into the lonely responsibility for risking everything on love ("My dismal scene I needs must act alone" [IV.iii.19]). Audiences may sympathize with Juliet enough that they accept Romeo partly for her; conversely, Romeo's tragedy increases to the degree that the play denies him our knowledge of her.

But how can it be, defiance from a "tallow-face," "whining mammet," and "green-sickness carrion" (III.v.157,184,156)? The audience's pleasure at Juliet's initiative should also raise doubts. Is this Juliet not the improbable impossible itself? After all, we witness Juliet in a fully created domestic environment, expected from babyhood to be the sexual object of men, with a suitable marriage as the signal event of her life, with all her choices and even emotions conditioned for her.[54] But though Juliet defies her parents' proximate demands, her revolt does not reject all they have taught her. Once Juliet loves, she makes love her whole existence. We may be jolted by the suddenness of her total acceptance: "My only love sprung from my only hate!" (I.v.138). But Juliet's well-trained adaptability to marriage inspires her unexpected adaptability to love. Marrying Romeo and dying for him extends radically and unforeseeably exactly what Juliet has been taught. While love itself, as critics rightfully note, transforms Juliet, her upbringing creates an unintended receptivity to that

53. Larry S. Champion argues that Shakespeare creates audience sympathy for Juliet by showing her, for one thing, serially deserted by others, in *Shakespeare's Tragic Perspective* (Athens: University of Georgia Press, 1976), 75–82.

54. Dash, stressing the adolescent female's independence, "arrogance" (69) and "confidence" (86), takes a different view of Juliet's childhood than the more conventional one offered here.

transformation. Here, as so often the case in Shakespeare, the known and managed world contains unrecognized possibilities both strangely consistent with and catastrophic to the values and desires that engender them. If Romeo is psychologically overdetermined, then Juliet is, we might say, surprisingly underdetermined by her environment; her "conditioning" contains the seeds of rebellion against her very trainers. Juliet's susceptibility presents to the audience an innocence that converts engagingly to strength. Her very malleability leaves her more freedom than Romeo's melancholy leaves him. When Romeo first espies his lady, he blurts out, "Beauty too rich for use, for earth too dear!" (I.v.47), a precarious attitudinizing about love. In contrast, Juliet's directness and practicality shine through her poeticized responses, making the communion possible: "Saints do not move, though grant for prayers' sake" (105). That invitation to kiss comes to the audience, as does so much of Juliet, with a gentle, expansive jolt of surprise. Likewise on the balcony, all that Juliet knows is to act upon her love without mediation: "send me word tomorrow / ... Where and what time thou wilt perform the rite" (II.ii.144–46). Juliet's simplicity contains an impetuous power, brought home to the audience by the sudden distancing of her unexpected leaps.

Yet Shakespeare invites the audience to see Juliet's trap, too. She promises Romeo to "follow thee my lord throughout the world" (II.ii.148). But immediately the Nurse calls "Madam!" and Juliet answers "I come, anon" (149–50). That exchange interrupts the mood and detaches the audience from Juliet's protestation. For laying her fortunes at Romeo's feet and following him throughout the world is just what Juliet does not do. She appropriates the freedom to love whomever she will, but she does not appropriate the freedom to renounce her family. Exactly upon that dilemma the play convinces the audience to accept tantrums from Romeo, mad dashes to and from Friar Lawrence, half-suicidal drawings of knives from the pair, and a disengagingly preposterous potion that counterfeits death when the couple might simply do what any reasonable lovers (Lysander and Hermia!) do: run away. (After all, the play allows the banished Romeo's easy movements in and out of Verona.) Juliet declares (with engaging simplicity) that she will follow Romeo to the ends of the earth, yet (distancingly) goes in when called. She hists Romeo back yet will not shout her love: "Bondage is hoarse, and may not speak aloud" (160). Juliet's tragedy is that she undertakes to reconcile her duty toward her family with her love for Romeo, the environment that created her against the self realized beyond its limits. As Kahn suggests, an undertaking so naïve about patriarchal "aggression" must fail: Juliet can never "speak the truth of her heart in her father's household" (16). But *Romeo and Juliet* enrolls the audience in its preposterous machinations because we engage sympathetically with both Juliet's freedom and the anchorage of her milieu, the former being really the double of the latter.

Juliet demonstrates the dangers and yet the liberating potential of unsophistication, a quality opposed to all the aphorisms and allegories of the wise fatalists. Shakespeare also gives Juliet an extranarrative range that links her with Mercutio's marginal address to the audience. Juliet engages us directly during her exchange with her mother after the poignant aubade and valediction with Romeo. The conversation between mother and daughter creates humor, an underlying text of quibbles, because Juliet expresses her love for Romeo in words that Lady Capulet takes as hate: "And yet no man like he doth grieve my heart" (III.v.83); "Would none but I might venge my cousin's death!" (86); "Indeed I never shall be satisfied / With Romeo, till I behold him—dead—" (93-94; cf. 96-99,99-102). These quips dominate the scene; they are funny (if sometimes grotesque), and audiences will laugh at Juliet—again unexpectedly. Such effect defines, in fact, the theatrical "purpose" of the scene. Juliet's comments are not Freudian slips; they are intended—but for whom? Her puns appeal outside the immediate narrative moment and contribute nothing to the action; they exceed Lady Capulet's comprehension. Juliet's jokes are wholly theatrical, and they stand out as the scene's most distinctive feature. She addresses her comic equivocations to the audience, and the audience alone. Juliet's exploding puns help release for the audience the sexual tension of the previous scene. We will share with her a small, festive thrill at her insouciance. Juliet's double entendres engage spectators in a subversive, unpredictable, extranarrational self-assertion in the face of oblivious, well-meaning oppression. Her comic quibbles extend her beyond the story, in conspiracy with the audience. Juliet is comic in spirit, and for that reason perhaps more tragic than Romeo. She expresses most deeply the play's overflowing vitality, the possibility of life, Eros over Thanatos. But her extraordinary and nearly successful efforts to realize their love go forever unknown by Romeo. That is the imperfection of—the measure of the irreducible spectatorial distance from—their romantic deaths.

Juliet evokes the carnivalesque possibility that the play concedes in spirit but not in fact. The carnivalesque, as pictured by Mikhail Bakhtin, embraces various parodic inversions of official or hierarchical life, including uncrownings, confusions of social identities, mixtures of classes, mock violence, grotesqueries, excess of eating and drinking, and (not least) dissolving of the distance between player and spectator in the performed event, formal properties whose effect is communal regeneration. *Romeo and Juliet* shows traits of the carnivalesque, such as grotesque bodily humor; the play especially capitalizes upon the marginal, or liminoid, betwixt-and-between status of theater to make spectators partial creators of the tragedy's vision. By effects that distance spectators from the narrative and engage them with the theatrical experience, *Romeo and Juliet* undermines necessity with carnivalesque creativity and volition. The different ontologies of characters, their locales in time and space, their suggestiveness beyond the containing narrative of the play all signal the active presence of the spectator.

The Chorus, a character neither of the plot nor of the audience, proclaims the tragic theme. Yet we proceed instead to the comedy team of Sampson and Gregory. The two enter armed "with sword and bucklers" (Q2). While the story of *Romeo and Juliet,* popularized by Arthur Brooke's *The Tragical Historye of Romeus and Juliet* (1562), takes place in fifteenth-century Verona, Sampson and Gregory have nothing to do with that. Their broadswords and target shields, which will shortly contrast visually with the rapiers of the well-born Benvolio and Tybalt, mark them as English, plebeian, and contemporaneous with the audience. Sword and buckler were the old-fashioned weapons of the English that the rapier was displacing in the 1590s. Sword and buckler matches still thrived as popular sporting events; they took place as elaborate, multiday bouts—by which combatants earned money and "degrees" from fencing schools[55]—performed at various public venues, including the Theatre, where *Romeo and Juliet* was likely first staged.[56] Sampson in particular parodies the swaggering professional fencer who on other days might tread the same boards. Their speech is the bawdy slang of Shakespeare's London, with its jokes upon collier-choler-collar, taking the sides of the street toward the wall or the gutter, maidenheads, weapons-as-tools, thumb-biting, and the legal niceties of the duello.[57] As Sampson and Gregory demonstrate, idiom can mark different degrees of dramatic reality among characters, some standing close to the audience, others distanced historically, geographically, psychologically. As with poetic necessity, Sampson and Gregory depend upon the spec-

---

55. Mercutio alludes to this contemporary practice when he calls Tybalt "a gentleman of the very first house" or fencing school (II.iv.24–25).

56. For a fuller discussion of these contests, see Mary McElroy and Kent Cartwright, "Public Fencing Contests on the Elizabethan Stage," *Journal of Sport History* 13 (Winter 1986): 193–211.

57. In the 1590s several books appeared in England on rapier fencing and the code of the duel, among them Sir William Segar's *The Booke of Honor and Armes* (1590), *Giacomo di Grassi His True Arte of Defence* (1594), *Vincentio Saviolo His Practise* (1595), and George Silver's *Paradoxes of Defence* (1599). Shakespeare seems to have been familiar with Segar's and Saviolo's books, if not with all of them.

tator's extranarrative sensibility to appeal, to amuse, to make sense. Shakespeare takes the audience's reality *inside* the play. With the onrush of Tybalt the play deftly reaches the narrative proper;[58] he is a character wholly driven by its action, unlike the servants, whose raison d'être is their extranarrative familiarity.

The balcony scene shows brilliantly how *Romeo and Juliet* intensifies the audience's involvement and detachment, to make real a preposterous, saccharine love-meeting. The spectators' delight in the blatant theatricality of the balcony scene allows its narrative success. The audience knows that Romeo's passion has progressed beyond Rosaline. Mercutio's ignorance prompts our generous reaction toward his humor's victim at the same time that Mercutio expresses on our behalf the absurdity of Romeo's generic romanticism. Mercutio thus affords the audience both identification and distance. His fruitless conjuration of the lover Romeo ("Appear thou in the likeness of a sigh!"[59] [II.i.8]), furthermore, operates as a prophecy, warming the audience to Juliet's gratuitous appearance, another instance of poetic necessity.[60] Any audience will know that something is coming, diminishing Shakespeare's need to explain what Romeo and Juliet are doing there. Mercutio's conjuration, like his Queen Mab speech, is consciously presentational (another play-within). It forces spectators again to note the theatrical spectacle itself as they simultaneously delight in it. Mercutio parodies Romeo not only as the "humor" of a lover but more specifically as the stage version of that humor: "Speak but one rhyme, and I am satisfied; / Cry but 'Ay me!', pronounce but 'love' and 'dove'" (II.i.9–10). The Mercutio-actor will "present"—act acting—by caricaturing the gestures and speaking style of a conjuration. Mercutio even has his two auditors, Benvolio and Romeo, registering the continuum of spectatorial response from open amusement to unseen annoyance. For the audience, these conjurations make the formal pleasures of theater the object of conscious pleasure in the theatrical moment. Mercutio's presentational style will also condition the spectators to indulge the lover's attitudinizing, exactly by recognizing its theatricality, a heightening of both engagement and detachment.

The balcony scene succeeds not by absorbing the audience in the narrative

---

58. The contrast between the fighting of Sampson and Gregory and that of Tybalt reflects an Elizabethan social debate about the effects of changing weaponry, the earlier weapons essentially English and sporting, the later foreign and conducive to bloody personal duels.

59. This image of the metamorphic Romeo echoes his own recurrent wish to be something (fantastical) he is not: "O that I were a glove upon that hand, / That I might touch that cheek!" (II.ii.25).

60. As Eric Bentley observes, "In plays, prophecies are not made for nothing. Anything prophesied in Act One is going to come true later, and the audience knows this," *The Life of the Drama* (1964; repr. New York: Atheneum, 1983), 29.

illusion but by drawing the audience's attention to the artificiality of that illusion. Romeo advances, turns, and discovers Juliet's light above: "It is the east, and Juliet is the sun" (II.ii.3). Fantastic foreshadowing, for Romeo does not know that the light belongs to Juliet, as his surprise will suggest (10).[61] Romeo has, in effect, conjured Juliet, more poetic causation. Romeo's next speech reinforces the audience's detached perspective. He dwells upon a fantastical Petrarchan conceit (15–22) about Juliet's eyes inhabiting the spheres and her brilliant cheek outshining the stars that he imagines exchanged in her eye sockets. This labored vision of carnivalesque dismemberment displays but hardly reveals; modern audiences will witness more than engage. Romeo's speech creates spectatorial distance also by playing *against* Juliet—an instance of Romeo's dissonance. For the Juliet-performer standing before us in the daylight or theater light can hardly fulfill the vision he enunciates across the stage.[62] We will grant Romeo his imagination (and generally piece out the theatrical imperfection), yet the extreme contrast will also make his odd dream slightly inaccessible to the audience. Here language and image divide our perspective.

Juliet, too, "presents." When Romeo takes her at her word ("Romeo, doff thy name, / And . . . Take all myself" [47–49]), she recoils with the chagrin of someone who has just been discovered fantasizing. Juliet's two "soliloquies" constitute an extended apostrophe to Romeo, an inherently theatricalized form of address. She appears, of course, on a balcony as on a stage, with Romeo again the secret audience completing the metaphor. The real audience, sharing Romeo's discrepant awareness, takes on that distance, too. No accident, I suspect, that in the popular imagination Juliet's "O Romeo, Romeo, wherefore art thou Romeo?" (33) has come down as a parody of love and that "wherefore" is thought to ask not "why" but "where." The stage image (Juliet gazing out above, Romeo hidden below) looks as if Juliet really does call *for*, not about, Romeo. Indeed, that unsophisticated distortion of "wherefore" reflects the sophisticated intuition that the stage illusion is set up to make jokes about itself.

The comedy proceeds to locate the relationship of the lovers both inside the narrative and also betwixt-and-between the narrative and the audience, further

61. Most editors, following Rowe, give Juliet her entrance at II.i.1. The light showing through the window, however, does not require Juliet's visible accompaniment. She may be in the window or passing before it so that the audience recognizes her and Romeo does not, for his next lines are abstract. On "It is my lady, O, it is my love" (10), she may step onto the balcony from the window, or enter the whole scene for the first time, or, if already present, simply become recognized by Romeo.

62. The presence of a boy-actor for Juliet will exacerbate even further, and throughout this scene, the difference between what the audience sees and what it must imagine.

heightening the scene's conscious theatricality. "What man art thou" (52), "How camest thou hither, tell me, and wherefore?" (62), "By whose direction foundst thou out this place?" (79), asks Juliet, returning repeatedly to the practical unlikelihood of this encounter. She adds, "The orchard walls are high and hard to climb, / And the place death, considering who thou art, / If any of my kinsmen find thee here" (63–65). Their exchange is funny on one level because it contrasts the factual Juliet with the fantastical Romeo, who answers: "With love's light wings did I o'erperch these walls" (66); love "lent me counsel, and I lent him eyes" (81). The exchange is funny outside the narrative, too, for it playfully calls attention to compressions of space and suspensions of probability that are the virtue of the Elizabethan stage. Romeo could scale the walls so easily because he had merely to walk around a pillar, and her bedroom was child's play to find because all he needed to do was step forward, turn around, and discover himself in a new locale. Juliet's practical questions have no practical answers, and Romeo's hyperbolically poetical responses are the true species of response. Audience members may register a degree of spectatorial detachment here at the theatrical joke in Romeo's replies. Such lines as "With love's light wings did I o'erperch these walls" invite Romeo to "point at" his love presentationally (and even affectedly) rather than experience it. Juliet's queries and Romeo's answers call attention humorously to the dramatic manipulations (poetic necessity) that ought to obviate just such questions.

The scene dramatizes love itself, furthermore, in a way that activates the spectator's creative collaboration in the dramatic "fact." Is it light or is it dark in this scene? Certainly the audience must visualize darkness. Juliet states modestly to Romeo, "Thou knowest the mask of night is on my face, / Else would a maiden blush bepaint my cheek" (85–86). She asserts oddly, "Thou knowest," perhaps to remind the spectators, who are outside the make-believe, that the setting is nighttime. (The lines also have the advantage of giving Juliet a concrete bodily reaction but of negating any need for the performer to attempt to blush at will.) But does Romeo really *know,* or act as if, night is on her face? Juliet (who is the sun), after all, has appeared in a lighted window, or perhaps with a taper, and he has recognized her—and her twinkling eyes and her cheek bright enough to fool birds into singing. His praise, of course, makes sense because Juliet is actually visible to the audience (and to the actor): We confer *our* knowledge unwittingly upon him, a fascinating and unexpected way in which Shakespeare causes the audience to engage with Romeo, even to "explain" his dialogue. On the other hand, emphasizing darkness, Juliet recognizes Romeo by his voice (58–60), and he declares that he has "night's cloak" (75) to hide him. Conversely, however, Juliet will also worry that "[i]f they [her kinsmen] do see thee, they will murther thee" (70), and Romeo, furthermore, declares that he lent love eyes (81), observes "the peril" in Juliet's eye (71), and entreats her by vision, "Look thou but sweet, / And I am proof against their enmity" (72-73)—all of which plainly suggest that the two now see each other distinctly (even more clearly than the audience sees them) and expect to be seen by others. This scene is sometimes dark and sometimes light, and Romeo and Juliet are visible or invisible to each other, moment to moment, as sentiments and events require.[63]

Such confusion is at the heart of Romeo and Juliet's love as the audience comes to validate and partially create it, a sophisticated exercise of spectatorial distance. Stanley Cavell describes the playgoer's relationship to a play in terms akin to engagement and detachment: We are in the characters' "present," but they are not in ours; they are in our "presence," but we are not in theirs.[64] We can experience their actions, that is, but we cannot step across the footlights into Romeo and Juliet's world and forestall their deaths. But do Romeo and Juliet really offer a complete, sufficient dramatic present? The two describe their love (here and everywhere else) as a brightness that they embody (but we cannot see) in contrast to a darkness that we (also) cannot see: "Two of the fairest stars" (15); "brightness of her cheek" (19); "bright angel . . . / As glorious to this night" (26-27); "I am afeard, / Being in night, all this is but a dream" (139-40). The audience must imagine their brightness and the scene's darkness. Romeo and Juliet present their love only as a contrast in which both terms are absent, removed from the audience's theatrical "presence." Their dramatic "present," love radiant in darkness, opposes the literal present, an open stage in daylight, and love grounds itself upon a glory—"as glorious to this night"—that we cannot affirm. Of course, we must always piece out the "imperfections" of a play with our thoughts, and most audiences will approve (create) as true, however inexplicable, that Romeo and Juliet indeed love each other. But the piecing out turns into an incriminating exercise here: Exactly where we must enter imaginatively (the threshold across which the stage illusion will not take us) is in grasping the extraordinary and compelling

63. Shakespeare practices such tricks with setting elsewhere. The Forest of Arden, for example, will seem both wintry and summery, both in England and in France, and inhabited by both domestic and exotic plants and animals. C. L. Barber comments, "The Forest of Arden, like the Wood outside Athens, is a region defined by an attitude of liberty from ordinary limitations, a festive place where the folly of romance can have its day," *Shakespeare's Festive Comedy: A Study of Form and its Relations to Social Custom* (Princeton: Princeton University Press, 1959), 223. Likewise, the Capulet orchard creates the magical environment appropriate to comedy.

64. Stanley Cavell, "The Avoidance of Love: A Reading of *King Lear,*" in *Must We Mean What We Say?: A Book of Essays* (New York: Charles Scribner's Sons, 1969), 332-37.

essence of their love itself. The love scene confronts the playgoers with its fundamentally contingent and provisional status and insists that the engrossing passion of the lovers can exist fully only in our imaginations. The play will not, cannot, confirm it. Just as we invent for Romeo his sight of Juliet in the near-total darkness, we must invent an idea of love parallel to the experience of the lovers. I would suggest that Romeo tells us the scene's truth: Love *really is* a dream! The audience assumes here, however unwittingly, a creative responsibility for the nature and existence of an extraordinary passion.

I have been describing a scene in which, carnivalesquely, the audience shares a joke and creates a vision, consciously or unconsciously, with the actors and characters. The carnivalesque quality of *Romeo and Juliet* emerges not only in the world of the imagination but also in the everyday world, which bobs through the play with sufficient dissonance to tease, even subvert, its context. Most importantly, the everyday world stands persistently for the play's festive potential, against its Lenten abstractions. Figures such as Capulet's servingmen and cooks (this household is always preparing for a banquet) remind us of the physical body as an object of celebration. Other plebeian characters such as Peter and the Musicians open up the lamentations over Juliet's presumed death to the rush of life and laughter. The musical instruments, food, songs, and flowers of a wedding lend their function to a burial: "And all things change them to the contrary," says Capulet (IV.v.90). But *Romeo and Juliet* consistently disrupts sententiae with experience: The Musicians will prove Capulet unexpectedly right by turning things again to their contraries. Like other comic realists, they comprehend just what is literally before them in time and space: The "pitiful case" to which the Nurse alludes, the First Musician recognizes as the shabby case in which he carries his instrument (96–101). The plebeian characters render feuding comic, as Peter threatens to fight with the Musicians over virtually nothing, a "merry dump" (107), an oxymoron. They contend by dim-witted insults ("gleek," "minstrel," "serving-creature" [114–17]) parodying those of a duello. Peter teases the audience's recollection of Sampson ("We'll not carry coals" [I.i.1]) with his "I will carry no crotchets" (118). He and the Musicians caricature the feuding of the privileged: But why, and why here? Shakespeare has already defused the pathos of grief with spectatorial distance; he then goes that gesture one better by reducing the very activating conflicts of the play's action to brainlessness. In such perspective lies the play's rejuvenating vision. The Musicians will "tarry for the mourners, and stay dinner" (146); thus the marriage meats do furnish forth the funeral tables. Peter and the Musicians illuminate the experiential heart of the play: the multifarious "meanings" of events, so multifarious that events have no inherent meanings, regeneration (dinner!) residing on the other side of loss. The comedy underneath the tragedy of *Romeo and Juliet* results in something beyond either, a carnivalesque residue of knowledge by which the warmth and hilarity of love never die from its catastrophes.[65]

IV

The tension between the audience's engagement with theatricality and its detachment from narrative determinism makes oxymoronic the last act of *Romeo and Juliet.* Romeo enters wondering if he might trust sleep's "flattering truth" (V.i.1), itself an oxymoron that both recalls and ignores Mercutio's critique of dreams. Likewise, Romeo lives again in the subjunctive: "If I may trust . . . " (1). On the other hand, Romeo will speak his sad joy in soliloquy (1–11) directly to the spectators, a revelation of self that yet activates their sympathy. Romeo may touch some playgoers and vex others with this scene; many might feel something of both responses: genuine pathos yet the signature dissonance. Yes, "some joyful news" really will soon be "at hand" (2), if Romeo could wait for it: His lines trap the audience in an ambivalent engagement and detachment, born of its discrepant awareness that tidings of disaster impend and yet remedies also hover. That Romeo chooses the worst of what we know to be two possibilities undermines our sympathy by means of our complicitous knowledge. His heart "sits lightly"; he feels lifted above the ground (3–5): Romeo presumes to comprehend his fortune gravitationally, a first gambit, for the spectator, in a murky and unreliable relationship between sensation and interpretation in the scene. The audience will learn a few lines later (49–52) that his suicide is already a fixed idea. "Is it e'en so?," says Romeo to Balthazar's dire news, "Then I defy you, stars!" (24). (He will express the same sentiment at Juliet's tomb: "And shake the yoke of inauspicious stars" [V.iii.111].) Romeo believes that his suicide will be a free, self-determined, and defiant action; he also believes that he interprets his sensations correctly. Yet the scene's irony, derived from both our discrepant awareness and Romeo's zeal for death, denies him the audience's full sympathy: He is making a mistake!

65. The auditorial experience might be likened to C. L. Barber's description of Rosalind: "Because she remains always aware of love's illusions while she herself is swept along by its deepest currents, she possesses as an attribute of character the power of combining wholehearted feeling and undistorted judgment which gives the play its value," *Shakespeare's Festive Comedy,* 233.

Romeo will create a destiny, no matter whether we call his action acquiescence or heroism, that merely confirms his interpretation of life—and at the expense of Juliet.[66]

Critics have viewed the Apothecary, a culler of "simples" (V.i.40) and a giver of poisons, as the Friar's double.[67] That interpretation argues from spectatorial detachment, positing a shock of recognition as the audience makes the mental, analogical leap between the two. The Apothecary's death-selling, in that view, unmasks the Friar as bankrupt duessa, revealing for the detached instruction (and poetic delight) of the viewer a symmetry and justice in the sudden appearance of an otherwise gratuitous figure. Gratuitous because the play sharply delineates the Apothecary beyond its mechanical needs (another image or presence from the world outside and oblique to the plot). As the analogue or double of the Friar, the Apothecary will activate a latent judgment (enhanced if the same actor plays both parts): that the Friar is himself guilty of rude will, a Pandarus. Yet such an interpretation may also shortchange the theatrical immediacy that the text creates for the Apothecary, shortchange the audience's engagement with this numinous character. The extended, detailed rendering of the Apothecary and his shop diminishes our allegorical identification of him with the Friar, for the Apothecary lives powerfully on the stage in his own selfhood. Shakespeare describes him physically ("overwhelming brows," "tatt'red weeds," bony [39, 39, 41]), categorically ("caitiff wretch," "needy man" [52, 54]), and environmentally ("empty boxes, / Green earthen pots, bladders, and musty seeds, / Remnants of packthread, and old cakes of roses" [45–47]). This "beggar" (56) engrosses the audience with his sudden realism and dramatic self-sufficiency. Although we may recall the Friar, we are not *compelled* to contemplate detachedly one in the other. The Apothecary becomes interesting—as the Apothecary. The play equivocates on the question of whether the Apothecary doubles for the Friar, equivocates because our engagement with the immediate, concrete presence of the Apothecary tends to erode the distance implicit in the allegory. The referential value of this wizened wretch stays open, an example of the intrinsic link between spectatorial position and interpretation.

If its engagement with the Apothecary confuses the audience's allegorizing, we might be surprised, too, by our engagement with Paris in the last scene

66. For an argument that in the second half of the play "we are made to feel satisfaction" in the identification of Romeo and the earlier externalized role of Despair, see Joan Hartwig, *Shakespeare's Analogical Scene* (Lincoln: University of Nebraska Press, 1983), 71–74.

67. For rich discussions of the Apothecary in relation to the Friar (and as another figure of Despair) and of the scene as part of a "continuum of scenic development" (70), see Joan Hartwig, *Shakespeare's Analogical Scene*, 67–112.

(V.iii). His very entrance offers an odd case, because the tragic deaths of the lovers do not require his presence at all, nor is he invited by Brooke's poem. Paris arrives, in part, to be interrupted; the audience knows that immediately.[68] Paris is a blocking-figure, and in the last scene he will be one literally. But the audience hardly requires that to happen—no poetic or narrative necessity here. He has entered the scene to be perceived differently than he had been before— not by Romeo but by the audience. The Paris-present works dissonantly against the Paris-past. We swing from prior detachment to engagement now. When Paris served as *alazon* to the marriage, his character remained flat, irrelevant. Now emerges something we might have only first felt in the deathbed scene, the depth of Paris's love for Juliet (he had patronized her at Lawrence's cell). Like Romeo a few moments before, Paris stands alone grieving before the audience, a theatrically ingenuous position. The audience will credit his straightforward "woe" at the "dust and stones" (13) of Juliet's canopy, and will acknowledge sympathetically, too, his devotion by the lonely "obsequies" (16) he promises nightly. Paris's self-image, "with tears distill'd by moans" (15), loses nothing to Romeo's. His braving of Romeo argues his devotion winningly. Paris's former function as a heavy created a spectatorial remove that made us incapable of *seeing* him then; now, without a conventional role, he stands forth as a touching, vigorous protector of an entombed body and a lost hope. Even more, Paris's manner of mourning contrasts to Romeo's, for Paris honors the beloved with an act of life (the remembrance of flowers and sweet water nightly) rather than an act of death.[69] Shakespeare has resurrected Paris. That a character might have a "life" that rises beyond his or her apparent narrative function offers one of the reasons for his presence. Paris's arbitrary entrance gives him an integrity outside our expectations; his dramatic success is a form of dissonance. Shakespeare aligns Paris with the Apothecary, with those carnivalesque strains that transgress *Romeo and Juliet*'s presumptive borders, the second voice hinting persistently to the audience that choices exceed those its formalists imagine.

68. Paris takes remarkable precautions against being discovered at Juliet's tomb, instructing his page in detail to keep his ear close to the hollow churchyard ground. Why? Paris knows nothing of Romeo's plans. What makes plausible Paris's behavior is us. The audience brings to the scene its recognition that Romeo is on his way—without considering that Paris has no warning and little motive for his stealth. We transfer our knowledge here to a character, as elsewhere our expectations create the play's internal coherence and inevitability.

69. Paula Newman and George Walton Williams, noting the parallel syntax between Paris's injunction to his boy and Romeo's to Balthasar ("Give me . . . " [V.iii.1,9,22]), conclude that, "The flowers represent Paris—freshness and youth and life; the mattock and iron represent Romeo—death," "Paris: The Mirror of Romeo," in *Renaissance Papers 1981*, ed. A. Leigh Deneef and M. Thomas Hester (Raleigh, N.C.: Southeastern Renaissance Conference, 1982), 17.

And just then, after the audience becomes engaged with him, Paris enacts Romeo's tragic pattern. Like the hero—or Mercutio and Tybalt—Paris will not hear the very words Romeo speaks in his ear, for his biases cannot admit that Romeo has come to do himself, not Juliet's body, violence: "For I come hither arm'd against myself" (65). Paris and Romeo face each other exchanging defiances: Paris, so suddenly worth our interest, invites the audience to recognize in his misprision the mirror-image of Romeo. Like his counterparts, Paris dies for his deafness. Here *Romeo and Juliet* works a paradox: The audience's identification with Romeo in his obsession with love-as-death encourages our consent to the killing of Paris, who has just touched us. Paris's very position as Romeo's antagonist, of course, makes him the reprise of Tybalt, and Romeo—who has entered the scene "savage-wild" (37)—reenacts his own fury. We may take Romeo's part, right or wrong, simply "because his embrace of desperate action is so vital" (Hartwig, 109). Yet in the moment, the audience's sympathies may also tug against its understanding, because Romeo displays his energy and vitality pursuing their destruction.

Paris dies, but he will not go away. He continues to fray the edges of the spectator's absorption in Romeo's dramatics, distracting us. Paris asks Romeo out of mercy to open the tomb and lay him with Juliet (72–73), and the audience learns suddenly that Paris is kinsman to another interposer, Mercutio (75)—a detail that recalls, like an electrical connection, our sense of Paris's narrative unmooring. Paris does not belong here; he has come misallied. "O, give me thy hand, / One writ with me in sour misfortune's book!" (81–82), says Romeo, emphasizing their mutuality as he lifts Paris (the weight of love!). Indeed, Romeo's death-speech dwells on the person of Paris, his relationship to Juliet. That Romeo bears Paris into the monument as an act of fellowship proclaims their doubleness, their alternative responses to like problems. Visually, the tomb's interior presents a vivid, asymmetrical tableau of death: Tybalt to one side in his "bloody sheet" (97), Romeo and Juliet embracing at center, Paris lying nearby, "the ground . . . bloody" (172). The audience sympathizes with the pathos of the lovers and their courage, yet Paris (the blocking-figure) detaches us, interrupts, his bloodiness drawn to our attention (140–43, 172–74). Paris distracts the audience from assuming fully the "position" of Romeo and Juliet; he constitutes a just intrusion that the exclusiveness of their love cannot comprehend. Paris represents a communal world that would not be admitted but cannot be denied; his invasion of the Capulet tomb amounts to a spectatorially distancing criticism of Romeo. Paris demands our attention, beyond the requirements of plot, as a subversive redundancy.

Audiences will sympathize with Romeo in his emotionally wrought death-speech. But our discrepant awareness along with Romeo's shifting focus, with its implied comparisons, and his tendency to "present" urge some spectatorial distance, the ironies clicking like remote control to limit our empathy. True, Romeo commands the audience with the fluidity of his thought, and his spontaneous, changing perspective colors the scene with psychic realism. But the speech engages the audience through the kind of suspense that qualifies its identification with the character: Will he recognize the truth? Our discrepant awareness may make us feel sorry for Romeo but not exactly sorry *with* Romeo. His attention moves from Paris (74–83) to Juliet (84–86) to Paris (87) to his physical "lightning" (88–91) to Juliet and Death (91–96) to Tybalt (96–101) to Juliet and Death (101–6) to his own death (106–12) to Juliet's body (112–15) to the poison (116–20) to Juliet's body (120). Though Romeo's focus grows narrower, the audience hears an expanding system of similitudes. Beyond his resemblance to Paris, Romeo discovers his kinship with Tybalt and appropriates the role of Tybalt's avenger. Romeo unseats, becomes Death, taking upon himself its disturbing, half-real necrophilia (104–6). He speaks of "bitter conduct," "unsavory guide," and "desperate pilot" with the vial of poison in his hand, objectifying the despair that belongs to him subjectively. He "presents," dramatizes himself: "Eyes, look your last! / Arms, take your last embrace! and, lips, O you / The doors of breath, seal with a righteous kiss" (112–14). In the theater, this attitudinizing calls attention to itself, tending to detach the audience from Romeo. His death-speech limits the spectator's empathetic validation of his actions.

Romeo's nearly grotesque vision of Juliet invokes the play's carnivalesque subtext. Their romance, indeed, had commenced festively: the antic invasion and suspended time of the Capulet banquet. A "feasting presence full of light" (86), the vault recalls the great hall of the Capulets. Death, as in carnival, will not quite be death, "That I reviv'd and was an emperor" (V.i.9). Romeo has entered the last scene in a liminoid kinetic state: "And all this day an unaccustom'd spirit / Lifts me above the ground" (V.i.4–5); "or did I dream it so? / Or am I mad" (V.iii.79–80). His violence has approached a ghastly bestiality: "By heaven, I will tear thee joint by joint, / And strew this hungry churchyard with thy limbs" (35–36). He experiences, too, a letting-go, a "lightning before death" (90), the liftedness of emotional peace, cued perhaps by a physical lightening as he releases Paris's body—or prepares to release his own. This portrait works repeatedly to engage the audience with Romeo's feverish bodily sensations, his tension, his expansiveness, his extraordinary betwixt-and-betweenness. The audience will experience Romeo's and Juliet's deaths not by means of some analogous enervation (like Cordelia's limp body) but as heightened sensuality. Our visceral stimulation, like a carnivalesque aura, runs counter to the sense of death as narrative closure.

Moments of great decision often distance the spectator, who will absorb the passion but listen for motive. Each lover conveys to the other a life-in-deathness that the spectator may find disturbing—and a little thrilling. The tomb-as-womb ("thou womb of death" [45]) offers no idle trope in this scene. In a bold image of necrophilia, Romeo even ponders Death as an actual lover, for Juliet seems so much alive: "Shall I believe / . . . that the lean abhorred monster keeps / Thee here in dark to be his paramour?" (102–5). Juliet's vitality comes to Romeo in submerged sonnetese, formulaic but also touching: "beauty's ensign yet / Is crimson in thy lips and in thy cheeks, / And death's pale flag is not advanced there" (94–96). The audience may recognize with a certain horror that Juliet is actually waking up; her revival is what Romeo beholds and what so astonishes him: "Ah, dear Juliet, / Why art thou yet so fair?" (101–2). Juliet's blossoming aliveness spurs him to suicide, for Romeo "dies" now to displant Death as her paramour. The audience will feel both agony and distance, even a sense of guilt, knowing the utter accuracy of Romeo's observations and the utter inaccuracy of his interpretation. His death-speech details Juliet's physical presence with powerful sensuality—his puzzled awe, his stately valediction to her eyes, arms, lips. The more the actor lingers, the more anxious the audience may feel at the delusion.

Yet Shakespeare interlaces another kind of engagement, with the possibilities contingent in Romeo's talk. Romeo does not simply enter the tomb, bid adieu, and drink off the poison. Instead, he re-creates, or rather, creates anew, the emotion and reason for suicide, a moment thrilling in part because Shakespeare anchors the motivation for death squarely in the immediate dramatic present. Romeo dies in the misprision of the instant, Death's paramour for life's body. Each tragic moment can be a moment of choice—and possibility. Such technique keeps the instability, the open-endedness, of the dramatic present alive. That Romeo reinvents the motivation for suicide when the narrative of the play least demands it means, likewise, that the opposite is possible as well, that what will happen in the dramatic event cannot finally be predicted by what has happened so far, that the present is not history, that the second life of the play burrows through every recognition and decision. Juliet, as she prepares to "die with a restorative" (166), gives the audience the final, searing image: "Thy lips are warm" (167). That phrase strips the world of its abstractions, creating an instant kinesthesia of wonder at the celebrative material body.

Romeo and Juliet refuses the audience a pause at Romeo's death; rather it switches perspective, with a welcome shock, to fussbudgetry. (Moments later, Juliet's death will yield to even broader comedy.) For who should come fussing and stumbling into this scene but Friar Lawrence: "Saint Francis be my speed! how oft tonight / Have my old feet stumbled at graves!" (121–22). At the drug's quickness, Romeo has cried out, "O true apothecary!," a virtual cue (perhaps a real one) to the bustling Friar and a deft aural and visual linking of the two herbalists (particularly effective if the same actor doubles for the two characters). Will audiences find a moral here? Evans reminds us that Elizabethans considered stumbling at graves a bad omen.[70] The Friar fulfills another prophecy, unexpectedly: "Wisely and slow, they stumble that run fast." Fittingly, his own hurry implies that his stratagems have spun away too rapidly for control. Yet the Friar's entrance is funny; audiences generally laugh, particularly if the actor executes a pratfall, perhaps stumbling over Balthazar: "Who's there?" (122). Pratfalls occur comically, in the green world, since they never injure the doer. The fresh theatrical electricity will bury the morality. As before, spectacle conflicts with thematics. We follow Lawrence now, though with our own discrepant knowledge of what awaits him. The play delays agonizingly the Friar's discovery of Romeo, building the audience's tension all over again: He pauses to identify the body in front of him (just waking — like Juliet), asks about the light in the sepulchre, asks whom Balthazar means by "my master," asks how long Romeo has been inside, requests Balthazar's company, states his fear, stoops to look at the bloody weapons and puzzle their meaning, and finally — finally! — enters the tomb and beholds the "lamentable chance" (146). Here the spectators' superior knowledge completes a new sense of horror at the unfolding. Knowing what awaits, furthermore, can make the auditors' sense of responsibility, reactivated in Lawrence's fearfulness, as painful for them as for him. The Friar's presence, then, causes the audience to invest its emotions in perspectives about Romeo's tragedy, rather than to absorb or contemplate or feel, on its own terms, the tragic experience itself.

Similarly, Balthazar constitutes a fascinating detail in this scene and in the play's second life. He accompanies his master to Juliet's tomb but retires on stage instead of obeying Romeo's threatening dismissal: "I'll hide me hereabout, / His looks I fear, and his intents I doubt" (43–44). Does he plan to help Romeo if needed? In the presence of the audience, Balthazar sleeps through the sword fight between Romeo and Paris and thinks he has dreamed it (137–39); he may

---

70. G. Blakemore Evans, *Romeo and Juliet*, 186 n.122.

also be on stage (and asleep) through all or some of Juliet's awakening, the hulabaloo of the Watch, and her death.[71] Balthazar's sleep is not funny, though he is comically weak-kneed. Nonetheless, as with Auden's ship that sails calmly on in the face of "something amazing," his sleep (like Paris's intervention) insists upon the social context of self-dramatized suffering. The moment of Romeo's extremity is Balthazar's of rest. Furthermore, as Romeo goes to his own "everlasting rest" (110), Balthazar apparently wakes up, tripped over by the Friar. Balthazar plays out an unpredictable, carnivalesque version of Romeo's allegory of death and transubstantiated life, another of the play's theatrical displacements of energy and spectatorial focus. The carnivalesque vein continues, even turning to broad humor, with the First Watchman, who observes, as ingenuously as might his fellows in *Much Ado About Nothing,* that here lies "Romeo dead, and Juliet, dead before, / Warm and new kill'd" (196–97). Lawrence, Balthazar, and the Watch dislocate sentimental empathy by means of a carnivalesque and communal afterlife; we progress toward theatrical parody.

If the audience's perspective pursues a quick succession of characters, its relationship to the single character can shift suddenly, as well. Before Juliet dies, Friar Lawrence has yet a desperate plan: "Come, I'll dispose of thee / Among a sisterhood of holy nuns" (156–57).[72] Fine word, "dispose"! Juliet will have none of it, her refusal instantly detaching the audience from this now-inept cleric (her last giver of commands and last deserter) who could think that she might temporize against a romance to which she has dedicated the very possibility of life. The Friar rushes away, leaving Juliet to her last crisis typically alone. He returns under suspicion, a broken man, trembling, sighing, weeping (184), "short" in "date of breath" (229), bereft of plans. Our sudden disengagement with the Friar, repeated dramatically in his sudden collapse, uncovers further the subversive nature of this play, where characters can reverse instantly, where the law of life is volatility. (Offstage, people cry out in the streets and rush toward the tomb; Lady Montague dies upon the gad.)

---

71. The copy text, Q2 (as well as the "bad" Q1), gives Balthazar an entrance with some members of the Watch (at 181), but no prior exit to effect it. He may leave as the Friar enters the tomb (unlikely), when the Friar rushes away (more likely), or after the Watch has entered, sneaking away behind them (just as likely).

72. Friar Lawrence knows that the Watch is coming no more than Paris had reason for posting guard. We as audience know it, however, because the page has announced that he would summon the Watch (71), just as earlier we knew that Romeo was on his way. As before, such statements work through a kind of reverse empathy: We make the Friar's words true and reasonable for him because they are already true and reasonable for us; unconsciously, we put Friar Lawrence in our place rather than ourselves in his.

Thematically, the last scene pays obeisance more to chance, particularly bad timing, than to destiny: Paris becomes a name in "sour misfortune's book" (82); the Friar exclaims "what an unkind hour / Is guilty of this lamentable chance!" (145–46); the Prince asks "What misadventure is so early up" (188) and demands that "mischance be slave to patience" (221); Friar Lawrence remarks that Friar John "[w]as stayed by accident" (251). True, the Friar also asserts that "a greater power than we can contradict / Hath thwarted our intents" (153–54), and the Prince can see "heaven" (293) acting out a civic morality, but the dominant tone of the last scene is chance, accident, and bad timing.[73] If some "greater power" guides life, still, the overwhelming human *experience* of life is unpredictability, change, speed, possibility. The tragic ending insists not only on comic thematics but also on comedic theatrics. The scene triumphs with split-second timing and physical agility, the kinds of virtuosity comedy typically foregrounds. The first two hundred–odd lines of the tomb scene contain at least fourteen entrances (not counting Juliet's or those of assorted attendants), three retirements, at least five exits, four offstage sounds (one whistle, two "noises," a speech), a sword fight, a body-dragging, three deaths, one probable pratfall, two entrances (and a waking) timed precisely against deaths, one tomb-opening (requiring tools), and the handling of an unusual quantity of props, including (beyond a dagger, a half-dozen swords, and a vial of poison) flowers or petals, sweet water, at least three (probably more) torches or lanterns, two crowbars, a spade, a mattock, and a considerable quantity of fake blood. This tragic ending emphasizes comic stage business and paraphernalia. Performatively, the bad timing of chance requires the great (comedic) timing of actors. The audience's engagement with the pathetic yields constantly to interruptions, diversions, and feats (what's next, what's next!) demonstrating the comic flair. Inevitably the audience becomes involved in the spectacle, which draws attention away from the nature of character and to its presentation.

With all the survivors finally on stage, the tragic tone dominates again. Yet the tragedy fails oddly to complete itself. The Prince cuts short the mourning (216–21), just as Friar Lawrence had done at Juliet's feigned death. He leads the characters out of the play to "Go hence to have more talk of these sad things," warning that "[s]ome shall be pardon'd, and some punished" (307–8), but leaving the audience in suspense as to what and whom. His last lines,

---

73. "The final scenes of *Romeo and Juliet*, although tragic in outcome, are comic by nature inasmuch as everything hinges on accidents of timing," Martha Tuck Rozett, "The Comic Structures of Tragic Endings: The Suicide Scenes in *Romeo and Juliet* and *Antony and Cleopatra*," *Shakespeare Quarterly* 36 (Summer 1985): 154.

furthermore, fall into the sestet of a sonnet, formulizing his emotions. The rival monument-building of the Capulets and Montagues misses the spirit of Romeo and Juliet's love. But more important, the ending provides no emotional recognition of the lovers' grandness or their tragedy; indeed, neither their historian nor even Romeo and Juliet themselves have comprehended it fully.[74] Shakespeare's tragedies typically conclude with a reporter and an outside spectator, such as the Friar and the Prince. To some degree, their exchange will "make true," as it were, what the audience has witnessed; any reportorial shortcomings also leave a residual spectatorial energy—a doubt, a question, a desire for the unsaid. Such dissonance lingers in *Romeo and Juliet*. Most disturbing, Romeo never "recognizes" Juliet, either her tragic stature or the alternative comic ending for which she stands. Nor does the play's closure illuminate that darkness. The ending leaves the spectator, walking out of the theater, with the nagging suspicion that the characters have concluded the narrative but missed the point. Such dissonances entertain the play's second life of open contingency against closed necessity.

The carnivalesque of *Romeo and Juliet* will never quite go away. It strews like seeds the potential that Garrick's ending and James Howard's tragicomic version make actual. The possibility of a set of meanings radically different from those of the play's official fatalists persists through all the action: in Sampson and Gregory's bravado, Mercutio's laughter, the musician's banter, Juliet's heroism, Balthazar's sleep. This second life is immediate, sensual, regenerative, and ultimately theatrical. The play calls attention to the contextual gratuitousness of many of its forebodings, undermining them, creating in the spectator a narrative detachment (or extranarrative engagement) even as characters march toward the disasters they have imagined. The hilarious and the sentimental live in particular symbiosis in this play, one whereby the spectator becomes complicitous in the dramatic illusion. In the spirit of the dialogic, the play parodies the very romance it endorses. *Romeo and Juliet* works structurally through contrasts of presence and dissonance, contrasts that the spectator often recognizes, and whose recognition becomes even further ground for the moving figure of the play.

---

74. On this point, see Champion, *Shakespeare's Tragic Perspective*, 90.

2

Remembering *Hamlet*

Hamlet is a play of memory.[1] Memory shapes *Hamlet* inside and out, becoming a burden for the characters, a challenge for the actor playing Hamlet, and an uncanny experience for the spectator. To the protagonists, remembering renews the pain of separation and loss. To the Hamlet-actor, remembering entails foresight; he must consciously balance his emotional spontaneity in the present against the big scene just ahead, begetting in the whirlwind of passion a "temperance that may give it smoothness" (III.ii.8–9). To the audience, remembering begets the surprise of discovering in analogous events, shared language, and mirroring characters, the haunting of the dramatic present with the play's own past.[2] As the audience encounters and remembers Hamlet, it moves

1. For some related, recent studies emphasizing memory in *Hamlet,* see Edward Pechter, "Remembering *Hamlet:* Or, How it Feels to Go like a Crab Backwards," *Shakespeare Survey,* vol. 39, ed. Stanley Wells (Cambridge: Cambridge University Press, 1987), 135–47; and Richard Helgerson, "What Hamlet Remembers," *Shakespeare Studies,* vol. 10, ed. J. Leeds Barroll III (New York: Burt Franklin, 1977), 67–97. My chapter considers how characters, actors, and spectators remember, but like Pechter and Helgerson, I treat remembering as the entry to a nexus of qualities, such as mimicry in acting, imitation in behavior, and repetition in structure.

2. This auditorial memory bears comparison to Freud's "uncanny," which I shall address

through a ground-plan of "positional" similitude, displacement, and wonder.[3] Hamlet first creates the audience's context, then becomes "contextualized" by others, and finally offers the audience a new, transcendent perspective. Playgoers initially engage with Hamlet because his relationship to his world mimics their spectatorship to his play. In the second phase, auditors grow increasingly aware of how the play recollects its own actions and how characters, particularly Ophelia, become the uncanny refractions of Hamlet. We detach from Hamlet as the play denies him a privileged point of view and, commensurately, as he denies his moral kinship with others. The third phase elevates the audience's engagement and detachment, as Hamlet achieves both discreteness and interconnectedness. Wonder marks that phase, as, for example, the playgoer half-recognizes in the dying Hamlet the uncanny embodiment of the King that's dead—not his father so much as our theatrical ghost. For the spectator, wonder constitutes the conjoining of belief with mystery, uncertainty—the intensification of both engagement (identification) and detachment (separateness).[4] That ground-plan, perhaps a pattern for spectatorial "development" in the tragedies, invites the audience

---

later in the essay. Freud saw the uncanny as the shadowy repetition in the present of something familiar from the past that has been repressed, whether infantile feelings or primitive beliefs; see Sigmund Freud, "The 'Uncanny' " (1919), repr. in *On Creativity and the Unconscious: Papers on the Psychology of Art, Literature, Love, Religion,* ed. Benjamin Nelson (New York: Harper and Row, 1958), 122–53.

3. I borrow the use of "ground-plan" from Ralph Berry, *"Richard III:* Bonding the Audience," in *Mirror up to Shakespeare: Essays in Honour of G. R. Hibbard,* ed. J. C. Gray (Toronto: University of Toronto Press, 1984), 114. I propose here a general pattern shaped by the text, the development of the audience *Hamlet* hypothesizes or "implies." Different performances, productions, and sensibilities will necessarily ring changes upon this ground-plan, some emphasizing the audience's parallels with Hamlet, others not. Not all spectators, for example, will feel the same disengagement from Hamlet, or even annoyance toward him, in the scenes immediately following the playlet. On the other hand, that Hamlet's murdering of Polonius will put the audience off to some degree has become a "given" of response, the kind of consensus behind the "no doubt" in David Bevington's statement that "Hamlet's unfeeling response to Polonius's death is no doubt deplorable," *Action Is Eloquence: Shakespeare's Language of Gesture* (Cambridge: Harvard University Press, 1984), 183.

4. J. V. Cunningham argues that wonder holds equal place with pity and fear as a Renaissance effect of tragedy, connecting it with Aristotle's approval of an action that is both impossible and yet probable, *Woe or Wonder: The Emotional Effect of Shakespearean Tragedy* (Denver: University of Denver Press, 1951), 62–105. Other scholars have suggested that Renaissance terms such as "wonder" introduce an air of Renaissance shock-value into tragic resolution. Bruce R. Smith, for example, treats wonder in Renaissance tragedy as the heightened emotional effect that grand sententiousness and grand stage sensationalism can create—stern moral clarity and theatrical novelty working together: *Ancient Scripts and Modern Experience on the English Stage: 1500–1700* (Princeton: Princeton University Press, 1988), 217.

to recognize that *Hamlet*'s reenactments of itself may finally make the play as open-ended and tinged with possibilities as it is closed and repetitious.

For the characters, memory comes insistently, like the drums that beat so sharply through the play.[5] The action of remembering generally brings melancholy, a sense of loss. Worse, memory disrupts, demands, and manipulates. The ghost enjoins murder with "remember me" (I.v.91); Gertrude sins by a failure of memory; Polonius offers Laertes precepts, correct but lame, to "character" in his memory; Ophelia longs to redeliver "remembrances" and later laments to have seen what she has seen; the actors from the city must instantly remember and reexperience speeches of wrenching emotion; villains are plagued by their memories; Hamlet worries about the legacy of a man's reputation; and Fortinbras takes Denmark with "rights of memory." In this prop-heavy play, moreover, physical objects—the armour of a ghost, a portrait, a skull—are like alien vessels washed up from the past. Documents—contracts, letters, plays—become hopeless legislation against the forgetfulness of time. Memories have a kinetic objectness in *Hamlet,* as if weight, burden.

Beyond memorizing all those lines, the actor of Hamlet must solve the problem of playing the present as unpredictable and free, yet somehow on an emotional continuum with what has preceded and what must come after. John Gielgud captures trenchantly the actor's dilemma toward this Hamlet-problem: "The arrival of the players, easier again, natural, true feeling, but the big soliloquy is coming in a minute, one must concentrate, take care not to anticipate, not begin worrying beforehand how one is going to say it, take time, but don't lose time, don't break the verse up, don't succumb to the temptation of a big melodramatic effect."[6] The role challenges the actor, as perhaps no other does, through its repeated dislocations of sensibility—shifts in mood, physical quality, self-awareness, emotion, and energy—so that Hamlet constantly startles his fellows and the audience yet remains whole. Acting requires both remembering the lines and experiencing them afresh in the moment. Hamlet heightens that performance problem; he vibrates with the electricity of discovery. Gielgud accomplishes the role in similar terms: "It was not until I stood before

5. Marjorie Garber observes that "*Hamlet* is indeed a play obsessively concerned with remembering and forgetting," *Shakespeare's Ghost Writers: Literature as Uncanny Causality* (New York: Methuen, 1987), 147; see especially 147–63. Garber focuses on "the relationship between memory and revenge" (148) and "memory and forgetting" (153): "Rather than facilitating action, remembering seems to block it, by becoming itself an obsessive concern, in effect fetishizing the remembered persons, events, or commands so that they become virtually impossible to renounce or relinquish" (154).

6. Toby Cole and Helen Krich Chinoy, eds., *Actors on Acting* (rev. ed., New York: Crown, 1970), 400; from John Gielgud, *Early Stages* (New York: Macmillan, 1939).

an audience that I seemed to find the breath and voice which enabled me suddenly to shake off my self-consciousness and live the part in my imagination, while I executed the technical difficulties with another part of my consciousness at the same time" (401). Acting turns particularly challenging with Hamlet, because the character must continually surprise himself and the audience with passion and synchronous "recognition."

Hamlet himself models an exaggerated spectatorship. His emotions swerve from the far end of passionate engagement to the far end of detachment experienced as lassitude. As Gertrude observes of him, "thus a while the fit will work on him," and then, like a dove, "His silence will sit drooping" (V.i.285–88). Hamlet becomes alternately engaged with and detached from his very destiny, an audience-figure to his own drama. Similarly, the audience proceeds from an early positional (though not necessarily psychological) identification with Hamlet, succeeded by a structural and moral decontextualization or detachment, to a sympathy more mysterious and less personal than before. The opening Watch scene places the audience at a middle distance from the action, interested yet cautious, awaiting evidence. We observe the fear and wonder of the Watch more than we participate in it. With the court scene, the audience first engages with Hamlet's own removed, audience-like perspective, his "position," as he asserts that nothing "can denote me truly" (I.ii.83). Hamlet now manages the audience's context. Through *The Murder of Gonzago,* the spectator attends sympathetically to his emotional swings and dislocations. But with the nunnery scene and until Hamlet's departure for England, the audience lessens its positional identification with him, despite our share in his secrets, as other perspectives structurally "frame" his and as playgoers see characters, paradigmatically Ophelia, betrayed by Hamlet because of their identification with him. After his sea-escape, Hamlet returns steadier and more focused, inspiring in the audience a new quality of wonder. That wonder tingles with a sense of the uncanny. Hamlet's words and gestures echo his earlier actions and those of others, who have come also to share emotional properties, to double, with one another. Climactically, as his death "remembers" the ghost, Hamlet achieves, too, a separate *arete. Hamlet* invites spectators to their own double response: a fear and wonder akin to the Watch. The play erodes Hamlet's epiphany with its grim echoings of the past; yet paradoxically Hamlet's final victory over Claudius stands as an authenticating action. Like the Hamlet-actor, spectators engage with the spontaneous present even as they recognize more distantly the coercion of history.

I

In the nineteenth and twentieth centuries, playgoers and readers have tended, like Coleridge, to feel a special kinship towards Hamlet[7]—though often for incompatible psychological reasons. In the theater, however, we understand characters in terms of our spectatorial distance from them as much as through psychological or other "facts" of their personalities. Thus the audience aligns with Hamlet's position, whatever additional attractions may pertain. Hamlet dominates the spectators' experience of the first half of the play, and their sympathy gains from parallels between his spectatorship (his engagement and detachment) and theirs. Playgoers begin their positioning with Hamlet before they hear his name. The pattern develops in the opening Watch scene in two contrasting ways: first, through the engaging rhythm of physical tension and release, of social intrusion and assimilation, to which the audience surrenders empathetically; and second, through the "arm's-length" distance, the detachment, that the scene also establishes for the audience through its implied rituals, the ghost, and time. In its architecture, the first scene functions as a primer for "distance" in the play. (Horatio will liken the ghost to a "prologue" [123] and a "harbinger" [122].) The opening draws the audience into the special physical energy and perspective of the characters. On the other hand, the scene confirms the spectators' self-awareness and independence of thought. The first scene virtually demands detached comparison and judgment on the part of the audience—preparation for a thinking hero.

The first twenty lines of *Hamlet* (the first "beat"[8]) launch rhythms of the body and of social relations that the scene as a whole will repeat: muscular contraction yielding to relaxation, motion to stasis, aggression to community. Reiteration lodges this pattern in the spectator's sensory expectations. Dialogue works to lodge the motif of reiteration in our consciousness, as well: The play will move forward by recollecting itself. T. S. Eliot called *Hamlet's*

7. T. S. Eliot calls attention to this symbiosis and blames it on the misplaced creativity of certain "dangerous" critics who "often find in Hamlet a vicarious existence for their own artistic realization. Such a mind had Goethe, who made of Hamlet a Werther; and such had Coleridge, who made of Hamlet a Coleridge," "Hamlet," in *Selected Essays 1917–1932* (London: Faber and Faber, 1932), 141.

8. I use this term in its popular theatrical sense, to denote the smallest unit of dramatic action, as in an exchange between two characters on a single subject that moves from disagreement to resolution.

opening poetry musical.[9] "Imitative counterpoint" forms one useful musical comparison; characters such as Francisco and Barnardo mimic each other as in crescendo and decrescendo. They seem, finally, almost to exchange qualities of the heart. The famous reversed protocol of the change of the guard causes each sentinel to repeat sequentially the other's tension and release, even their standing and moving. Barnardo may enter cautiously, "carefully" (6); unlike Francisco, he has seen the ghost the night before. On "Who's there?" Barnardo will pull himself up physically into a taut, defensive stance, probably with weapon posed, perhaps stepping forward. Francisco follows suit with, "Nay, answer me. Stand and unfold yourself," and the two guards face each other, bodies mirroring their fighting postures. That muscular contraction yields to release as the dialogue ricochets: "Long live the King!" "Barnardo," "He." First official, then tentative, then friendly, speech suddenly breaks further beneath its own formulaic surface, releasing private feelings, like night sounds, echoing beyond their circumstances: " 'Tis bitter cold, / And I am sick at heart." The tension rises for a moment—"Have you had quiet guard?" asks Barnardo, still wary—and then subsides. Imitation turns into exchange: The two guards switch stage positions, with Francisco starting in the direction from which Barnardo came, and Barnardo assuming Francisco's physical, and perhaps emotional, station. Vocally and kinesthetically, the action of one character is the tripwire to like action by the other—in stops and starts, in muscular tension and release, in public voice and private tones—so that the alternating lines suggest bodily responses in imitative counterpoint. The episode engages the spectator, who will echo muscularly the changes of the soldiers, and whose interest will be piqued by the mystery behind the movement and dialogue.

The second action of challenge, as Horatio and Marcellus enter, repeats the confused protocol. Horatio apparently offers a spontaneous response, an incomplete password—"Friends to this ground"—whose formulation Marcellus may step in to clarify in the next half-line: "And liegemen to the Dane." The tension of momentary confrontation (Francisco will draw up defensively in challenging the two) gives way again to a friendly exchange of stage positions, as Francisco approaches Marcellus and Horatio and moves past. Marcellus's "Who hath relieved you?" may cue the Francisco-actor to appear relieved in spirit as well as at post. Likewise, "Barnardo hath my place" directs audience

9. "There emerges, when we analyse it, a kind of musical design also which reinforces and is one with the dramatic moment. It has checked and accelerated the pulse of our emotion without our knowing it. . . . The transitions in the scene obey laws of the music of dramatic poetry," T. S. Eliot, "Poetry and Drama" (1951), in *On Poetry and Poets* (London: Faber and Faber, 1957), 76–77.

attention back to Barnardo, who now assumes Francisco's stage position and, perchance, its contamination of locale: cold and sick at heart.[10] Confusion, tension, likeness: The first twenty lines repeat their pattern.

The gestures of the play's first beat recur in the scene: the intrusion of the ghost like that of the relief; the "password" that Horatio demands ("Speak, speak, I charge thee speak" [51]), and the apparition's vain striving to communicate; the aggression toward the ghost by the soldiers with their partisans. These famous passages establish a rhythm for the audience: repetition yet unpredictability, confrontation and assimilation, muscular tension and release, formality and intimacy. Actions recall their precedents, as in a world of finite gestures of infinitely variable nuance. Characters intrude upon one another and then trade roles, exchanging emotional properties as they change places. The skeptical Horatio takes on the guards' "fear and wonder"; the guards in the second encounter with the ghost switch from their initial passivity to an aggressiveness exceeding the intruder's. That rhythm will become familiar, particularly as Hamlet mimics and contaminates the actions and language of those around him.

The first scene shifts between the action of the story and the action of telling stories (sometimes the two intersect), creating an episodic sense of both recurrence and unpredictability that will persist through the play. In that episodic spirit, *Hamlet* frequently alludes to information outside its borders, from the politics of Denmark and Norway to Roman history to the folklore of cock-crowing to theater itself. Yet the past may suddenly become the present: "The bell then beating one—" (39), Barnardo narrates, and last night's encounter turns into tonight's. Events, like human characteristics, migrate, contaminate. History is ritualistic and recurrent, yet with moments of freedom from its own laws—both circle and arrow. The ghost recalls the sheetless dead gibbering in the Roman streets before the fall of mightiest Julius (113–16). Yet the crowing of the cock reminds Marcellus of that hallowed season free from the malign influences of planets, fairies, and witches (161–64). And suddenly the play opens upon just such a moment, "the morn in russet mantle clad," walking over the dew of an eastward hill (166–67).

Hamlet further establishes the form of spectatorial expectation in the Watch scene's fluctuations of physical energy and the social values that accompany those fluctuations. The whole scene builds orchestrally through increas-

---

10. Where is Barnardo when Francisco greets Marcellus and Horatio? Marcellus's "Holla, Barnardo!" and the latter's slightly delayed response, "Say—/ What, is Horatio there?" suggest that he may stand off from the others, perhaps the same obscuring distance from the three that Francisco was from him.

ing levels of bodily tension and relaxation. It starts with the local, two-part changing of the guard and repeats with the twin visits of the ghost, the violent action exploding outward to encompass the whole stage, as characters twice sit in close circle upon the ground, then leap out of their repose, and finally whirl after the ghost with their weapons. In its first visitation, the ghost seems to control the physical action, presumably passing within a "truncheon's length" (I.ii.204), as it has before, "warlike" (47) and armed, distilling the soldiers to jelly with fear. In the second encounter, the watchers turn suddenly aggressive, initiating the action, blocking the ghost, striking at it: Roles reverse. Motion, speed, energy accelerate with the intrusion and confrontation. The world of this play, then, comes to the audience as escalatingly physical and dynamic. Timidity may revert into an aggressiveness that lurks beneath the surface, offenses at every character's beck and call. All is changing, yet one. The audience becomes here powerfully engaged with the playworld through its very physicality.

Yet spectators move in and out of phase with this speeding train. The second main feature of the spectators' experience of the Watch scene is their moments of detachment. Sometimes the audience may only grasp that it does not grasp all. Take the change of guard. That the play confuses the protocol of the change of guard may be more an afterthought of the critics than an immediate perception for the audience. What, after all, is the real password: "Long live the King," or "liegemen to the Dane," or even "Friends to this ground"? If any will suffice, then does the Watch really require a formulaic phrase at all? Indeed, the opening moments take their special tension partly from the audience's sense that some form is off, without its knowing what the proper rite is, so that the spectator remains groping to understand the exact conditions of the playworld.

Perhaps the scene's most fascinating dissonance for the spectator involves the apparition. Just how ghostly is this figure anyway? It enters in full armour, probably originally rising from a trap door downstage (which would signify to an Elizabethan audience that the entering figure was indeed an apparition). The ghost moves with "martial stalk" (66), in a stately Elizabethan slow-motion (I.ii.201). The "illusion" will be pale-looking (I.ii.233), will frown angrily or sorrowfully (62 and I.ii.231–32), will gesture emotionally (I.ii.216–17), and will keep its eyes riveted on Horatio and the soldiers (I.ii.233–34). But most important, the watchers remark not so much upon its ghostliness as its human resemblance to "the King that's dead" (41). Indeed, to the spectator, the ghost will probably not look much like a ghost at all.[11] Instead of reacting to his otherworldliness, the soldiers are dumbfounded by the ghost's verisimilitude

---

11. As if suggesting a staging weakness in the text, eighteenth- and nineteenth-century

to the Elder Hamlet: "Looks 'a not like the King?" (43); "Most like" (44). Shakespeare takes advantage of the lifelike appearance of the actor, which renders the ghost ambiguous, potentially even unconvincing, to the audience. Shakespeare makes the familiar furnish the illusion, by stressing that very familiarity as shocking and remarkable—uncanny. Spectators understand the ghost not by their own perceptions but by the soldiers' reactions to it; the watchers, that is, become the mirror through which we look inside the play at the true nature of the figure before us. The audience assumes a triangular relationship to the ghost, with both a direct and a refracted line of vision. Even as the audience retains its own distanced impressions of the personage in armour, it will simultaneously see that figure through the mediation of the sentinels. The ghost terrifies the Watch onstage and may amuse the watchers off. Here the audience will experience (in a scene concerned with the reliability of the senses) the insufficiency, even the oppositeness, of its own senses for explaining the world before them. The playworld's truth comes not directly but indirectly. This "triangulation" of response, of course, holds for much drama, but it seems particularly common to Shakespeare and other playwrights who create spectacle through language. Audience response will be both direct and mediated, both sensual and vicarious, and the two avenues may conflict in the qualities they reveal.

The audience's dissonances in the first scene extend to time as well as characters. Producers have historically taken Barnardo's " 'Tis now strook twelf" (I.i.7) as a stage direction and introduced the two sentinels by the tolling of a bell. Reverberate and repeated sounds—drums, cannons, trumpets—invoke the publicness and large effects of the play's actions. The clock's gong also initiates a series of time measures in the first scene: the pole star (36), the clock beating one (39, 46, 65), the crowing of the cock announcing morning (at 139, 147, 157). Shakespeare accelerates narrative time in defiance of real, spectatorial time. The time-motifs force spectators to notice repeatedly their separation from the play, the way they are out of phase with the action (some may find it irritating). Such self-consciousness actually establishes an early kinship between the audience and Hamlet, whose pointed declaration later on the same parapet that "The time is out of joint" (I.v.188) will reflect, among other things, his sense that events are moving faster than he wishes. While spectators will experience the play in their own time frame, they can only "possess" the play by surrendering to its internal time.

---

productions went to great pains to make the ghost's appearances look mysterious, with scrims, special screens, and shadowy lighting techniques.

Horatio is a friend not only of Hamlet but of the audience, assuming its spectatorial distance in the first scene and throughout the play. He comes as a reliable observer, a scholar, skeptical and ironical yet also receptive, an ideal us. The difference between the cautious Horatio and the believing soldiers makes the ghost credible to the audience—especially when we imagine the dread sight exposed on an Elizabethan bare stage, in broad daylight, faintly old-fashioned, at the beginning of the play, with spectators still settling themselves. Horatio takes on the inevitable, first-scene distance between the responses of characters and the responses of the audience and makes that difference official inside the playworld. *Hamlet* invites the spectator, that is, to engage with Horatio's reaction to the ghost, his exclamation of "fear and wonder" (44), his pallor and trembling (53), without experiencing the ghost directly in the same way. As Horatio verifies the ghost, he also relieves the audience of any responsibility to be terrified. Indeed, the apparition may not become fully real to the audience until it is real to Hamlet.

Hamlet's opening scene, then, engages the audience in the suspenseful muscular and emotional rhythms of the play; simultaneously, the audience experiences its own detachment, its private view of the ghost, its private sense of time, its Horatian skepticism. As with the circle and arrow of history, the Watch scene emphasizes the playgoer's experience of community and also autonomy. The scene forces the audience to recognize its independent sense impressions and judgments, its interior consciousness, as incumbent to the play's spectatorship. That mode belongs properly to Hamlet, whose reactions fall consistently short of or in excess of the vehicles available for his expression: No public forms, moods, or shapes can denote him truly. Our nerve endings will mimic those of the characters, but that mimicry will also not denote us fully. As with the triangulation of the ghost, *Hamlet* pursues the differences between the mediated and the direct vision.

II

Hamlet creates a "character" for its spectators so as to build their positional engagement with Hamlet, the first phase in the audience's development. *Hamlet* will shape the audience into something resembling Hamlet, just as he will behave as a critical observer of his own tragedy. *Hamlet's* spectators must relish playgoing while retaining a self-conscious independence; the drama depends upon it. They are the theater's pulse and memory, activated by Hamlet. The role of Hamlet, because it demands virtuosity, leaves considerable interpreting to the skills of the actor, with the result that stage incarnations vary perhaps more than with any other Shakespearean part.[12] Through the actor's choices in the first phase, however, runs a certain position: Hamlet's distance from the court and his closeness to the audience. Shakespeare's ingenious presentation of the ghost anticipates the spectators' desire for immediate excitement coupled with their restlessness and initial resistance. *Hamlet* pays attention to its playgoer's behavior and theatrical knowledge: The play assumes audience interjections, intense emotions, quick opinions, mixed responses—just as Hamlet and Polonius turn outspoken (and differing) spectator-critics as the Player recites the death of Priam. Hamlet's comment on audience reactions to the "War of Theaters," that "many wearing rapiers are afraid of goose-quills and dare scarce come thither" (II.ii.343–44), suggests how *Hamlet* can cajole playgoers to interpret action personally. The fickleness of the audience provides subject matter for Hamlet's first conversation with Rosencrantz and Guildenstern, and to the players Hamlet will recollect the quick demise of a play that did not please the multitude (II.ii.434–37). If the audiences discussed by Hamlet and his school chums relish theatrical controversies, the poet and playwright "to cuffs in the question" (355–56), then the allusion to the warfare berattling the common stages introduces that very subject upon this common stage. Likewise, Shakespeare seems to make jest with his own tragic canon through his allusions to *Julius Caesar*'s sheeted dead (I.i.113–20; cf. *Julius Caesar,* I.iii and II.ii, and indeed, *Julius Caesar* may have played in sequence with *Hamlet*) and to Richard Burbage having enacted both Brutus and Hamlet and John Heminges both Caesar and Polonius (III.ii.98–106). Such dialogue fashions the audience's witty remove—its knowledge of theater or the Lord Chamberlain's Men—into a form of engagement, so that the stage action becomes slightly "liminoid," inside and a bit outside the narrative world.

Hamlet's theatrical in-jokes and allusions predicate seasoned spectators conspiratorial and self-aware enough to delight in remembering plays: Marlowe's

12. Hamlet "calls on an actor's full armoury of craft: vocal, physical, mental and emotional. It is also a canvas that can be painted in so many ways and with so many different colours. The fact that many questions are posed in *Hamlet* and very few answers given makes the title role one of the greatest acting parts. You are allowed to attempt to give some of the answers through the performance," Derek Jacobi, "Hamlet," in *Shakespeare in Perspective,* vol. 1, ed. Roger Sales (London: Ariel Books, 1982), 291.

Dido, Queen of Carthage; Kyd's *The Spanish Tragedy* and other revenge tragedies; mongrel genres; the dumb shows still used by the Lord Admiral's Men;[13] mystery plays; the morality Vice of rags and patches; Herod; Termagant; stock characters; chopins, feathers, and rosettes as standard costume accessories. Hamlet's vision of Polonius as old Jephthah hints at the Lord Chamberlain's Men's production of Thomas Dekker and Anthony Mundy's *Jephthah Judge of Israel;*[14] the "croaking raven" lines (III.ii.253–54) that Hamlet shouts spectator-like during *The Murder of Gonzago,* come from the *True Tragedy of Richard III*—phrases from a play hurled at a play inside a play.[15] Hamlet's warning against the lead actor's rant and the "pitiful ambition in the fool" (III.ii.44) poke at Burbage's rival Edward Alleyn and former company member Will Kempe.[16] Yorick's skull may recall the 1588 death of Tarleton[17]—as Burbage addresses Robert Armin, the new comedian playing the gravedigger. Horatio alludes to pickpockets at the theater (III.ii.88–89). *Hamlet* also creates intimacy with the audience by rummaging its popular memory: the famous ape, the forgotten hobbyhorse, the ballad of Jephthah, the siege of Ostend,[18] and possibly Essex's rebellion (the "late innovation" [II.ii.333]). *Hamlet's* playgoers can never forget where they live and what they know. The *Murder of Gonzago* remembers the murder of the Duke of Urbino in 1538, an incident that Hamlet holds up to the audience of Claudius's court as the source of the playlet and that Shakespeare may be displaying to his assembled gentry and groundlings as the germ for his story of the Elder Hamlet's murder, the extradramatic genesis of *Hamlet* thus partly internalized in the play. Such theatrical clubbiness trips a quick and knowing, nonnarrative delight in its spectators. *Hamlet's* extraordinary number of soliloquies and audience-addresses also forge a special closeness with the audience: Virtually every major character speaks to the playgoers (Claudius, Polonius, Ophelia, even Laertes), and the Prince soliloquizes for the record books. A soliloquy draws an actor out of his or her character; the character, that is, becomes more like the actor. When the

13. G. B. Harrison, *Shakespeare's Tragedies* (London: Routledge and Kegan Paul, 1951), 101.

14. David Pirie, "*Hamlet* without the Prince," *Critical Quarterly* 14 (Winter 1972); repr. in *Shakespeare's Wide and Universal Stage,* ed. C. B. Cox and D. J. Palmer (Manchester: Manchester University Press, 1984), 175–76.

15. Howard Felperin, *Shakespearean Representation: Mimesis and Modernity in Elizabethan Tragedy* (Princeton: Princeton University Press, 1977), 47–48.

16. Harrison, *Shakespeare's Tragedies,* 110.

17. M. C. Bradbrook, *Shakespeare The Craftsman* (New York: Barnes and Noble, 1969), 135.

18. Harrison, *Shakespeare's Tragedies,* 105.

players sweep from the platform, and Hamlet turns toward the audience and says, "Now I am alone" (II.ii.549), the actor starts to reveal himself to that audience, no longer wrapped within the bubble of mise-en-scène or the stage conflict that creates and sustains character. He must play less out of the situation and more out of himself. To some degree, a soliloquy invites the audience to see beyond the actor-as-character into the actor-as-self. Such addresses to the audience repeat *Hamlet's* liminoid shortening of the distance between audience and "illusion."

Hamlet's "What a piece of work is a man" speech (II.ii.295–310), half directed towards the auditorium, illustrates the playgoers' awareness of the theatrical event underway. Hamlet sizes up his world: "this goodly frame, the earth, seems to me a sterile promontory; this most excellent canopy, the air, look you, this brave o'erhanging firmament, this majestical roof fretted with golden fire, why, it appeareth nothing to me but a foul and pestilent congregation of vapors." "Frame," "canopy," and "firmament" recall the Elizabethan playhouse; playwrights commonly used "promontory" as a metaphor for the stage;[19] and "fretted with golden fire" sounds like "the heavens," the stage roof painted with gold stars. Jenkins argues that such language need not refer directly to the stage.[20] Yet Hamlet's repeated, gestural "this" tends to make the references to frame, canopy, firmament, and roof immediate and concrete, the pronoun inviting the actor to point toward his stage surroundings as he speaks. Hamlet's reductive "foul and pestilent congregation of vapours" evokes a different Shakespearean metaphor, shadows and dream, for the theater (his reference, moments before, to "outstretch'd heroes" as "shadows" imagines heroes as they might be theatrically overacted [263–64]).[21] Yet the audience will see before it the looming corporeality of the place where shadows play. This famous moment calls forth a theatrical self-consciousness from the audience: essentially, sufficient detachment from the character's psychology to embrace a recognition of theatrical occasion. Dramatic language and extra-dramatic phenomena stalemate, inviting spectators to hold Hamlet's sentiments at arm's length as much as to sympathize with them. Such investing of the verbal with a visual significance that extends it contradictorily gives the

19. Ralph Berry, *Shakespeare and the Awareness of the Audience* (New York: St. Martin's, 1985), 6–9.

20. Harold Jenkins, ed., *Hamlet* (London: Methuen, 1982), 468.

21. "[F]oul and pestilent congregation of vapours," though it begins as a reference to sky, could be delivered in such a way as to include the smell of assembled bodies on stage and in the theater.

speech a powerful Elizabethan memorability[22]—a memorability here predicated on spectatorial disengagement from the illusion. *Hamlet* characterizes its audience in terms of a lively emotional responsiveness, a critical alertness to performative environment as well as narrative, and an eagerness for shared jokes, topical allusions, and acting that recognize the playgoer in the theatrical event. *Hamlet*'s "implied" spectators might be expected to interject their comments into the performance, as the Prince and Polonius interrupt the First Player or Hamlet speeds up the playlet, calling out, "Begin, murtherer, leave thy damnable faces and begin" (III.ii.252–53). *Hamlet*'s constructive auditors know the theater like veterans, with a detailed and delighted memory for plays, speeches, and the seesaw of theatrical taste. If players are the "abstract and brief chronicles of the times," then *Hamlet*'s playgoers might be called the chronicles of the theater. Indeed, such audience members are not altogether unlike the actors (and, not coincidentally, the literate majority of *Hamlet*'s Elizabethan audience could be expected to have themselves performed in grammar school or university plays).

Hamlet engages the audience by his detachment from his own story, a detachment that imitates through exaggeration (mimicry) the detachment the play engenders from its spectators. Hamlet is Shakespearean tragedy's most charismatic hero and its most knowledgeable playgoer: That conjunction is no accident. Michael Goldman's observation notwithstanding, that "[a]n actor is a man who wants to play Hamlet,"[23] Hamlet himself might be described as a man who wants to be a member of the audience. Hamlet separates himself from the characters and events of his story. He dresses differently from others, stands to the side, interprets actions, speaks to the spectator, himself an onstage audience mediating across the theatrical threshold, both inside and outside, liminoid. In the play's triangulation of effects, Hamlet mimics others, registers their humors by parodying them.[24] Hamlet stands in the relation of an audience-figure to other characters. But events also assign him an actor's role. The play sets out a "part" for Hamlet with certain formal expectations—that he declines:[25] For revenge we have delay; for passion, irony; for deep plots,

22. On the way Elizabethan plays combine bold visual effects with dialogue to create memorable moments, see Michael Hattaway, *Elizabethan Popular Theatre: Plays in Performance* (London: Routledge and Kegan Paul, 1982), 57.

23. *Shakespeare and the Energies of the Drama* (Princeton: Princeton University Press, 1972), 74.

24. Pirie argues that Hamlet displays a witty, comic detachment towards the morally unworthy play in which he has landed, a quality that modern "realistic" productions tend to obliterate, "*Hamlet* without the Prince," 164–84.

25. Pirie puts it this way: "The ghost has cast Hamlet for the role of ruthless hero in a

soliloquies. Ultimately Hamlet's assumed and his assigned roles, to represent himself truly and to "remember" his father, converge; he will make a revenge spectacle of *not* acting revenge.

The audience engages with Hamlet's special stance, his "distance." For openers, he disclaims acting. His role cannot be compassed on the stage: Nothing, not inky cloaks, sighing, weeping, or downcast eyes, "can denote me truly. These . . . are actions that a man might play, / But I have that within which passes show" (I.ii.83–85). That declaration attacks the conventions by which characters communicate with the audience, the bias elsewhere in *Hamlet* and in Elizabethan drama generally for understanding emotional states metonymically by their physical symptoms. In the opening seventy-odd lines of the first court scene, a noticeable passage of stage time, Hamlet has only two lines. What is he doing? Hamlet's behavior must be compelling enough to syphon away some spectatorial attention during Claudius's section, so that the scene can fulfill itself only by pivoting finally toward the Prince. His actions should also contrast with the stage style of Claudius, who orates, commands, envelopes the court in his emotional geography, always slightly overdoing it: "presentational" acting. Claudius's manner, like his too-reiterated "Laertes" (42, 43, 45, 50), will keep the audience at bay. How might Hamlet show his difference? For one, by underplaying, not acting—little promenading, little gesticulating. Though the Hamlet-actor may sigh and look downcast, he can energize the scene truly with focused quietness, an alien and concentrated minimalism.[26] Hamlet, of course, depicts himself to Claudius and Gertrude as an actor, costumed, with an inventory of actorly "points" (windy breath, tears, and "vailed lids"). Yet his protest against the inadequacy of acting demarcates his mental distance from his physical presentation. Hamlet's reserve maintains a spectator's detachment toward the scene. Indeed, Hamlet instinctively

---

conventional revenge tragedy. Claudius expects him to pursue the plots of an ambitious claimant to the throne in a political drama. Polonius sees him playing Romeo to Ophelia's Juliet in a tragedy of star-crossed lovers parted by their fathers. Fortinbras . . . challenges the Prince to accept the role of a Danish Henry V. . . . Hamlet's instinct is to reject all these scripts," "*Hamlet* without the Prince," 165.

26. Arthur Colby Sprague, for example, cites a description of Henry Irving as Hamlet: " 'leaning on his elbow, motionless, making no show of grief, but gazing, it would seem, half pensively, half cynically, not so much into vacancy as into the heart of some oppressing mystery or sorrow,' " *Shakespeare and the Actors: The Stage Business of His Plays* (1660–1905) (Cambridge: Harvard University Press, 1945), 133. For a helpful study that treats "business" and acting choices in twentieth-century film, television, and audio productions, see Bernice W. Kliman, Hamlet: *Film, Television, and Audio Performance* (Rutherford, N.J.: Fairleigh Dickinson University Press, 1988).

opposes: "A little more than kin, and less than kind" (65); "Not so, my lord" (67). He makes his grief an accusation. He is as reactive as he is assertive, as much in society with the audience as the characters on stage. We take the position of this strange creature so quickly because he places his relationship to the play in the same domain as our own—attentive yet detached, glib, critical, interjective. The audience engages with Hamlet's distance. Indeed, that distance substitutes for what his costume and "points" cannot denote. The missing objective correlative for Hamlet's secret "that within" reappears, like the pea under the shell, in the subjective correlative, Hamlet's theatrical position.

Hamlet holds the world at arm's length, his most characteristic physical gesture. It is how he holds Ophelia in her closet or Yorick's skull or, verbally, Rosencrantz and Guildenstern.[27] He will keep his distance and peruse a face.[28] The ghost, addressing Hamlet, knows his man. Hamlet's initial fear and wonder melt into pity (I.v.4-5), and the ghost must work to keep Hamlet's attention and to overcome his mere passive sympathy, calling upon him to "List, list, O, list!" (I.v.22; cf. 5-6, 34, 38), invoking filial love (23, 81), encouraging him to be "apt," willing to stir, not dull (31-34).[29] At "[a]dieu, adieu, adieu! remember me" (91), Hamlet staggers backward, imitating old age: "And you, my sinows, grow not instant old, / But bear me stiffly up" (94-95). He will remember as a spectator: "whiles memory holds a seat / In this distracted globe" (96-97). And his next gesture is to put the ghost's "word" at his arm's remove, to externalize it, by writing it down in his commonplace book.[30] He will later keep Ophelia's redelivered "remembrances" at a similar arm's length. To the Renaissance playgoer, Hamlet's writing would

27. I am indebted to Kathleen Campbell for drawing my attention to Hamlet's recurrent arm's-length gesture.

28. Hamlet in Ophelia's closet, of course, holds Ophelia at his arm's length and peruses her face as if he would draw it. The gesture may have gained potency as a signature image for the character because, to its Elizabethan audience, it may have also identified the Hamlet-actor, Richard Burbage. Edwin Nungezer notes that "Burbage was famous not only as an actor but as a painter" (76). Indeed, Burbage himself might have often been known to peruse a face as if he would draw it: "There is in the gallery at Dulwich a picture presented by William Cartwright [an actor], which is described as 'A woman's head, on a board, done by "Mr Burbige, ye actor"; in an old gilt frame,'" *A Dictionary of Actors and of Other Persons Associated with the Public Representation of Plays in England before 1642* (New Haven: Yale University Press, 1929), 77.

29. The ghost's "duller shouldst thou be than the fat weed / That roots itself in ease on Lethe warf" (32-33) is a prescient assault on Hamlet's state of mind: "How weary, stale, flat, and unprofitable / Seem to me all the uses of this world! / . . . 'tis an unweeded garden / That grows to seed" (I.ii.133-36).

30. The Variorum connects Hamlet's new "word" with a military "Watch-word" (Steevens on "word," *A New Variorum Edition of Shakespeare*, vol. 3, *Hamlet*, vol. 1, *Text*, ed. Horace

recall a real audience activity, for "the original player of the Prince would at this moment be doing exactly what some members of the audience were doing: jotting down the best lines."[31] The First Quarto *Hamlet* alludes to exactly such spectatorial behavior, as there Hamlet chastises the clown whose jokes are so predictable that "Gentlemen quotes his jeasts down / In their tables, before they come to the play."[32] But the anticlimactic action of writing will frustrate the audience kinesthetically after the torrid, "O most pernicious woman! / O villain, villain, smiling, damned villain!" (105–6). The energy goes askew. Similarly, much later, when Hamlet comes upon Claudius in prayer he says, "Now might I do it pat, now 'a is a-praying; / And now I'll do't" (III.iii.73–74). And yet that wonderful Elizabethan plosive, "do't," does not explode into vengeance. To say I might do it now is at that "now" exactly not to do it, but rather to keep the consummation a raised arm away.[33] At another anticlimax, after the playlet, Horatio's "note"-making ("I did very well note him" [III.ii.290]) cues the Prince to shift his thoughts from vengeance to postperformance entertainment. And so would an Elizabethan playgoer, for dramas ended with dance or music: "Ah, ha! Come, some music! Come, the recorders!" (291). Hamlet now virtually recapitulates his behavior after seeing the ghost, with also a distant pun: "trivial fond records" (I.v.99) and recorders. As he holds out the recorder to Guildenstern with his signature arm's-length gesture, Hamlet displaces his aggression towards Claudius into connoisseurship about music.[34]

Howard Furness [London: J. B. Lippincott, 1877], 108 n.110). If so, then "Adieu, adieu, remember me," that equivocal code, becomes a play upon the confusion over passwords at the play's beginning.

31. Pirie, "*Hamlet* without the Prince," 167. Hamlet's writing in his commonplace book is also, of course, student behavior. But in the sixteenth century, schooling and spectatorship had elements in common. University students at Oxford and Cambridge after their second year, for example, attended thrice-weekly disputations, formal academic debates among senior students, and would take notes on useful phrases and arguments in their own commonplace books.

32. *Hamlet,* First Quarto (1603), in *Shakespeare's Plays in Quarto: A Facsimile Edition of Copies Primarily from the Henry E. Huntington Library,* ed. Michael J. B. Allen and Kenneth Muir (Berkeley: University of California Press, 1981), F2r–F3v; noted by Pirie, "*Hamlet* without the Prince," 167.

33. Goldman discusses this moment as one of several "stop-actions" in *Hamlet* that provide powerful and engaging stage images: "The frozen action allows us to register simultaneously an intense impulse to action, an incompleted action, and no action—action whose meaning may be the opposite of what we see" (77); see *Shakespeare and the Energies of Drama,* 77–80.

34. The text invites, rather than requires, the Hamlet-actor to hold out the recorder to Guildenstern. A colleague informs me of a production in which Hamlet wraps his arms around his schoolmate like a puppet-master showing him how to play the recorder. Nonetheless, the text contains a notable number of opportunities, at key moments, for an arm's-length gesture.

III

Because Hamlet makes drama out of his disengagement, his spectatorship becomes acting, like the audience's occasional interjections or its persistent muscular imitation. That Hamlet "stage-acts" has become a critical commonplace. Not only does he enact, with the players, the part of Aeneas in his tale to Dido (II.ii.446), he also performs his life as roles. While acting can illuminate Hamlet's self-definition and heroism, or the play's larger theatricalizing of reality, I wish to consider an aspect of Hamlet's performing that suggests spectatorship as much as the absorption of acting: mimicry. Mimicry predicates listening. Audiences will always echo a play kinesthetically,[35] imitating characters, trying out their gestures, if less parodically than does Hamlet. Our muscles tense with those of the Watch; we tilt our heads to that of a character whom we are observing, or echo other stage movements with our muscles or muscular imaginations—forms of memory.[36] Such echoings in the playgoer's body "authorize" the performance; they endorse kinesthetically the actor-as-character's privilege to stand in for the audience. Hamlet's mimicry reveals a satiric detachment, which inspects, spectator-like, the very style of the play. Hamlet as a mimic filters and distances the play, always maintaining a position slightly closer to the audience—more *like* the audience's—than any other character's. Hamlet's mimicry suggests a species of extreme spectatorial commentary. It involves no Stanislavskian self-discovery nor any architechtonic temperance that will give each passion smoothness. Mimicry is not quite acting; it eschews realism for the isolated and exaggerated characteristic. It makes no moral claim to "show virtue her own feature, scorn her own image." Mimicry offers presentation rather than representation, and recalls the kind of stuffed histrionics that Hamlet abhors. To catalog examples, Hamlet mimics Marcellus's bird calls (I.v.116), his mother's reproofs (III.iv.9–12), the cry of hide and go seek (IV.ii.30–31), Laertes's bombast at the grave (V.i.273–84), and Osric's Euphuistic rhodomontade (V.ii.112–20). He impersonates a madman for the court and a melancholic lover for Ophelia in her closet. He mimics a student, an old man (after the ghost and perhaps to Polonius

35. See Bruce Wilshire's argument that the relationship between audience and actor resembles that between actor and character, *Role Playing and Identity: The Limits of Theatre as Metaphor* (Bloomington: Indiana University Press, 1982), 21–29.

36. The audience's muscular imitation affords the communicative and emotional power of dance as a theatrical form, and critics such as John Martin have argued that an actor should be viewed as a species of dancer, in *The Modern Dance* (1933; repr. New York: Dance Horizons, 1965), 96–97.

[II.ii.196–200]), and a stage-manager at the playlet; copies a courtier hinting at secrets (I.v.173–79); improvises false conversations (II.ii.387–88, 390–91); and asks Horatio to rate his theatrical singing of ballads as worthy a "fellowship in a cry of players" (III.ii.277–78). Likewise, Hamlet quotes inveterately— proverbs, ballads, plays—drawing from the kind of memory he requires of his audience. Though he *acts* an actor with Aeneas's tale of Dido, Hamlet later mimics bad acting by sawing the air with his hand (III.ii.4–5)—just the obvious gesture a spectator such as he would remember. He stops the First Player to repeat, "The mobled queen" (which Polonius requotes [II.ii.503–4]). He either quotes or paraphrases the book he reads by the "satirical rogue" (II.ii.196–200), and, in a strange rhetorical negative-positive, he verbally (and perhaps physically) enacts the wanton pinches and paddling fingers of the bloat king (III.iv.181–88). Quotation is Hamlet's "word": "Adieu, adieu! remember me" (I.v.110–11).

Hamlet's mimetic actions are really reactions, vehicles for judgment more than empathy. The audience allies with Hamlet's mimicry without having to agree with it. Characterized as critics, we stand closer to the position in which his impersonations take place than to his objects. Hamlet's gestures of delay—he steps onto the stage with "To be," its set-piece form recalling an undergraduate rhetorical disputation[37]—also reiterate his detachment from his play. Hamlet's most common style of entering a scene is alone, reflective, or in attitude: imitating mourning, reading a book, delivering "To be," instructing actors, hesitating at vengeance, chatting with traveling soldiers, watching a gravedigger, retelling a story. Repeating the architecture of the opening scene, Hamlet often interrupts the story with the telling of stories. Certain of Hamlet's speeches such as "To be" or "dram of ev'l," are so familiar as to sound, on the modern stage, quoted themselves. At those moments, the Hamlet-actor will appear to be impersonating an actor playing Hamlet. Perhaps the conditioning of audi- ences for such "presentation" reflects their deeper intuition about a presenta- tional aspect of the character itself. The urge to mimic amounts to a kind of remembering (as if Hamlet hearkened to an ever-present "remember me") but his parodies also disfigure what we see. Hamlet exaggerates the spectatorship imagined by the play: the audience's remove, its imitations, its running judgments, its awareness of stage-figures as acted. The Elizabethan "privileged playgoer,"

---

37. G. B. Harrison argues that in "To be" Hamlet is not contemplating suicide but only reading his book and "meditating on the words before him, which are set out in the normal form of an academic argument, beginning with the usual formula for such exercises— *Quaestio est an* (the question is whether)—followed by the alternative question which is the topic for debate," *Shakespeare's Tragedies*, 100.

with an excellent school-trained memory, with an expert's knowledge of the actors, stage manners, and stock parts of the several London companies, and with a theater that anticipated active spectatorial opining, might have felt an affinity with Hamlet.

But Hamlet also practices the immodest, air-sawing style of acting that he condemns (as the problem of delivering such lines as "periwig-pated fellow tear a passion to a totters" may suggest [III.ii.9–10]).[38] The play both rejects and employs the Senecan manner of revenge drama common among its popular predecessors. Cues to physical business in Hamlet's lines can invite broad acting, even overdoing. Upon the ghost's departure, Hamlet's "hold, hold, my heart, / And you, my sinows . . . bear me stiffly up" (I.v.93–95), has inspired physical collapse, lurching, and writhing upon the stage. Even the charge, "These are but wild and whirling words" (133), suggests Hamlet's "mouthing" (overplaying) of his preceeding lines. When Hamlet sights the ghost in Gertrude's closet, his mother observes, "Forth at your eyes your spirits wildly peep," and "Your bedded hair, like life in excrements, / Start up and stand an end" (III.iv.119, 121–22). These lines recall the ghost's claim on the parapet that his tale of purgatory could "Make thy two eyes like stars start from their spheres, / Thy knotted and combined locks to part, / And each particular hair to stand on end" (I.v.17–19). The Queen's imagery posits a violently theatrical reaction from her son, bugging his eyes and doing wild things with his hair against the glaring (III.iv.125) spirit. At the graveyard, with Laertes declaiming at his Senecan best and leaping into the trench to embrace the corpse, Hamlet interrupts the histrionics to outdo them: "Nay, an thou'lt mouth, / I'll rant as well as thou" (V.i.283–84;cf. "but if you mouth it . . . " [III.ii.2ff.]). Hamlet, as audience to Laertes's bad acting, ridicules it by stepping across the theatrical threshold and striving to outdo it, an exposé utterly lost upon the court. While Hamlet's bombast hints at the shock of grief ("I lov'd Ophelia" [269]), Gertrude perceives only madness.

How does the audience know Hamlet, then, or engage with his overt self-dramatizing? The role looks unplayable, utterly resistent to a "temperance that may give it smoothness" (III.ii.7–8), with awkward silences; equally awkward long speeches at moments when we expect action; dense clauses followed by declarative simplicity; relentless, sudden, radical swings in emotion; and changes of focus as the wind blows. The pattern of the role is its unpredictability, its sweeping from high style to simple sincerity. That "pattern"

---

38. For a discussion of Hamlet's own o'erdoing Termagant and his employment of older forms of acting and modes of theater, particularly his efforts at turning his story into a medieval morality play, see Howard Felperin, *Shakespearean Representation*, 44–67.

charms the audience; we strive to encompass his point of view even as it slips just beyond our grasp, moving to his inner engagement and detachment. Gielgud observes that acting Hamlet was unlike any other role: "In rehearsing Hamlet I found it at first impossible to characterize. I could not 'imagine' the part, and live in it, forgetting myself in the words and adventures of the character, as I had tried to do in other plays."[39] Gielgud likens the part to a relay race, the actor hurtled from emotion to emotion, climax to climax, great scene to great scene. He feels, too, the Senecan invasion: "I knew that I must act in a broad style, that I must be grander, more dignified and noble, more tender and gracious, more bitter and scathing, than was absolutely natural" (401). The part seems to promote a double-consciousness in the actor, engaged and simultaneously self-aware. The role invites the actor and the character both to experience the surprise of recognition. Such moments go off like submerged firecrackers throughout the play: for example, "Ha, ha! are you honest" or "It *hath* made me mad" (Jacobi's reading, emphasis added) or "They fool me to the top of my bent" (III.ii.384) or the emotional segue from "Ay, so, God buy to you" to "Now I am alone" to "O, what a rogue and peasant slave am I!" (II.ii.549–50). Hamlet's associational style of thinking prompts his surprise: "To die, to sleep—/ To sleep, perchance to dream" (III.i.63–64). Here Hamlet holds the image in his mind long enough to reexperience its connotations, and to follow whatever bend in the road they indicate. Just this quality gives "To be," the play's most formal speech, its sense of spontaneity and discovery. Such "recognition" engages inherently in the theater; it approximates the thrill of spectatorship, particularly in a play stocked with auditorial jokes and allusions.

Hamlet, one might argue, formalizes a style of acting beyond presentation or representation, something of a cross between them. That style draws spectatorial attention to expression as such yet presumes to represent experience; it might be termed self-surprise. While Kyd and Marlowe gave characters a new theatrical self-recognition, *Hamlet,* as Goldman argues, particularly expands the possibilities for representing mental life on stage.[40] One of Hamlet's "histrionic motifs" in the soliloquies "is a buried current of emotion that takes its time working to the surface" (30). I would add that Hamlet establishes a process of discovering new (or renewed) emotion or insight in what he has just said or is about to say. Though the emotion may be "buried" or newly created,

---

39. Cole and Chinoy, *Actors on Acting,* 401.

40. Michael Goldman, *Acting and Action in Shakespearean Tragedy,* 34–35; see his chapter on *Hamlet,* " 'To Be or Not To Be' and the Spectrum of Action," 17–45, especially the discussion of the "To be" soliloquy, 28–45.

it arrives with the shock of surprise; for the audience such surprise discovers (or invents) a contrast between the old rhetorical and the new psychological modes. Generating such spontaneity again and again offers a major challenge to the Hamlet-actor. Self-surprise works to personalize the role for the actor, contributing to the famous variability of successful Hamlets, for the actor must give a local emotion to his free-floating outbursts. Self-surprise takes the character out of the immediate social interaction or narrative and calls for a response generated elsewhere, from inside. Moments of self-surprise make the character slightly more like a real person, the actor—and analogous to the audience's intermittent burst of insight and recognition.

The problem of acting Hamlet's discoveries and emotional shifts raises the problem of his audience: To whom does Hamlet speak? The Prince has perhaps four audiences. Intimates make one audience (as in "Horatio—or I do forget myself" [I.ii.161]), whom Hamlet addresses with directness and feeling. The public world of the court provides a second audience, for whom Hamlet is the observed of all observers, calling from him a certain formality of speech. A third audience includes the theatrical audience, as when Hamlet says "A little more than kin and less than kind" or "These tedious old fools!" [II.ii.219]; his voice here is often judgmental or surprised. Yet Hamlet has another audience that is no-audience, a kind of talking to no one in particular. Indeed, the counterpart of Hamlet's moments of surprise, when the actor and character are suddenly wholly focused in the present, are moments when the character seems to disappear, to go "out" of the present even though he is speaking into it. The play is peppered with large and minute examples, as in "You, as your business and desire shall point you, / For every man hath business and desire, / Such as it is . . . " (I.v.129–31) or, seconds later, "And now, good friends, / As you are friends, scholars, and soldiers" (140–41). Hamlet gets lost, speaking to no character in our midst, only half conscious.

Hamlet's first soliloquy (I.ii.129–59) presents his multidirectional technique—full of breaks, shifts, emotional interjections, lists, doublings back, and self-surprise—that still manages to enroll the audience's sympathy. The soliloquy divides its progress: exposition ("But two months dead," "So excellent a king," "so loving to my mother") spliced with external address or recognition ("That it should come to this!" "Heaven and earth, / Must I remember?" "Frailty thy name is woman!"). The speech, that is, disrupts its historical recounting with explosions of self-surprise: dissonant spontaneity within a narrative format. The audience understands Hamlet more in the interaction of these stylistic poles than in the "information." The soliloquy develops from world-weariness to anger, and from vagueness to specificity. These poles reflect the detachment and engagement of Hamlet's relationship to his play. Hamlet's cascading interjections, as he struggles to express himself, also make the speech exciting—the sense of the imminent, the unpredictable, taking shape. His inchoate language forms the verbal counterpart to his visual undenotability. At first, we grasp Hamlet's emotion in his verbs and adjectives—sallied, melt, thaw, weary, stale, flat—without grasping their contextual implications. What, after all, are "the uses of this world" or "things rank and gross in nature"? The image of flesh thawed into dew plumbs dejection, yet the conceit's grotesqueness also disengages, and to what could "sallied" refer? Hamlet, moreover, calls our attention back and forth from his exposition to himself, constantly shifting the focus of our engagement. His language doubles and repeats, particularly his emotional interjections: "too too sallied"; "O God, God"; "Fie on't, ah fie!"; "nay, not so much, not two"; "within a month . . . A little month." The doubling extends to syntax, with two "within a month . . . she married" clauses. Such repetitions call for virtuosic acting, the creating through pitch, timbre, and intensity the spontaneously felt distinction that words cannot convey, verbal self-surprise and recognition charging Hamlet's lines. Such surprise and recognition engage spectators with Hamlet in an analogy of spectatorship; he discovers his reactions almost simultaneously with the audience.

Hamlet's soliloquy progressively includes his spectators as objects of address, tightening their identification with him. His turn from abstractions to specifics helps. His twin *this*es invite a physical gesture pointing the audience toward the vanished court: "That it should come to this!," "that was to this." Likewise "Heaven and earth, / Must I remember?" supplies an interjected question as an explanation to the audience, the shift in tone and the momentary self-surprise offering motivation for continued exposition. He recalls the funeral image of his mother in sharp detail, as if driven uncontrollably by memory. The soliloquy establishes a contrast in emotional intensity between exposition and interjection, between detachment and engagement, that ultimately collapses. Hamlet, like an Elizabethan spectator, can see vividly with the mind's eye ("My father—methinks I see my father," says Hamlet, "In my mind's eye" [I.ii.184–85]), and can engage emotionally with what he imagines. Ultimately in the first soliloquy the past surrenders to the present; the vehemence of interjected, unpent emotion becomes the vehemence of the exposition itself. The shifting perspectives of Hamlet's divided style and divided soul, these rhythms of distance, merge in a whole and essentially spectatorial relationship toward his world: "But break my heart, for I must hold my tongue."

Critics have been historically drawn to Hamlet because they see something of themselves in the character: procrastination, melancholy, craftiness, over-thoughtfulness, sensitivity of soul, despair for a seedy world, existential choice. But spectators can identify with him for a different reason, deriving from something other than the proper analysis of his afflictions. Our tendency to read the play favors those critiques that interpret him as if he were a fixed object, out there, separable from us. Yet theatrically, Hamlet engages playgoers significantly through his *relationship* to the rest of the play. He is audience-like; he appropriates our shifting distance, our mimesis, our inclination to comment and judge, and he invites us to sound the mystery of the inchoate point of view (like our own). Indeed, Hamlet coopts the perspective of the spectator and engages us with its shifting, processual, and transformational quality.

IV

The audience loosens its attachment to Hamlet morally, as the play illustrates his interrelatedness with others, and aesthetically, as it "frames" him with those characters who resemble him and whom he touches. I wish to focus on the positions of two figures as Hamlet-reverberators and Hamlet-frames: Ophelia and Claudius, lover and enemy. The nunnery scene (III.i) will invite audience-members to recognize consciously, perhaps for the first time, some positional disengagement from Hamlet. But long before that scene, spectators receive subterranean hints of the contextualizing power of remembering and the unreliability of spectatorship that will later build detachment. The two Polonius family scenes (I.iii and II.i), for example, employ important motifs of memory, repetition, and imitation that they also subtly parody or complicate. Laertes instructs Ophelia to "fear" (I.iii.16), "fear" (said twice, 33), and "fear" (43) Hamlet's protestations, but when she turns the table, advising him to follow his own teaching, he answers breezily, "O, fear me not" (51). Laertes perceives (in duplicate) a "double blessing" (53) and "double grace" in his "second leave" (54) with Polonius, who urges his son to hurry and then delays him: "these few precepts in thy memory / Look thou character" (58–59). Polonius, that is, instructs Laertes, as Laertes has just instructed Ophelia. The voyager then turns back to remind his sister to "remember" [84] what he has said—Laertes effecting a Polonian double leave-taking. (" 'Tis in my memory lock'd [85], Ophelia replies.) Next, Polonius plays Laertes again, by asking about his advice to Ophelia and tendering his own parallel instruction regarding Hamlet. The scene moves forward by musical chairs, as characters continually displace each other as teacher and student. "Remembering" provides the scene's subject and action both. Worth noting, Laertes and Polonius give largely bad advice: it is all about keeping aloof, withholding oneself, or reserving relationship, a position toward others that the play renders fatuous. Worth noting too, the Hamlet "charactered" by these two memories changes, as Laertes depicts the Prince's vows of love as compromised by his destiny, while Polonius degrades them to "brokers" (127) and "unholy suits" (129) bent on mischief. Here remembering works not for clarity but for instability in the portrait of Hamlet.

Such imitation and repetition recall the "imitative counterpoint" of the play's first scene. They suggest the transferability of "parts" that will come to haunt the audience's experience of Elsinore. Other characters echo in a minor key the motif of impersonation, and its derivative, quotation (though only Hamlet shows a parodic edge). The ghost repeats Hamlet's "swear" (I.v.149, 155, 161, 181); Ophelia acts out Hamlet in the closet ("And with his other hand thus o'er his brow, / . . . And thrice his head thus waving up and down" [II.i.86–90]); Polonius improvises dialogue for Reynaldo (II.i.14–15, 17–19), then impersonates an imaginary Dansker (46, 52–58), and Reynaldo parrots back Polonius's lines (51). To the King, Polonius quotes Hamlet's letter and then even quotes himself (II.ii.109–124, 141–42). Later he quotes the actors' playbill (II.ii.396–402). Both Horatio and the King read aloud Hamlet's letters (IV.vi.13–31, IV.vii.43–48). Ophelia inhabits her madness with ballads; the eccentric gravedigger sings ballads and quotes scripture (V.i.36–37). Such mimicing and quoting make Hamlet's all the more central.

And unreliable. Ophelia's reenactment of Hamlet in her closet displays the engagement and detachment, inherent biases, and subjectivity of spectatorship, rendering it problematic. Hamlet's mimicry is unfathomable, Ophelia's remembering tainted by desire, and the audience's awareness soiled in the working of "discrepant" knowledge. Ophelia's view of Hamlet matters in the play, because she is a prime source for its memory of him before he became the melancholy Prince. Her report here provides the only sighting of Hamlet between his ghost scene and his entrance reading a book. The episode also sounds another distant trumpet to the spectator's later disengagement with Hamlet in its second phase of development. Is Hamlet going mad for Ophelia's love, playing the antic, or perhaps bidding her farewell as he turns avenger? Ophelia enters the scene as a postperformance spectator: She has "noted" Hamlet's best gestures. She has been moved herself by tragic emotion: fear ("I have been so affrighted!" [II.i.72]; "But truly I do fear it" [83]) and its complement, pity ("a look so piteous in purport" [79]; "a sigh so piteous and profound" [91]).

Ophelia's fear or pity express her critique, as "purport" and "profound" suggest. But given its discrepant awareness, the audience may suspect that desire colors Ophelia's spectatorship. She reacts as if Hamlet were responding only to her denial of his access. She also reacts from other private feelings: her fear that the deprivation of love disorients the body (94–97) and destroys being (90–93)—fears that she will later live out. Ophelia's reenactment of Hamlet makes report about herself, one spectatorial effect of Ophelia's impersonation.

But discrepant awareness taints the audience, too. Because we know of Hamlet's antic disposition and Ophelia does not, we distrust her credible but discrepantly held explanation, love-ecstasy (credible, at least, until Polonius endorses it). Our positional superiority urges a weakly reasoned bias and detachment. Yet the audience will engage with Ophelia, too, and with the Hamlet she envisions. The scene registers her pain and disturbance, so great that they call Polonius to action. Ophelia has the ability to see, better than anyone else, a soul in torment. Hamlet's anguish reaches us through Ophelia, climaxed in the description (and perhaps in her imitation) of his "sigh so piteous and profound / As it did seem to shatter all his bulk / And end his being" (91–93). Ophelia offers a seismograph to powerlessness, to ineffectual pain in *Hamlet,* for no other character experiences them as she does. After the nunnery scene Ophelia will stand alone on stage, "of ladies most deject and wretched" (III.i.155), while her father and Claudius debate, virtually unaware of her.

The episode displays Hamlet's "contamination" of Ophelia: She becomes more like him. She "takes his part" (later she will assume some of his stage position). Ophelia gets to play Hamlet physically. Her repeated "thus" suggests her own imitative gesture: "and with his other hand thus o'er his brow, / He falls to such perusal of my face" (II.i.86–87), and most likely she takes Polonius's wrists and holds him as Hamlet had held her at "the length of all his arm" (85). With another "thus," she continues to impersonate Hamlet, waving her head and likely shaking Polonius: "At last, a little shaking of mine arm, / And thrice his head thus waving upon and down" (89–90). The episode presents its key action, what we actually see, not as Hamlet's antics but Ophelia's mimicry: Hamlet's haunting of her. Ophelia illustrates the dialogic seepage of "forms, moods, shapes" (I.ii.82) from one character to another that undermines Hamlet's (the audience's, anyone's) presumption of autonomy and remove. Ophelia will become like Hamlet.

Ophelia's report "deconstructs" the objectivity of spectatorship further. Hamlet's unbraced doublet, fallen stockings, and backwards eyes parody the conventions of the melancholy lover, yet they also half-denote his real outsized and "piteous" grief. Ophelia's picture of Hamlet places him in the "teapot" school of acting—knees knocking, hand on brow—and her imitation makes sure that we get it. Ophelia's physical impersonation, that is, provides the medium for the audience to make its own sympathetic muscular response to Hamlet. Our doubt makes our senses alive; we "try out" Ophelia's Hamlet with slight adjustments of our own body or with our muscular imagination. The audience remains empathic yet uncertain; we get a possible truth simultaneously with the satire of it, authenticity and exploded form going hand in hand.

A specter haunts Hamlet, too. He appears like a ghost "loosed out of hell / To speak of horrors" (II.i.80–81). For the audience, he recalls not Ophelia's generic ghost, but the theatrical ghost of act I. Hamlet mimics before Ophelia the ghost's initial scrutinizing of the Watch, its lifting of its head (I.ii.216), its fixing of its eyes "most constantly" on Horatio (I.ii.233–34).[41] The ghost contaminates Hamlet's gestures, just as Hamlet contaminates Ophelia. But Hamlet echoes the ghost only incidentally to his portrayal of lover or antic. The audience alone, not Ophelia or any Claudian courtier, can appreciate his ghostly mimicry. It lacks public-relations value. The ghost-echoes explain Hamlet's visit to Ophelia's closet, moreover, in a way that makes his visit to her closet irrelevant. Here the audience's knowledge disrupts its sense of narrative. Perhaps *Hamlet* constitutes a play about an audience that cannot make up its mind, as Stephen Booth suggests,[42] partly because its audience sometimes knows too much. Ophelia makes spectatorship the episode's theme and action, with the effect of rendering it problematic: The spectatorial position itself (Ophelia's, Hamlet's, the audience's) takes on hints of desire, partiality, bias, and paradox.

The nunnery scene (III.i) launches the audience's conscious estrangement from Hamlet, a scene that can serve as a model for the shift toward detachment in the play's spectatorial ground-plan. As prelude to that encounter, Rosencrantz and Guildenstern report on the "crafty madness" (III.i.8) of Hamlet. The King refers to Hamlet's "turbulent and dangerous lunacy" (4), and Gertrude echoes with "Hamlet's wildness" (39). Such imagery prepares more than reports, there to shape our view of Hamlet and to direct our expectations. So far, Hamlet has been ironical, suspicious, elusive, witty, rude, reflective, distracted, exasperated; but toward the court, he has not been

---

41. John Hunt, "A Thing of Nothing: The Catastrophic Body in *Hamlet*," *Shakespeare Quarterly* 39 (Spring 1988): 38.

42. Stephen Booth, "On the Value of *Hamlet*," in *Reinterpretations of Elizabethan Drama: Selected Papers from the English Institute,* ed. Norman Rabkin (New York: Columbia University Press, 1969), 137–76.

turbulent, wild, dangerous, or even particularly crafty. The nunnery scene turns away, temporarily, the audience's identification with Hamlet, even as, after "To be," Hamlet on the stage physically turns away from the audience he has addressed and encounters Ophelia. The pattern of the scene is of interruption (first by Ophelia, then by Hamlet), confrontation, and Hamlet's attempt to overwhelm Ophelia, to dominate her, to transform her into his image rather than to acknowledge her (the general structure here recalls that of the opening scene). Hamlet in conflict with Ophelia stands for Hamlet in conflict with his audience, thus with himself. Ophelia initiates the exchange. But control shifts to Hamlet on "are you honest" (102), and his comments become a widening gyre, encompassing Polonius, marriage, all women, and all married couples (one in particular). For the first time, we see Hamlet's cruelty and violence; not accidentally, the Prince draws our attention to it by suggesting his own dangerousness (121-28). Some stage Hamlets even grab Ophelia and shake her. The scene pivots on the axis of honesty: "when givers prove unkind" (100) . . . "Ha, ha! are you honest?" (102). Ophelia accuses Hamlet of breaking faith, and he responds not by answering but by antically turning the accusation against her. Props and gestures make the moment memorable, as Ophelia attempts to hand Hamlet letters—"words" (97), "remembrances" (92)—and he (as the action is usually interpreted) recoils from them. Later in the mad scene she will again distribute props as remembrances (flowers to Laertes), recalling the ghost's injunction to Hamlet. Ophelia becomes associated in this play with the pain and problem of memory;[43] indeed, she becomes herself a misinterpreted or misremembered memory. Hamlet's refusing the object here amounts to rejecting the burden of "honest" memory, responsibility for the past. He sublimates his frustration about the ghost and his own integrity—"I am myself indifferent honest" (121), he confesses—by venting it on Ophelia ("are you honest" recalls his complicating of the ghost: "It is an honest ghost, that let me tell you" [I.v.138]). Hamlet's talk of honesty disengages; he evades honesty by disrupting the dialogue.

The scene progressively enrolls the audience in Ophelia's—not only Hamlet's or perhaps not even Hamlet's—point of view. He is manifestly cruel to her, and in a way that she cannot comprehend: His anger is ineffectual, useless, merely cruel (not cruel only to be kind). Hamlet starts to storm out of the scene (132), comes back, starts to storm out again (140), comes back with heightened invective, finally completes the turbulent exit (at 149). He now becomes the interruption rather than the normative presence in the scene, and Ophelia

---

43. Marjorie Garber remarks similarly that "Ophelia herself is constantly associated with the need to remember," *Shakespeare's Ghost Writers*, 148.

solidifies that reversal with two addresses to the audience (141, 150–61). The audience's point of view, that is, shifts from Hamlet ("To be") to Ophelia, just as we engage emotionally with her. Ophelia's asides sound her affection and her impotence, as she calls upon the heavens to help and restore Hamlet. Ophelia is herself Hamlet's finest audience; his fall is, empathically, no less than her own. Indeed, if we feel for Hamlet in the scene, we do so partially through Ophelia. Our stage image at the end of the exchange is of Ophelia in despair, by herself, speaking in a formality of style that lends her anguish an elegiac dignity and memorability. She stands alone, perhaps to the side of the stage, perhaps weeping, through Claudius's and Polonius's busy huddling. They barely notice her: "How now, Ophelia? / You need not tell us what Lord Hamlet said, / We heard it all. My lord . . . " (178–80). Ophelia may draw spectatorial attention in those moments as magnetically as did Hamlet in the initial court. The nunnery scene presents the play's first exchange of Hamlet's perspective for another. Heretofore Hamlet was, on stage, the frame of events for the audience; in act II characters pass across *his* stage. Now we begin to see, as if behind the scenes, the residue of Hamlet's actions.

The nunnery scene offers a model of the audience's growing estrangement from Hamlet: We start to share the position of his victims, and thus we grasp more and more the ineffectualness of his actions. The playlet's aftermath, for example, is anticlimactic, turning away from action toward more playing; " 'Tis now the very witching time of night" (III.ii.387–99) refashions Hamlet in a titillatingly ghoulish but hardly empathic set-piece of Senecan revenge; the prayer scene effects a frustrating "stop action" (in which some spectators recoil at Hamlet's sentiments); the closet scene exposes Hamlet's refined moral sense yet also his wildness and even his distance from the significance of his own acts ("For this same lord, / I do repent" [III.iv.172–73] yields to "I'll lug the guts into the neighbor room" [212]). Though different spectators may respond at different paces in these scenes, cumulatively the audience will share a certain erosion of identification with Hamlet's position. What we took sympathetically as the inchoate of Hamlet's antic disposition looks more and more like chaos.

V

The audience detaches from Hamlet partly because in acts III and IV the play increasingly "contextualizes" him, denies him separateness, interestingly so in relation to Claudius.[44] We experience Hamlet in the deepening web of narrative effects—action, counteraction, and interpretation—not just through an exclusive closeness with him. Changes in scenic rhythm outline that contextualization. While Hamlet holds the stage continuously for three-fifths of act II (437 of its 723 lines), acts III and IV displace that mode with another. Act III begins with Claudius and Polonius "framing" Hamlet in the nunnery scene, whose perspective also shifts away from Hamlet and toward Ophelia. After the playlet sequence, the act accelerates with a briefer Claudian scene (including Hamlet's "Now might I do it pat" [III.iii.73–96]), as Claudius's final couplet completes another frame (97–98). Likewise, with Hamlet's departure from the closet, Gertrude carries his repercussions into the space of the King (IV.i), whose real anguish over the killing of Polonius, his fear for himself and others, and his doubt about the course he has pursued with Hamlet filter the next scenes and make the audience his emotional confidant (a transition begun in the prayer scene). Rosencrantz has already warned the audience of the ambivalent value of murdering Claudius, for "The cess of majesty / Dies not alone" (III.iii.15–16). Act IV begins with three short scenes featuring Claudius (45 lines), Hamlet (31 lines), and then Claudius "framing" Hamlet again (68 lines). Claudius, like Ophelia, registers Hamlet's turbulent entropy, the King's stage isolation and anguish modulating somewhat the distancing effect of his counterplot. Hamlet departs with "How all occasions do inform against me" (IV.iv.32–66), and the court dominates the rest of the act, paced by a mounting tide of entrances (Gertrude, mad Ophelia, Claudius, and the rebellious Laertes in scene v, for example) and punctuated with news of Hamlet. Short scenes and interludes serve as shock waves to the explosions of the playlet and Polonius's slaying, and the stage time of other characters increases, particularly that of Claudius, as the play shifts focus to the effects of Hamlet's behavior.

Claudius's stage image alters after Hamlet's *Mousetrap*. Early in the tragedy, Claudius commands the platform, surrounded by retainers and the accoutrements of his position: chair of state, drums, trumpets. He enters and exits by flourishes and processions, as he "dispatches ambassadors and receives petitioners" and "sits in regal splendor in the midst of courtiers and torchbearers to behold a play."[45] The contrast between Claudius's ceremonies and Hamlet's improvi-

---

44. Terence Hawkes, focusing upon Claudius's complex roles, particularly his avuncular one, treats the king as an element disrupting the linear plot progression, pulling auditorial attention to him and away from Hamlet; see his *"Telmah,"* in *Shakespeare and the Question of Theory,* ed. Patricia Parker and Geoffrey Hartman (New York: Methuen, 1985), 316–17.

45. David Bevington, *Action is Eloquence,* 185.

sations establishes a basic theatrical rhythm of the play.[46] Yet as the middle scenes proceed, Claudius's courtly entourage diminishes to Rosencrantz and Guildenstern (III.iii), plus the Queen (IV.i), just Polonius (III.iii.26), or some few others (IV.iii). Claudius will even hold the stage alone (III.iii.36-72, 97-98 and IV.iii.58-68), as Hamlet has. The king loses some of the protective draping of ceremony, approaching the play's alternate mode, associated with Hamlet, of exposed emotions and "isolation, darkness, and terror" (Bevington, 174).

Robert Hapgood argues that through act III Claudius commands a measure of auditorial sympathy, despite Hamlet's contempt, culminating in his poignant "My offense is rank."[47] Thus, only after the king reveals his plot against Hamlet's life (IV.iii.58-68) does he become the damned villain that his nephew conceives. (In productions that choose not to exaggerate Claudius as a sensualist and heavy drinker, such imagery as the "bloat king," paddling fingers, and "reechy kisses" [III.iv.182-85] registers something about Hamlet as well as about his uncle.) The audience's response to Claudius will illustrate further the disruption of its identification with Hamlet, for Claudius mirrors, at an extreme, the audience's experience of a chaotic Hamlet. The action insists upon the interdependency, rather than the autonomy, of each mighty opposite, eroding the audience's private affair with a spectator-like Hamlet.[48] Claudius's uncanny similarities to Hamlet, whose words and patterns of action seem to transmigrate psychically to the King, paradoxically keep Hamlet himself at some distance from the audience. We come to experience other characters, such as Claudius, not simply *through* Hamlet (as he mimics or interprets them) but as *extensions* (often negative) of Hamlet's consciousness. Here a pattern of the first scene reappears, as confrontation transforms into assimilation. Finally, the spectator grasps Hamlet, back from the voyage, with a new, comparatist's distance, achieved through a series of contrasts: with Horatio (who is now always onstage with Hamlet), the gravedigger, Yorick,

46. See the well-known essay by Francis Fergusson, "*Hamlet, Prince of Denmark:* The Analogy of Action," in *The Idea of a Theater: A Study of Ten Plays: The Art of Drama in Changing Perspective* (Garden City, N.J.: Doubleday, 1949), 109-54; see also Bevington, " 'Maimed Rites': Violated Ceremony in *Hamlet,*" in *Action Is Eloquence,* 173-87.

47. See Robert Hapgood, *Shakespeare the Theatre-Poet* (Oxford: Clarendon, 1988), 117-18; Hapgood argues convincingly that Hamlet's harsh estimation of characters does not always square with the play's presentation of them, though by the end they turn into what he has imagined (115-20).

48. René Girard discusses the similarities and reciprocity between Hamlet and Claudius in terms of his paradigmatic "circle of mimetic desire and rivalry," "Hamlet's Dull Revenge," in *Literary Theory/Renaissance Texts,* ed. Patricia Parker and David Quint (Baltimore: Johns Hopkins University Press, 1986), 280-302.

Laertes, Osric, Fortinbras. Spectators will recover much of their affinity for Hamlet, yet not their proximity to him as an exclusive audience-figure.

Both Hamlet and Claudius share certain dramatic functions: Each turns avenger; each becomes an object of revenge; each seeks to dominate the same woman, Gertrude, against the other. Also, each delays. While Hamlet accuses himself of delaying his revenge toward Claudius, Claudius accuses himself of delay in removing Hamlet.[49] The King here reveals a special resemblance to Hamlet or, one might say, a "contamination" by Hamlet. Though for two scenes running (III.ii, III.iii) the King has announced his plan to send Hamlet to England, the dangerous Prince strikes out before Claudius accomplishes it: "Alas," says Claudius to the Queen, "this bloody deed . . . will be laid to us, whose providence / Should have kept short, restrain'd, and out of haunt / This mad young man" (IV.i.16–19). Later Laertes raises that same question: "But tell me / Why you proceeded not against these feats / So criminal and so capital in nature, / As by your safety, greatness, wisdom, all things else / You mainly were stirr'd up" (IV.vii.5–9). Claudius's long self-extenuation implicitly accepts Laertes' criticism: He did delay. The audience catches, moreover, the insufficiency of Claudius's reasons in Laertes' weighing of the cost: "And so have I a noble father lost, / A sister driven into desp'rate terms" (25–26). In such a context, Claudius's abstract meditations on desire and delay a few lines later reflect inevitably backwards upon his own actions, sharing in that moment Hamlet's famous generalizing habit of mind. "That we would do, / We should do when we would; for this 'would' changes, / And hath abatements and delays as many / As there are tongues, are hands, are accidents, / And then this 'should' is like a spendthrift's sigh, / That hurts by easing" (118–23): A piece of the play's floating sense of loss and longing sticks to Claudius. Such lines offer the actor flashes of opportunity to catch the audience's sympathy, before Claudius quells it with the next conspiracy.

Claudius gives Laertes "two special reasons" (IV.vii.9) for his delay: Gertrude's love for Hamlet, and "the great love the general gender bear him" (IV.vii.18), who overlook all his faults (cf. IV.i.19–23, IV.iii.3–7). First, Claudius, who has killed for love, now for love desists from killing. The trap of his conspiracies is that Gertrude almost lives by Hamlet's looks and Claudius lives by hers, so that to destroy Hamlet would be to endanger the woman in whose sphere he has his life and soul (IV.vii.14–16). Second, Claudius, shrewd in his paranoia, fears the multitude's love for Hamlet. But adjacent to those motives may be a third. As he laments his inaction to the Queen, Claudius avers that, toward Hamlet,

---

49. For comments upon Claudius's delay, see Hapgood, 100–101, and Girard, 296–97.

"so much was our love, / We would not understand what was most fit" (IV.i.19–20). Those lines may be interpreted as a lie, something convenient to say to Gertrude, but the actor may also play them as the truth (since a lie serves no necessary dramatic function). Claudius, of course, has courted Hamlet in their first scene together, and he expresses deep concern about Hamlet *before* he has cause to fear him ("O, speak of that, that do I long to hear" [II.ii.50]). As Hamlet has lost a father, Claudius may desire him as a surrogate son, a way to bind Gertrude further and a tidy form of expiation for his sins: "think of us / As of a father" (I.ii.107–8). Claudius, though fearing Hamlet, can be played as caring for him too, just as the king states a humane distress over the killing of Polonius. Nonetheless, with "wisest sorrow" he thinks on the good old man together with remembrance of himself (e.g., IV.i.12–23). Claudius's selfishness need not render him uncaring toward others: That is the very warfare of his soul. The role of Claudius provides the actor with sparks, repeated moments, of auditorial sympathy, though a stage interpretation could also smother them for a more inveterate villain.

For modern, psychologically minded spectators, Claudius may hide a fourth reason for delay, that at some subterranean level he seeks his own unmasking, as Hamlet seeks suicide. Claudius, after all, epitomizes those guilty creatures sitting at plays whose crimes are virtually on their lips. Claudius, too, finds his "painted word," his hypocrisy, abhorrent (III.i.50–52) and seeks his salvation as fervently as the rewards of his crimes. His guilt weighs intolerably upon him. Claudius, moreover, who fears a popular rebellion, nearly prompts one with his "green" attempt to hugger-mugger the death of Polonius—an erratic performance for the politician who has outmaneuvered Fortinbras. Hamlet's enforced voyage looks to Laertes like Claudius's complicity or extenuation. The King's overcomplicated plot with Laertes, like his plan to have the English do his bidding, cannot succeed without attracting notice. A *public* poisoning!? His very concern for discretion calls attention to the plot's excesses. For Claudius unconsciously to seek his own destruction would be, after all, much within the spirit of this play: "For goodness, growing to a plurisy, / Dies in his own too much" (IV.vii.117–18).

Hamlet contaminates Claudius. The latter part of the play impresses upon the audience a sense of the King as diseased, with Hamlet as the hectic raging in his blood. Hamlet's diseased wit virtually activates the other's sickness. Claudius's obsessional view of Hamlet emerges, for example, when he calls him, "this fear, / Which now goes too free-footed" (III.iii.25–26). "Fear" is here a metonym for "Hamlet": Claudius treats his emotion about Hamlet as if it were Hamlet himself; his internal fear takes on an objective, external existence interchangeable with Hamlet.[50] A few moments later, Claudius approaches Hamlet's position in relation to the audience: "My offense is rank" (III.iii.36–71) echoes Hamlet as audience-figure in his most famous soliloquy, "To be" (III.i.55–89). Both soliloquies move dialectically and meditatively. Like Hamlet, immobilized in the choice of being or not being, Claudius is a man to a double business bound, snared between consciousness of sin and desire for forgiveness. Both seek a certain oblivion. Claudius's self-entrapment exposes his moral relativity: The man who preached a "golden mean" now finds in the equal weighing of delight and dole the dilemma of unfulfillment in either direction. Claudius's public high-wire balancing act has left him in suspended agony. For Hamlet, too, consciousness makes resolution sick and urgent enterprises lose the name of action. Indeed, Hamlet's "lose the name of action" and Claudius's "there the action lies / In his true nature" suggest that each is not only troubled by his own inaction but troubled to clarify the nature and repercussions of action itself. The two soliloquies also ponder consciousness after death: Claudius fears an absolute, divine accounting, Hamlet a sentience more dreadful than death. Each speaker rehearses the corruptions of justice in the mortal world. Claudius's image, "Offense's gilded hand may shove by justice," recalls Hamlet's "proud man's contumely" and "The insolence of office"; the latter speaks of "the law's delay," the former of how "the wicked prize itself buys out the law." Claudius repeats Hamlet's diction—"currents," "shuffling"[51]—as if his overhearing of "To be" crystallized the language and structure of his own predicament. They speak almost identically of their immobility: Claudius stands "in pause where I shall first begin / and both neglect," while Hamlet's thought of dreams after death "must give us pause." Claudius's soliloquy, too, like Hamlet's, casts light on his delay, displaying his revulsion at murder. While Claudius secretly spies upon Hamlet during "To be," Hamlet comes upon Claudius unbeknownst during "My offense is rank." Claudius ends his long speech with angels, prayer, and hopeful submission; Hamlet turns toward Ophelia as his ministering angel, "Nymph, in thy orisons / Be all my sins remember'd." We respond to both speakers similarly, not just because their dilemmas parallel, but also because of the similar emotional

---

50. Claudius's language reverses the play's Elizabethan habit of naming an emotional condition by its physical features, for example, "the teeth and forehead of our faults" (III.iii.63). Here Claudius names a physical object by its emotional connotation. Claudius will speak similarly when he talks of retaining "th' offense" (III.iii.56), by which he means the "benefits."

51. Cf. Claudius's "or with a little shuffling" (IV.vii.136) in the strategem of the foils: Though there may be no shuffling "above," Claudius will not renounce it on earth. Hamlet's "shuffled off this mortal coil" uses "shuffle" to suggest shedding; Claudius uses the word to connote deception.

vividness of their thoughts. Each populates the world with his feelings, associations, and judgments. The two are moved by their metaphors as if by the thing itself, so that the soliloquies take us into not only powerfully distressed and baffled minds but minds given also powerfully to coloring, shaping, interpreting all before them. Claudius, that is, echoes Hamlet in content as well as in a quality of mind with which we have come to empathize. Whatever sympathy an audience may feel for Claudius here gains, perhaps derives, from its identification with Hamlet.

Claudius resembles Hamlet in "O my offense is rank" by another, more subtle means that theatrical performance can best confer. Claudius ends by decrying his own evil: "O bosom black as death! / O limed soul that struggling to be free / Art more engag'd!," and he proceeds even to command himself to action: "Bow, stubborn knees, and heart, with strings of steel, / Be soft as sinews of the new-born babe! / All may be well." To whom does he speak, and who does the speaking? Claudius's soliloquy culminates in a perspective about himself as the sum of his thoughts and actions, which necessarily stands outside those thoughts and actions. The "speaker" is not his Faustian better angel addressing his worser part, for it includes the recognition of both ineffectual sin and ineffectual remorse. In his consciousness toward his "limed" soul, Claudius reveals a consciousness, a presence, a penumbra of the self, beyond and greater than sin and remorse. That presence must remain indescribable, mysteriously open-ended; it stands always just discontinuous with what admits of description. The effect is particularly theatrical. Only with the live Claudius-actor on stage does the audience receive the full impact of a character addressing himself so as to evoke suddenly a more opaque presence—a mystery enhanced analogically by the equivocal relationship of actor to character. The presence that always recedes before each encroachment of description or definition, that unplucked heart of the mystery, goes by another name in this play: Hamlet. Hamlet turns most opaque at those moments of greatest self-revelation in his soliloquies: his antiphonal voices in "Too, too sullied flesh" or his elusive self-discoveries in "Rogue and peasant slave," or the luminous sensibility that utters, "Nymph, in thy orisons / Be all my sins remb'red." Indeed, by this missing Hamlet does an audience, particularly the modern one, empathize with Hamlet most.

Hamlet, then, haunts Claudius, for what the audience senses about Hamlet, his delays, his speech, even his mystery, organizes our experience of Claudius. That Hamlet has a delay problem prompts any fleeting reflection that Claudius has one, too. Hamlet's strange relationship to his father primes the audience for Claudius's curious paternalism. We would never entertain the hint of a

Claudian death-wish without Hamlet's. Claudius would lose much of whatever mystery he wraps himself in without Hamlet's darker mantle. As Claudius becomes more rounded, more exposed in the middle scenes of the tragedy, he also becomes uncannily more Hamlet-like. Hamlet is the audience's condition for knowing Claudius. The spectator will not likely recognize these effects directly or systematically, but they enhance the feeling, such as Bradley's, that the *Hamlet*-world grows into an extension of Hamlet himself. Claudius's symbiosis with Hamlet encourages spectatorial detachment toward the Prince, denying his separateness from others and compromising his exclusive proximity to the audience.

Despite Hamlet's contamination of Claudius, the King never garners the spectator's identification that Hamlet claims so habitually. No structural or psychological similarities can make Claudius so empathic as Hamlet. Nor can Hamlet's more numerous murders make him so odious as Claudius becomes. Hamlet's distance vis-à-vis the spectators determines their identification more powerfully than does the moral or character profile. While the audience disengages variously from Hamlet during the middle scenes of the play, it always remains in part Hamlet's confidant, sharing his jokes, his scorn, his stratagems, his special knowledge. Claudius lacks such a position, beyond his momentary flashes of spectatorial affinity. But *Hamlet,* nonetheless, urges a new comparatist's detachment upon the playgoer. Though Hamlet and Claudius are not equivalent in our sympathy, we recognize each by his relationship to the other. The audience perhaps never grasps Hamlet's emotional condition so surely as when he exults in Gertrude's closet that " 'tis sport to have the enginer / Hoist with his own petar" (III.iv.206–7) and "O, 'tis most sweet / When in one line two crafts directly meet" (209–10). Hamlet increasingly identifies himself as Claudius's nemesis. What is sweetness to Hamlet is sickness to Claudius, who becomes increasingly obsessed with Hamlet as the "hectic" in his blood (IV.iii.66). Claudius's whole life takes disease from the mighty opposition: Until England "cure[s]" him, "How e'er my haps, my joys were ne'er begun" (67–68). Claudius, that is, identifies himself as "possessed" by Hamlet. If a little less than kind, Hamlet and Claudius are perhaps now more than kin: They call one another into action and into a new sense of being, in this play where "use almost can change the stamp of nature" (III.iv.168). Indeed, Hamlet's own final indifference to Rosencrantz and Guildenstern imitates his vision of how the King uses them, as sponges or as nuts in the corner of an ape's jaw. To feel in one the presence of the other qualifies the spectator's relationship with either, forcing an ongoing displacement and mental revision of our theatrical "recognition."

VI

Ophelia's departure after act IV culminates the play's detachment phase and allows its new beginning and last stage of spectatorship. Ophelia stands for memory—and forgetting. By Ophelia's vision particularly do we come to glimpse the Hamlet who was once the expectancy and rose of the state. Hamlet's tragic overthrow consumes her, a loss as enormous to her as the possibilities of life; the prelapsarian Hamlet, the unmatched mold of form, hovers for us in Ophelia's anguish for the past. As a figure of memory, she imitates—recalls and thereby reinterprets—Hamlet. Ophelia retells history and becomes its subject, bearing the story of the antic Hamlet, a messenger loosed from hell, into the play, just as she will herself become a figure in a story of her own demise (IV.vii.166–83). Ophelia's props, like Hamlet's, are "remembrances," letters, "[t]heir perfume lost" (III.i.98). She distributes flowers: rosemary to Laertes,[52] "that's for remembrance; pray you, love, remember" (IV.v.175–76); to Gertrude and Claudius double flowers that recall their sins. Indeed, Ophelia's talk to Laertes, the incipient revenger, echoes an earlier psychic traveler, the ghost who claims revenge with "remember me." Ophelia in her madness seems to recollect her father and Hamlet, yet indecipherably, the two tumbled into ballads that evoke an undenotable private grief. Memory truly contaminates Ophelia.

Ophelia's other function is to be misremembered and forgotten. As Ophelia stands alone on stage at the end of the nunnery scene, in the impotent anguish of her memory of Hamlet, Polonius and Claudius forget her, simply miss the closed circle of pain in which she stands. Here Shakespeare uses the versatility of the stage space—its capacity to be simultaneously two distinct yet undivided locales—to create a poignant contrast of noting (ours) and forgetting (theirs). Ophelia has already, in some sense, been forgotten in the scene by Hamlet, who makes her, instead of herself, an emblem of womankind. She will discover madness as a sleep and a forgetting. Mad, she does not identify Laertes, Claudius, or Gertrude except in a preternatural way. Hanging her memorial garland on a willow tree, she will not recognize the danger of such drowning, a death traditionally associated with forgetfulness.

The burial scene (V.i) crystallizes Ophelia's dramatic function, for there she is both memorialized and forgotten. Her history is already a subject of confusion, the fate of history in this play: Is she a suicide or not; does she deserve

---

52. Jenkins, *Hamlet*, 536–42, suggests an inventory of which characters receive what flowers.

Christian burial or shards, flints, and pebbles?[53] Laertes turns the occasion into an attack on church legalisms and a self-dramatization, as if he would out-Herod Herod; Hamlet makes his love of Ophelia his theme to out-Laertes Laertes. The audience loses Ophelia to the dramatic occasion; she is now her symbol: "Sweets to the sweet" (243); "And from her fair and unpolluted flesh / May violets spring!" (239–40).[54] Finally, of course, the hard-won rites for Ophelia become displaced by a brawl and a shouting contest over who loved her most—in which the subject is not Ophelia but rhetoric, "emphasis" (255).

The play confuses the "facts" about Ophelia and then forgets her at her own burial service. How does the audience respond? Most immediately, we forget Ophelia too, engaging with Hamlet's unexpected (and strange) emotional outburst and the physical struggle on stage. Yet Ophelia establishes a lingering incompleteness in *Hamlet,* a denial to the audience of the full measure of resolution. Hamlet, for example, never acknowledges Ophelia, never under-stands the course of her destruction or the sensitivity and devotion that her catastrophe bespeaks. The undertow of *Hamlet* is loss—ultimately unlocalizable, undenotable grief—an emotional crossroads at which both audience and hero meet. We forget Ophelia, but she leaves behind a residue of ineffable sadness and longing, just as the fading of the memory of Hamlet's father leaves for the son a loss of mirth beyond showing. The audience to the play becomes, in some measure, like Hamlet toward the ghost. Revealingly, we as audience never wish Ophelia avenged, even though Laertes makes a pointed accusation of Hamlet at the graveyard (246–49). As Hamlet loses his father, so does Ophelia lose Hamlet, and so does the play lose her. Yet the counterside is that the death of Ophelia may also open up new possibilities in the play. Ophelia is a lens to Hamlet's past; when she disappears, in a sense, so does Hamlet's history. Her departure from the play may make possible the emergence of a different Hamlet: if not exactly changed, then somehow transformed, unfettered by all that he has passed through.[55] From her death, violets.

53. That Shakespeare chooses to show the hugger-mugger burial of Ophelia, while passing over that of Polonius, itself recommends Ophelia's thematic importance.

54. The audience's sense of Ophelia reduced to the function of dramatic victim increases with the play's metaphoric echoes: Laertes early in the play warns her to beware "[a] violet in the youth of primy nature, / Forward, not permanent, sweet, not lasting" (I.iii.7–8). She has receded into the image of what would undo her.

55. Linda Bamber comments that "the very issue of Woman fades into the background toward the end of the play. This greatly lessens the sense of disjunction that we feel [between the early idea of woman as a 'monster of lust and deception' and the later image of woman as 'good and true, worthy of love']. Hamlet has forgotten about Woman *as* an issue, and so do we," *Comic Women, Tragic Men: A Study of Gender and Genre in Shakespeare* (Stanford: Stanford University Press, 1982), 76.

VII

A new inclusiveness in Hamlet, the manner in which his consciousness catches the light of other characters, corresponds to the "development" in the audience's perspective toward him. The audience's detachment grows toward Hamlet, a lessening of its singular positional involvement—which might be indicated connotatively by the difference between empathy and sympathy— allowing a new sense of wonder.[56] *Hamlet's* wonder is akin to Freud's description of the "uncanny."[57] The "double" in literature conjures up the uncanny, for doubles involve "transferring mental processes from one person to the other—what we should call telepathy—so that the one possesses knowledge, feeling and experience in common with the other, identifies himself with another person, so that his self becomes confounded.... And finally there is the constant recurrence of similar situations, a same face, or character-trait, or twist of fortune, or a same crime, or even a same name recurring throughout several consecutive generations" ("The 'Uncanny,'" 140–41).

A principle of repetition gives rise to the uncanny, the repetition of something threatening and thus repressed, for which Freud postulates a "repetition-compulsion" in the unconscious mind (145). Freud finds the uncanny in such experiences as animism, magic and witchcraft, omnipotent thoughts, fear of the return of the dead, the castration-complex, dismemberment, and epilepsy and madness (147–51). Overall, "the 'uncanny' is that class of the terrifying which leads back to something long known to us, once very familiar" (123–24). Psychologically, the uncanny appears especially when repressed infantile complexes are revived or when primitive beliefs, long discarded, seem confirmed: "What is concerned is an actual repression of some definite mate-

56. For a stimulating, phenomenological study of wonder, see Cornelis Verhoeven, *The Philosophy of Wonder*, trans. Mary Foran (New York: Macmillan, 1972; first published in Dutch in 1967). Verhoeven observes, for example, that "What we call wonder is not one clearly definable feeling but a range of possibilities.... Wonder admits of a range of possibilities since it is an experience of self on the way to and groping for an attitude with regard to the reality with which we are confronted.... Confronting reality at this point [wonder] is the state of suspension between the grasped and the ungrasped. It is one and the other or neither one nor the other, never one without the other.

"Wonder is a certainty which has only just been established and has not yet lost the expectation of seeing its opposite appear" (26–27).

57. For a discussion of Freud's "uncanny" in *Hamlet*, see Marjorie Garber, "*Hamlet:* Giving Up the Ghost," *Shakespeare's Ghost Writers*, 124–76. Garber discusses the uncanny in relation to the tension between the call to remember and the call to revenge (which requires forgetting), and with considerable reference to writings of Lacan, de Man, Derrida, and Nietzsche (and to Shakespeare's own haunting of the works of Western culture).

rial and a return of this repressed material, not a removal of the *belief* in its
objective reality" (157). Freud considered uncanny effects particularly rife in
literature, for literature can juxtapose and interlace poetic reality and quotidian
reality so as to keep its audience in the dark about the conditions of its "world,"
activating the audience's anxiety, its "conflict of judgement whether things
which have been 'surmounted' and are regarded as incredible are not, after all,
possible" (158). The gathering mood of *Hamlet* bristles with a sense of
wonder and strangeness—as in the aroma of doubling between Hamlet and
Claudius—resembling Freud's uncanny. Uncanniness is a half-remembering.
Return of the dead, madness, transference of thoughts, unconscious repetition
of actions: These are the stuff of the half-rememberings of *Hamlet*. With
these elements, the play creates its own uncanniness: the spectator's engaged
sympathies and simultaneous half-consciousness of distant resonances.

Hamlet appears in the graveyard like a man who has discovered something
unknown to the audience, a remove; at the same time, the spectators' awareness
that the gravediggers have convened for Ophelia reminds them that they know
things that Hamlet does not, about the imminence of death. The scene, of
course, begins from the position of the gravediggers, a radical displacement of
perspective from any heretofore in the play, particularly Hamlet's, for what he
has found heavy, they find light. That juxtaposition of engagement and
detachment, heaviness and lightness, rendered through a sharply fresh purchase,
promotes the spectatorial wonder of the ending. Hamlet and Horatio arrive, as
if at a starting point, as outsiders. Hamlet interests, even "charms" the
audience, but inevitably detaches it, too, as playgoers seek to recognize him
anew across the distance of sea voyage and dramatic perspective. The gravediggers have also coopted Hamlet's ground (our ground for knowing him), the
carnivalesque: "Has this fellow no feeling of his business? 'a sings in grave-
making" (V.i.65–66). The humor of the gravediggers' exchange resides in
their tacit assumption that law is always "shuffling": Ophelia's suicide for them
is a "fact" preceding any legal choplogic. They offer conundrums and inhabit
them unconsciously: The truth of the physical world recedes equally from
these two realists as from the "authorities," their purchase more novel than
reliable. Similar to Hamlet, the First Clown improvises like an actor, mimicking the argumentation of a lawyer.[58] As Hamlet plays straightman to the
delver, we come subtly to assume Hamlet's stance in the conversation, sharing
his pleasured frustration at the witty (and unwitting) dodges of the Clown.

We react not so much to Hamlet as with him, and the audience may become

---

58. Jenkins notes in the First Clown's discussion of drowning a "burlesque of the legal
arguments in the actual case of Sir Jas. Hale, who drowned himself in 1554," 377; see also 547.

aware of its own role paralleling his but separable from him: as, for example, when the First Clown makes his playwright-to-audience joke about the madmen of England. Most important, while we respond similarly to Hamlet, we are also detached from him, for our greater attention, like his, focuses on the Gravedigger in the exchange. Here the audience's spectatorship no longer takes Hamlet's spectatorship as its main object. As the focus thereafter shifts to Hamlet, his spontaneous and free-ranging mind charms the audience with its invented histories for the skulls tossed up. But the Prince remains also enigmatical, forcing the spectatorial analogue now upon Horatio, who, as the scene progresses, stands to Hamlet as Hamlet has to the Clown. The First Clown has preempted Hamlet's antic style, the kind of games the latter had worked upon Polonius; the play, then, must establish a different relationship between Hamlet and the audience. Horatio takes the role in the last act of displacing subtly the audience's empathy for Hamlet, because he is always present with him: Horatio comments, agrees, demurs, and steadily modulates Hamlet's thought from his quiet remove: "'Twere to consider too curiously, to consider so" (205-6). Horatio's stillness of character verifies Hamlet's essential sanity to the audience, despite his later outburst at Laertes. Horatio's equanimity allows Hamlet, furthermore, playfulness—less destructive than earlier—toward what he discovers. Horatio corrects what might otherwise be our dissonant perception of Hamlet's morbidity. He distances and disarms Hamlet, re-creating in a different key his triangulation of the ghost. As with the "facts" of Ophelia's suicide, the audience's knowledge of Hamlet depends now upon the authority of others as well as its own observation: The audience loses an unmediated sense of Hamlet; only a network of relationships now can denote him truly.

The gravediggers displace the spectators' understanding, too, by bringing into the play a wholly new, external, plebeian history. As distanced interpreters of the plot, they are themselves audience-like. The gravediggers provide a carnivalesque history of the dead once they are dead ("a tanner will last you nine year" [168]), the reductio ad absurdum of remembering. Their vision offers, then, a context for the *Hamlet*-world, yet they blur into it, too, as the First Clown identifies Yorick's skull and with it a history common to Hamlet and to him. The play suddenly incorporates a different, even obverse, narrative occurring at the edges of its own: of plebeians, of the dissolution of princes rather than their nascence. The urgency of Hamlet's problems resolves into a dew before the gravediggers. The scene focuses upon remembering and forgetting, the imaginative and the concrete, fathers and sons. While Hamlet imagines a politician, a lord, a lady, and a lawyer, their aspirations, strategems, and documents, the scene displays its own physical quiddity in the skulls and bones so rudely jowled about by the gravedigger. Despite all Hamlet's wit and imagination, the bones resist stories, histories, and take on a separate reality in their irreducible factness. These relics dominate Hamlet's attention, setting the contrast between what is remembered and what is really "there." Fact displaces story. The grave, center stage, commands the field: The characters and audience turn spectators to the Gravedigger's business. The bones acquire almost a comedic half-life: The Clown loudly batters the skulls about as he digs and flings ("knock'd about the mazzard with a sexton's spade" [89–90]; "Why does he suffer this mad knave now to knock him about the sconce with a dirty shovel" [101–2]). The craneums may spray dirt as they fall ("Is this the fine of his fines, . . . to have his fine pate full of fine dirt?" [106–8]). The assorted bones may also bang off each other ("Did these bones cost no more the breeding, but to play at loggats with them?" [91–92]). They are broken, jawless (89), and they revolt the stomach ("my gorge rises at it" [187–88]), disgust the nose ("And smelt so? pah!" [200]), and cause Hamlet's own bones to ache (92–93). They are weight and motion, performing the physical action—and the humor—of the scene. The skulls and bones are inescapably *there,* and the scene lights them up in all their irreducible, sensual, grotesque factuality.

Such are the relics of memory and the facts of destiny. Hamlet holds Yorick's skull at arm's length—his signature gesture—the living and the dead, the present and the past-future, the father and the son, staring at each other. Though we might see suddenly that Hamlet has found, in the jester-figure, his true begetter, though we have laughed with Hamlet at the hopelessness of conveyances, deeds, and titles to forestall the commerce of time, though we see too that even a tanner's corpse will rot, that everything is forgotten underground, that even Alexander can stop a bunghole, the moment adds not a jot more wisdom about the meaning of life to the common fund. Yorick's skull gives us not information but spectacle, not knowledge but acknowledgment, the mirror held up to nature. Yet the scene's reductiveness also creates community. Hamlet, the Gravedigger, and Yorick seem now bound to each other, reflections —as the Gravedigger marks his career by Hamlet's life, as we discover Hamlet's carnival father in Yorick, as Hamlet has enacted a jester, all three of them "clowns." Indeed, the Gravedigger serves as audience to Hamlet's madness while Hamlet now audits him. Politician, courtier, lady, and lawyer have, as well, come alive in Hamlet's imagination as he weighs the bones, even though the human histories are lost, forgotten. As Bruce Wilshire states, "Imagining is a kinesthetic involvement with others."[59] When Hamlet jokes with the Clown, likewise, he takes on the rhythm of the latter's imagination; indeed,

---

59. *Role Playing and Identity,* 18.

like the Gravedigger, he takes Yorick's remains in his hand, then recollects him, then tosses away the fetid bones. Staring at the jester's skull, the speculative Prince achieves, perhaps, not insight but philosophy: "[A]s a form of desire (love)," philosophy is a "pathos," the state of wonder; it is "the radicalization of wonder in all directions."[60] One sign of Hamlet's wonder is his imaginative engagement with the living as well as the dead—a radical engagement in all directions. Upon the entrance of Ophelia's processional, Hamlet brims with question and inference: "The Queen, the courtiers. Who is this they follow? / And with such maimed rites? . . . 'Twas of some estate. / Couch we a while, and mark" (218–22). Such behavior defies the stoicism of Horatio. Hamlet's fascination with immediate life survives his acceptance of forgetting: The latter may even be the condition of the former.

Hamlet offers two potential endings. In one ending, Hamlet, bathed in a new resolution and equanimity, makes peace with those whom he has wronged, rises to the mighty opposition, strikes down Claudius after his public exposure as a villain, transforms his own posturing and hesitation into a completed action of revenge, takes on his father's mantle of heroic kingship, and achieves selfhood in the imminence of death. In the other ending, Hamlet, despite innumerable excitements of his reason and blood, hangs back from action, walks obliviously into a drygulching, allows his energy to be deflected into the imbroglio with Laertes, kills the king only as a forced reaction when he is himself virtually dead, and surrenders all the promise of his own kingship to the calculating Fortinbras. In the first ending, Hamlet achieves honor; in the second ending, he achieves suicide.

However playgoers may feel such a dilemma of endings, they will also experience a sense of both involvement and independence greater than during their earlier spectatorship. As light on the denouement, we may recall that one rhythm of the play flows from conflict to assimilation (not exactly resolution). The audience will become the consciousness of the play, though still maintaining a detachment toward Hamlet, as characters continue to emerge as "double perspectives," echoes of each other. As the last scene commences, Horatio's presence still distances the audience's view of Hamlet. The scene begins as a gathering-up, largely expositional—"You do remember all the circumstance?" / "Remember it, my lord!" (V.ii.2–3). Though Horatio occasions the telling of the adventure at sea, he remains noticeably reserved on two subjects. "So Guildenstern and Rosencrantz go to't" (56) must be delivered in a tone that Hamlet can infer as disapproval, for he reacts defensively: "Why, man, they did make love to this employment" (57). And when Hamlet asks (twice) whether

60. Cornelis Verhoeven, *The Philosophy of Wonder,* 10–11.

he is not acting in perfect conscience to kill Claudius and risking damnation if he does not, Horatio dodges, observing that the King will shortly know the business from England (67-72). Horatio refuses to validate Hamlet's past and prospective actions, and the audience may pick up a reservation over Hamlet's harshness or even a doubt that Hamlet will take revenge. Horatio repeats here his relationship to the Watch in the first scene: "So have I heard and do in part believe it" (I.i.165). The audience may acquire some detachment from Horatio's. Perhaps he—and we—also detect something unconvincing in Hamlet's manner, as when he says, "the interim's mine, / And a man's life's no more than to say 'one' " (73-74), the " 'one' " cuing not his urgency for revenge but his oneness with Laertes.

In the ending as a whole, the passion for "remembering," for rectifying the past and discharging its burdens, lessens for all the principals. The audience will experience, accordingly, both a completion of form and a sense of possibilities beyond form, engagement and creative dissonance. The very resemblances among characters vitiate the revenge imperative. Claudius and Hamlet, Hamlet and Laertes, Laertes and Fortinbras assume a strange half-kinship. For the audience, Hamlet's denoting relationships turn graphically multiple. Hamlet will play for the king and follow his pleasure; he salutes his mother, appreciates her instruction, and apologizes to Laertes, a *communitas* utterly alien to the melancholy Prince who at the beginning of the play defined himself by his opposition to others: "Not so, my lord" (I.ii.67). Hamlet's fellow-feeling makes present what we will lose, the potential for better terms of relationship, the arrow of the new rather than the circle of revenge. Hamlet's apology to Laertes translates into a fascinating act of forgetting: "What I have done / ... I here proclaim was madness. ... If't be so, / Hamlet is of the faction that is wronged" (230-38). When Hamlet killed Polonius he was impassioned to the top of his bent. But was he mad? Hamlet's apology reinvents the past (chooses *one* interpretation), a form of dramatic "reeducation." The rhetoric, moreover, flirts at breeziness and choplogical: "Was't Hamlet wrong'd Laertes? Never Hamlet! / ... Then Hamlet does it not, Hamlet denies it. / Who does it then? / His madness" (233-37); "That I have shot my arrow o'er the house / And hurt my brother" (243-44). Hamlet's third-person perspective reflects the brain but not the heart. Critics sometimes argue that beneath the disingenuousness of the speech, Hamlet wishes to negotiate an apology, without disclosing the truth of the murder to the listening King.[61] Yet will this speech really

---

61. See, for example, Philip Edwards, ed., *Hamlet* (Cambridge: Cambridge University Press, 1985), 235 nn. 204-11: "[H]is regret is entirely genuine, even if his expression is considerably less than candid."

sound "clever" on stage? The audience may hear the speech as transparently false yet convincing. We have arrived where the strict accounting of madness and revenge no longer matters. Our detachment reveals a new kind of assent. Hamlet's apology makes us conscious that we accept it at the same time that we recognize its shallowness, that we accept it because we want it, that at the heart of truth are not "facts" but desires. We choose our memories.[62] The audience may feel, with Hamlet, a sudden freeing of energy in the apology. With the same winning illogic, Laertes will later say to Hamlet, "Mine and my father's death come not upon thee, / Nor thine on me!" (330–31).

Hamlet hardly seems to wish the tragic completion toward which events are surging; Laertes a short time before would have cut Hamlet's throat in the church (IV.vii.126) but now finds that "it is almost against my conscience" (V.ii.296). Even Claudius may lose desire. When Gertrude drinks from the tainted chalice—he has called out to her, but not with the voice or gesture that would stop her—he recognizes, "It is the pois'ned cup, it is too late" (292). For the man who has announced that his entire life hinges upon Gertrude's, who sees the abatement of love in time and the anguish of undone "shoulds" (IV.vii.119–22), "it is too late" brings him face to face with the worst of fears. When Laertes says he will hit Hamlet now, Claudius may even turn away from his own revenge: "I do not think't" (295). The tragic eruption takes on a life of its own; it fulfills the audience's need for physical resolution, for violence and the expiation of blood, but it does not exactly fulfill our sense of the passion and intention of resolution.

Hamlet's completion of his destiny in the final act will reach the audience as uncanny, even unnerving. Hamlet becomes ghostly. In the subtext of assimilation, Hamlet comes to resemble not so much his heroic father as his father's spirit, the King that's dead.[63] In perhaps the most stunning instance of one character's language and mental processes contaminating another's, of what Freud might have considered an uncanny "transference of thoughts," Hamlet's dying speeches (332–340, 342–349, 352–358) resonate with the thoughts, words, and images of the ghost. Hamlet's valediction to Horatio sounds like the memory of his conversation with the ghost. Hamlet speaks as if from beyond the grave: "I am dead, Horatio . . . Horatio, I am dead." That the "poison quite

---

62. Terence Hawkes, with a somewhat harsher tone, argues that, "Throughout, it seems to me, the audience of *Hamlet* might legitimately feel that it is being buttonholed, cajoled, persuaded by participants in the play to look back, to 'revise,' to see things again in particular ways, to 'read' or interpret them along specific lines to the exclusion of others," *That Shakespeherian Rag: Essays on a Critical Process* (London: Methuen, 1986), 98.

63. Bernice Kliman notes that in Kozintsev's film of *Hamlet,* the ghost music plays when Hamlet kills Claudius, in Hamlet: *Film, Television, and Audio Performance,* 93.

o'er-crows" his "spirit" rings with the crowing of the cock on the ramparts: "It faded on the crowing of the cock" (I.i.157), just as Hamlet's "I do prophesy" the election of Fortinbras recalls his "prophetic soul" at the ghost accusing his uncle (I.v.40). Hamlet assumes a role imitating the ghost's. He forgives Laertes, "Heaven make thee free of it!" as the ghost has forgiven Gertrude, "Leave her to heaven" (I.v.86), and indeed Hamlet follows Laertes, "I follow thee," as he has followed only one other character before, "I'll follow thee" (I.iv.86). The Prince imitates, too, the ghost's dramatic intention, its actorly objective, expressing the urgency of his story, his desire to have his history remembered, exactly in the manner of the ghost. Hamlet's "Had I but time— . . . O, I could tell you—/ But let it be" recalls the apparition's constraints and press of time: "But that I am forbid / . . . I could a tale unfold" (I.v.13–15) and "But soft, methinks I scent the morning air, / Brief let me be" (I.v.58–59). Hamlet's anxiety to "Report me and my cause aright" and for his "wounded name, / Things standing thus unknown" reiterate the ghost's overarching motive: "remember me." (Even Hamlet's "adieu" to the wretched Queen may evoke that word's most insistent user: "Adieu, adieu, adieu! remember me.") Hamlet, moreover, fears that Horatio will not "remember" him, just as the ghost had feared the Prince: "If thou didst ever hold me in thy heart" echoes the ghost's "If thou has nature in thee, bear it not" (I.v.81). Finally, the response that Hamlet sees in those around him reduplicates exactly that of the Watch to the ghost—the emphasis now shifting to Hamlet's audience. "You that look pale and tremble at this chance," says Hamlet, precisely as Barnardo has observed, "How now, Horatio? You tremble and look pale" (I.i.53). Again, Hamlet's reference to "You . . . / That are but mutes or audience to this act," echoes Horatio's description of the Watch, "distill'd / Almost to jelly . . . / Stand dumb and speak not to him" (I.ii.204–6).

The ghost haunts Hamlet. The trajectory of the play is in that sense successful, fulfilled: Hamlet has acheived the embodiment initiated on the ramparts, hinted by Ophelia's report, and faced in the graveyard. On the other hand, to describe that Hamlet as self-discovered or self-realized sounds strange, if we mean by self an identity separate, somehow "free." Hamlet has become "himself" by becoming that spirit, "My fate," that cried out to him. Destiny is triumphantly fulfilled at the same time that Hamlet arrives at what could crudely be called a psychic suicide. (In those productions of *Hamlet,* such as Sir Johnston Forbes-Robertson's or Richard Burton's, where Hamlet dies in the King's vacated chair, I find the uncanny effect particularly strong.) Something finishes, yes, but in such a way that it further disturbs. We do not directly connect the Hamlet of the dying speeches to the ghost; if we did then the ending would lose the eerieness of the déjà vu, the half-remembered, the uncanny. We feel instead the preternaturalness of Hamlet, the sense of possession, mystery, wonder. His "translation" fascinates the audience and holds it spellbound, at the same time that the audience may feel slightly unnerved and distanced.

Hamlet's imitation of the ghost creates a remarkable, complex engagement and detachment for the audience. We are catapulted between the present moment and our half-conscious memory of the past, engaged with the dying Hamlet yet detached, experiencing Hamlet also as other, not himself. Such a condition suggests wonder, when reality "is one and the other or neither one nor the other, never one without the other." The audience's emotions and intuitions bathe the action, heightening its sense of arrival. Yet Hamlet-as-ghost represents a recognition in which only the spectator participates, not because the audience *happens* to possess the appropriate "facts" while the characters do not possess them, but because the characters are ontologically incapable of recognizing what the playgoers sense, their complex wonder. Psychic resemblances, uncanny or otherwise, are largely outside the consciousness of *Hamlet*'s characters. Mad Ophelia does not know her own mimicry of Hamlet or her ghostliness. Even had Horatio been present for Hamlet's interview with the King that's dead, the *Hamlet*-Zeitgeist would not allow him in the last scene to say, "Aha! That sounds like the ghost!" The differences in recognition between characters and audience are not accidental but ontological, and the "play," the arbitrary rules of connection and relationship, can exist only in the spectatorial consciousness.

We become *Hamlet*'s memory, as Hamlet had been the ghost's. The audience's sense of the drama's realism increases with the ending, so that the emotional boundaries between play and audience blur. The duel itself draws the playgoer powerfully into the play. It presents an action that would have been realistic to the spectators at the Globe, many of them, like the actors, trained at fencing schools, accustomed to seeing real fencing matches offered on the public stages, and keenly interested in displays of this gentlemanly skill.[64] The duel, thus, has a double existence, first as a stage action, a "virtual" action, and then as something real, a display of actual prowess. The twin woundings and the complicated exchange of rapiers showcase that authentic virtuosity. (A considerable amount of blood seems spilled in the fencing contest, suggesting vehemence of action and heightening the audience's reactions: "They bleed on both sides" [304]; "She sounds to see them bleed" [308]; "so many princes at a shot / So bloodily hast strook" [366–67].)

64. See Kent Cartwright and Mary McElroy, "Expectation, True Play, and the Duel in *Hamlet*," *Arete: The Journal of Sport and Literature* 1 (Fall 1983): 39–56.

Only the audience experiences in Hamlet's speeches the poignance of his death simultaneously with the strange wholeness of his life. We no longer watch the Watch from outside the event, as we did in the opening ghost scene, but watch the characters onstage now from inside the essential dramatic experience. In the final gesture of the pattern initiated in the opening scene, the audience becomes assimilated into the play. When Hamlet addresses those who "look pale, and tremble" and are "mutes or audience to this act," and when Horatio similarly declares the "woe or wonder" that the havoc might evoke, they are describing the stage audience but not exactly the theatrical audience.[65] The awe the audience feels is not of being struck dumb in surprise and ignorance. Indeed, the spectator takes a position paralleling Hamlet and Horatio in these addresses, vicariously facing the onstage audience, as if the knowledge we possess were more real than anything the court could know. We and only we share Hamlet's and Horatio's secrets (and more). The audience's relationship to stage events has reversed from the first scene. For that reason, the staginess of the denouement—its declamatory style addressed to the "public," from Hamlet's dying speeches through Horatio's oratorical response to Fortinbras ("What is it you would see? / If aught of woe or wonder, cease your search" [362–63]) to Fortinbras's directives—invites presentational acting to which spectators can respond sympathetically. Such acting expresses their sense of public demonstration and positioning. The audience in the theater, indeed, may become an analogue for that wholeness of recognition in the play toward which all the characters grope like audiences, full of doubts and opinions ("Even while men's minds are wild" [394]).

We receive the play sequentially, and we, like Hamlet, forget: We forget Ophelia at her burial, we forget Hamlet's guilt, we approve Laertes's exonerations of himself and Hamlet, no matter how they distort what we have seen. As the experience of the play suggests, there may be an exhilaration, even a freedom, in the forgetting. The ground-plan of the spectator's distance from Hamlet evolves from a positional engagement, through a new contextualization of him, to a heightened experience of kinship and difference both, where spectators see Hamlet not only in proximity to them but in a network of qualifying relationships—the wonder of newness and familiarity both. Hamlet remains always "contingent," perhaps increasingly so. To see Hamlet's nature as bound up with spectatorial distance suggests an "un-determining" of Hamlet, the admission of an essential dynamism beneath the destiny. *Hamlet,* I would

65. For the classic discussion of Horatio as *directing* the responses of the audience, as opposed to the view taken here, see J. V. Cunningham, *Woe or Wonder: The Emotional Effects of Shakespearean Tragedy,* 16–37.

propose, states a paradigmatic pattern of spectatorial response to Shakespeare's tragic heroes, one echoed by Romeo, Juliet, Othello, Lear, Antony, and Cleopatra despite their local differences. Such "distance," as in *Hamlet,* leaves the audience with a new emotional vividness toward the world, as well as a sense of possessing that world.

3

The Scenic Rhythms of *Othello*

In contrast to *Hamlet*'s episodic and discursive structure, *Othello* advances climactically in an accelerating, headlong march, compressed in time. Few pauses to gather itself up; few meditations; no side plots. *Othello*'s scenes overwhelmingly favor the "active" rather than the "reactive" or "reflective" mood, to apply Bernard Beckerman's terminology.[1] Spectators surrender to the rapid, varied, shocking emotional movement of the play within its narrow predicament. Yet in the wake of catastrophe follows the audience's profound need for understanding as relief from the "burden of witness" that *Othello* imposes with particular acuteness.[2] The great problem in responding to *Othello* is not simply what

1. "Shakespeare's Dramatic Method," in John F. Andrews, ed., *William Shakespeare: His World, His Work, His Influence*, vol. 2 (New York: Charles Scribner's Sons, 1985), 397–416; for a related distinction between "leading" scenes and those with anticlimactic conclusions, see Bernard Beckerman, *Shakespeare at the Globe 1599–1609* (New York: Macmillan, 1962), 54–57.

2. Marjorie Garber discusses the "burden of witness" in tragedy, how it compels spectators to "retell," to re-create the play interpretively as a way of satisfying their dramatically induced need for expression, in " 'Vassal Actors': The Role of the Audience in Shakespearean Tragedy," in Leonard Barkan, ed., *Renaissance Drama*, n.s. 9, 1978 (Evanston, Ill.: Northwestern University Press,

to think but rather *how* to know what to think. Despite all its grand gestures, wild passions, and hints of magic, the tragedy can hold the audience at bay: hiding motives, shifting points of view, reversing judgments. Perhaps nowhere in Shakespearean tragedy do characters so seldom give vent to the emotions of the audience; even Emilia at the end barely manages to "stand for" us. The spectacle of passion often overwhelms our understanding. We experience *Othello* profoundly as having meaning, yet of all Shakespeare's tragedies it perhaps most resists discovery, grist for T. S. Eliot's maxim that "a work of art cannot be interpreted; there is nothing to interpret."[3] In the face of *Othello*'s resistance to definition, we might consider instead the dynamic process and nature of the audience's experience. I shall take particular interest here in the structure of scenes, in a rhythm to scenes that pits opposing tones and values of the play against each other. The dramaturgy of scenes, we might say, manifests their meanings.[4] Performance-oriented criticism of Shakespeare sometimes appears limited because it is tied to an actor's need to choose one interpretation for a word or one gesture for an action from a range of compelling possibilities. An approach such as rhetoric, on the other hand, entertains a multiplicity of meanings; for example, the ideas of amplification, accusation, and delay implied by the word "dilation" as they arise, qualify, and undermine each other in shaping *Othello.*[5] But scenic structure offers its own copious rhetoric. I have in mind rhythms to scenes by which the audience experiences empathy and moralisms; or low and elevated styles of speech; or contrasts of value, such as the famous one of Othello as traitor-within-the-gates or noble Moor; or even the audience members' own muscular tension and release. *Othello* makes spectators aware of their special participation, one

---

1978), 71–89. Peter Erickson notes how *Othello*'s ending avoids aiding the spectator or critic: "There is an unwillingness not only on Othello's part but also on the part of others to draw the appropriate critical conclusions about Othello's tragedy. . . . The disproportionate emphasis on Iago's torture provides a release that distorts Othello's major contribution of the tragic outcome," *Patriarchal Structures in Shakespeare's Drama* (Berkeley: University of California Press, 1985), 102–3.

    3. "Hamlet," *Selected Essays 1917–1932* (London: Faber and Faber, 1932), 142.

    4. Michael Hattaway argues that Elizabethan actors created "character" not according to naturalism or depth psychology but according to the demands of individual scenes, and that Shakespeare and Marlowe worked through strong scenic effects: patterns repeated from scene to scene, set pieces and formal groupings, archetypal personages, and the bold linking of iconographic and verbal effects, in *Elizabethan Popular Theatre: Plays in Performance* (London: Routledge and Kegan Paul, 1982), 56–61.

    5. Patricia Parker, "Shakespeare and Rhetoric: 'dilation' and 'delation' in *Othello,*" in *Shakespeare and the Question of Theory,* ed. Patricia Parker and Geoffrey Hartman (New York: Methuen, 1985), 54–74.

that by the end bridges their distance from Othello through analogous experiences, if not exactly through empathy.

Othello looms as Shakespeare's most sensational tragedy, yet audiences may also find something clinical—observational rather than experimental—in their sympathy with its characters. Sensational, yes: Performances can create a pity so great that it provokes a reflex of moral outrage, pathos begetting ethos. Spectators have reacted to the so-called temptation scene with excruciating pain, have shouted for Othello to throttle Iago, have yearned to halt Desdemona's solicitousness for Cassio. The death of the heroine stands as drama's classic occasion for the spectator-as-bumpkin to intervene in the action. From its earliest performances, the scene has excited extreme reactions: Desdemona, falling back upon her deathbed and imploring, by the very expression on her face, tearful pity from spectators at Oxford in 1610; and "a very pretty lady" sitting beside Pepys at the Cockpit in 1660 calling out "to see Desdemona smothered."[6] Accounts of performances of Othello, moreover, resonate to the heightened passions of the actors: Thomas Betterton in "wonderful agony"; Spranger Barry passionate "to the utmost extent of critical imagination"; John Kemble "grand and awful and pathetic"; Edmund Kean raising the audience's "admiration and pity" with "repeated bursts of feeling and energy which we have never seen surpassed."[7] Even allowing for historical differences of taste in acting styles, Othello frequently delivers to its audience a pathos and wild passion (even "savagery") unusual in drama.

Yet audiences will feel this thrill of passion at a distance. We seldom surrender wholly to a character's point of view. Against the empathy of seventeenth-century spectators, Rymer felt compelled to villify the play for its inanities.[8] While *Othello* has innocent characters, it has no innocent spectators; we are always the audience who knew too much. The strangeness of the plot is that "Othello cannot see his opponent until too late. But the audience sees with extraordinary clarity."[9] The play's limited moments of reflection and commentary are reserved largely for the villain. Thus, one reason why audience members might wish to shout out at *Othello* is that seldom does a character within the play stand for us, express emotion on our behalf. Through

---

6. Cited in Gamini Salgado, *Eyewitnesses to Shakespeare: First Hand Accounts of Performances 1590–1890* (London: Sussex University Press, 1975), 30, 49.

7. Cited in Salgado, *Eyewitnesses to Shakespeare*: Richard Steele on Betterton, 258; Francis Gentleman on Barry, 259; James Boaden on Kemble, 261; William Hazlitt on Kean, 261.

8. *A Short View of Tragedy* (London, 1693), repr. in *The Critical Works of Thomas Rymer*, ed. Curt Zimansky (New Haven: Yale University Press, 1956), 132–64.

9. Francis Fergusson, *Shakespeare: The Pattern in His Carpet* (New York: Delacorte, 1970), 222–23.

fourteen of the fifteen scenes of *Othello,* the audience shares its discrepant awareness with Iago; indeed, Iago's swiftly succeeding practices, as they propel the action, uphold the merciless gap of awareness between characters and audience and create "virtually incessant flashes of irony" from the tragedy's start to finish.[10]

In the temptation scene the play's focus pivots: Engagement with character through "internalization"—as indicated by soliloquies and (presumed) asides—shifts decisively from Iago to Othello,[11] and Othello's emotional and physical locomotion increasingly dominates the stage.[12] One result for the audience is painful self-consciousness: sensitivity to the agonies of Othello played against the moral hatefulness of his delusion and victimizing of Desdemona. Beyond a vicarious share in Emilia's later outbursts (herself tricked and tainted, too), we must largely compass our anger and frustration ourselves. The audience sympathizes with Othello, even after his jealousy takes hold, despite our grieved awareness of Iago's manipulations. Yet we do not "take his part" in the same manner that we do with Hamlet. With Othello we know where we are: "This is what it means to be jealous," we say, as if we were in an exotic but familiar vehicle, studying its controls, switches, accomodations. With Hamlet, we do not know where we are; our empathy for him is the discovery of "where," as if we were to wake up not knowing that we were in a spacecraft and to learn so by experimentation. We have in advance the coordinates of Othello's misery; the spectator watches him aware that he or she is "watching." That detachment toward character affords a complementary engagement with acting as acting. In Olivier's *Othello,*[13] for example, we watch him "playing" the Moor in the temptation scene: in command, knowing, supremely assured that he can extract the information from Iago, patient, physically manipulating Iago. There the word "jealousy" strikes like an injection. Our sympathy for

10. Bertrand Evans, *Shakespeare's Tragic Practice* (Oxford: Clarendon, 1979), 116–119.

11. See Larry S. Champion, *Shakespeare's Tragic Perspective* (Athens: University of Georgia Press, 1976), 141–42.

12. Lawrence Olivier, noting the "sighing and groaning, and moving and making faces" of Othello in the play's latter half, concludes, "In *Othello,* the passage from the handkerchief scene through to flinging the money in Emilia's face is, pound by pound, the heaviest burden I know that has been laid upon me yet by a dramatist," from an interview with Kenneth Harris, *Observer,* 2 February 1969, cited in John Russell Brown, *Discovering Shakespeare* (New York: Columbia University Press, 1981), 123.

13. *Othello* (Britain: B.H.E., 1965), film, directed by Stuart Burge, starring Laurence Olivier, Maggie Smith, and Frank Finlay. Lawrence Olivier's portrayal has been considered this century's "outstanding 'realist' " Othello (though not without great romantic sympathy) and Paul Robeson's "the outstanding 'romantic,' " Martin L. Wine, *Othello: Text and Performance* (London: Macmillan, 1984), 45, 51–52.

Othello is a form of "recognition" induced by acting. We "stand in" with such an Othello, but he never stands for us in the way Hamlet does.[14] The audience's detached recognition will evoke frustration and anger, as well as apprehension and pity. Behind many statements of "meaning," I suspect, stand such divided spectatorial emotions, and we might argue that the vast dispute between Bradley's noble Moor and Leavis's traitor-within-the-gates reflects two ways, the one emotionally immediate and empathic, the other rationalistic and distanced, of managing the spectator's anxiety.

Divided rhythms within the play give rise to divided responses without. The audience "gets" *Othello* as much in its supercharged scenic dynamics as in its difficult characterizations. For that reason, I shall examine principally three scenes or parts of scenes in the play: the arrival at Cyprus (II.i); the early stages of the "temptation scene" (III.iii.1–279); and the denouement (V.ii.105b–371). The arrival scene comments upon the play's beginning; the temptation scene enacts its climax; and the denouement takes us to the tonalities of "recognition." These three sections will recall others in the tragedy. Playing upon earlier Venetian scenes, the arrival scene presents a strongly imposed and spectatorially engaging authority, embodied in a hierarchy of "big" entrances, undermined by a detaching anarchy of verbal styles. The temptation scene, which seems almost random in the exits and entrances of its principals, reveals in the characters a persistent, subtextual through-line of "taking each other's parts," so as to make convincing a fantastical result from a casual encounter. Here the audience's own engagement conflicts with its intellectual and moral perspective. Finally the denouement summarizes the overarching divisions of *Othello*: its strained "judgments," deferred resolutions, and ultimate opaqueness. In such passages the audience may recognize finally its relationship to the drama as the mirror of Othello's to his world.

I

The scene of arrival at Cyprus (II.i), formal in its buildup, creates a dramatic event wholly absent in Cinthio's *Gli Hecatommithi* (1566). The scene inter-

---

14. I adopt here Bruce Wilshire's use of such phrases as "standing in" and "standing for" to describe transactions between actor, character, and audience; see Bruce Wilshire, *Role Playing and Identity: The Limits of Theatre as Metaphor* (Bloomington: Indiana University Press, 1982), 13–20 and elsewhere.

ests in part because, as a whole, it has so uninterested critics: Nothing much happens. Unlike the chance comings and goings of the temptation scene, the arrival brims with formality and publicness, characters accumulating in a carefully anticipated rising action of "big" entrances. In this regard, the scene progresses in a crescendo of spectatorial engagement. But the between-entrance passages—first stiffly heroic in language, then affectedly courtly, then pedestrian—detach the audience and undermine the escalating hierarchic pattern, which, finally, "leads nowhere."[15] Spectatorial focus divides, as we listen to some characters while anticipating others, or observe a conversation on one part of the stage and a vicious commentary about it on another part. The arrival scene does dispose of the Turks and provide Iago the material for setting Roderigo against Cassio. Yet these matters receive perfunctory treatment. The characters arrive, and that is essentially all; by way of plot, the big entrances contribute virtually nothing. Granville-Barker argues that while "Shakespeare breaks the continuity of the action," he also completes the preparation for tragedy: first, by revealing character traits (such as Cassio's fealty and Desdemona's courageous calm); second, by showing Iago's disintegrating effect manifested in his verse and prose; and third, by picturing Desdemona and Othello weathering a violent sea and "storm of fortunes" (I.iii.249) only to arrive in a "more treacherous calm."[16] Perhaps more interesting, the scene yokes passages of strange and different tones within a pattern that cannot quite comprehend them. What looks to the audience like advancing order one way looks like increasing digressiveness another way.

The arrival pursues a "climactic" structure, to use Jean Howard's term, "climactic" because organized in a rhythm of anticipated entrances of rising importance, whose tensions and resolution create for the spectator a sense of "order, hierarchy, and control."[17] Here structure presents a worldview—that

15. In some sense, speech undermines action in the arrival scene: The linguistic styles of Montano, Cassio, and Iago erode the entrance-events that give the scene its overt structure. By the end, as we shall see, Iago's speech subjectively reinterprets, re-creates, the activities of the scene; such a problematic relationship between speech and gesture is suggestive for *Othello* as a whole. In a careful study of the women's voices in the play, Eamon Grennan observes, that "*Othello* is not only a play *of* voices but also a play *about* voices" (275), in "The Women's Voices in *Othello*: Speech, Song, Silence," *Shakespeare Quarterly* 38 (Autumn 1987): 275-92. In the same issue, James L. Calderwood also studies speech in *Othello,* particularly the distancing "division of Othello into a narrating and a narrated *I*" (295): "Speech and Self in *Othello,*" *Shakespeare Quarterly* 38 (Autumn 1987): 293-303.

16. Harley Granville-Barker, *Prefaces to Shakespeare,* vol. 4, *Love's Labour's Lost, Romeo and Juliet, The Merchant of Venice, Othello* (Princeton: Princeton University Press, 1946), 130-34.

17. Jean E. Howard, *Shakespeare's Art of Orchestration: Stage Technique and Audience Response* (Urbana: University of Illinois Press, 1984), 101-5. Howard discusses the Signiory

of Venice and Othello—as scenic form. The climactic arrangement engages the audience, by shaping our overall expectations and tensions throughout the course of the scene. The contrapuntal undertow, on the other hand, detaches the audience with its digressive tones and hints of parody, undermining our engagement with the reassuring authority of the climactic entrances. Ultimately that latter, "privatizing" vision inherits the earth. This scene transforms the play's crisis of action into form. The arrival scene comes in six episodes: first, the exposition of the storm by Montano and the gentlemen (1–42); second, Cassio's entrance, concern for Othello, and description of Desdemona (43–82); third, Desdemona's entrance, the praise game, and Iago's aside (82–181); fourth, Othello's arrival and "contentment" (182–212); fifth, Iago's suborning of Roderigo to a quarrel with Cassio (213–85); and sixth, Iago's soliloquy of further motive-hunting (286–312). While the first two segments virtually equal each other in lines, the third is more than twice as long, retarding noticeably the forward momentum of the action (Granville-Barker suggests kindly that this slowness allows the spectator to share Desdemona's "sense of how the time lags while she waits for news" [133]). Contrarily, the fourth segment, the big theatrical entrance, ends abruptly: Othello's transition into the exit, "O my sweet, / I prattle out of fashion" (205–6), hardly fits his behavior. The scene moves briskly at first, revved by the excitement of the storm and the characters' concern for the safety of Othello's flotilla, each arrival allaying some fears and heightening others. The first five entrances after the opening, for example, come at intervals of twenty or fewer lines. Then for approximately a hundred lines, the scene proceeds to forget its most expected voyager. The energy disperses into games of wit, only to soar with Othello's climactic appearance, and then to subside suddenly as villain and gull inherit the stage. In the very structure of the scene, order, hierarchy, and control yield to private disorder dominated by Iago.

The climactic structure of the arrival recalls both the Sagittary scene (I.ii) and the Signiory scene (I.iii). At the Sagittary, Iago and Othello enter discussing Roderigo's incitement of Brabantio. The audience expects the father next, but, surprisingly, Cassio arrives instead, summoning Othello to the Duke. Finally, Brabantio appears brimming for a fight and fulfilling our anticipations. The rising tension at the Sagittary follows the successive entrances, with Othello calming each fresh and bigger crisis. In a variation on the climactic ending, however, the Sagittary scene refuses to satisfy fully the

---

scene (I.iii) as an example of a climactic structure used to create "order, hierarchy, and control" (104), although a climactic structure, Howard stipulates, can also lend itself to very different effects.

kinesthetic tension it arouses in the audience (similar to the Cyprian arrival and also the play's finale). The impending brawl collapses, and Brabantio and Othello exit with no immediate resolution to their conflict. The Signiory scene, too, operates through a climactic pattern of entrances, initially of messages to the Duke concerning the maneuvers of the Turkish fleet, then through the entrance of Brabantio with Othello and, finally, with Desdemona's great, first arrival in the play. In the Signiory scene, each intrusion, each upheaval, turns into a further advance toward clarity and order, so that by the end of the scene both the Turkish threat and Desdemona's marriage are deciphered and answered. The three scenes in question align, as well, in the pattern of a diptych of private and public panels:[18] The Sagittary scene commences as a private exchange and becomes public; the Signiory scene begins in council and turns secretive with Iago and Roderigo; likewise the arrival scene surrenders its public ceremoniousness to the intrigues of the two Venetians. The Signiory scene and the arrival scene, as well, share a chronological division into initially active sections (the commotion of entrances) and then reflective ones (the stage left to Iago and Roderigo), the latter sections supplying critiques that reinterpret the former sections.

Overall, each of the three scenes begins in a threat to order or life and culminates (at least temporarily) in reaffirmed order. Also important, these episodes all constitute Othello-scenes, his first three of the play. Mark Rose observes that the scenes of the first act "are so closely knit that after a performance or reading it is difficult even to recall that they are separate scenes."[19] In that light, we might consider the Cyprian arrival as structurally a variation and commentary upon the patterns of the Venetian first act. Shakespeare's plays often show a domination of a particular scenic shape, as James Hirsh observes: "two or more scenes with similar structures in the same play almost invariably reflect upon one another in a variety of ways and create patterns that serve to bind together the play as a whole."[20] Waves of characters entering in a rising pattern constitute such a structure for *Othello*. Beyond the ways that the climactic movement of the arrival comments upon the opening scenes, it also looks forward to Cassio's drunken fight with Roderigo, where, Rose notes, "the scene's first segment builds in intensity and in number

18. I take this use of "diptych" from Mark Rose, *Shakespearean Design* (Cambridge: Belknap Press of Harvard University Press, 1972).

19. *Shakespearean Design*, 89; I emphasize here the similarity among these individual scenes; Rose, rather differently, treats the three as one extended movement (88–94).

20. James E. Hirsh, *The Structure of Shakespearean Scenes* (New Haven: Yale University Press, 1981), 209.

of characters, climaxing with Othello's entrance and his restoration of peace" (73). Even *Othello*'s last scene moves twice from a lone figure onstage to an accumulating many. The arrangement—reason, authority, wise equanimity ascendent in a rising tide—represents the worldview that the play turns topsy-turvy. That overthrow begins in the atonalities of the Cyprian arrival.

The opening episode of the arrival at Cyprus hints at the structure of the whole. The setting transports the audience to Cyprus, to an unspecified location (out of doors or semienclosed) near the harbor but not in direct sight of it. One of the gentlemen with Montano apparently keeps lookout from the stage balcony.[21] Our point of view widens with our physical world. From the simple and straightforward diction of Iago seconds before (I.iii.383–414), new characters now speak in heroic figures and elusive rhetoric. Montano's synecdoches and metonymys demand a moment's deciphering: "What ribs of oak, when mountains melt on them, / Can hold the mortise?" (8–9); other figures billow unexpectedly: "As to throw out our eyes . . . Even till we make the main and th' aerial blue / An indistinct regard" (38–40). These characters speak in a presentational style that will tend to detach the audience from them. The tempest evokes the energy of an invading army in a military encounter: "battlements" (6), "ruffian'd" (7), "guards" (15), "defense" (45), for example. (This line of dialogue culminates fittingly in the hopeful vision of "the warlike Moor Othello" [27; cf. 35–36]). The heroical, then, permeates both manner and matter, in the Cyprians' style of speech and the martial tempest itself.

But such unreliable weather! A "desperate tempest" (21) stirs abroad, with the sea "high-wrought" (2), "wind-shak'd" (13), and "enchafed" (17) and the battlements on shore shaking to the wind that seems to have "spoke aloud" (5–6).[22] Except that this tempest, like the scene as a whole, "goes nowhere," indeed, simply disappears. Trains of people enter the stage, none of whom look or act as if they had just escaped a storm, unlike the effect of similar weather in *The Tempest* or *King Lear.* With Cassio, the material storm will metamorphose into a symbolic-sounding, literary one, a shift toward antirealism. The tempest bangs the Turks and inspires spectatorial anxiety for Desdemona and Othello. Nonetheless, the Cyprians' windy rhetoric and the storm's absence of physical effects upon the

21. The scene seems located above as well as away from the harbor ("What from the cape can you discern at sea?" [1]). At the Globe, it could have been played so that the lookout peered out above the audience, and Cassio, Desdemona, and Othello could have entered through the audience, using it, in fact, to create the sense of passing through a crowd, which Cassio's first line and the reference to citizens on the shore suggest.

22. Is it night or day in this scene? The Second Gentleman speaks of waves casting water on the "burning Bear" (14) and "th' ever-fixed Pole" (15), as if the tempest were at night, yet the scene generally suggests daylight.

characters render the tempest, for the audience, as something declaimed, told rather than shown, something "not there." The heroic motif appears overblown.

Cassio's speeches hint at the symbolism of the storm ("For I have lost him on a dangerous sea" [46]), for a moment, situating the audience's understanding. But Cassio then replaces the heroic with the courtly. His paeans to Desdemona take literary language to the verge of obscurantism: She "paragons description," exceeds "blazoning pens," and "in th' essential vesture of creation / Does tire the ingener" (62–65) (as these last lines have tired explicators). In Olivier's film of *Othello,* when Derek Jacobi envisions rocks, seas, and winds omitting "Their mortal natures, letting go safely by / The divine Desdemona" (73–74), the backdrop of sky on the set suddenly brightens, the storm evidently clearing at the mention of divine Desdemona's name. Such sentimentality now surrenders to an equally strange, powerfully sexual speech in which Cassio invokes Jove to swell Othello's sail, bless the bay with his "tall ship," and "[m]ake love's quick pants in Desdemona's arms" so as to "[g]ive renew'd fire to our extincted spirits" (77–81). When divine Desdemona does enter, Cassio makes everybody kneel! (84)—as he further conjures "the grace of heaven" wheeling round her (85–87).[23] At some point, the spectator may wonder if he or she has landed in Cyprus or Faeryland.

Cassio's symbolic language diminishes his psychological realism and hints at the possibility of theatrical humor. Though he expresses sincere concern for Othello and Desdemona, he also sounds like a mouthpiece for the play. His homage to divine Desdemona and his apostrophe to "Great Jove," moreover, aim at no one precisely before him; stage Cassios will tend to utter the lines facing the audience. Such oblique set-pieces will reduce the spectator's identification with the speaker. Cassio's presentational style reflects his current standing in the play. He succeeds as symbol-bearer because we accept intuitively that artificial, literary language fits his courtesy-book persona. To the extent that Cassio's talk does characterize him, it disengages the audience. Cassio's interlude may hint at self-satire. As Cassio completes his mannered rhapsody for Desdemona, for example, Montano (who has only seconds before asked

---

23. Analyzing the contrasts between movement and stasis in *Othello,* Michael E. Mooney underscores the artificial, literary nature of Desdemona's entrance: "Here the kneeling men encircle her. The action 'stops.' Desdemona is set apart, held in everyone's eyes. . . . And here Desdemona's mythological and religious iconography as Venus and the virgin is established. She silently stands at the still point of a turning circle of figures. The Neoplatonic, syncretic traditions Shakespeare draws upon to create this chrysolitic 'jewel' crystallize in her dramatic entry," "Location and Idiom in *Othello,* " in Othello: *New Perspectives,* ed. Virginia Mason Vaughan and Kent Cartwright (Rutherford, N.J.: Fairleigh Dickinson University Press, 1991).

about Othello's wife) must inquire, "What is she?" (73), perhaps momentarily dumbfounded by Cassio's adjective-inflated vision of Desdemona's escapes.[24] Does Cassio speak for the occasion, or does his talk parody "big entrances"? Both possibilities inhere in the scene, "[t]hough," as the Gentleman says of mad Ophelia, "nothing sure." Against our fearful anticipation of Desdemona, the rhythm of courtly love reified and satirized distracts our attention with its literary manners—distancing us, perhaps humorously, from the climactic structure of the scene.

Desdemona will have nothing of such fustian: "I thank you, valiant Cassio. / What tidings can you tell me of my lord?" (87–88). Her entrance corrects Cassio's errant sensibilities. Yet while the scene now reorients the audience's tension to Othello, the action siderails anew with Iago's improvised rhymes. The problem of appropriate praise continues in a different key. What just was action becomes now subject, as we move from mannered speaking to a discussion of utterance: "What wouldst thou write of me, if thou shouldst praise me?" (117). Such a movement will heighten the spectators' comparative awareness, their detachment (not unlike the temptation scene's effect, with "thought" as both process and subject). Iago's version of praise provides the antidote to Cassio's, substituting the reductive for the inflated, yet without arriving at a satisfactory balance. The contrast demonstrates the way in which *Othello* will undercut characters who seem to offer, at least provisionally, responses or perspectives with which the audience might identify itself. The scene makes Cassio increasingly silly; Iago turns toward us in soliloquy, yet his realism, a mood with which the spectator might sympathize, also belittles. And how funny—or witty—is Iago really? Iago's avowal that his "Muse labors" (127) implies that his jokes develop spontaneously, improvisationally. Yet Desdemona accuses him of following a hackneyed script: "These are old fond paradoxes to make fools laugh i' th' alehouse" (138–39). Iago's rhymes do seem to work variations upon common Elizabethan epigrams.[25] In the theater,

24. Peter Erickson notes that the scene presents "three images of Desdemona": Cassio's poeticized exalting of woman's power, Iago's deflation of Desdemona in favor of male wit, and Othello's turn on the courtly love convention, transfering his warrior identity to Desdemona: *Patriarchal Structures in Shakespeare's Drama,* 89–91. Ann Jennalie Cook suggests that the arrival scene provides the audience with continuing, "ambivalent evidence on Desdemona," so that we do not know yet if she is "saint" or "seductress"; here the feminist critique of the play's ambivalence toward Desdemona might find added context in the ambivalent structure of the scene as a whole: see Ann Jennalie Cook, "The Design of Desdemona: Doubt Raised and Resolved," in *Shakespeare Studies,* vol. 13, ed. J. Leeds Barroll III (New York: Burt Franklin, 1980), 187–96, esp. 190–91.

25. See, for example, Norman Sanders, ed., *Othello* (Cambridge: Cambridge University Press, 1984), 90 n.136.

interestingly, familiar and worn-out jokes can garner laughter, even though the audience recognizes their triteness and, here, their misogyny. Iago's jokes can engage the spectator with their humor but detach with their ugliness, just as Iago himself can engage with his apparent spontaneity but detach spectators who, like Desdemona, suspect prepackaging. The ambiguity of improvisation versus scripting (one that recurs in the play) gives the audience a distinct experience (as Othello will receive his later) of Iago's opacity. Desdemona offers some refreshing clarity—"O, fie upon thee, slanderer!" (113), "most lame and impotent conclusion! . . . a most profane and liberal counsellor" (161–64)—that encourages the spectator to think, or to hope, that she hears herself. Yet the scene, as it follows Iago's verse, slips into the comfortableness of Venetian raillery and manners. For the playgoer, the interlude is both amusing and—in its length and ambivalence—disengaging, even disturbing. The audience laughs indulgently (with Desdemona) at what it does not want indulged.

Just before Othello's big moment, the arrival scene defines its contrapuntal undertow, its antistructure, visually in Cassio's interview with Desdemona (upstage or to a side) set against Iago's downstage soliloquy.[26] The audience's attention divides, with the now-tediously affected Cassio whispering in Desdemona's ear, kissing his fingers, bowing, and the vicious Iago dredging his scatalogical psyche (167–77). When Othello bursts onto center stage, he will do so with Cassio and Desdemona on one side and Iago on the other. (The Signiory scene gives Desdemona a corresponding entrance visually between Othello on one side and Brabantio on the other.) The contrapuntal "beat" that precedes Othello will thus affect how the audience experiences the entrance. First, the counterpoint will take the play's unsatisfying spectatorial alternatives— the lieutenant or the ensign—into the heart of a scene contoured for completion, hierarchy, and reassurance. Exactly such sabotaging of structure constitutes the deep resonance of the Cyprian arrival. (The early Signiory episode contains similar hints in Brabantio's unexpected mockery of the Duke's run-on maxims of reconciliation.) Secondly, the contrapuntal beat will heighten the audience's perception of a current of disengaging "presentation" or contrivance running through the scene. Iago virtually stage-manages Cassio's actions in his asides: "ay, well said, whisper. . . . Ay, smile upon her, do" (167–69). Later, of course,

---

26. Jean Howard uses the term "dramatic counterpoint" in a similar, if slightly more restrictive sense: "the sustained juxtaposition, within a scene, of two separate lines of stage speech that unfold concurrently and prevent the audience from focusing its undivided attention upon either. Often the two lines of stage speech differ markedly in tone, diction, or emotional intensity, thus heightening the audience's impression of their separateness," *Shakespeare's Art of Orchestration,* 52.

he will explicitly stage-manage Cassio with Othello looking on. Here Iago stands before the audience as more real than Cassio, framing the mannered and "constructed" lieutenant and (to a lesser extent) Desdemona, distancing the audience from their tableau. Later, in the scene-within-the-scene (IV.i.93–169), Cassio's stagy laughter at Iago's successive and unfunny mentionings of Bianca will create a similar jarring artificiality. Now with the villain's aside, the play manuevers the audience to identify its point of view with a repugnant realism and to disengage with a finer (if fantastical) civility.

The scene's climactic trajectory manifests itself visually (as does the antistructure): Each entering character will come to center stage, snatch the attention of everyone, and then begin to merge into the groupings of characters already assembled. In a swelling of pageantry, Cassio enters alone, Desdemona with three others, Othello with "Attendants." Though Othello brings a crowd with him, the previous arrivals will have created an onstage throng. His constitutes the big theatrical event, the high tide of spectatorial excitement. But what might be the point of giving Othello a grand entrance this late in the play? The elapsed time between now and his last appearance in the Signiory scene will have allowed the Othello-actor time for a costume change, and most productions will present him semi-armored in battle gear. Salvini's version suggests the large effects available in this occasion, as the Victorians staged it:

> First a cannon is discharged, outside. Then shouts and martial music, to welcome the general on shore, are heard, as if at some distance. These sounds grow louder and louder, and presently the quay is filled with natives of Cyprus, and with soldiers and sailors, cheering, and waving their caps. At the height of this triumphal clamor, with the loud clang of cymbals and blare of trumpets, Othello appears, in full armor, upon the quay.[27]

He comes, for the first time in the play, as a conquering hero. The shattering of the Turkish fleet has the aura of military victory, as does surviving the storm (the scene imagines the tempest in martial terms, as we have noted). In contrast, Othello's first entrance in the play (I.ii) passes with noticeably unheroic understatement. There he appears in night-garb, actually following Iago, who is in midconversation, onto the boards, so that the spectator's attention will be drawn first to the speaker and then (with a slight shock) to

---

27. Edward Tuckerman Mason, *The Othello of Tommaso Salvini* (New York: Putnam's, 1890), 21.

Othello. Their opening lines, moreover, tie the audience's attention magnetically to Iago, for he enters on what we catch as a boastful, self-negating lie.
Othello will have materialized without the spectator quite knowing it—which
is, of course, the way things happen in this play. While this first entrance has
dramatic surprise, the Cyprian one gives Othello the aura of military triumph
that he deserves. Indeed, without the latter occasion, the audience would have
virtually no immediate, physical experience in the play of Othello's heroic
stature.

The anticipated moment comes—and collapses. Othello sees before him
what he did not expect (for a "se'nnight" [77]): "O my fair warrior" (182). His
surprise at finding Desdemona overwhelms him, breaking the aura of heroic
power with wonder's doubt and awe: "It gives me wonder great as my content /
To see you here before me" (183-84).[28] The climactic event turns contrapuntal,
after all, and Othello's militarism yields to the music of utter joy and the
promise of domestic bliss. Cyprus is Venice. Othello's own lines catch this
shift in tone from soldier to civilian: "News, friends: our wars are done; the
Turks are drown'd." (*cheering*) "How does my old acquaintance of this isle?"
(202-3). After a few more lines the heroic pageantry vanishes, leaving the
stage to its true Venetians. Othello's big heroic entrance fulfills our expectations
—just—but it transmutes into an opposite tone, the general himself taken,
overturned, by an emotional storm. The audience may well feel appeased and
slightly robbed, left wanting more of what we will barely glimpse again.

Alone with Roderigo, Iago conducts an exegesis of the events just passed,
the scene's final privatization of truth. Iago reinterprets Cassio, for example, in
his own image: "a slipper and subtle knave, a finder-out of occasions; that has
an eye can stamp and counterfeit advantages, though true advantage never
presents itself; a devilish knave" (241-45). Iago recreates the arrival in the
crudely materialist vision that consumes him. By suborning Roderigo to this
vision, Iago begins actually to reshape the external world itself. Here Iago

28. Feminist criticism underscores Othello's shift in tone away from the heroic. Marianne
Novy argues, for example, that Othello's "my fair warrior" suggests a "fusion of Desdemona's
essence into his" and his sense of "content," evoking "calm" and "comfort," connotes a "regression
to a relationship like that of mother and infant," *Love's Argument: Gender Relations in Shakespeare* (Chapel Hill: University of North Carolina Press, 1984), 129. Writing from a semiotic
perspective, Alessandro Serpieri also notes Othello's detaching movement of thought: "Even in
this happy moment in which he is reunited with Desdemona after the separation at sea, Othello is
not able to represent himself *in* the flow of the present, but he has to distance himself in some way
in . . . the transcription of the image," "Reading the Signs: Towards a Semiotics of Shakespearean
Drama," trans. Kier Elam, in *Alternative Shakespeares,* ed. John Drakakis (London: Methuen,
1985), 140; for a discussion of Othello's distancing style of utterance, see Calderwood, "Speech
and Self in *Othello.* "

enunciates in his own psychologizing the scene's structural undermining of order and manifest reality. Iago's battering insistence on the salt lechery and hypocrisy of others has a further, more surprising effect upon himself. His soliloquy offers the audience bewilderingly redoubled explanations for his revenge: his own lust to destroy Desdemona, his suspicion that Othello and then Cassio have cuckolded him, his desire to demonstrate a superiority to Othello: "And nothing can or shall content my soul / Till I am even'd with him, wife for wife" (298–99). Those words echo strangely Othello's, moments before: "My soul hath her content so absolute" (191), as if Iago unconsciously appropriates Othello's speech. Likewise, his accusations about his own wife seem to arise out of the scene itself: his fascination with Desdemona's sexuality, with the idea of adultery. Iago's banter with Desdemona has unleashed and amplified his voyeuristic conjurings of sexual depravity in women, and his observing of Cassio and Desdemona may have heightened his jealousy: The contrapuntal lacunae of the scene enlarge Iago's obsession and he contrapuntally revises the scene's ending. Just as Iago has reinterpreted Desdemona and Cassio, his explanations seem to reinterpret his own history of hatred through the lens of his current emotion, his immediate experience in the scene. Iago's errant motives express the scene, as if what has passed before his eyes and mind has somehow refashioned him. If so, then this soliloquy illustrates the final, rudderless subjectification of order, hierarchy, and control. The arrival scene offers a particularly fascinating example (in a place where we might least expect it) of the shifting tonalities, rhythms of structure and antistructure, and precarious satisfactions of *Othello*. The primary pattern of authority cannot contain the language, activity, and texture of the scene. Granville-Barker says that "The preparation for tragedy is complete" (134). Instead, perhaps the tragedy, reflected as scenic form, has already been launched.

II

Later, after Othello has already begun his plunge into jealousy, he ransacks his insecurities: his blackness, his lack of a chamberer's tongue, his difference in years from Desdemona (III.iii.263–67). On these grounds, Iago and Brabantio have already found him "defective" (II.i.230–31). Just as Othello rifles such matters for the linchpin to Desdemona's infidelity, so critics have sought in them, with fascinating results, explanations for his vulnerability to Iago. Yet one aspect of Othello's inventory—so much a given as to be almost invisible—is its placement in the scene. His listing comes essentially after the fact, after the fall, as an effort to explain what he has already decided to believe. For the audience, however, Othello's descent gathers its own plausibility as it happens.

That plausibility arises from the very structure of the temptation scene. Iago's implanting of jealousy holds the audience by pitting its sympathy against its thinking, its moral awareness. I am particularly interested here in the early exchanges of the temptation scene culminating in Iago's first exit and Othello's soliloquy (III.iii.1–279). The scene's first two actions consist of Desdemona's interview with Cassio (1–28) and Othello's with Desdemona (29–92). As "actions," they launch the pattern of temptation. These two episodes establish empathy as a paradigm of human interaction in the scene, by a model that I refer to as "taking another's part." Yet this "subtext" of empathy will lock horns with a "text" verbally concerned about thinking, the two directions dividing and straining spectatorial response. As the scene progresses, the audience's intellectual detachment builds to exasperation at the emotional susceptibility that has just engaged it. But we do not walk out on the temptation scene, and neither does Othello.

Iago's "little act upon the blood" (328) enthrones the plausible impossible: Spectators recognize the steady, thorough poisoning of Othello's mind, but they never quite see it happen.[29] Instead the audience feels the jump, like electricity between copper plates. Othello answers Iago's query about whether Cassio knew of the courtship, for example, with just such an arcing from the safe to the precarious: "He did from first to last. Why dost thou ask?" (96). The words are monosyllabic; the Othello-actor must speak them relatively slowly, and the caesura in the middle invites a pause: That break can stand for the gap between trust and doubt, health and sickness, the credible and the incredible in this scene. Othello's response fundamentally "divides"; his answer and question link not logically but centrifugally. The current leaps from one plate to another because the scene and the play will create the momentum of such leaping.

That momentum arises from "taking another's part," a paradigmatic action in the temptation scene that renders the jealous infection horribly real even though the spectator cannot pinpoint the exact moment at which Iago implants

29. Michael Goldman observes that, "one is drawn to pore over these passages, combing them for the very instant of malignant transfer. That there need be no single point—because minds may not behave that way—is no matter. Our belief that such a point must exist is part of our mythologizing of the process, one more reflex by which we honor the mystery of human action," *Acting and Action in Shakespearean Tragedy* (Princeton: Princeton University Press, 1985), 50.

it. In Shakespeare's drama, "part" frequently refers to an actor's role (as in "The humorous man shall end his part in peace" [*Hamlet,* II.ii.322–23]). "Taking another's part" identifies a mental, emotional, and even physical transference of roles, from one character to another character who serves as audience-figure to the first. Such transference will hardly trouble the theatrical audience, for sympathy even to the point of advocacy constitutes an aspect of spectatorship itself. The image dots the tragedies: "Lest then the people, and patricians too, / Upon a just survey take Titus' part" (*Titus Andronicus,* I.i.445–46); "but the kind Prince, / Taking thy part, hath rush'd aside the law" (*Romeo and Juliet,* III.iii.25–26); "My tears begin to take his part so much, / They mar my counterfeiting" (*King Lear,* III.vi.60–61); and "Did heaven look on, / And would not take their part?" (*Macbeth,* IV.iii.223–24). Statements of sympathy, such as Edgar's for Lear or Macduff's for his wife and children, prompt a reciprocal pathos in the spectator: Audiences become incriminated in one character's sympathy for another. Taking over parts assumes an almost topographical quality in the temptation scene. Despite its apparently informal mix-and-match of entering and exiting characters, they displace each other like chess pieces: Cassio yields his position with Desdemona to the entering Othello; Iago steps into Othello's thoughts as Othello contemplates the retreating Desdemona. Later in the scene, such transference of parts will find its objective embodiment in Desdemona's handkerchief as it passes from Desdemona to Othello to Emilia to Iago.

The scene's opening "beat" between Desdemona, Cassio, and Emilia (1–28)—a "beat" because it completes a short movement of intention or conflict between a set of characters unified by a single subject or emotion—conditions crucially the audience's theatrical responses to the scene as a whole, though critical discussions normally bypass it. Desdemona's assurances to Cassio will exacerbate the spectator's "discrepant" alarm, as her enthusiasm to help the lieutenant unwittingly forwards Iago's plot. That burden of knowledge may invite the audience to hesitate at Desdemona's promise, or even to spy a fault, such as that she meddles inappropriately in Othello's generalship. Mitigating such possible detachment, the emotional negotiation of the Cassio–Desdemona interlude will engage the audience in the subtextual "taking of another's part" that will help explain Othello's fall. The audience may feel in its own sympathy the discomfort of an almost involuntary complicity.[30]

---

30. Marjorie Garber discusses how Iago imposes a "burden of witness" upon the audience, his unwanted confessions to the audience placing us "in an uncomfortably confidential and intimate relationship with Iago, whether we want it or not," in "'Vassal Actors': The Audience to Shakespearean Tragedy" (80). Garber observes that "Our suffering in *Othello* is not only an

Doubt begins with assurance. The episode takes its structure from Desdemona's progressive upping of her assurances, because of the sacked lieutenant's anxiety. "Assure," "warrant," "do not doubt," and "vow" flicker through the interchange. Assurance inspires doubt, as if the more Desdemona repeats the words the less Cassio believes her. Desdemona's qualified guarantee launches the beat: "Be thou assur'd, good Cassio, I will do / All my abilities in thy behalf" (1–2), the vagueness of "All my abilities" lingering faintly in the air. The pathetic Cassio seems unable to speak, perhaps out of anxiety; despite Desdemona's addressing him, the next lines go to Emilia, who encourages her mistress and notes her own husband's grief. Cassio collects himself: "Whatever shall become of Michael Cassio" (8)—and he evidently doubts that much will become of him—he professes indebtedness to Desdemona: Thank you for trying. Perhaps catching his despair, she increases the ante with her second assurance: "be you well assur'd / He shall in strangeness stand no farther off / Than in a politic distance" (11–13). But the lieutenant remains inconsolable, fearing that this politic estrangement will last so long that "My general will forget my love and service" (18). Cassio will not buy her promise; he predicts, rather, that Othello's thoughts will take on a life of their own. Here Cassio's image of policy feeding upon a nice diet and breeding itself out of circumstances (15–16) initiates part of the very action of the scene; later, Iago's transplanted thinking will seem to take on its own life in Othello's mind. Thus prodded into her third assurance, Desdemona raises the stakes over the top: "Do not doubt that; before Emilia here, / I give thee warrant of thy place. Assure thee, / If I do vow a friendship, I'll perform it / To the last article" (19–22).[31]

These opening bars display a dynamic of reciprocity: Desdemona's early qualifyings undermine her assurances, and Cassio's doubts egg Desdemona into taking his emotional position for her own. Such a psychological transference foreshadows that between Iago and Othello, as Iago's qualified assurances incite Othello's doubt: "I dare be sworn I think that he is honest" (125). Desdemona's sympathy leads her to appropriating Cassio's part.[32] Her com-

---

empathic sharing of Othello's own agony; it is also a private and particular suffering of our own, wrought of the repressed desire to intervene" (75); perhaps part of our suffering and our "repressed desire to intervene" arises from our glimpse of the disastrous consequences within the play of the very kind of sympathy we exercise as audience.

31. In Othello's murder of Desdemona, exactly her sympathy for Cassio pushes Othello over the edge and into violence: "Out, strumpet! weep'st thou for him to my face?" (V.ii.77). At this line, Edward Tuckerman Mason tells us, Tommaso Salvini's Othello dragged Desdemona to her feet and grappled her, his first molestation of her in the scene, *The Othello of Tommaso Salvini*, 95.

32. The play has already subtly prepared the audience for Desdemona's sympathy in her unusually active listening—her "greedy" and "devouring" ear (I.iii.149–50)—to Othello's story;

mitment escalates in specifics and emotion proportionally to Cassio's reservations: His hypothetical doubts fire her assurances. Such rising temperature leads to combustion, as Desdemona climactically assumes responsibility for Cassio's state of mind with her life-and-death vow (anticipating Othello's more murderous one). Desdemona's last assurance seals her destruction. In her largesse of sympathy, she becomes Cassio's factor, takes on his hopes, and will "intermingle" (25) them into her relationship to her husband. For the spectator, the interlude displays the idea and creates the experience of persuasion: Cassio's hinted pessimism calls forth Desdemona's certainty; she takes his part because he will not. Later Othello, searching for the missing thoughts, will rise to Iago's silent doubt as Desdemona has to Cassio's. Desdemona's care and generosity toward Cassio will prompt the audience, on its side, to take her part, to approve her, despite its discrepant knowledge. The spectator's sympathy endorses hers, a species of response upon which the scene will play brutally.

Desdemona and Cassio provide the scene's first transplant of "causes": a word that connotes ambiguously both beginning (cause as origin) and ending (cause as goal, vision). The next dialogue concludes in a second "taking another's part," as Othello takes his wife's. Desdemona keeps the metaphor overtly before the spectator. In upholding Othello's praise during the wooing, Desdemona reminds him, Cassio "[h]ath ta'en your part" (73), just as she takes Cassio's here: "he hath left part of his grief with me / To suffer with him" (53-54). Othello yields more to the arguer than the argument: "I will deny thee nothing" (76, repeated at 83). Jane Adamson has objected that Desdemona here manipulates by winsomeness and charm and that she meddles improperly in military procedures, though some feminist critics have defended Desdemona.[33] However that may be, the audience will also simply experience

---

see Peter Erickson, *Patriarchal Structures in Shakespeare's Drama*, 84-85. Timothy Murray argues that Othello's suspicion of Desdemona reflects his "perception of her as the personification of theatricality" (70), her capacity for "dramatic mimesis," for feigning ("Sir, she can turn, and turn; and yet go on / And turn again" [IV.i.253-54]). Murray notes that Renaissance commentators considered women more susceptible than men to imitative responses to theater, *"Othello's Foul Generic Thoughts and Methods,"* in *Persons in Groups: Social Behavior as Identity Formation in Medieval and Renaissance Europe,* ed. Richard C. Trexler (Binghamton, N.Y.: Medieval and Renaissance Texts and Studies, 1985), 66-77.

33. *Othello as Tragedy: Some Problems in Judgment and Feeling* (Cambridge: Cambridge University Press, 1980), 137-38. Blunting the harsher view, Marianne Novy observes that, "Desdemona knows that in some ways she is transcending patriarchal categories in pleading for Cassio"; nonetheless, her imagery of nourishment and warmth "suggests either that she is imagining total identification with him . . . or that she sees herself as taking care of him as a nurturing mother does a child," *Love's Argument: Gender Relations in Shakespeare,* 139-40. Here the feminist perspective underscores the politics of empathy structuring the scene. For

Othello's yielding, yielding not only locally to her entreaty but expansively to his own wonder and delight in her.[34] The two introductory movements in this scene acclimate the audience to the instinctive and even pleasurable susceptibility of characters to each other. Desdemona departs on exactly such a note of release and surrender: "Emilia, come.—Be as your fancies teach you; / What e'er you be, I am obedient" (88–89).

Othello's exchange with Desdemona reveals an additional wrinkle to "taking another's part," its inherent "dialogism."[35] Desdemona, for example, invests Cassio's cause with her confidence, his worry with her assurance: "Good my lord, / If I have any grace or power to move you, / His present reconciliation take" (45–47). Desdemona's suit on Cassio's behalf, then, is a "dialogue" of Desdemona and Cassio. The dialogic creates itself, acquires its own life. Desdemona's assurance has its counterpart in Othello's confidence in his own rightness, one half of the dialogue he will bring to the part he takes from Iago. Othello possesses a self-flattering desire to prove himself right, a trait he shares with other characters in this play of intermingling "parts." When Olivier's Othello asks Desdemona about Cassio, "Went he hence now?" (51), he follows Desdemona's "Ay, sooth" with a self-congratulatory glance at Iago, as if to publicize that he had been correct in judging, against the ensign's hesitation, that the figure stealing away was indeed Cassio. The beat between Othello and Desdemona contains, in that moment, two simultaneous conversations, one silent, the other vocal. Olivier's gesture works, and makes sense of

---

feminist overviews of the divided critical assessment of Desdemona's purity, responsibility, and sexuality, see W. D. Adamson, "Unpinned or Undone?: Desdemona's Critics and the Problem of Sexual Innocence," in *Shakespeare Studies,* vol. 13, ed. J. Leeds Barroll III (New York: Burt Franklin, 1980), 169–86; and Ann Jennalie Cook, "The Design of Desdemona: Doubt Raised and Resolved," 187–96.

34. Othello's request to Desdemona to "leave me but a little to myself" (85) may express mild annoyance and even a primitive fear of female absorption. Othello may here recognize uneasily Desdemona's power over him—but a recognition in which his reproof gives way immediately to his wonder as she departs. In a somewhat extreme argument for Othello's sexual anxiety, Edward A. Snow observes that "[Desdemona's] suit excites Othello's jealousy not only because of the concern it shows for Cassio but also because of its evocation of the overprotective mother and the son's anxious fantasy of threatening sexual demands," "Sexual Anxiety and the Male Order of Things in *Othello,*" *English Literary Renaissance* 10 (Autumn 1980): 405.

35. I take this term from Mikhail Bakhtin. For an extended exploration of the "dialogic" in literature, see M. M. Bakhtin, *The Dialogic Imagination: Four Essays by M. M. Bakhtin,* ed. Michael Holquist, trans. Caryl Emerson and Michael Holquist (Austin: University of Texas Press, 1981). Put crudely, utterances appropriate each other, infuse each other, so that any utterance is a kind of dialogue of self and other; pure, uninfluenced, unpenetrated utterances cannot exist. Speech thus becomes dynamic, open-ended, an ongoing reformulation of the self in the intoxication of other utterances and selves.

Othello's questions about Desdemona's suitor (such as, "Who is't you mean?" [44]), which otherwise sound obtuse given his own glimpse of Cassio (37, 40) and Desdemona's explicit identifying of him (45). While Othello surrenders to Desdemona's desire to win a contest, he also wins his own with Iago, who has seemed to deny Cassio (38–40). Iago's doubt calls forth Othello's assurance. The scene registers a secondary rhythm that will exacerbate the essential empathy, for after Othello takes Iago's hemlock he will labor to be right. Egotism conspires with susceptibility.

Declarations in the temptation scene evoke their opposites. Assurance and doubt haunt each other like object and shadow. Watching Desdemona depart, Othello returns to an earlier state of wonder, echoing his "content" from the arrival scene: "Excellent wretch! Perdition catch my soul / But I do love thee! and when I love thee not, / Chaos is come again" (90–92). Some critics take Othello's "when" as an unconscious prediction, a telling appearance of the traitor-within-the-gates; others, conversely, see the speech as affirming the absoluteness of his love. The subtextual vibrations of the scene arouse both responses: Othello's "I do love thee" is unequivocal, yet it is uttered into a system of conversation launched by Desdemona and Cassio in which affirmation inspires doubt. The dramatic context gives "and when" its special electricity. The characters' suspicions instruct the audience. One law of speech in this psychic mise-en-scène is that efforts to assure undermine assurance: Iago will use this negative-positive subtext to devastating effect: "For Michael Cassio, / I dare be sworn I think that he is honest" (24–25). Thus when Othello sizes up his love by imagining its opposite, he utters his faith into a theater of spectators trained for the nonce to invert it.

Wonder, too, divides the consciousness, as "cause" embodies opposite meanings or assurance and doubt come to haunt each other. In his "Perdition" speech, Othello experiences wonder's double nature as both awe and doubt. Wonder suggests an epiphanic, even dazed loss of self-consciousness, as well as an aware questioning, the paradox that John Donne balances artfully in "I wonder, by my troth, what thou and I / Did, till we loved?" ("The Good-Morrow"). As Othello's eyes follow the exiting Desdemona, she may suddenly appear to him as the separate and inscrutable "Other" on whom he has pinned his life's dream.[36] Wonder reintroduces the dialogue of susceptibility and self-assertion already at play in the scene, and indeed in the earlier "content"

---

36. For the theory of woman as "Other" in the tragedies, see Linda Bamber, "Comic Women, Tragic Men," in *Comic Women, Tragic Men: A Study of Gender and Genre in Shakespeare* (Stanford: Stanford University Press, 1982), 1–43.

speech (II.i.183–93)[37] that the "Perdition" lines recall. The awe of wonder affirms one's susceptibility to the transforming power of another; the uncertainty of wonder activates the fear of loss and the desire to reassure oneself. Wonder admits vulnerability.

Othello senses himself, moreover, as "lost in thought," evoking the geography of thought elsewhere in *Othello.* [38] Thought is a place of habitation (where one can be lost), as Iago suggests with "Utter my thoughts? Why, say they are vild and false, / As where's that palace whereinto foul things / Sometimes intrude not?" (136–38). For Othello, thought acquires additionally the corporeality of a landscape of objects, such as when he takes his "farewell" through the sounds, sights, and sensations of the "Pride, pomp, and circumstance of glorious war" (354). Similarly, Desdemona has just now imagined a suit "full of poise and difficult weight" (82); such language might even invite a gesture of heaviness by the actress or boy-actor. Othello's lost-in-thoughtness arises from Desdemona's mesmerizing sensual power over him, his taking her part. His wonder proceeds from his empathy.

Exactly the dynamics of "taking another's part" outlined here facilitate Iago's transplanting of jealousy in the next duet (the image of transplanting, thought-as-organism, fits the audience's experience and Iago's own sense of poisoning the blood). By the very nature of theatrical response—spectatorial wonder—the playgoer will empathize with Othello's wonder; Iago's machinations abuse, insult the audience because, among other reasons, he abuses just that response.[39] Iago himself pretends to be "lost in thought" with his hesitant "My noble lord—" (93), his interior-centered "[b]ut for a satisfaction of my thought" (97), and his "stops" (120). Iago, that is, mimics Othello's wonder, appropriates his mood and its motions: Iago acts absorbed yet doubtful. Othello's language in rising now to Iago's "wonder" reflects the Moor's vulnera-

---

37. Cf. "I fear / My soul hath her content so absolute / That not another comfort like to this / Succeeds in unknown fate" (II.i.190–93).

38. Michael Goldman notes the play's "particularly riddling concern with *thinking* and *knowing* as the roots of action," *Acting and Action in Shakespearean Tragedy,* 48.

39. In his discussion of *Othello* in "The Improvisation of Power," *Renaissance Self-Fashioning: From More to Shakespeare* (Chicago: University of Chicago Press, 1980), 222–54, Stephen Greenblatt analyzes Iago as the embodiment of Western empathy, arguing that empathy, against our presumptions of its benignity, can be put in the service of "rapacious" improvisations for power: "What is most disturbing in Iago's comically banal and fathomless expression ['Were I the Moor, I would not be Iago'] . . . is that the imagined self-loss conceals its opposite: a ruthless displacement and absorption of the other. Empathy . . . may be a feeling of oneself into an object, but that object may have to be drained of its own substance before it will serve as an appropriate vessel. Certainly in *Othello,* where all relations are embedded in power and sexuality, there is no realm where the subject and object can merge in the unproblematic accord affirmed by the theorists of empathy" (236).

bility to taking another's part, reinforced by the sense of thought as locale and thing: "thou echo'st me, / As if there were some monster in thy thought / Too hideous to be shown . . . As if thou then hadst shut up in thy brain / Some horrible conceit. . . . Show me thy thought" (106–16), "for I know thou . . . weigh'st thy words" (118–19). Jealousy in the exchange becomes true— transferable—because it possesses for Othello all the validity of a weighted object (a green-eyed monster) in space. Iago induces Othello to "take his part," enter the arena of Iago's mind as if it were his own, an action represented in Othello's verbal echoing of Iago: "Iago: Indeed! Othello: Indeed? ay, indeed" (101–2); "Iago: Honest, my lord? Othello: Honest? ay, honest" (103–4); and "Iago: Think, my lord? Othello: Think, my lord?" (104–5). Othello believes only that Iago has echoed him. The moment of love's wonder doubles as the moment of oblivious danger.

By the time Othello, left alone, ruminates insecurely over his blackness, his lack of "soft parts," his age (III.iii.257–76), all such explanations for his jealousy are beside the point; they are now mere retrospective inventions to control something already finished and beyond his grasp.[40] The "causes" of Othello's fall are more in the dynamics of human relationship in this playworld than in the peculiar features of Othello's psyche. That point bears stressing. For all Othello's barbarism, his blindness about marriage, his ignorance of the ways of Venice, even his anxiety at female sexuality, the spectator's experience of the shocking action of jealousy hinges upon none of them. It arises, rather, in the model of empathy that orchestrates the scene itself. The audience responds incrementally, progressively. "Temptation" does not occur as an event—pinpointed, precise—because susceptibility, "taking another's part," underlies the entire scene: the doubt that haunts assurance; the dialogue of sympathy and self-certainty; the awe and question of wonder; the geography of thought. The way people speak and respond creates the possibility of Desdemona's noble concern for Cassio and Othello's disasterous plunge into jealousy. Normative scrutiny of the scene, however valid, tends to miss its undertow, the "act upon the blood" (328) to which the audience responds more than to single speeches or moments. Iago continually accuses himself of exactly what he wants Othello to do—"As I confess it is my nature's plague / To spy into abuses, and oft my jealousy / Shapes faults that are not" (146–48)—and Othello reciprocates by assuming the part.

---

40. In discussing Renaissance improvisation and Iago's malevolent empathy, Greenblatt offers a comment that might also bear upon Othello's "cause": "Conversely, all plots, literary and behavioral, inevitably have their origin in a moment prior to formal coherence, a moment of experimental, aleatory impulse in which the available, received materials are curved toward a novel shape," *Renaissance Self-Fashioning,* 227.

Iago's treacherous role-modeling, as well as a lethal insult to Othello, constitutes a felt insult to the spectator. The audience's wriggling distress in *Othello* expresses their sense of something done to them and not to the hero alone. Our engagement with characters in the theater takes the form of imagining (however remotely) ourselves as them, so that in abusing Othello, Iago abuses the mechanism of our own response, the very openness and vulnerability whose laying bare has been the burden of the scene.[41] That laying bare will ultimately engender its reflex: spectatorial self-consciousness, detachment. The verbal spotlighting of thought and thinking invites the audience's detached reflection on the mind's workings. In the 170-odd lines between Desdemona's exit and Iago's, variants of "think" and "thought" appear twenty-four times, besides numerous related words such as wisdom, conceit, ruminate, apprehensions, meditations, guess, doubts, suspicions, surmises, inference, and the like. With a distancing effect, Iago baffles the audience as he would Othello. He preempts us by demonstrating the power of ratiocination and also by arguing for its pitfalls, activating Othello's susceptibility to the weightiness of thought and at the same time warning him against the insubstantiality of thinking. In drama, the independent reactions of a third-party witness can cue and even release, as would an escape hatch, the reactions of spectators. But no such party joins this duet, where Iago occupies both sides of every question. The audience might feel a frustration of impotence here, as Iago's hypocrisy occludes each alleviating idea even as he expresses it.

By making the audience conscious of thought as a source of action for the characters, the temptation scene encourages thinking as an action of detachment by the audience. As the scene progresses, so does our detachment. Made to reflect upon thought, we feel, as we would a bludgeon, Othello's self-contradictions of fact, inference, and judgment. For all Iago's insinuations, the text, often through Othello, provides straightforward, commonsensical refutations: (1) Desdemona herself answers in advance Iago's suggestion of a "guilty-like" Cassio: "A man that languishes in your displeasure" (43); (2) Desdemona's very elopement with the Moor also counters Iago's insinuations about Cassio's freedom as go-between in the wooing; (3) Othello fairly interprets Desdemona's free sociability, which she has just demonstrated in taking Cassio's part with him: "Where virtue is, these are more virtuous" (186); (4) That Othello had

---

41. As the scene moves toward Iago's exit (257), the language of seeing and watching increases, but overcast with the suspicion of jealousy: As with "taking another's part," Iago's appropriation and abuse of watching further contaminates the mechanics of spectatorship: "Note if your lady strain his entertainment / ... Much will be seen in that" (250–52). To Othello's pain upon his forehead, Desdemona replies, "Faith, that's with watching" (285).

no sense "of her stol'n hours of lust . . . saw't not . . . thought it not" (338–39) argues, in his own terms of "ocular proof," that they existed not; (5) Othello's comment, "For she had eyes, and chose me" (189), answers in advance Iago's argument that the marriage violates nature in "clime, complexion, and degree" (230). This last example will disengage the spectator particularly; here Othello allows Iago to substitute one sense of "unnaturalness" for another. The general muses, "And yet how nature erring from itself—" (227): Othello conceives "unnaturalness" as Desdemona's love falling away from him.[42] Iago reverses that conception by treating not marital infidelity but the marriage itself as unnatural. Othello may not take this representation well; indeed, Iago's quick backtracking suggests an intervening look of anger from his partner: "But (pardon me) I do not in position / Distinctly speak of her" (234–35). Yet Iago's crude insinuation works. The moment offers Othello the simple choice between two opposite definitions of nature, and he chooses the wrong one. Othello takes Iago's part, even his "nature"—the scene's most human imperative, and also its disaster.

The spectator must witness Othello enunciating solemn standards of evidence and judgment and then instantly violating them: "I'll see before I doubt; when I doubt, prove" (190). Without further (or any) proof, of course, Iago's "exsufflicate and blown surmises" (182) sink Othello inextricably deep in jealousy. Othello's disclaimers exist solely to be dramatically contradicted. They orchestrate audience detachment blatantly. As measuring rods of logic and self-awareness, Othello's claims to probity distance the audience from his character. The juxtaposition of Othello's asseverations with his behavior appeals beyond the playworld to the audience's most rudimentary common sense and everyday ethics. Othello claims nothing so much as his own common sense and his resolute adherence to it: "Exchange me for a goat, / When I shall turn the business of my soul / To such exsufflicate and blown surmises" (180–82). Though G. Wilson Knight, among others, has suggested that a drama will defuse or supplant the moral values with which we enter the arena—allowing what we consider weakness in life to appear as strength upon the stage—any such suspension crumbles here.[43] Almost Brechtian in their alienation-effect, Othello's self-contradictions compel the auditor into the kind of pedestrian

---

42. Many critics have presumed, mistakenly I think, that Othello's line imagines Desdemona's love for him as unnatural, as if her nature had erred in loving him. But Othello might just as easily be imagining the opposite, a reading that offers a far greater drama and danger in the exchange—as if something truly were at stake. Even a critical doubt about Othello's meaning would improve upon the common presumption.

43. *The Wheel of Fire* (1930; repr., London: Metheun, 1961), 9–11.

judgments and responses that we expect the theater to transcend. The temptation scene verges on taking the audience out of the theater because it arouses mental and moral reactions that explode the theater's confines.

That some spectators will wish to leap from their seats and disrupt the action pays tribute to the way the play can demand an unusually personal and ethically charged response, exacerbated by the absence of a character or a mechanism allowing audience release inside the scene. The temptation scene's emphasis upon thinking distinguishes the spectator's (now-heightened) self-awareness from Othello's. We yearn for the attentiveness, the recognition, in these characters that the scene forces upon us. *Othello* provides numerous examples of protagonists—Desdemona, Emilia, Roderigo—acting dense of mind, lost in thought, dumb to the implications of their own perceptions, or relieved by comforting rationalizations.[44] For them, too, passion and desire displace comprehension. Here the audience's perspective—its spectatorial distance—makes Othello guilty of complicity. The audience's detachment now even prompts it to draw large judgments from small discrepancies. Othello, for example, defends Desdemona's behavior before Iago attacks it: "Tis not to make me jealous / To say my wife is fair, feeds well, loves company, / Is free of speech" (183–85). If Othello sounds prematurely defensive here, he sounds so because we hear him from far outside. The bizarre fascination of the temptation scene is that it activates both spectatorial engagement (by making sympathy a subtext) and ethical detachment (by making judgment a text). We share sympathy with the very process of Othello's fall, even as the scene makes war upon that sympathy. The "temptation scene" divides our response to the emotional spectacle from our judgments about it. That experience gains such power for the audience, moreover, because ultimately it parallels Othello's complex response to Desdemona.[45]

---

44. After Othello explodes out of the "brothel scene," for example, Desdemona answers Emilia as if in a daze (IV.ii.97–106). Though Othello has called her "strumpet" and "whore," Desdemona leaps after Iago's rationalization, that "[t]he business of the state does him offense" (166). "If 'twere no other—" (168), she concludes, grasping at straws, even though she has understood intuitively Othello's threat to her very life (160). The Willow scene (IV.iii), immediately following, begins on an elegaic note. Desdemona speaks of her death; she sings Barbary's dying song; the wind knocks. Yet the focus diverges from death to manners, from itching eyes, to inscrutable men, to women who cuckold their husbands, and Desdemona ends the scene with a lame couplet about mending one's ways. Here scenic form expresses psychology. The structure of the Willow scene turns contrapuntal as the audience loses beneath a tonal sea change its sense of what Desdemona may or may not understand. Emilia becomes transparent, Desdemona inscrutable—to us and perhaps to herself.

45. For a fine discussion arguing that the playgoer's methods of interpreting Othello parallel

III

Othello opens the door of the murder chamber, and the world, in the form of Emilia, rushes in (V.ii.105). I mark *Othello*'s denouement from that point. Emilia's harsh and disruptive voice commences the unraveling, the Aristotelean reversal and recognition, of the play. And such reversals and recognitions! Their sensationalism will engage any audience: entrances and exits; hidden weapons; murder attempts and a killer's escape; letters of revelation and a demonic unmasking; poetry of exalted suffering; and a suicide approaching prestidigitation. But sensationalism can also leave the audience just *watching*, agape with wonder yet externalized, involved yet adrift for meaning. Here spectacle can overwhelm understanding. The denouement's sensationalism comes in its rapid-fire and sometimes simultaneous stage events and in the passions of its characters, such as Emilia and Othello himself. But the ending of *Othello* limits spectatorial empathy: Emilia speaks too coarsely, Othello speaks too obliquely, and Iago speaks finally not at all. In terms of detachment, on the other hand, the denouement denies the audience the illumination and perspicuity that mark some of tragedy's richest experiences. Yes, the final episode boils over with "judgments." But the principal thrust of judgment, that Othello has played the fool, hardly satisfies our sense of the temptation scene's tragic unfolding. The structure of the denouement thus evokes a double response from the audience. That double response, figured in the rhythm of delays, quick shifts, and incomplete points of view, consists of an engagement that falls short of empathy and a detachment that falls short of clarity, an excitement of passion and a doubt of understanding—something not unlike Othello's own wonder.[46]

The denouement maintains a tension between sympathetic engagement and detached understanding that can lead the audience to recognize the experience of spectatorship itself. The ending of *Othello* divides the audience's response through techniques of speech, stage configuration, and acting, such as (1) the vehement accusations against Othello-as-fool; (2) the relief yet irritation of

---

the process of Othello's inferences about Desdemona, see James Hirsh, "*Othello* and Perception," in Vaughan and Cartwright, Othello: *New Perspectives*.

46. About Othello as he approaches the murder, Jane Adamson writes, "our view here of what is happening both includes and (as it has ever since Act III) also conflicts with his. Our judgments and feelings themselves conflict, making it equally impossible for us to 'identify' with him or to remain wholly detached from him," *Othello as Tragedy*, 264.

Emilia as an audience-figure; (3) the unfinished kinesthetics of violence; (4) the centering of moral indignation on Iago and the visual severing of Othello from him; (5) the physical, objective otherness of the bed; and (6) Othello's presentational and representational acting.[47] Assessments of Othello's character have historically often separated into camps of sympathy and detachment: the Bradleyan noble Moor against the traitor-within-the-gates of Leavis and Eliot.[48] But no wonder the problem of "judging" Othello has consumed critics, for that problem consumes much of the dialogue and hysteria of the last scene. Judging Othello amounts to the overt subject of the close (as "thought" has of the temptation scene). Here character upon character echoes the same revisionist interpretation, Othello-as-fool. What *Othello* presents as the hero's irresistible attraction to jealousy in the temptation scene it detoxifies to blindness and folly in the denouement, inviting the spectator to forget or adjust its earlier response. Much of the scene's audience-engaging sensationalism arises from the characters' indignation at Othello's folly. Yet characters express this revisionist judgment with a passion so great as actually to undercut it. The rhythm of the scene reverberates between the two views of Othello, sympathetic and detached. The divided denouement confronts spectators with their own desire for simple clarity and judgment toward the hero; yet for all its sensationalism, the tragedy leaves Othello nearly as opaque to them as the body of Desdemona, pale and cold, looms for him.

The diminution of the general into a fool culminates with Othello's final extenuation of himself: "Then must you speak / Of one that lov'd not wisely but too well; / Of one not easily jealous, but being wrought, / Perplexed in the extreme" (343–46). Othello's verbs, "wrought" and "[p]erplexed," hint at what T. S. Eliot considered an "aesthetic rather than a moral attitude" (130–31). "Wrought" connotes emotional agitation, of course. According to the *Oxford English Dictionary,* Jacobeans also applied the word to commodities—textiles, leathers, metals, and scores of hand-manufactured wares—to emphasize the fashioning, shaping, and finishing that distinguished them. Othello suggests, that is, that he has been as finely "worked upon" by Iago as he is "worked up."

---

47. For a unusually stimulating essay that, by comparing historical performances, illuminates many of the clues to staging and audience response imbedded in Shakespeare's text, see James R. Siemon, " 'Nay, that's not next': *Othello,* V.ii in Performance, 1760–1900," *Shakespeare Quarterly* 37 (Spring 1986): 38–51.

48. A. C. Bradley, *Shakespearean Tragedy: Lectures on* Hamlet, Othello, King Lear, Macbeth (London: Macmillan, 1904), 169–98; F. R. Leavis, "Diabolical Intellect and the Noble Hero," *The Common Pursuit* (1952; repr., New York: New York University Press, 1964), 136–59; and T. S. Eliot, "Shakespeare and the Stoicism of Seneca," in *Selected Essays 1917–1932* (London: Faber and Faber, 1932), 129–31.

"Perplexed" connotes a similar susceptibility. For early seventeenth-century meanings of "perplexed," the *Oxford English Dictionary* cites "involved in doubt," "bewildered," "puzzled." As with "wrought," "perplexed" also applied to material objects, and specified intricate interwining and entanglement. "Perplexed" used in its agonistic sense, as in "tormented" or "vexed," emerged later in the seventeenth century. Othello's present bewilderment falls short—a psychic and moral diminution—of his earlier wonder, such as his "content" upon seeing Desdemona at Cyprus, a wonder whose conjoined awe and doubt express his greatness of heart. Othello, then, sees himself in his valedictory as a figure of extreme confusion, crafted so by Iago. Such language depicts Othello as baffled (like a comic antagonist) and victimized.[49]

Verbal anticipations of Othello's "wrought" and "perplexed" go off early in every corner of the play's ending, like navigational lights defining the terrain. Secondary characters, especially Emilia, who stand as "response-regulators"[50] to the audience, repeat this vision of the victimized Othello. Emilia becomes one of the play's voices of truth, lifted almost to tragic stature as she uncovers her husband's evil. She assumes Desdemona's mantle of heroic womanhood, her self-discovery and martyrdom—"I'll kill myself for grief" (192)—privileging her own point of view. Instantly shocked over Desdemona's murder, Emilia brands Othello "devil" (131, 133). That tone shifts, however, with her first glimmerings of Iago's treachery, to accusations of "O gull, O dolt, / As ignorant as dirt!" (163–64). "Gull" and "dolt" are epithets that dismiss Othello's independent power of decision, like the bafflement implied in perplexity. "O thou dull Moor" (225), Emilia charges as preamble to revealing the truth about the handkerchief. Even as she affirms her own veracity against Iago's "thou liest," she repeats her verdict upon Othello: "O murd'rous coxcomb, what should such a fool / Do with so good a wife?" (233–34). Emilia is not alone. As she falls, the theme of Othello-as-fool continues symphonically in Lodovico, who steps forward as the voice of Venice and authority. "Where is this rash and most unfortunate man?" (283), he demands upon reentering, and, again, after Othello is once more disarmed: "O thou Othello, that was once so good, / Fall'n in the practice of a damned slave, / What shall be said to

---

49. For a recent "lexical" study of *Othello,* see Martin Elliott, *Shakespeare's Invention of Othello: A Study in Early Modern English* (London: Macmillan, 1988). Elliott examines "wrought" and "perplexed" similarly to the treatment here, with Othello imaging himself as the handiwork and at least partial victim of the artificer Iago, his words suggesting a passive view of himself and his actions (82–83).

50. I take this term from E. A. J. Honigmann, *Shakespeare: Seven Tragedies: The Dramatist's Manipulation of Response* (London: Macmillan, 1976), 27–28.

thee?" (291–93). Othello completes this picture of himself: "O fool, fool, fool!" (323).

Wrought, perplexed, gull, dolt, ignorant, dull, fool, unfortunate, practice — such language inveigles the spectator to see Othello as more dupe than engineer, more victim than self-victimizer. The portrait is appealing yet reductive. It appeals because it erects a sharply etched, public interpretation of Othello's jealousy, allowing him the tragic stature of flawed nobility. It diminishes because Othello-as-fool composes too small a vessel for the characters', and our, abhorrence of the recently experienced murder of Desdemona. The tragedies have their fools — Roderigo, Polonius, Rosencrantz and Guildenstern, even Gloucester — who die for their folly. But the shallowness of their souls disarms our anger at them or our interest in calling them to a harsh accounting. Emilia sputters her outrage repetitiously and to inarticulateness: "O gull, O dolt, / As ignorant as dirt! Thou hast done a deed — " (163–64). "[M]urd'rous coxcomb" is almost oxymoronic. Words can barely express her anger, so that we sense subtextually a frustration with speech itself. The audience thus can experience both the most intense emotion and the insufficiency of its terms, sensationalism denying understanding. The language of Emilia, Othello, and Lodovico offers one latticework of "judgment" about the victimized Othello; it also wobbles like thin planking in a high wind.

Emilia's freighted words launch a series of emotional juxtapositions in the rhythm of *Othello*'s ending that establish the bi-polar or divided awareness in which the audience concludes the play. Alone after the murder, Othello staggers (probably physically) to see what he has done: "O insupportable! O heavy hour!" (98), thinking that the universe should respond to his deed with earthquake and the "huge eclipse / Of sun and moon" (99–100). His solipsism may startle spectators (yet not, I think, provoke them in the Leavisian sense). But to Othello's call the universe returns Emilia, boisterous, prosaic, heated, coarse, hurrying her way from act IV. Emilia's reactions to Desdemona's death and Othello's confession are courageous, immediate, and intuitive: "Help, help, ho, help! O, lady, speak again!" (120); "Thou dost belie her, and thou art a devil" (133); "I'll make thee known, / Though I lost twenty lives. Help! help! ho, help! / The Moor hath kill'd my mistress! Murther, murther!" (165–67). Emilia stands here as an audience-figure, perhaps not so much a response-regulator as a response-ventilator. With the murder of Desdemona so bloodless, so cold, and so recent, spectators need the loud, commonsensical, aggressive, and heedless burst of outrage that Emilia provides. She perfectly captures the audience's reflexes, its utter intolerance of any of Othello's defenses and its need to have the murder shouted from the rooftops.

Audiences may be particularly desperate for explosive relief: Othello's murder of Desdemona, as an act of violence, lingers as maddeningly incomplete. Though he has promised to spill her blood moments earlier (V.i.36), he declines the full expression of the sacrificial act: "Yet I'll not shed her blood, / Nor scar that whiter skin of hers than snow" (3–4).[51] Indeed, Othello fails to complete the smothering, and his language (as well as the Desdemona-performer's movements) can leave the audience in an agony of unknowing as to whether Desdemona really is dead: "She's dead. / . . . Hah, no more moving? / Still as the grave . . . / I think she stirs again. No" (91–95). The murder scene swings the spectator's attention back and forth between the knocking Emilia and the questionably dead Desdemona four distinct times, as the audience wonders, perhaps, if Desdemona's signs of breathing refer to the character or merely to the acting.[52] Such unresolved tension exactly typifies the last scene. Here, also typically, the release comes not in the action of murder itself but in a dislocation, a projection, as it were, of that need sideways into Emilia's bellicosity.

Audience tension demands an Emilia. Yet Emilia also divides our response, for she constitutes the character perhaps least capable in the play of understanding Othello. The complexity of his fall not only exceeds her knowledge, it also exceeds her psychology. That Emilia exposes Othello in itself condemns him. Of visions of the noble Moor she will remain forever innocent; she is no Bradleyan. Emilia's unshakable faith in Desdemona, her cutting accuracy regarding Othello, and her unmasking of her own husband puncture Othello's "self-idealization." But the point is not simply that Emilia demonstrates to Othello the virtues in which he has failed; equally to the point, it is Emilia who does so. Her very philistinism tarnishes Othello, for a sensibility cruder and yet less erring than his own dismisses him on behalf of the play. But some audience members will already dislike Emilia for her service to Iago and her tawdry opining with Desdemona; even her first appearance tags her as sharp tongued (II.i.103–7).[53] The right truth, the wrong messenger: just the way we sometimes experience Iago, as when, for example, he exposes Cassio's

---

51. One stage tradition has Othello finishing off Desdemona with a blade on "So, so" (89), an action of uncertain propriety: After all, no characters in the scene observe blood, as they typically do in such plays as *Romeo and Juliet* or *Hamlet*.

52. Concerning the problems and spectatorial effect of Desdemona's "playing dead," see the Introduction, 1–3.

53. Emilia's exposure of Othello also raises response issues of social class. The plebeian members of a Jacobean audience, for example, might have reacted quite differently to her denouncing of this upper-class general than would one of Shakespeare's "privileged playgoers," and the mix of those responses in the audience might have differed, too, from the Globe to Blackfriars.

fatuousness in the Cyprian arrival. Indeed, Emilia's character rightly belongs to comedy (where servants know the truth), and, in a context less pathetic, her repetitions of "My husband?" ("What needs this iterance, woman?" [150]) would have the effect of a comic double-take. Emilia lacks exotic romanticism and Signiorial reason; Shakespeare chooses her both to expose Othello's arrogant self-righteousness and simultaneously to disrupt spectatorial perspective. The play refuses to unravel and judge Othello's crime on the level of Othello's sensibility—a dislocation typical of the fascinations and frustrations of this tragedy. Emilia's juxtaposed point of view will temporarily displace Othello's for the audience, particularly as the drama focuses more and more upon her discovery of Iago, her self-recognition, and her heroism. Yet *Othello* creates, contrasts, and destroys its own perspectives: When Emilia dies, the audience largely loses the independent voice of outrage, the passionate commentator who stands slightly to the side of the principals and sees the "truth."

Othello's exchange with Emilia completes Desdemona's murder emotionally, yet it also continues the overall pattern of tension aroused and unrelieved. The physical action of the last scene presents a series of failed attempts at kinesthetic release. In tragedy, spectators generally expect violence in the final act not only to resolve the play's conflicts but also to purge their own aggressive tensions. But *Othello* gives us half-gestures: Othello threatens Emilia with physical harm but halts (158–59); Iago reaches for his sword against Emilia but Gratiano forestalls him (223–24); then, only in the aborting of Othello's rush at him (235), does Iago succeed in fatally wounding her (236); Othello threatens Gratiano with his Spanish blade but collapses in middeclamation (264); he wounds but does not kill Iago (287), and is disarmed for a second time (288). These assaults excite the audience repeatedly, but their failures deny it the visceral satisfaction of completed physical confrontation. Before Othello's suicide, the only successful acts of violence happen against women. Desdemona's murder repulses the audience morally yet also feels too uncertain to release us kinesthetically. Emilia's death hardly satisfies more, for she is no sooner wounded than forgotten. "The woman falls," says Gratiano, and then, in a remarkable leap to conclusion, "sure he hath kill'd his wife" (236). Emilia, of course, possesses enough life to agree: "Ay, ay! O, lay me by my mistress' side" (237), upon which Gratiano delivers into the perfect tense the manifestly undead Emilia: "He's gone, but his wife's kill'd" (238). Immediately the Venetians rush offstage, leaving Emilia unattended in the last throes of agony: Even Othello barely seems to notice her. These passages may be more weird in the reading than in the rapid-fire of the theater, but they are, at best, awkward.

And callous, I think, from the audience's perspective, as we are left suddenly to watch Emilia die alone, unremarked. Emilia's Willow song heightens the pathos of her desertion; likewise she must lengthen out the announcement of her real death because no one else in the play marks it: "So come my soul to bliss, as I speak true; / So speaking as I think, alas, I die" (250–51). Were Emilia expiring in a crowd, such speech might strike the audience as presentational acting, but her isolation actually privileges the self-dramatization. The spectacle barely slows. Indeed, the moving camera lingers upon Emilia long enough to register only that her death will be our forgetting.

In Shakespeare's tragedies, a crucial form of audience fulfillment accompanies last-act acknowledgments, those moments when characters pause to recognize publicly the worth of others, even adversaries. Acknowledgment has both moral and psychological value. It confirms, within the society of the play, the generous stirrings that the audience may have felt toward characters, often through glimpses accessible only to them. Thus the justice of the tragic world comes not only in heroes exalted or villains punished, but in a recognition of characters by each other that reaches deeper than the paradigms by which they have lived. Before the duel, Claudius observes Hamlet's free and generous nature; at the duel Hamlet acknowledges Laertes's honor with his apology; later Horatio lingers over Hamlet's body with words of recognition that leap beyond the surrounding carnage: "Good night, sweet prince, / And flights of angels sing thee to they rest!" Lear dies in a long tribute to Cordelia; indeed, his capacity to appreciate her measures his very greatness. True, tragedies do not always achieve the recognition of characters that the spectator might desire. But the absence becomes part of the effect of the play. *Macbeth* makes that point unmistakably. When Macbeth receives news of his wife's death, he halts long enough to underscore his inability to acknowledge: "She should have died hereafter; / There would have been a time for such a word. / To-morrow, and to-morrow, and to-morrow … " In *Othello*, the women, Desdemona and Emilia, never receive in life or in death sufficient acknowledgment. Such silence, I would argue, speaks profoundly to the audience.

The forsaking of Emilia demonstrates the denouement's masterly switching of points of view—from character to contrasting character, from group to individual—and its residue of mixed spectatorial feelings. Corollary to its revision of Othello from traitor-within-the-gates to victim and fool, the play isolates its moral indignation on Iago. Although in act III Othello joined his ancient in a brotherhood of murder, here the action severs Othello from Iago in our judgment and our eyesight. Emilia, the audience-surrogate, directs our attention to her husband: "You have done well, / That men must lay their

murthers on your neck" (169–70). Emilia asks the quintessential question—
"But did you ever tell him she was false?" (178)—though the question's very
literalness (from the literal-minded Emilia) inevitably misses the quintessential
truth, the synergy of the temptation scene. Even as Emilia announces the
murder of Desdemona, she also rechannels audience attention to the unmasking
of Iago: "My mistress here lies murthered in her bed—/ ... And your reports
have set the murder on" (185–87). Emilia will have crossed the stage toward
Iago ("Disprove this villain" [171]), who has just entered with Montano and
Gratiano; Othello's lines position him near the bed. While Emilia on one part
of the stage (perhaps centrally) contests her husband with impassioned heroism (190–97), Othello, on another part, commences to fall upon the bed in
roaring desolation ("O, O, O!" [198]) and then to rise again in self-righteousness
("O, she was foul!" [200]). This is heady stuff, and the audience has the
excited sense of leaping between two electrically charged currents. As not the
least of these effects, the play successfully splinters Othello's fate from Iago's;
their physical locations diverge on stage, and Iago no longer stands, quite, as
the "explanation" of Othello.[54]

In the denouement of *Othello,* characters—Emilia, Othello, and Iago—become
less and less accessible by reference to each other; their juxtaposition renders
them mysterious. Much of the action of unraveling remains, perhaps for that
very reason, emotionally external to the audience, something we observe as
much as participate in. Part of this externalizing, distancing effect comes in
the exposure of the mechanics of Othello's fall. Those characters who step
forward with pieces of the truth focus the spectator's attention upon the action
reduced to objects: the handkerchief, the letters in Roderigo's pockets. Indeed,
the handkerchief now cues Emilia's denunciation of Iago (214–22) and Othello's
attempt on him (234–35). Othello will return to the handkerchief later with
Cassio (319–23). Likewise, Lodovico pulls out one and then another of Roderigo's
letters (with the casual information that Roderigo also has died twice), explaining
to Othello, "Sir, you shall understand what hath befall'n, / Which, as I think,
you know not" (307–8). Othello understand?—Right.

While Othello's responses may be passionate and spectacular, the audience
may scrutinize him for signs of self-realization, for acknowledgments of
Desdemona. Othello's dialogue consists largely of self-extenuations and accusations ("She turn'd to folly, and she was a whore" [132]), outbursts of grief ("O,

---

54. Summing up the effect of Iago in the last scene, Carol Thomas Neely observes, similarly,
that "Iago's silence, his imperviousness, his un-made-upness, his refusal to suffer, all mitigate his
scapegoat function throughout the last scene," *Broken Nuptials in Shakespeare's Plays* (New
Haven: Yale University Press, 1985), 132.

O, O!" [198]), or expressions of emasculation ("Man but a rush against Othello's breast, / And he retires" [270-71]). To grasp what Othello comes to understand, we might well turn to what Othello actually does. From his line "Peace, you were best" (161) through the entrance of Gratiano, Montano, and Iago, through the announcement of Desdemona's murder, to his exchange with Gratiano ("O she was foul!" [200ff.]) almost forty lines later, Othello has two lines: "Nay, stare not, masters, it is true indeed" (188) and "O, O, O!" (198). Emilia and Iago run with the dialogue; what behavior does the text invite from the Othello-actor? Othello becomes angered enough by Emilia to reach for his sword ("I care not for thy sword" [165]), but to Montano's greeting, "How now, general?" (168), he offers no verbal response. Later, as we have noted, he roars out and falls upon Desdemona's bed (198), then rises again to accuse her. Yet Othello's falling and rising happen in a private world of grief independent of the evolving conflict between ensign and wife. When Emilia exclaims, "O thou dull Moor" (225), she may be addressing not only his folly but a physical dullness at that moment, a remoteness, his mind "lost in thought." Indeed, Othello's "O"s are the culmination, one might infer, of his intense concentration on the dead Desdemona. His comment to Gratiano and Montano, "Nay, stare not, masters," suggests that he remains physically close to the bed. Emilia's "I will ne'er go home" (197) may trigger a parallel recognition in Othello, and open the floodgates of his loss. Such distraction suggests, again, Othello's earlier "wonder" at Desdemona, neutered into "perplexity." While the audience can watch Othello's face, however, it cannot precisely know his mind.

The bed exercises a magnetic, trance-like power over Othello, it attracts and holds him, vitiates him. As a prop, the bed stands out as unusual, perhaps unique, in the tragedies. It possesses an anthropomorphic presence quite beyond that of the other properties and settings of tragic endings—Claudius's throne or Juliet's tomb or Cleopatra's monument. Against the rushing of characters to and fro, the bed steadfastly keeps the stage.[55] It holds the pathetically dead Desdemona and draws more bodies to it. Ultimately the object acquires the potency to poison sight; it becomes the physical embodiment of *Othello*'s horror. As an object on stage, the bed appears in the last scene with a prior functional identity—a marriage-bed—whose meaning then falls prey to corrosive amending by language and action. Because it will never lose its initial pictorial significance even as it becomes loaded with tragedy, the

---

55. For the argument that the bed was not contained within the "discovery space" of the Elizabethan stage, but was "thrust out," or carried forward, onto the stage, see Richard Hosley, "The Staging of Desdemona's Bed," *Shakespeare Quarterly* 14 (Winter 1963): 57-65.

bed accumulates poignance, realized powerfully on stage, from the tension between its late visual function and the now active and linguistic distortion of it.[56]

Othello's fixation upon Desdemona's bed, furthermore, expresses a key facet of his character in the last scene. If the denouement of *Othello* as a whole tends, for the audience, to both sensationalize and externalize, one might say, too, that Othello's own mind moves to the rhythm of external objects present to sight or imagination. Othello's mind is much in the physical world. The abstract address and speculation of "To be or not to be" are not his idiom. In "It is the cause" (1–22), Othello, to have a voice, must locate something to address: first "my soul," then "you chaste stars," then the candle in his hand, then the sleeping Desdemona herself. Indeed, the very rhythm of his thought, its object-centeredness, as much as its particulars, brings him to the smell and touch of Desdemona. Othello must imagine an audience in order to speak. He relates directly with the world in its concreteness, discovering an immediate, external focus of attention, as the springboard to speech, self. Here Othello marks the sensibility toward which the audience itself evolves.

The power of the bed as the object of Othello's object-centered attention explains his collapse of valor in "Behold, I have a weapon" (259–82). "Be not afraid," he says to Gratiano, "Here is my journey's end, here is my butt / And very sea-mark of my utmost sail" (266–68). Destination, target, and peninsula: They are the bed, whose sight (recollections of his arrival at Cyprus) melts Othello's martial resolve. The bed across the stage, indeed, is where Othello goes in asking "Where should Othello go?" (271). He addresses Desdemona: "Now—how dost thou look now? . . . / Pale as thy smock!" (272–73); he seems to touch her, "Cold, cold, my girl? / Even like thy chastity" (275–76). Her deathly beauty haunts him: "Whip me, ye devils, / From the possession of this heavenly sight" (277–78). The audience desires in Othello an appreciation of Desdemona's virtue commensurate with his earlier dread imaginings, something beyond the material reductiveness of "cold as thy chastity."[57] The play

56. For a discussion of dramatic tension between picture and language, see Bert O. States, *Great Reckonings in Little Rooms: On the Phenomenology of Theater* (Berkeley: University of California Press, 1985), 53–54.

57. Feminist criticism has emphasized Othello's failure to recognize and acknowledge Desdemona. Carol Thomas Neely argues, for example, that the disengaging effects of *Othello*'s ending, greater than usual for Shakespeare's tragedies (134), arises ultimately from the failure of women's ameliorating power to transform the men: "The men . . . persistently misconceive the women; the women fatally overestimate the men" (127); "The men's profound anxieties and murderous fantasies cannot be restrained by the women's affection, wit, and shrewishness. The play ends as it began in a world of men—political, loveless, undomesticated" (111); see "Women and Men in *Othello,*" *Broken Nuptials in Shakespeare's Plays*, 105–35.

denies us this public recognition, in the way that it consistently keeps obscure Othello's self-realizations.[58] Yet in its stead the denouement provides a passionate, harrowing recognition of utter loss from a soul that knows itself largely by knowing the world around it: "O Desdemon! dead, Desdemon! dead! / O, O!" (281–82). Perhaps the most telling moment in the episode comes when Othello feels Desdemona's still flesh—"cold"—a gesture that can unnerve members of the audience and that illuminates the physical separateness of Othello inside his grief.

Othello is rich in such great theater (and it is no surprise that historically the more successful Othello-actors have been, like Kean and Salvini, the more passionate). The ending of *Othello,* like other of its moments, those dealing with witchcraft or the handkerchief, for example, invests the physical universe with a preternatural power (here realized in the bed and Iago's demonism). That primitivism enhances the ending's sensational immediacy and its mystery. The dialogue's hints for the stage movement of the Othello-actor suggest, as well, a kind of physical possession. While he will stand almost entranced for one or two intervals, Othello's language at other times invites convulsive movement by the actor, as if "driven": "Whip me, ye devils. . . . Blow me about in winds! roast me in sulphur! / Wash me in steep-down gulfs of liquid fire!" (277–80). Beyond Othello's frozen concentration on the bed, the scene's imagery and kinetics project him as whipped, blown, washed, and hurtled about from revelation to revelation, passion to passion, falling on Desdemona's bed, rising to accuse her, rushing at Iago, attempting an escape, collapsing again at the sight of Desdemona, recovering himself before Lodovico, wounding Iago, crying out at each new unraveling of the details of villainy, berating himself, gathering together every ounce of heroic composure for the valediction. If not a noble Moor, he is certainly a busy Moor, and one is not surprised that even Eliot and Leavis acknowledge the audience-winning high theater of the last speech.[59] Such action invites broad acting, and the ending of Othello strikes me as highly gestural, successfully "presentational." Desdemona's killing may anticipate what comes later. There Othello rolls his eyes murderously (37–38)

58. "In one sense, collapse into emotional numbness is the only appropriate response Othello can make to the shock of realizing his delusion," Peter Erickson, *Patriarchal Structures in Shakespeare's Drama,* 99.

59. One way that *Othello* compensates for any extremes in the audience's detachment from the plot is to create a complementary engagement with acting. Othello is a virtuoso part, apparently one of Burbage's most famous and triumphant, for the actor can play a character of startling appearance, exotically dressed, heroic, romantic, and given to great speeches of subtle and passionate music. The spectacle and the structure of such scenes as the Cyprian arrival, the temptation, and the denouement further concentrate audience attention on the spectacle of acting.

and gnaws his nether lip (43); his whole frame shakes with bloody passion (44); he loses his temper (79). Othello's violent jealousy likely called for highly conventionalized, histrionic Elizabethan acting, corresponding in many details to Burton's cataloguing of the jealous humor, much grimacing and agitation.[60] Acting, indeed, marks Othello's career in the play. The general, so self-possessed in the play's opening acts—"Keep up your bright swords, for the dew will rust them" (I.ii.59)—now behaves as if possessed himself. The externalizing of Othello's passion launches considerable kinesthetic excitement at the audience, a volley of sympathetic muscular sensations crying for relief. These emotional gestures succeed in engaging the spectator, just as the denouement as a whole can absorb us and yet block the door to Othello's or Iago's psyche.

Acting obscures psychological action to greatest effect in Othello's valediction. The speech comes as an afterthought; Othello has already been invited to one self-summation: "O, thou Othello, that was once so good, / . . . What shall be said to thee?" (291-93). The parade of shocks and revelations now seems halted. Cassio ties up the loose ends of Iago's machinations. Lodovico (like the Albanys and Malcolms) lays our expectations to rest by telling us what will come next and directing the characters offstage. But Othello forestalls that exit, that version of the end: "Soft you; a word or two before you go" (338). He must call us back into his own play. He faces now the dramatic predicament of his identity ("That's he that was Othello; here I am" [284]). The psychological action of his suicide speech will be his reconstruction and commemoration of himself, the regaining of his "occupation." The speech is both grand and incoherent. While Othello calls for reportage in the plain style—"Speak of me as I am; nothing extenuate" (342)—he will instead present himself indirectly through simile and analogy. He aspires to a prelapsarian idealized self. Though Othello has, moments before, imagined himself as victim of a fate beyond his control and still considers himself "unlucky" (341)—ill fortune is an interpretation that Othello repeats early and late in the scene[61]—he now lays claim to his atrocities. In doing so, his valediction runs counter to the patronizing of his folly sounded by Emilia and Lodovico. Here, finally, Othello assumes his double role as both Bradleyan victim and Leavisian victimizer:

> And say besides, that in Aleppo once,
> Where a malignant and a turban'd Turk

60. Daniel Seltzer, "Elizabethan Acting in *Othello,*" *Shakespeare Quarterly* 10 (Spring 1959): 201–10.

61. "It is the very error of the moon, / She comes more nearer earth than she was wont, / And makes men mad" (109–11); "Who can control his fate?" (265); "O ill-starr'd wench" (272).

> Beat a Venetian and traduc'd the state,
> I took by th' throat the circumcised dog,
> And smote him—thus.
>
> (352-56)

Those lines are the play's most striking effort to resolve the conflict of "judgments" between acts III and V, for the self-distancing language and the action make Othello both wrongdoer and the party wronged.

But Othello presents himself as a sinner twice, in metaphors that divide rather than unify our understanding. Though one vision is of the malignant, violent, and blasphemous Turk, the other is

> of one whose hand,
> Like the base Indian, threw a pearl away
> Richer than all his tribe; of one whose subdu'd eyes,
> Albeit unused to the melting mood,
> Drops tears as fast as the Arabian trees
> Their medicinable gum.
>
> (346-51)

The "base Indian" recalls for us the unworldly savage, the natural man too naïve and unsophisticated to recognize the pearl of civilized value.[62] This image evokes, as does the Arabian-treelike mourner, a passionate and unaffected simplicity.[63] Indian and mourner suggest the innocence of ignorance. But that innocence contradicts rather than supports the image of the malignant Turk, who is evil by nature.[64] These two opposite representations of Othello stand side by side, joined by proximity, if not by logic. Indeed, the rhetoric of Othello's last speech tries to have it both ways, making him too innocent to be evil and too evil to be innocent.

Othello's valediction sounds narrated, "written." Leavis found in it the "self-dramatizing trick" marking Othello's egotism, failure of self-comprehension,

62. Most editors of *Othello* choose "Indian" as opposed to "Iudean." For a summary of the problem, see Norman Sanders, ed., *Othello*, 191–92.

63. Sanders, in the New Cambridge *Othello*, 191–92, prefers a reading of 'base' as low in rank or in the order of creation, rather than as 'vile.' M. R. Ridley, editor of the New Arden *Othello* (London: Methuen, 1958), 195–96 nn.348–49, follows a similar line, suggesting that Othello's image parallels "a current traveller's tale of an Indian who, in ignorance of its value, threw away a priceless pearl."

64. For the view that treats the Turk and the base Indian/Iudean as connotatively similar, see Alvin Kernan, ed., *Othello* (1963; repr., New York: New American Library, 1987), xxxiii.

and sentimentality ("an attitude *towards* the emotion expressed" [143]). Leavis's objections are essentially moral. To put it differently, how does the valediction play as acting, the self-dramatization as drama? Othello himself performs a species of acting. He must die publicly: The nature of Othello's self is that it requires an external point of reference—an audience—to reveal itself. Othello will say, then, what the presence of an audience most invites; his personality will tilt emotion toward oratory, self-revelation toward rhetoric. Othello speaks as a reporter to other reporters (or a priest at a funeral), objectifying himself as an absent third party: "Then must you speak / Of one . . . Of one . . . of one . . . Set you down this" (343–51). The manner is descriptive (the evening news) rather than expressive, the acting presentational rather than representational. "Of one that loved not wisely, but too well" may tip off the audience in the theater that Othello constructs his persona as he memorializes it.[65] The final gesture of suicide, the closing of acting into action, the sudden leap across the paradox of (re)presentation, thrills the audience with its heroism. At the same time, however, the gesture argues that all that preceded it was contrived for this *coup de théâtre;* the moment of realism reconfirms our sense of artifice and trickery. The suicide, then, is inescapably double-edged, both authentic and manipulated.[66]

Thus the spectator may make a double response to Othello's valediction, feeling first with Gratiano that "All that is spoke is marr'd" (357), alternately with Cassio that "he was great of heart" (361), and back again with Lodovico that "The object poisons sight" (364). The audience watches Othello imaginatively create himself in the valediction; heretofore he has simply inhabited the heroic self already created.[67] The speech may be the play's ultimate instance of the divided response: It detaches the spectators, in reaction to the sentimental, self-serving, and presentational in Othello, at the same time that it engages them in the heroism of his self-fashioning. What ought to conceal, also reveals. Our experience may be not unlike the awe and doubt of Othello's own lost

65. Seeing the play as a cynical tragedy, Edward A. Snow emphasizes the disengaging and presentational aspect of these lines: "It doesn't really matter, for instance, whether we accept or attempt to argue with Othello's final estimate of himself as one who 'lov'd not wisely but too well' . . . : the terms themselves are free-floating euphemisms designed to prevent us from even making contact with what is specific and disruptive in his story, much less understanding what is at stake in it," "Sexual Anxiety and the Male Order of Things in *Othello,*" 386.

66. Jane Adamson, arguing for a more empathic relationship to Othello than the view proposed here, finds in his valediction and suicide "his final acknowledgment of what he has sometimes fleetingly recognized as the absolute ground of his emotional and moral life . . . his absolute need for Desdemona's unalterable love," *Othello as Tragedy,* 297.

67. For an illuminating discussion of Othello in this regard, see Michael Goldman, *Acting and Action in Shakespearean Tragedy,* 62–70.

wonder. The valediction charms the audience on a second level, too, for it occasions an actorly tour de force and a spectatorial pleasure in the virtuosic delivery of vivid language, passionate tears, and the niftiest suicide in Shakespeare. Even Leavis could not resist the vicarious thrill of such a great actorly event: "Who does not (in some moments) readily see himself as the hero of such a *coup de théâtre?*" (153). While Othello's suicide speech is teasingly problematic as a dramatic action, it is irresistible as acting, the "presentation" serving up the delight of the deeper "representation."

The denouement of *Othello*—its various "judgments," switched focuses, kinesthetics of delay, visual isolations, all culminating in the hero's valediction—challenges the watcher with the difficulty of sense-making. The very spectacle keeps its characters at a distance from the audience, the chug of passion, action, and change seldom deviating into explanation. Perhaps the most sweeping effect of the ending is to structure the spectator's consciousness ultimately like Othello's: The play comes in its details, its objectness, its concrete otherness, always opaque. Inside this consciousness, we experience not so much understanding as the presences and absences by which we know its "world," where the fullest acknowledgment must be only the most sensate: "dead, Desdemon! dead! / O, O!" Spectatorship of *Othello* finally turns Othello-like, and the progressive unfolding of *how* onlookers know the play brings them deeper into a perspective analogous to that of the protagonist. Renaissance audiences (who, it is sometimes argued, favored spectacle and pathos as against realism, psychology, and "interpretation") may have been more pleased with *Othello* than are some of their modern heirs. In the twentieth century, we find frustrating the play's and the hero's final inscrutability. Perhaps that unease tells us how we moderns experience drama. Michael Goldman observes that "Action is a notion that allows us to think of a person as having what he does."[68] The tragic protagonist possesses his or her world through action. For the theatrical spectator, empathy provides a groundwork of interest, a calling, while the creative insight of detachment completes the possessing of a play. Spectators make the tragedy most fully their own in the action of interpretation—as Othello comes in his valediction to possess himself. *Othello's* sensationalism arouses, through a form of deferral, the audience's longing to understand. Such spectatorial experience can confer a certain liberty, a discovery of choice. *Othello* works to enlarge its spectators by re-creating Othello's most noble perspective inside their own, yet provoking, too, the comprehension, exceeding any inside the play, of what it fully means to be Othello.

---

68. Michael Goldman, *Acting and Action in Shakespearean Tragedy*, 10.

4

Kent, Edgar, and the
Situation of *King Lear*

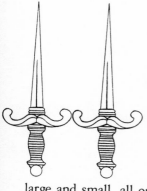

Much of the business of characters in *King Lear*[1] is reacting—tears, pity, anger, frustration, moral outrage almost inexpressible—and much of the business of the audience is responding to such responses. *King Lear* offers that one tragedy considered either too personally affecting (Johnson on the death of Cordelia[2]) or too metaphysically vast (A. C. Bradley on the play's imaginative range[3]) for the stage. Lawrence Danson notes the difficulty for the audience in rightly situating itself between the play's scales of metaphysical and personal, large and small, all or nothing.[4] Characters in *Lear*, like its audience, grasp for measurement ("dividing, weighing, valuing, choosing shares") to fix some

1. My discussion will be based upon the First Quarto version (1608) of *King Lear*. All textual references to the Quarto text will be made to *The History of King Lear* and all textual references to the Folio (1623) to *The Tragedy of King Lear*, both in *William Shakespeare: The Complete Works*, ed. Stanley Wells and Gary Taylor (Oxford: Clarendon, 1986). While *Romeo and Juliet, Hamlet,* and *Othello* also raise the problem of multiple texts, with none of them have scholars so widely acknowledged the existence of separate, authoritative texts as with *King Lear*. I start with the premise that *King Lear* offers two independent versions, the Quarto and the Folio. The conflated text (such as the *Riverside's*) offers a third alternative, but with a different kind of claim, deriving from the history of textual transmittal rather than of textual composition. Because this chapter deals primarily with how secondary characters mediate between the audience and the

proportion in a world of "proportionless reality," or, Johnson's apt phrase, " 'the desert of intermediate vacuity.' "[5] Such metaphors expose a spectatorial hurdle basic to Renaissance theater that *King Lear* makes an ongoing problem of the play: How does an audience "situate" itself, historically, geographically, morally, and psychologically? Finding the coordinates of Lear's strange world, for example, looms as the audience's principal challenge in the "abdication" scene. Here secondary characters help fill the role that Hamlet sometimes performed as a mediating hero. In drama, a secondary character present at an action played between other characters becomes a witness or surrogate for the audience. No matter whether the spectator accepts or rejects, exceeds or comes short of the witness's response, that character will nonetheless "situate" the auditor. Such response-guiding characters, standing between the audience and the action, affect spectatorial distance. If the "meaning" of a play restates the audience's engagement and detachment with its characters, events, scenic

---

tragic action, I have chosen to base my discussion on the Quarto, in which characters such as Kent, Edgar, and Albany assume roles more expansive than in the Folio. Concerning the dramatic virtues of the Quarto, I am not prepared to agree with Wells (and others) who consider the Folio "a more obviously theatrical text" (1063). Gary Taylor and Michael Warren's collection of essays, *The Division of the Kingdoms: Shakespeare's Two Versions of* King Lear (Oxford: Clarendon, 1983), has helped shape a critical preference for the Folio, but the relative status and merits of the Quarto and Folio versions are not yet a matter of critical consensus. Examining the performance values of the Quarto takes a less radical position than does dismissing it in favor of the Folio, and accepts Taylor and Warren's acknowledgment of "the independent dramatic integrity of the two texts" (vii). For a helpful parallel text of the two, see *William Shakespeare: The Complete* King Lear: *Texts and Parallel Texts in Photographic Facsimile,* prepared by Michael Warren (Berkeley: University of California Press, 1989).

2. "I was many years ago so shocked at Cordelia's death, that I know not whether I ever endured to read again the last scenes of the play till I undertook to revise them as editor"; cf. "But I am not able to apologize with equal plausibility for the extrusion of Gloucester's eyes, which seems an act too horrid to be endured in dramatick exhibition, and such as must always compel the mind to relieve its distress by incredulity," Samuel Johnson, *Johnson on Shakespeare,* vol. 8 in *The Yale Edition of the Works of Samuel Johnson,* ed. Arthur Sherbo (New Haven: Yale University Press, 1968), 704, 703.

3. "The influence of all this on imagination as we read *King Lear* is very great; and it combines with other influences to convey to us, not in the form of distinct ideas but in the manner proper to poetry, the wider or universal significance of the spectacle presented to the inward eye. But the effect of theatrical exhibition is precisely the reverse. There the poetic atmosphere is dissipated; the meaning of the very words which create it passes half-realised; in obedience to the tyranny of the eye we conceive the characters as mere particular men and women; and all the mass of vague suggestion, if it enters the mind at all, appears in the shape of an allegory which we immediately reject," *Shakespearean Tragedy: Lectures on* Hamlet, Othello, King Lear, Macbeth (London: Macmillan, 1904), 269.

4. Lawrence Danson, "*King Lear* and the Two Abysses," in *On* King Lear, ed. Lawrence Danson (Princeton: Princeton University Press, 1981), 119–35.

5. Danson, 124–25, 133.

rhythms, and acting, then characters alter attributes of the play as they regulate distance. But *King Lear* makes the mediation of such personages both fundamental and problematic: Characters who set the play's moral coordinates (for better or worse) sometimes proceed to fall away from or contradict the very qualities they seemed to represent.

In *Othello,* spectators anguish in the temptation scene in part because no character stands for them, expresses their anger, anxiety, frustration. By contrast, *King Lear* directs the audience with a near-superfluity of witnesses and responses, so that *reactions* move us perhaps as much as actions themselves[6] (*Lear*'s catastrophes are less horrible yet more affecting than those of, say, *Titus Andronicus*). In the *Lear*-world, moreover, causes vanish while effects linger: Cordelia's "No cause, no cause" (sc. 21.72) can remind the spectator how vastly the catastrophe resonates beyond its activating conflicts. We lose track of comings and goings in a wash of emotion. Bradley observes that "The outline is of course quite clear; anyone could write an 'argument' of the play. But when an attempt is made to fill in the detail, it issues sooner or later in confusion even with readers whose dramatic memory is usually strong" (260). Who can keep the storm scenes straight? Who in the theater, for that matter, can fully grasp what Lear is saying as he contends with the fretful elements (thunder sheets rippling overhead), beyond pointed phrases such as "ingrateful man" (sc. 9.9) or "two pernicious daughters" (22)? Out of this cacophony, the audience feels, as must the actors, that in scene 20 we arrive finally at some shore of the play: "Dover beach."[7] That scene astonishes us with the sense that we have stepped through a window into a clearing where all that has come before suddenly matters less or not at all, a new "situation." Response and recognition structure Lear's appearance in the scene. *King Lear*'s "causes"—and any Aristotelean sense of action—fade, leaving the audience awash in the residual present.

King Lear leaves the audience aware of the present in another way: present to its regenerative community of acting. For length of playing time and emotional hardship, *Lear* holds a special place in the canon of Shakespearean tragedy. As Lear suffers, the verb "endure" becomes central in the action. Lear endures; secondary characters endure witnessing his endurance; the actors invest long and arduous work, and so does the audience. To reach the end of a

6. See Emrys Jones, *Scenic Form in Shakespeare* (Oxford: Clarendon, 1971), 152–59.

7. Though "Dover beach" or, alternatively, "Dover cliff" misname the scene, for they suggest a narrative action, Gloucester's fall, that explicitly does not happen, both names honor an experience for the audience that very much does happen.

tragedy is a feat, an accomplishment for players and auditors both, "heroic" in the way that theater can be so. With *Lear* this feat is not only a matter of surviving the play, but also of coming to possess it. Characters, actors, and spectators become a community of the occasion: this performance, this day, these people. That consecrating of the concrete moment arrives, in part, through the particularity of *King Lear*'s theatrical (or "histrionic") imagery,[8] in which a feather, a stone, an awkward button can manifest a tragic universe. The characters (and actors) around Lear create this occasional community through a reticulation of responses that entangle, then expose, and finally free the audience. To that end, *King Lear* makes especially keen use of the power of ensemble acting characteristic of Renaissance drama.

For the audience, *King Lear* converts the problem of "situation" into a recognition of the present moment for all its strangeness or surprise. *King Lear*'s fragmented dialogue, for example, attunes spectators to the tintinnabulations of suppressed emotions. Characters speak but fail to connect, becoming isolated on the stage—a pattern of dialogue that I call "oblique" rather than interactive: indirect, delayed, or incomplete responses between characters, whose emotions rivet the audience to their present. Characters situate us only to discomfort or surprise us. A secondary character such as Kent demonstrates the spectator's oscillating distance from Lear,[9] for Kent frequently intervenes as an audience-surrogate and moral counselor, only to become tarnished by his actions. If Kent frustrates spectatorial engagement, Edgar unexpectedly invites it. Edgar's shallowness, even his own detachment, provide surprising ground for our engagement with those heroic qualities that he does possess, although heroism in *Lear* tends to express collective rather than individual attributes. Likewise his penchant for disguise actually confirms the play's rising action. Kent and Edgar cue a movement of audience response that other characters advance and that the play's ensemble acting urges as a theatrical experience: a certain detachment from the Lear-group (figured by Kent) yielding to an engagement with the play's heroes (prompted by Edgar). Ensemble acting combines with properties of dialogue and portrayal (as in Lear on

8. Danson, "*King Lear* and the Two Abysses." For a discussion of histrionic imagery that the Lear-actor might play to or against in creating range of emotion and for a discussion of the difficulty in speaking much of the language in *King Lear*, see Michael Goldman, *Acting and Action in Shakespearean Tragedy* (Princeton: Princeton University Press, 1985), 71–93.

9. S. L. Goldberg argues that "the action of *King Lear* does not essentially consist in Lear's story," hence the importance of secondary characters, whose "specific selves" create the "very condition" of Lear's heroism: "[W]e cannot identify with him, or see him in a special, privileged way, or respond to him or his speeches with a different kind of sympathetic understanding and critical detachment from that with which we respond to anyone else," *An Essay on* King Lear (Cambridge: Cambridge University Press, 1974), 68.

"Dover beach") to draw the audience toward a powerful sense of immediate life. Various secondary characters—the heath-group or even the dead
Cordelia— attune the audience to acting itself as a symbol of regeneration and
spontaneous adaptability. By the end, the play's many responses and respondents,
the very fact of their multiplicity, validate the *Lear*-world's vitality. Engagement with theatrical spectacle becomes the "situation" for seeing the world
feelingly.

I

Kent is Lear's and *Lear's* principal respondent, registering the progress of the
"hero" and the play: "Is this the promised end" (sc. 24.259).[10] He does not
achieve what he seeks. Kent stands for service, yet self-sacrificing, persistent,
and deeply felt as his service is, it verges on the futile and sentimental. He will
die, it seems, of sympathy (not a very encouraging prospect for the audience!).
At first, Kent's responses define moral terrain for the audience, even voicing
its exasperation at Lear. Yet Kent can become downright annoying himself. He
represents both the rectitude of the *Lear*-world and its unmalleability, its
violent stasis.[11] In the course of the play, Kent's travails may prompt in the
audience a desire to intervene that underscores its own powerlessness, the
tension of theatrical response.[12] Rather than the realism that Poor Tom can
evoke, Kent recalls ideal stage retainers such as Eubulus in *Gorboduc* (1562)
or Perillus and Mumford in *The True Chronicle Historie of King Leir* (1605).[13]

10. Michael Warren analyzes the differences between Kent's role in the Quarto and the Folio,
noting particularly that the Folio severely cuts Kent's part in the last two acts and that in the
Quarto he is more visible but marginalized, his dramatic functions absorbed by others such as the
madmen, Gloucester, Edgar, and Albany. In the last acts of the Quarto, writes Warren, "Kent is no
longer interesting for what he does so much as for what he says: he becomes a spokesman for
humane values, acting an almost choric role" (63), "The Diminution of Kent," in *The Division of
the Kingdoms,* 59–73.

11. Goldberg observes of Kent's language that it is "plain, rather terse, unambiguous. . . . It is
a language not much *open* to experience," 71.

12. Marjorie Garber discusses the audience's "burden of witness" in *Lear* and other tragedies,
our feelings of complicity and desires to intervene, in Marjorie Garber, " 'Vassal Actors': The Role
of the Audience in Shakespearean Tragedy," *Renaissance Drama,* n.s. 9, 1978, ed. Leonard
Barkan (Evanston: Northwestern University Press, 1978), 71–89.

13. Certain Elizabethan political dynamics form the deep background of an aristocratic
retainer such as Kent. As Lawrence Stone states, a major accomplishment of the Tudor dynasty
was to wrest power from nobles with large and dangerous independent retinues, one effect of

But Kent will give the audience a "situation" that it will not entirely want: engagement with his morals (his defense of Cordelia, for example) yet detachment from his behavior (his manner of defending her).

For the audience, the Quarto *King Lear's* opening scene is an off-balancing act. Lear at his "grand entrance" impresses the audience with his imperiousness but also the political danger of that manner.[14] Kent's explosive defense of Cordelia only intensifies the spectator's visceral experience of discomfort with the escalating suddenness of dramatic conflict. The initial moments activate but defer the audience's desire for "situation." First the quick allusions by Kent and Gloucester to the "division of the kingdoms" (sc. 1.4) just elude our grasp (and their mention of Albany and Cornwall misleads us about the importance of the two sons-in-law in the scene). When he arrives onstage, Lear proclaims his "darker purposes" more rapidly and elliptically than in the Folio: He launches the love-test without stating a political intent, or promising that each of his daughters will receive some territory as dowry, or outlining the curtailment of his power.[15] Similarly, his disinheritance of Cordelia erupts before we are sure what has happened, a reversal with barely a buildup. Played with the speed and directness the text invites, these gestures can alarm the audience with a sense of overacceleration.[16] A dramatic incident may sometimes proceed at a measured pace that teases the audience into longing for completion,[17] as with

---

which was a shift of old feudal loyalties away from territorial lords and toward the crown, *The Crisis of the Aristocracy: 1558–1641*, Abridged Edition (Oxford: Oxford University Press, 1967), 96–134. Kent suggests that atavistic private loyalty inimical to the Tudor hegemony. Scholars typically note that the breakup of large aristocratic households contributed to the problems of masterless men and poverty in the late Tudor era.

14. I draw the idea of Lear's "imperiousness" from Peter W. M. Blayney's literary comparison of Quarto and Folio texts, "Chapter 9: The Folio's Major Alterations," in his forthcoming *The Texts of* King Lear *and Their Origins: Volume II,* which I have read in manuscript form. A 1986 stage production of the Quarto at the University of Rochester, reported by its director, David Richman, confirms the Quarto Lear's imperiousness. Commenting on Lear's opening speech on stage, Richman notes Lear's vigor, clarity, and strength (376–77); for the complete discussion, see David Richman, "The *King Lear* Quarto In Rehearsal and Performance," *Shakespeare Quarterly* 37 (Autumn 1986): 374–82.

15. In the Folio, unlike the Quarto, Lear implicitly promises portions to Albany and Cornwall, proposes to prevent future strife, and makes clear that he is divesting himself of rule, territory, and cares of state (I.i.41–44, 49–50), moderating the terrible impetuosity of the Quarto.

16. Richman, discussing his production of the Quarto, notes its dramatic economy and directedness: "[Lear] rarely diverts attention from his daughters. . . . The scene in Q, simpler and sparer than its better known counterpart, proved a strong and playable dramatic sequence," "The *King Lear* Quarto In Rehearsal and Performance," 377.

17. For an analysis of how Shakespeare's scenes can evoke in the spectator the desire for either an accelerated or a decelerated pace, see Emrys Jones, *Scenic Form in Shakespeare,* 23–40.

the statue scene in *The Winter's Tale.* The love-testing here works oppositely; it is too rapid and cryptic for the hefty matter at hand. Even the Folio's brief digressions disappear, as Lear repeats that he intends to divest himself of rule (I.i.49–50) or alludes to France and Burgundy offstage (I.i.83–85).[18] The audience undertakes the love-test with too few anticipatory reactions and too little subtext. We lack orientation; we lack the "why" of Lear, both the why of his abdicatory politics and the why of his psychological angling. Here Shakespeare guides the audience to experience in the kinesthetics of scenic structure— our emotional foot-dragging before inadequate preparation—the rashness of Lear's decision. Our discomfort serves as engagement; we invest emotionally in wishing that the pace of the conflict not abandon our understanding. Such ambivalences heighten the value of Kent and others as they promise to situate the audience.

Critics generally take the tenor of the first scene as frozen or wooden, displaying qualities of a fairy tale.[19] In this light, characters such as Kent come to be read as symbolic: "He is not, for the moment, a real (an eccentric) man. . . . He is, and by design, a flat character, highly conventionalized."[20] Yet in the theater, no matter how formalized the initial events may seem, audiences will engage with the immediate stage tension and the delights of acting. So far from feeling "machine-like" in its ritualism, the Quarto love-test, lacking the Folio's hints of Lear's self-indulgence (such as "unburdened crawl toward death" [Folio I.i.41]), brims with political uncertainty and danger: the daughters compete without, importantly, the audience's assurance of their preassigned portions. The scene reverberates with feeling: Along with its shocking suddenness, we witness slick insincerity, bluntness, anger, threatened

18. Richman, "The *King Lear* Quarto In Rehearsal and Performance," 377.

19. See, for example, Russell Fraser, "If subsequent scenes are so realistic as hardly to be endured, the opening scenes have not to do with realism but with ritual and romance. Their abiding characteristic is niggling formality. They do not wear the aspect of life so much as the aspect of art. . . . The impelling action of *Lear* is made to resemble a fairy tale, which is, I suppose, its ultimate provenance. . . . He makes his characters unreal initially because he means them, at least in part, to be symbolic," Introduction to *The Tragedy of King Lear,* ed. Russell Fraser (New York: New American Library, 1963), xxvi–xxix. For an elaboration of the iconographic and emblematic approach to *King Lear,* see Russell Fraser, *Shakespeare's Poetics in Relation to* King Lear (London: Routledge and Kegan Paul, 1962). William Frost discusses the "machine-like" quality of ritual" (197) in "Shakespeare's Rituals and the Opening of *King Lear,* " repr. in *Shakespeare: The Tragedies: A Collection of Critical Essays,* ed. Clifford Leech (Chicago: University of Chicago Press, 1965), 190–200. In a reading of the play interested in the "combination of parable and parable situations with acute realism" (57), Maynard Mack calls the opening atmosphere of Lear's court "emblematic, almost dream-like" (94), King Lear *in Our Time* (Berkeley: University of California Press, 1972).

20. Fraser, Introduction, xxvi–xxvii.

violence, chagrin, and the sweep of grand personages on and off the stage, as the playwright spotlights successive actors-as-characters for brief, virtuosic solos. Against the mannered set-pieces of Gonoril and Regan, for example, Cordelia must deliver her two telegraphic asides with a spontaneous urgency that commands spectatorial assent. We engage with acting early in this play, for acting, rather than exposition, tips off who-stands-for-what. While the action of the scene does proceed by its own ritualism, Shakespeare invites actorly performances that play against such formality by engaging spectators in the creative pleasure of the passing moment. Theatrically, the abdication scene's "meaning" cannot be severed from its vitality on stage, qualities that the readerly perspective behind terms such as "symbolic" and "flat" tends to miss.

The paucity of exposition leaves the audience groping for "situation." The spectacle is no more tractible: No inky-cloaked witness interprets the solemnity from the sidelines; rather, we attend the court in its stage arc, as it stands in official display.[21] Cordelia speaks to us, but her asides come from *inside* that tableau: "What shall Cordelia do? Love and be silent" (57). Love and be silent is a tactic (that the play will not validate) alerting the spectator to something amiss. But it does not condemn Lear's staged event, only his judgments within it.[22] The audience needs such assertions from Cordelia as, "I am sure my love's / More richer than my tongue" (72-73), exactly because her awarding of love's duties may sound rather parsimonious. Cordelia exposes the egocentrism of Lear's court by disrupting its ceremonial speech, but she still keeps the audience distanced by speaking inside the charade and inside the formal stage configuration. Shakespeare here declines to solve the problem of spectatorial "situation" with a comfortably antiphonal character.

In contesting with Lear, Kent becomes, like Cordelia, a response-regulator *manqué*. As if to certify Cordelia's moral position, he interjects fresh outrage, but in what sounds like an old pattern. "Good my liege—" / "Peace, Kent" (113-14): In a quick five syllables the audience might foresee the escalating impass, as the long-acquainted earl and liege leap before each other's mutual

21. For a discussion of this configuration as part of the "spine" of visual grouping in *King Lear*, see Jean E. Howard, *Shakespeare's Art of Orchestration: Stage Technique and Audience Response* (Urbana: University of Illinois Press, 1984), 119-21.

22. While characters will criticize Lear's plan to divide the empire, his rejection of Cordelia, and his banishment of Kent, none ever questions the love-test itself. That bounty should follow where merit claims most (47-48) is the proposition the tragedy as a whole disputes.

contentiousness.[23] The two are playing out an old scene: Surely Kent has attempted before to come "between the dragon and his wrath" (114), if never at such a heated crisis. To arguments from Kent, we know instantly, Lear will prove impermeable. The two seem to complete a past that has preceded the play: bent bow, true blank indeed. As with Cordelia, the audience is in, but disconcertingly out. Emotionally relieved, playgoers approve Kent's intervention and its accuracy, "See better, Lear" (150), but may balk at aligning with his self-righteousness. Kent, like Cordelia, proffers a desired voice and a new problem.

Lear and Kent echo the intransigence and escalating anger established by the King and Cordelia. Lear dramatizes himself, as acting continues to deploy meaning: His images of dragon and bent bow or subsequent power-shakings, such as "on thy life" (146) and "Now, by Apollo" (151), invite a physically rigid self-righteousness, and deafen his hearing. To each of Kent's half-dozen challenges and arguments—the King hardly recognizes their content—Lear only gets angrier. Kent, like Cordelia, advances a pattern of disastrous interaction rather than stopping or redirecting it. "Now, by Apollo, King, thou swear'st thy gods in vain" (152), for example, is insulting only and helps provoke the sentence of banishment. Kent nonetheless signals to the audience that Lear can command absolute loyalty from the most rigorous of men, though now "majesty stoops to folly" in the "doom" of Cordelia (141).[24] Yet the listener may catch an abruptness, even a false note in Kent's speaking. Such phrases as "Be Kent unmannerly" (137) or "Think'st thou that duty shall have dread to speak" (139) or "To plainness honour's bound" (140) are self-laudatory in advance, deriving from personality as much as circumstance. Kent's scruples have the force of hand-to-hand combat. To the extent that audience members refuse to identify themselves with the manner of Kent's bludgeoning syllables, his speech must compromise his point of view.

Kent's self-defeating style points toward a feature of dialogue dragging the rocky ground of this play: a solipsism of communication matching the fragmenting of the kingdom. The Gonoril scenes, in particular, will demon-

23. "Between these two men, both hot-tempered, a curious, persistent conflict will recur to the very end of the play," Marvin Rosenberg, *The Masks of King Lear* (Berkeley: University of California Press, 1972), 70–71.

24. The Quarto reads "Reverse thy doom," as opposed to the Folio's "Reserve thy state." Peter Blayney notes in "The Folio's Major Alterations" that Lear's "doom" will "have disastrous personal consequences." The Quarto version carries a dramatic irony and sudden distancing different from the Folio, for "thy doom" suggests not only his sentencing of Cordelia but also the destiny he here creates for himself. That Lear fails to "hear" this distancing hint to the audience further emphasizes his hardened stance.

strate the pattern of oblique dialogue, the failure of characters to reach each other fully in conversation. Likewise in the abdication scene, characters speak but cannot hear. To each of his elder daughters' protestations of love-as-such ("Beyond all manner of so much I love you" [56], "And find I am alone felicitate / In your dear highness' love" [70–71]), Lear answers—nothing. Perhaps he knows the truth well enough (Lear's silence may guide the audience). Similarly, the play gives Gonoril and Regan (and Albany and Cornwall) no reaction when Kent says that "power to flattery bows" (140), a dangerously direct insult, or suggests that they are "the foul disease" (154). Kent's formal, rhymed valediction also chides them to live up to their testimony. Such lines address the playgoers more than the characters whom they describe and to whom Kent nominally speaks. Here his acting toward the audience claims a moral position. On the stage Gonoril and Regan should probably remain physically impassive. They do not flinch because words spoken of them cannot penetrate their solipsism (beyond Lear, no one reacts verbally to Kent). Lear's language to Cordelia defines the companion overreaction, as he does to her what he fears from her: "And as a stranger to my heart and me / Hold thee from this for ever" (108–9). As *King Lear* dislocates its characters one from another, for they are hard of hearing, it substitutes an implied address to the audience. Shakespeare orchestrates interaction between characters to define the social reality of the *Lear*-world: The scene is all overreactions and underreactions disturbing to the spectator because never proportionate or connected. The audience feels perhaps as unsituated as some characters feel vulnerable—not situated in this o'erhasty, expositionless ceremony whose contours we must decipher even as it unfolds; not situated in events that seem both happening spontaneously and already determined; not situated by characters such as Kent who launch out to reform excesses and merely repeat them; not situated by a dialogue of moral passion that largely fails to register.

Yet Shakespeare lifts the spectator from these precarious straits: The fortunate fall of this scene brings its fortunate dialogue, from a character who arrives as a much-needed audience-surrogate. France enters as Kent leaves, true reason replacing false reason. Though France criticizes Lear ("or your fore-vouched affections / Fall'n into taint" [211–12]) in praising Cordelia, the lady herself intervenes next, so that Lear's succeeding comment takes hostile aim only at her: "Better thou hadst not been born than not to have pleased me better" (226). France's statement of faith (212–14) prompts Cordelia's suit, and onstage she might physically interpose, move toward Lear; if so, she and France act out before the audience the instinctive, sympathetic partnership so absent in others. France attempts to mediate with his clear-mindedness about Lear's actual charge: "Is it no more but this—a tardiness in nature" (227). France shows a particular dignity among this cast of characters, not just because he reverses Cordelia's fortunes but because he stands back in egotism and dramatics, offering Burgundy first chance at Cordelia's hand. His love, kindling "to inflamed respect" (246), appears now both freshly discovered and proved of old, giving the spectator a positive, spontaneous value against the scene's earlier hint of repeated conflicts.

At the scene's close Shakespeare leaves not Gloucester, France, or others of the Lear-group to comment, but rather the two sisters whose evil we already recognize. When Iago inherits the early scenes of *Othello*, he exposes himself as duplicitously "honest." Not so now in *Lear*, where evil really does speak as "common sense." This moment, informal, conversational, intimate on the stage, is again disengaging for the audience, for the two propose a "reading" of the action. While we endorse the sisters' exposition of Lear's temperamental infirmities and their indictment of what has just passed, we nonetheless reject their point of view, the conspiratorial calm that stands for an evil intention larger than their excuses. We are left "situated" between rash injustice and calm injustice, cannons to the right, cannons to the left. While the audience has been present to insults and explosions, to intense love and moral outrage, we seldom completely "take the part" of the protagonists, though the acting keeps us engaged. The abdication scene holds the audience partially at bay, through its abruptness, patterned exchanges, and emotional disconnections. Shakespeare prompts spectatorial desires, whether for moral comfort or comfortable pacing, and leaves us as attentive as we are frustrated. The significance of the scene rises through its tensed engagement and detachment.

II

Scenes 3–5, the crisis between Gonoril and Lear (the "Gonoril sequence," as I shall call it) constitute one dramatic unit.[25] The ambivalences of the spectator's situation expand here: rash and calm injustice, self-compromising

25. For an extended discussion of Lear's scene with Gonoril (Folio I.iv) see Gary Taylor, *To Analyze Delight: A Hedonist Criticism of Shakespeare* (Newark: University of Delaware Press, 1985), 162–236. Taking into account the two antagonists, the audience's perceptions of the issues, and its reactions from earlier events, Taylor examines the moment-by-moment "revolutions of perspective" for the audience as it moves from blaming Lear to pitying him.

audience surrogates, oblique dialogue, and further engagement with virtuosic acting. Why does Shakespeare give the first scene of the brewing explosion to Gonoril and Oswald, dislocating the audience from the play's hero? For one, Gonoril's intention to force the crisis, to "breed from hence occasions" (sc. 3.24), breeds suspense, anticipation; we look forward to her maneuvers and Lear's response. Because Shakespeare puts Gonoril's intentions before us first, Lear will always be, to some extent, her victim, the object of our exasperation and alternately our leniency because we know too much. Secret knowledge can create guilty tension in the spectators (who acquire a complicity unwished for) and a commensurate superiority toward the intended victim, both distancing effects. Likewise, the "breed occasions" scene adds plausibility to Gonoril's charges against Lear.[26] This private and candid moment creates a dramatic verity for the audience, for Gonoril has nothing to pretend before Oswald. Gonoril's first line—"Did my father strike my gentleman / For chiding of his fool?" (1-2)—establishes her as rightly upset, confirming an insult she has apparently just discovered. Gonoril brings genuine exasperation.

The marvel of this scene, a distinction often evident in *King Lear,* is that Gonoril's actions appear both spontaneous and premeditated.[27] Her energy and exactness convey emotional immediacy, as if she had just this moment reached a crisis, a turning point in her own forebearance: "By day and night he wrongs me. Every hour / He flashes into one gross crime or other / That sets us all at odds. I'll not endure it" (3-5). Her intentions expand in each repeated charge. First she invites Oswald to a counteroffensive more comprehensive than Lear's crimes: "If you come slack of former services / You shall do well; the fault of it I'll answer" (9-10). Then her plan escalates a notch to include the other servants and to goad an explosion: "Put on what weary negligence you please, / You and your fellow servants. I'd have it come in question. / If he dislike it, let him to our sister" (12-14). Finally Gonoril's revenge takes in Lear's retainers, too, as she explains away her actions as an entrée for protest: "And let his knights have colder looks among you. . . . I would breed from hence occasions, and I shall, / That I may speak" (22-25). At each of these stages, Gonoril's anger escalates and her strategy crystallizes, as if her emotion were driving her (as Lear drives her emotion) to do what circumstances demand. (Lear's hunting horns in the background increase, for the audience, this tension and immediacy.) On the other hand, Gonoril's action sounds premeditated. Her assurance to Oswald that Regan and she are of one mind and

---

26. For the opposite view, see Gary Taylor, *To Analyze Delight,* 174-76.

27. This quality is more developed in the Quarto than in the shorter Folio version of the scene. The Quarto affords Gonoril the more politically rationalized and nuanced motives.

her sentencing of Lear, "Now, by my life, / Old fools are babes again, and must be used / With checks as flatteries" (18–20)—each idea standing slightly outside the reactive flow and dripping of contrived self-justification—suggest that she now breeds occasion to execute what she has long since concocted. She plans to dominate Lear viciously rather than to resolve the conflicts of two households under one roof. The scene simultaneously engages and distances the spectator toward Gonoril: We feel both the justice of her reactions and the wrongness of her nature, an emotional stasis descriptive of the *Lear*-world.

Spectatorial ambivalence again: Kent becomes witness (engagement) and instigator (detachment) of the rising conflict. The conflict in the Gonoril sequence, as well, will appear as an action both happening for the first time and already having happened. Entering alone when we expect Lear, Kent suspends in midair the fight brewing between daughter and father. Kent makes announcement of his "good intent" (sc 4.2) and of "that full issue / For which I razed my likeness" (3–4), but what does he wish to forge by his "labour" (6)? Kent never explains (leaving the audience a touch expectant), and his actor must invent the "through-line." Lear enters calling imperiously for dinner— "Let me not stay a jot" (7)—and discovers Kent. Again Shakespeare displays the King in his habitual willfulness and Kent arresting it. Kent calls Lear to kingship: That is his immediate function. A rite of bonding, Lear's long and formalistic interrogation entitles Kent to serve Lear, validates his witnessing for us, and details his rather medieval, literary character. Kent's virtue is that he is without graces: "That which ordinary men are fit for I am qualified in; and the best of me is diligence" (33–34). (Kent's plainness may improve upon Lear's current retainers, though he may also simply mimic them; likewise, the manners of Lear's Servant [50ff.] improve upon Kent.) Lear rises to the presence of Kent, displaying his own perspicacity and instinctive authority. Kent is our witness, then (for we share his secret), and yet a witness who also brings forth the best in Lear. For the audience, Lear gains dramatic range, volatility; Kent, implicated in that shift, seems to create what he endeavors only to observe.

Our dramatic sympathies may make us laugh when Kent trips up Oswald, who will often be played (helpfully) in the scene as a supercilious fussbudget. The abuse, however, can also look too one-sided, too easy. Kent, that is, now joins the King's retinue in spirit, even leads it, inviting some spectatorial discomfort with him. Lear's blow and our response invoke the problem that Gonoril introduced at the outset of these scenes: Are Lear and his knights "riotous" or scrupulous of dignity? The Servant observes that "to my judgement your highness is not entertained with that ceremonious affection as you were wont. There's a great abatement appears as well in the general dependants as in the Duke himself also, and your daughter" (54–59). Lear concurs: "I have perceived a most faint neglect of late" (65). The Servant, presumably Lear's own, argues against Gonoril's accusation by his very manner of speech. As a spectatorial problem, the strife between Gonoril and Lear appears both imminent, actions and responses just now initiating it, and already well under way. The behavior of Lear (and possibly his retinue) in the present scene may be high-handed, his imperiousness at the abdication finding its childish counterpart. But whether Lear deports himself because of Gonoril's present slights or from an ancient insufferableness that justifies her slights cannot be sifted. Lear's rowdiness seems alternately a first reaction and an established fact, just as Gonoril's revenge or the results of the love-test seemed both spontaneous and preconceived. Rather than resolving the dualism of the scene, Kent helps create it; he equally evokes Lear's kingship and joins in beating a servant. Characters, speeches, elements that appear at first to "situate" the play's auditors become absorbed in its ambivalent drift.

The Gonoril sequence gives the Fool his "big" scene.[28] From his entrance (90) to Gonoril's (181), he initiates the verbal play and dominates the stage. Upon his appearance, the tone of the scene shifts from Kent's and Lear's false heroics to satire, from the physically strong and aggressive to the weak and reflective, from action to its concave mirror: "Let me hire him too," says the Fool of Kent, offering his own "earnest," "Here's my coxcomb" (92). Turning the scene over to the Fool has two effects on the audience. First, it builds the spectators' secure delight in the ensemble acting before us. In Scene 4, Shakespeare repeatedly hands the stage over to greatly differentiated characters— Kent, Lear, the Fool, Gonoril—each time with a shift in tone, emphasis, and distance. Playing this scene, as well as the entire Gonoril sequence, requires from the actors mutual sensitivity and balance in energy, pacing, and intensity, one actor preparing for another even as his or her own character temporarily controls the stage. In the action, however, we start to bear witness to the disintegration of the kingdom: Spectators will accept (even enjoy) the degeneration and its emerging bestiality because they will be buoyed by a demonstration of surrogate community in the acting ensemble. In the heath scenes, the virtuosic communal acting, on full display, will begin to converge once more with the reintegrating community of characters. Generally the Quarto, with its developed roles for secondary characters, emphasizes ensemble acting more than does the "star"-oriented Folio. Shakespeare's deployment of group acting

---

28. For a discussion of the Fool's entrance, his appearance, and accoutrements, see Rosenberg, *The Masks of King Lear*, 102–9.

to hedge, support, or build the conditions of the story shows to particular advantage here and with other late plays, such as in *The Winter's Tale's* "sheep-shearing" scene. As a second effect upon the audience, the Fool's stage domination dramatically diminishes Lear. In the energy and shifts of the sequence, Lear follows the Fool; the King turns reactive, dependent, the powerful thrust of his stage mastery dramatically surrendered now to the least in his retinue. The theatrical diversion represented by the Fool actually marks the King's "progress": Lear's growing impotence constitutes not only an expositional but also a theatrical fact.

Lear's banter with the Fool (92–194), the longest duet of the scene, occupies the middle ground between Lear's conversations first with Kent and the Servant (Lear's followers) and then with Gonoril (Lear's antagonist). The Kent-conversation accentuates Lear's positive "authority," that with Gonoril his negative "admiration." Similarly, the King's responses to his "all-licensed" Fool oscillate, in a remarkably consistent back-and-forth rhythm, between amusement and resentment, the call for diversion and the threat of the whip: "Why, my boy?" (103), says the engaged Lear, eager for a joke; "Take heed, sirrah—the whip," rejoins the detached monarch, disliking what he hears (103, 106). The oscillation continues: first, an indulgent, "Why, no, boy" (128), followed resentfully by "A bitter fool" (131); then Lear inviting another riddle, "No, lad. Teach me" (134), countermanded by, "Dost thou call me fool, boy?" (143); or finally the good-humored, "When were you wont to be so full of songs, sirrah?" (164), followed by, "An you lie, we'll have you whipped" (174). As spectator-participant, Lear displays delight and surrender, on one hand, fluctuating with anger and opposition, on another. The Lear–Fool duet captures perfectly the kinetics of tension and release structured into the entire Gonoril sequence. For the spectator, the exchange with the Fool may seem like an interlude of comic distancing between the skirmish with Oswald and the impending storm of Gonoril. Yet even within this relative disengagement, the tickling of Lear's anger keeps the audience on edge to the larger emotional dynamics of the scene.[29] Even deeper, we feel the immense volatility and passion of Lear's personality.

---

29. The exchange between Lear and the Fool in the Quarto exceeds the Folio by some 14 lines, including a section (135–50) containing a complete movement of oblique dialogue, along with Kent's interjection, "This is not altogether fool, my lord" (146). Richman comments upon exactly that section in his Quarto production: "In our performance this was one of the Fool's most successful sequences. 'All thy other titles thou has given away; that thou wast born with' elicited a strong reaction from the audience throughout the run. Every night the spectators laughed and gasped, fully understanding the comedy and growing pain of Lear's situation," "The *King Lear* Quarto In Rehearsal and Performance," 381.

Perhaps the most fascinating aspect of the Fool is that he is actually not funny. Laughter at him often sounds slightly forced. He is "not altogether fool" and (for modern audiences) not even altogether intelligible.[30] While he serves as court jester by acting comically daft, we sense that daft he really is with melancholy: "Since my young lady's going into France, sir, the fool hath much pined away" (70–71). The Fool plays Lear's commentator, an outsider, a satirist, full of opinions and judgments about Lear's folly, launched all the more sharply because by indirection and analogy. In that capacity, the Fool functions to distance the spectator from Lear. Yet the Fool's entrance is a "big" moment in the scene, and he himself rivets the audience's attention. The Fool is more than *eiron;* we quickly grasp his deep emotional investment, his anguish at Lear's folly. So that all that he says is both satire and pain of heart: "Truth is a dog that must to kennel" (107). The Fool's jokes hurl grief, buried rage, and impotence at the King, and Lear's annoyance responds to the Fool's subtextual pain: "A bitter Fool" (140). While the Fool distances the audience on one level, he engages it in deep sympathy on another: We listen intently to his unfunniness because we hear in it the suppressed integrity of his own life (the Cordelia-actor doubling the part of the Fool powerfully underlines this effect). Thus, like others, the Fool stands inside as well as outside, engaged Lear-reverberator as well as detached Lear-corrective. His dual point of view confuses the context for his humor.

Lear's "admiration" later in response to Gonoril (as he becomes more like the adolescent she has accused him of already being) will bring to the surface a pattern of "oblique" dialogue at work with the Fool. When the Fool enters, Lear turns to him playfully, expectantly: "How now, my pretty knave? How dost thou?" (93). But the Fool pointedly ignores Lear, pursuing his line with Kent: "Sirrah, you were best take my coxcomb" (94). Ignoring a king is exactly the kind of high-handed effrontery that only a fool might get away with; for the audience, it nails the Fool's anger in place. On the stage, the Lear-actor must hold physically for the answer or for a way back into the conversation, or release himself muscularly (a shrug, a frown) from expecting a reply. The actor must fill the absence of an answer with himself. That local, technical problem represents, I would venture, a larger condition of action and acting in *King Lear* that the ordering of speeches in the Gonoril sequence stresses.

Lear and the Fool phase in and phase out of immediate contact. The Fool toys with Lear by means of his coxcomb; Lear threatens with the whip. The

---

30. Gary Taylor, *To Analyze Delight,* 195–206, explores the teasing half-sense of the Fool in this scene, both for modern playgoers and Renaissance ones.

two engage: speech and response. Next the Fool imagines truth and falsehood as the whipped dog and the stinking bitch, and Lear utters, "A pestilent gall to me" (107–10): Here the pair disengage from each other, address themselves to others. Lear's line, in particular, answers nothing and seems aimed at no one on the stage, a burden of heart, simply, that demands release. That dialogue of Lear and the Fool might be called oblique more than interactive, and the two characters go out of direct relationship with each other and into a relationship generalized to include the audience.[31] Oblique speech is reflective, internal, summary; its style and thought register a sudden detachment with the spectator.[32] This rhythm comes round again. The Fool next conducts Lear through an exposition of "nothing" that finishes with the Fool's apparent address to Kent, "Prithee, tell him so much the rent of his land comes to" and Lear's "A bitter fool" (129–131). Their engagement, that is, breaks off once more, spotlighting Lear in a suddenly lonely reflection, itself "bitter," answering no one and addressed to no one. Kent's interjection, "This is not altogether fool, my lord" (146), suggests a similar break and nod to the audience. The engagement of characters with each other leads, as its climax, only to detachment, a instant isolation of character and severing of stage community. Such a making and breaking of community presents drama at its elemental best. These moments hang in the air, expressing formally the pain for which relationships in the *Lear*-world have no room.

The appearance of Gonoril follows a similar pattern of delay and misdirection. "How now, daughter," asks the father, "what makes that frontlet on?" (183). But the frowning Gonoril does not get the next speech and never answers directly; rather, she must physically hold (or more likely develop and vary) her frontlet, her "point," while the Fool comments on it. With icy diction, she threatens to "censure" Lear (204), but, exemplifying the pattern of misdirection, the Fool rather than Lear gets the next speech (or song), a parable of cuckoos. The Fool takes us momentarily "out," while Gonoril may be left stamping her foot, as it were, and Lear assuming a daze: "Are you our daughter?" (213). The dialogue here, from Gonoril's entrance (181) to Lear's second exit (304), is an elliptical talking at cross-purposes, not engagement, face-to-face statement and

31. Daniel Seltzer demonstrates that the soliloquy diminishes in frequency in Shakespeare's late plays, its function accomplished more subtly. The example of what I call "oblique" dialogue here might be viewed as a similar sophistication of the "aside." See Daniel Seltzer, "The Actors and Staging," in *A New Companion to Shakespeare Studies*, ed. Kenneth Muir and S. Schoenbaum (Cambridge: Cambridge University Press, 1971), 34–54.

32. As Gary Taylor notes, "The structure of the dialogue encourages us to observe how Lear reacts to the Fool, to watch Lear attempting to follow him, to imagine Lear *thinking*," *To Analyze Delight*, 204.

response, but the breakdown of dialogue. The exchanges consistently frustrate Gonoril. She enters determined to air her grievances publicly and to command Lear's recognition of her power and threat. Her "through-line" in the scene might be described as asking so as to command: "I would you would make use of that good wisdom" (214) or (the mix of request and order) "I do beseech you / Understand my purposes aright" (232–33). But these characters do not answer each other directly. Instead, the Fool interposes his satirical responses to Gonoril in place of Lear's (218–19) and to Lear in place of Gonoril's (229). Lear, rather than replying directly, perfects his "admiration": "Doth any here know me? . . . Doth Lear walk thus, speak thus?" (220–21; the last line invites delaying stage business); "Your name, fair gentlewoman?" (230). Lear thus reduces Gonoril to repeating herself in a growing rage of frustration: "You strike my people, and your disordered rabble / Make servants of their betters" (250–51). Shakespeare deflects these characters away from engagement with each other. Lear alludes cryptically to his larger error ("We that too late repent's" [252]), shifts address to the entering Albany (252–53), and without reply turns to, "Ingratitude, thou marble-hearted fiend" (254). When he finally does answer Gonoril's charge, defending his train as "men of choice and rarest parts" (257), his claim may weaken with the audience's recognition that he reacts to the hideousness, worse than a sea-monster, of filial ingratitude (254–56), as much as he reacts to Gonoril's actual accusation.

Oblique dialogue affects the audience in several ways. First, the delays inherent in the scene—a character waiting, even fuming, for an answer while the dialogue darts off elsewhere—create tension and suspense for the audience, so that the scene arrests us emotionally and kinesthetically even as characters act as if in different worlds. That zigzagging movement can undercut the credibility of an argument, as it does with Gonoril's self-righteousness on entering. Such indirection disengages the audience from the characters' positions, so that we lose our bearing toward right and wrong. As a result, though the scene erupts with moral judgments, it cannot be compassed morally. Instead, we witness, merely and completely, the ruin of human contact in the *Lear*-world. Such "meaning" manifests particularly through acting, for the theater forces actors-as-characters to deal physically with the fact that they are not answered, heard, attended to. Actors must stand in place, hold their tension, give it over, walk away, throw up their hands, scowl; they must, unlike people in life or characters in a novel, respond with gesture to the disregard of others. Their choices, no matter how individualized, will inevitably register the escalating kinetic danger of the *Lear*-world. The theatrical event itself, then, draws attention to characters caged in anger and place. Shakespeare capitalizes on the fact that actors ignored must themselves respond; the spectacle "shows" the frustrations that characters only partially voice.

The oblique rather than interactive dialogue sufficiently detaches the audience so as to heighten its sense of Lear's accelerating childishness. What Gonoril styles as Lear's "pranks" and "admiration" really do look that way, for the diverging tracks of dialogue isolate and decontextualize his behavior, making Lear, in this case, look unresponsive, self-centered, solipsistic. His long speech, "Doth any here know me?" (220–28), offers irresistible opportunities for "presentational" acting. Because the dialogue places Lear out of, rather than in, engagement with others, his self-dramatizing shock at Gonoril appears as "acting," and even "fooling," given his physical and emotional contiguousness to the character in motley. (As Lear has contaminated the Fool, so the Fool contaminates him.) The oblique dialogue can lend support to the accusations with which Gonoril begins the sequence, as Lear appears to invent exactly the kind of capriciousness and deafness of which she has accused him. Oblique dialogue—this delayed response, intervening commentary, and isolation—will persist through the Gonoril scenes, making deft and silent comment upon its participants. When Albany enters, for example, Lear queries him in midstride but denies him an opportunity to answer: "O sir, are you come? / Is it your will that we—prepare my horses. / Ingratitude . . . " (252–54).[33] By the time Albany can muster a rebuttal ("My lord, I am guiltless as I am ignorant" [267]), Lear's passion has led him to beat his own head in remorse at what he has done to Cordelia (265). This delay makes Albany's sincere and simple answer appear not wrong but irrelevant (rather the way Gonoril treats him). The structure of dialogue, by distancing the audience, casts a vote about his character.

Kent's "big scene" (sc. 7) satisfies—initially—the audience's desire to take control of these events. Yet Kent also emerges here distancingly as response-regulator *manqué* in his confrontations with Oswald (1–40) and Cornwall (41–145), and his soliloquy (154–67). Kent's personality now controls the action, and other actors respond to him. In the first interchange, Kent operates, refreshingly, as an audience-figure, giving the spectators a brief release from the moral and emotional perplexities of Lear and his children and offering a simplistic opportunity to take sides. Acting contours situation. Oswald is an

---

33. Line 253 in Wells and Taylor is the edited version of "is it your will that wee prepare any horses" in the Quarto (D2v), as reproduced in *Shakespeare's Plays in Quarto: A Facsimile Edition of Copies Primarily from the Henry E. Huntington Library*, ed. Michael J. B. Allen and Kenneth Muir (Berkeley: University of California Press, 1981). As Peter Blayney has suggested to me, Lear's remark about horses may not (as in F) break off dialogue but rather take aim somewhat sarcastically at Albany.

affected, cowardly weasel, and Kent rails upon him with a hilariously Falstaffian catalog of epithets requiring virtuosic ("heroic") breath-control: "a base, proud, shallow, beggarly, three-suited, hundred-pound, filthy worsted-stocking knave; a lily-livered, action-taking knave; a whoreson, glass-gazing, superfinical rogue; one-trunk-inheriting slave" (13–17). Besides an audience-figure, Kent is also an extension of Lear, as Oswald extends Gonoril, so that the scene assures spectators of their basic alliances. Kent has intervened for Cordelia, followed Gonoril on stage; now he enters after Edmund has signed on with Cornwall: Against the play's "tide of disorder," as Robert Egan observes, Kent "sets an unambiguous, hard-edged code of assumptions and values"[34] that engages the audience temptingly. The whole scene presents in Kent a set of actorly problems and grand opportunities. Kent's verbal and physical baffling of Oswald particularly exhilarates actor and playgoer alike. Altogether, the role requires the Kent-actor to speak with wit and passion, to conform his emotional tone and characterization to the varying prose and verse, to move forcefully, and to impersonate three ways (Kent, Caius, and the "Osric-like courtier"), all demanding stamina and discipline of breath and body (Egan, 151).

Yet Kent's dual tasks as representative of Lear and as interlocutor for the audience come to blows. Egan argues that the stocking of Kent stiffles frustratingly the audience's desire to intervene (150–52). But the stocking and the exchange with Cornwall leading up to it also can reactivate the spectators' frustrations with Kent as a figure mediating the *Lear*-world for them. Certainly the stocking scene could be directed and acted such that audiences side with Kent against the upstart Cornwall and his insolent humbling of the King's messenger. On the other hand, a second voice calls through the Cornwall exchange as well, one that might disturb its auditors as it implicates them in the emotional politics of the Lear-group. Kent's rudeness and self-righteousness can bother us. This Janus-effect parallels those of the Gonoril sequence. To Cornwall's effort to ascertain the facts—"Why art thou angry?" (69); "Why dost thou call him knave? / What's his offence?" (85–86)—Kent answers with a high-handed dissertation ("That such a slave as this should wear a sword" [70–78]) and an arrogant ellipsis: "His countenance likes me not" (86). The structural analogue for this sequence is a judicial inquiry, a

34. "Kent and the Audience: The Character as Spectator," *Shakespeare Quarterly* 32 (Summer 1981): 147. Egan argues that Kent, particularly in the early parts of the play, "repeatedly . . . will intervene in the play's action only to be expelled from it and forced to remain a powerless onlooker"; thus, "he is the embodiment of a particular empathetic anxiety . . . which must be central to an audience's experience of *King Lear*" (148).

trial, *King Lear*'s recurring protocol, whose abuse or observance marks the stations of the plot. In Scene 1, Lear scorned judicial fairness; here Kent scorns Cornwall's proper inquest.

Kent's moral position resembles his opponent's more than the audience might find comfortable. In his extended reply to Cornwall, Kent describes Oswald as the-trouble-with-Gonoril: "Such smiling rogues / . . . smooth every passion / That in the natures of their lords rebel, / Bring oil to fire, snow to their colder moods" (71–75). His extremities of speech ("A plague upon your epileptic visage!" [79]) will detach us slightly, enhanced by Oswald's smile, even though we side with Kent's depiction. Minutes later, the tables turn, and Oswald charges Kent with the same kind of "service" of which Kent has accused him: "When he, conjunct, and flattering his displeasure, / Tripped me behind; being down, insulted, railed, / And put upon him such a deal of man / That worthied him, got praises of the King" (113–16). This description sounds disconcertingly like the truth (even more accurate than Kent's portrayal of Oswald). But Shakespeare, instead of distancing us from the presumptuous steward, next gives Kent a line exasperating enough to Cornwall (who may look as if taking sides with Oswald) that the fiery Duke calls for the stocks on the instant (119–20). The distance at which the audience hears charge and countercharge likens Kent to Oswald. The scene demonstrates unavoidably, furthermore, that Cornwall's fault, also Lear's, is also Kent's: their belief that "anger has a privilege" (68). The hot Duke's stocking of Kent only mirrors Kent's own behavior, this pattern of escalating umbrage recalling hopelessly the Earl's ineffectual anger at Lear's equally ineffectual anger upon a previous public accounting.

In the two-part rhythm of audience response outlined here, the play-goer begins empathizing cathartically with Kent. With varying intensities, however, the scene qualifies that disposition, exposing the Lear-group's kin-ship with Cornwall and forcing the audience to recognize, as well, our habitual approbation for what we merely prefer. Thus, the play continues to work its surprises and reversals, challenging the audience's situation, as initially clear-cut divisions between characters begin to blur. The audience, of course, will stay on Kent's side by the end of the scene: Regan's nastiness, Gloucester's intervention, and Kent's final equanimity all ensure that. But with that alignment lingers the nagging sense of the insufficiency of such opposi-tions. Shakespeare presents Kent both as lightning-rod for audience sym-pathies and as self-incriminating apologist for Lear, a dual role that erodes a playgoer's single perspective. Our shifting distance from Kent mirrors ultimately our shifting distance from Lear, just as the audience's frustration in the stocking scene precedes our anguish at watching the King, in the verbal gauntlet of the evil daughters, barter his dignity for the largest number of retainers.

III

Audiences experience the passion of *King Lear*'s storm sequence (scs. 8, 9, 11, 13). But would it be too irreverent toward Lear's grandiloquent railings—"Blow, wind, and crack your cheeks! Rage, blow" (sc. 9.1); "Rumble thy bellyfull; spit, fire; spout, rain" (14)—to suggest that no playgoer in the theater, Elizabethan or modern, ever quite comprehends them? These scenes distance the audience from Lear more than do any others in the play, and do so during his moments of greatest psychological trauma. Generally, the storm scenes refuse to endorse heroic individualism, at least as Lear exemplifies it.[35] Instead, the values of the sequence emerge substantially through secondary characters, who signal communal possibilities to the audience. They establish spectatorial detachment from Lear, and also a grudging respect. For all Lear's giganticism, the scenes' subtler heroes emerge through the community of secondary characters, and their actors, whose integration on the heath actually privileges Lear.

The heath episodes begin (sc. 8), not with Lear, but with Kent and the First Gentleman entering severally, glimpsing each other amidst the storm (which will "rumble" continuously or "crack" intermittently, or something of both, through the sequence).[36] The Lear-group first appears separated, materializing to one another, then vanishing. We shall quickly "see better," recognizing that Kent has been gathering news and making arrangements. A community of support knits underneath the chaos, one point of that beginning. The First Gentleman characterizes Lear, preconditioning our response to him: We catch Lear's vast histrionics at a distance. The Gentleman stresses verbs and action

35. For a materialist reading of *King Lear* that rejects the valuing of heroic individualism or "essential" humanity, see Jonathan Dollimore, "*King Lear* (c. 1605-06) and Essentialist Humanism," in *Radical Tragedy: Religion, Ideology and Power in the Drama of Shakespeare and his Contemporaries* (Chicago: University of Chicago Press, 1984), 189-203. Dollimore considers the humanist view misguided because "it mystifies suffering and invests man with a quasi-transcendent identity whereas the play does neither of these things" (190).

36. For an extended comparison of Quarto and Folio versions of this scene from a dramatic perspective, see Steven Urkowitz, *Shakespeare's Revision of* King Lear (Princeton: Princeton University Press, 1980), 67-79. Urkowitz's book takes a particular interest in the stage effect of interrupted speeches and interrupted exits.

words, "Contending" (3), "Bids the wind blow the earth" (4), "swell the curléd waters" (5), "tears his white hair" (6), "Catch in their fury" (8), "Strives in his little world of man to outstorm" (9): Lear in high dudgeon. Lear takes definition from the Gentleman and Kent, who reduce the audience's need to explain Lear amidst the stage thunder-balls rolling in the heavens. Though in the Folio version Kent's statements about "the old kind King" shades Lear with pathos (III.i.19), the Quarto provides a different anchor for our engagement through the countertactics now afoot (the Folio remains silent at present about the coming of French power).

Kent and the Gentleman "tell" what Lear "shows." We need make little investment in deciphering Lear and can respond rather to his theatrical energy, the Fool's counterpoint, and even the weather—Lear's context. Lear's first storm speeches do not lend themselves to our quick mental apprehension. He enters crying for hurricanoes to drown the tallest buildings (sc.9.2–3) and for thunder to smite flat the rotund world (7), much as the Gentleman has forewarned. Yet lines such as "You sulphurous and thought-executing fires, / Vaunt-couriers of oak-cleaving thunderbolts" (4–5) are so densely impacted and mouth-filling that they come to their auditors more as enormous sounds than as precise sense.[37] We catch the violence of, "Singe my white head" (6), picked up in his next speech in, "Why then, let fall / Your horrible pleasure" (18–19). After that, the tone suddenly switches to pathos—"Here I stand your slave, / A poor, infirm, weak and despised old man" (19–20)—and then as quickly rises again to defiance ("But yet I call you servile ministers" [21]). For the audience, the storm loses by now a specific "meaning"; Lear interprets it instead as the available object for moment-by-moment emotions.[38] We bear witness to this *Sturm und Drang* rather than participate in it. Watching this spectacle, the playgoer sympathizes, but less likely empathizes, with Lear's agony;[39] no wonder, then, that modern critics have sometimes taxed Lear for self-serving rant. Auditors will recognize, if anything, that Lear is making cosmic "points" from indignant self-concern: "Crack nature's mould, all germens spill at once / That make ingrateful man" (8–9).[40] His speeches

37. See Michael Goldman's discussion, already cited, of Lear as a speaking part in *Acting and Action in Shakespearean Tragedy.*

38. Dollimore puts it more harshly: "Indeed, Lear hardly communicates with anyone, especially on the heath; most of his utterances are demented mumbling interspersed with brief insight. Moreover, his preoccupation with vengeance ultimately displaces his transitory pity," *Radical Tragedy*, 193.

39. The spectatorial reserve suggested here may fit the cool, modern playgoer more naturally than his or her active Renaissance counterpart, but whatever the given dispositions of different audiences, the text seems to guide them in the same direction.

40. "Lear experiences pity mainly as an inseparable aspect of his own grief," Dollimore, *Radical Tragedy*, 192.

challenge the playgoer, for a play can acheive "dramatic" effects by cannonad-
ing the incidental into the cosmic, and playgoers come with a taste for such
leaps. But Lear's solipsistic cosmos—"servile ministers, / That have with two
pernicious daughters joined / Your high engendered battle 'gainst a head / So
old and white as this" (21–24)—hardly seems an unmasking of the universe
(particularly to the modern sensibility). Lear's bravery, unconverted for the
spectator into convincing insight or self-knowledge, appears as passion—and
largely just that.

If Lear's passion in the storm is exhilarating though impersonal, a thing to
watch more than engage with, that passion's exhaustion may yet accord the
sequence its greater interest. Readers often consider Lear's sudden sympathy
for the Fool as the heath scenes' first transitional moment, marking the slow
return to community: "My wit begins to turn. / Come on, my boy. How dost,
my boy? Art cold?" (68–69). That turnabout counts.[41] But while Lear
"explains" the tempest, secondary characters may be already "explaining" and
situating him. The Fool's medial remarks between Lear's first two storm
speeches, for example, help excuse the audience from embracing Lear's bombast:
"O nuncle, court holy water in a dry house is better than this rain-water out o'
door. Good nuncle, in" (10–11). (We will not wish with the Fool, however, that
Lear return to his daughters and ask blessing [12].) In the storm sequence,
"endurance" becomes a primary dramatic value: Secondary characters, first the
Gentleman, now especially Kent, direct our attention away from what Lear is
saying and toward the fact that he is bearing the affliction (48–49) of this roaring night. "I am a man more sinned against than sinning" (60), claims Lear, and
Kent answers, "Alack, bare-headed?" (61). Kent opens their next scene with his
"text" for the sequence: "The tyranny of the open night's too rough / For
nature to endure" (sc. 11.2–3). While the audience shares Kent's attention
to Lear's fortitude before the physical tempest, the king specifies his own subject of endurance: "This tempest in my mind / Doth from my senses take all
feeling else" (12–13). These two tempests differ, and the spectator who feels
sympathy for the affliction of the former can feel ambivalence regarding the latter.

Lear wins our admiration less for his point of view than for his persistence in
it. His gyves convert to graces. Lear's stubbornness and pride, the qualities
that launched him in disaster, come back dressed out as heroic perseverance.
But these scenes do not exactly reify individualism; rather they showcase
equally the exasperated community around Lear. His rehabilitation succeeds

---

41. For a reading, however, that denies the efficacy of pity or empathy in *King Lear,* see
Dollimore, *Radical Tragedy,* 189–203, esp. 191–95.

through the shift in emphasis, engineered by the secondary characters on the heath, in favor of spectacle and theatrical energy (in which they all share) and away from Lear's dubious parsing of sinners and sinned against. We engage with Lear for the tour de force of acting that manifests his strength of will. Shakespeare craftily frustrates Kent, Gloucester, and even the Fool, so that they may recapitulate the audience's offstage community of frustration. Lear treats Kent particularly harshly, half-ignoring him (sc. 9.49), pulling away from his physical assistance (sc. 11.3), refusing his entreaties to take shelter (5, 22), hurling, "Death, traitor!" at him (63), and insisting on the company of his "Theban" (144, 159). Kent's line, "He hath no daughters, sir" (62), works as a verbal throwing up of hands. Even the Fool echoes that exasperation, as he momentarily drops the veil of "outjesting" in favor of more direct audience address with, "This cold night will turn us all to fools and madmen" (70).

The storm scenes thus highlight the characters around Lear enduring his highly "presentational" endurance. To the extent that these characters shape audience response, they provide a release valve for exasperations at Lear's histrionics, a conduit for admiration of his stage power, and a validation for the spectator's heroism in sitting through all of it (endurance is also a playgoing virtue). Interestingly, the neatly paced adjurations of the Fool, Kent, and Gloucester for Lear to please come out of the tempest, and his maddening refusal, create in the audience a desire for the weather scenes to move faster, a desire that forges further solidarity between the audience and the sequence's response-regulators. The party around Lear, including the audience, then, *already* constitutes a community before he recognizes it. Indeed, Lear does not so much create a sense of community in tending to the sufferings of the Fool as discover a community of the theatrical moment waiting to be acknowledged. The secondary characters gain heroism through their fidelity to Lear in the face of his hostility. Since the Fool, Kent, and Edgar serve Lear by playacting, that heroism is particularly theatrical. Edgar's "My tears begin to take his part so much / They'll mar my counterfeiting" (sc. 13.55–56) recognizes for the audience the actor's *arete* as well as the character's. The heath scenes, then, stand as a tour de force in ensemble performance that engages the audience deeply with the stage's spontaneous community.

In the arraignment of Gonoril and Regan (a Quarto episode [sc. 13.16–51] absent in the Folio), the passion of that community becomes virtually inexpressible in the form of acting. The arraignment scene exhausts the motif of histrionics running through the storm sequence. Acting turns into silence, on the one hand, and burlesque, on the other. Lear enrolls his "justicers," Edgar and the Fool. Then, imagining the bestiality ("she-foxes") of his daughters, he breaks off into a trance: Edgar's "Look where he stands and glares" (19) may denote Lear's trance; Kent's later "Stand you not so amazed" (29) also implies it.[42] Lear may direct his "No, you she-foxes—" (18) toward empty space, stage furniture, or even Edgar and the Fool. Those two "cover" the trance with almost vaudevillian stage business: Their shared song followed by Edgar's comic verbal double-take on the Fool's singing—"The foul fiend haunts Poor Tom in the voice of a nightingale" (25–26)—is sure to get laughs. We might consider Edgar's remark "metadrama"; it exposes a stage illusion (the nightingale) from inside a narrative illusion (Tom of Bedlam) inside the abiding theatrical illusion. The comment distances momentarily, as Edgar winks at the audience through Tom.

"Playacting"—Lear's, the Fool's, Edgar's—reaches its end, and characters achieve a sorrow more authentic and cleansing than any pretensions to sorrow. Lear's arraignment of Gonoril is a dialogue duet with the Fool (42–51). It may culminate in a passionate and climactic stage gesture. One 1980s Royal Shakespeare Company production of the conflated text, for example, had Lear madly stab the Fool.[43] Kent registers Lear's now-total abandonment of patience (53–54). The Fool falls mute again (as he has in scenes 7 and 11), but now forever (he might appropriate Lear's trance to mark the difference) becoming Lear's enervated, sacrificial other (at the exeunt, Kent must usher him offstage). The episode exhausts disguise, acting, and all efforts to divert Lear's sorrow. Edgar signals this exhaustion by repeatedly breaking his Bedlamite character with the audience: "Bless thy five wits" (52); "My tears begin to take his part so much / They'll mar my counterfeiting" (55–56); "Poor Tom, thy horn is dry" (69). If Lear earlier reaches out to the resurrected community on the heath, here the characters around him reciprocally take on his sorrow as their own. The collapse of disguises such as Edgar's makes the audience emotionally and intellectually aware (engaged and distanced together) of the authenticity of

42. Richman's production of the Quarto *Lear* used a similar staging to great success. After commanding the judges to take their places, Lear continued to stare at what he thought were his daughters: "Lear stared, Edgar and the Fool exchanged obscene ditties, and a moment later Lear, seeing that he had not been obeyed, shoved them violently to their places," "The *King Lear* Quarto In Rehearsal and Performance," 382.

43. Richman's Quarto production took a less obvious tack of directing Lear's rage against Kent. Though the Fool is Lear's partner in the dialogue of Gonoril's arraignment, and thus a fitting and proximate object, Lear has also struggled against Kent through the tempest scenes. At any rate, the Quarto scene works brilliantly on stage with a physical climax to the storm sequence: "Lear flew into a terrible rage, directed mostly at Kent, whom he blamed for letting her [Gonoril] get away. Finally Lear collapsed in exhaustion beside Edgar. In our production, the mock trial achieved stunning effects. It was indeed an epicenter," "The *King Lear* Quarto in Rehearsal and Performance," 382.

Lear's resounding anguish more than Lear alone could ever express: acting's graphic insufficiency as expression itself expresses. The arraignment, then, takes the audience once more powerfully into the present moment, beyond the self-conscious artifices of characters. Edgar's soliloquy (95–108) at the close of the scene—"But then the mind much sufference doth o'erskip / When grief hath mates, and bearing fellowship" (99–100)—presumes to explain the scene but may leave the audience uneasy. Edgar's conclusions, deeply reflecting our experience of fellowship but, in context, too glibly o'erskipping sorrow, feel, like so much in *King Lear,* just as wrong as right. The speech, of course, carries the audience into an upswing that will deepen the cruel plunge of the next scene, the blinding of Gloucester.

IV

Kent exits, Edgar lurks. Kent's career in *King Lear* is a descent; Edgar's is a fall and rise. Kent disappoints the audience's hope that intense sympathy or "good intent" will preserve Lear. In a typically *Lear*ian transference of spectatorial energy, Edgar offers the redeeming chance unlooked for.[44] Without ignoring or apologizing for his limitations, playgoers will take some satisfaction in Edgar's strengths.[45] Easily duped and dismissed by Edmund, attached abnormally to disguises, naïve to fortune's tricks, Edgar demonstrates with his buoyancy, nonetheless, an alternative response to the degradations of the *Lear*-world. Odd that, as some modern critics have argued,[46] Shakespeare invests the

44. Michael Warren compares the role of Edgar in the Quarto and Folio texts, concluding that Edgar serves as a "philosophical agent" in both versions, but that in Q, Edgar is more callow, self-indulgent, and immature than in F, ending the play "devasted by his experience" (104–5), while in F, "Edgar grows into a potential ruler" (105): Michael J. Warren, "Quarto and Folio *King Lear* and the Interpretation of Albany and Edgar," in *Shakespeare: Pattern of Excelling Nature,* ed. David Bevington and Jay L. Halio (Newark: University of Delaware Press, 1978), 95–107.

45. Edgar is a particularly controversial Shakespearean character. I would agree that the tragedies often portray their "alternative" heroes ironically (Fortinbras, Malcolm, Octavius). Edgar's role relative to the audience, nonetheless, may differ from the roles of other alternative heroes. I suggest that Edgar's part offers the kind of opportunities for acting that engage audiences with his heroism, a different response than might occur from reading.

46. Rosenberg, for example, speaks of Edgar's "cruelty" (263) toward the blinded Gloucester, see 263–66. For one of the most interesting discussions of Edgar's reluctance to reveal himself to his father, see Stanley Cavell, "The Avoidance of Love," in *Must We Mean What We Say?: A Book of Essays* (New York: Charles Scribner's Sons, 1969), 267–353, esp. 272–85. Michael Warren

resilience and rejuvenation of that world in characters as limited as Albany and Edgar. Albany's upright nobility somehow handicaps him before the diabolical energy of Gonoril. Edgar appears amiable but light, given to "stage business" as a response to life. The one lacks range, the other depth, yet they are "heroes" of the narrative. Shakespeare often makes such gestures—"And Cassio rules in Cyprus" (*Othello*, V.ii.333)—but with *Lear* the audience's sense of the numb-headedness of good looms as particularly acute. Onstage, however, Edgar has his pluses. In Richman's Quarto production, "Edgar and Albany shared moral authority," apparently with dramatic success.[47] Indeed, beyond his obvious affinity with Albany, Edgar's dramatic proximities, such as, even, his closeness to Edmund or his distance from Lear and Gloucester, lend him stature and spectatorial plausibility. Edgar profits through the economics of theatrical energy.

Edmund introduces Edgar: "and on's cue out he comes, like the catastrophe of the old comedy" (sc. 2.129–30). In one of *Lear's* curious displacements, Edgar inherits a parcel of Edmund's stage dynamism. Edmund's very wish to supplant Edgar, of course, makes his dynamism the flatterer to the yet-unseen brother. Shakespeare emphasizes the links between the brothers Ed. Edgar fills a role in Edmund's comedy (Edmund even stage-tests Edgar's future madman in his "sigh like them of Bedlam" [130–31]). They stress their brotherhood: "How now, brother Edmund"; "I am thinking, brother" (133, 135; also 159, 166 and sc. 6.19, 32). Edgar has enough humor ("How long have you been a sectary astronomical?" [145]) that the audience will engage with him as with Edmund's improvisational energy. Shakespeare also bonds Edgar with the spectator along Edmund's great divide of youthful irreverence against aged superstition. As the legitimate enters, the bastard mimics their father derisively: "O, these eclipses do portend these divisions" (131–32), a science that Edgar dismisses as utterly as his brother. Edgar will, no more than Edmund, lay man's "goatish disposition to the charge of stars" (122–23). The audience has, moments before, shared Edmund's contempt for the self-deluding heavenly compulsions of Gloucester, a contempt that aligns thriving youth against tired age and, importantly, maintains in *King Lear* an opening for the efficacy of zestful action. Edgar participates in this revivifying, if dangerous, energy through his proximity to Edmund and thus the audience.

---

presents a sensitive summary of Edgar's emotional distance from many of the events around him, in "Quarto and Folio *King Lear* and the Interpretation of Albany and Edgar," 102.

47. Richman, "The *King Lear* Quarto In Rehearsal and Performance," 380. Richman did diverge from the Quarto in assigning the play's last speech to Edgar (following F) rather than Albany.

How we approve of Edmund provides some ground for approving of his brother.

Edgar also resembles the audience. In scene 2, Edmund does to Edgar—manipulated and "left darkling," with virtually no lines, in a consciously theatrical way—exactly what scene 1 has done to the spectator. Edgar's confusion echoes the playgoer's desire that action clarify and pace decelerate, so that the stage presents us with a character occupying our earlier discomfited situation. The bastard's treachery allows the audience to sympathize through Edgar with itself, to release its residual frustrations. Inevitably, too, we will sympathize with Edgar's victimization, because of our forced complicity of knowledge with Edmund. While the scene barely details Edgar above "a brother noble," unsuspecting of harms, and foolishly honest (166–68), the audience will recognize him as our incipient hero. Our sympathy here is positional as much as conventional or characterological.

After the stocking of Kent comes the proclaimed Edgar (sc. 7.167–87), the one caught, the other "Escaped." On the boards, Edgar will likely step forward to the stage's *platea* as opposed to Kent's *locus.* Soliloquy's natural intimacy between actor and audience, as well as Edgar's straightforward distress, appealing to an audience already anxious over a figure just humiliated with pillorying, gives Edgar added positional empathy. Against the impotent medievalism of Kent, Edgar turns suddenly real, Elizabethan: He will become a Bedlam beggar and, with begrimed face, blanketed loins, knotted hair, and "presented nakedness outface / The wind and persecution of the sky." Edgar's "outface" presages Lear's "outstorm" (sc. 8.9) and the Fool's "outjest" (sc. 8.15). That declaration, lingering in the shadows of Kent's and Lear's humiliation, promises both preservation ("While I may scape / I will preserve myself") and heroic defiance.

Edgar's disguise embodies a theatrical ambivalence: It constitutes an invented "part" more grimly realistic than any characterization in the play.[48] It likely did engage the Elizabethan and does engage the modern audience for its

---

48. In a recent article, William C. Carroll explores much of the same evidence surveyed here—literature of the underworld, ballads, historical analyses of sixteenth-century vagrancy—for the Elizabethan depiction of and response to the generic Tom of Bedlam, but for different purposes and with different conclusions from my own. Carroll argues that "[f]or most of Shakespeare's audience, Tom o' Bedlam would not have been a figure to pity" but "a stereotype of the con man" (431), a "fraud" (434). By contrast, I see an ambivalence—mixed of sympathy, pity, fear, and contempt—in Elizabethan responses to Poor Tom, and I view the stereotyping of the underworld literature as, to some extent, an exercise in distancing author and reader from a too-affecting subject. Carroll's essay illuminates the significance of the corporeal body in the play; see " 'The Base Shall Top Th'Legitimate': The Bedlam Beggar and the Role of Edgar in *King Lear,*" *Shakespeare Quarterly* 38 (Winter 1987): 426–41.

naturalism. Edgar's own detachment from his vile disguise spurs the audience's acceptance of his heroic position. This duality—realism and self-detachment—lends Edgar a haunting, important stage presence, and spectators attend him with some anguish and anticipation. Edgar's portrait of the Bedlam beggar, the filthy and "horrible" spectacle with "roaring" voice and "numbed and mortified bare arms," is so realistic that it has acquired a definitional status in the history of madness.[49] Though actual Bethlehemites did not roam the countryside begging alms, "Tom O' Bedlam" was a popular name, like Abraham Man, for crazed vagabonds in Renaissance England. Vagrants and beggars rummaged London's streets and the English countryside, increasing in number during Shakespeare's life.[50] While Elizabethan estimates of the begging poor cannot be relied upon, the Lord Mayor of London placed their numbers at 12,000 in the city in 1594.[51] With the Poor Laws, Parliament undertook periodic nationwide searches and apprehensions of vagabonds, for whom punishment ranged from whipping and branding to hanging.[52] Edgar's Poor Tom does not exaggerate the perpetual threat of reprisal for vagrancy when he describes himself as "whipped from tithing to tithing, and stock-punished, and imprisoned" (sc. 11.122–23). Edward Hext, a justice of Somersetshire, in a 1596 letter to a member of the Privy Council depicts a countryside rife with vagabondage and crime, numerous felons executed but others turned loose or escaped.[53] Hext

49. Edward Geoffrey O'Donoghue, in his history of St. Mary's of Bethlehem Hospital, London's ancient asylum for the insane, draws substantially from *King Lear* for his account of "Tom O' Bedlam," in *The Story of Bethlehem Hospital: From Its Foundation in 1247* (London: T. Fisher Unwin, 1914), 132–140. O'Donoghue conjectures that Shakespeare, who was associated with the area around Bishopsgate and likely visited Bethlehem Hospital, learned to classify madness personally from Timothy Bright, physician of St. Bartholomew's as well as author on melancholy, with whom he may have viewed the inmates of Bethlehem, 132.

50. Writing in 1913, Frank Aydelotte argued that "in the sixteenth century the numbers of rogues and vagabonds were larger in proportion to the population than they have ever been before or since," Frank Aydelotte, *Elizabethan Rogues and Vagabonds*, vol. 1 in *Oxford Historical and Literary Studies* (Oxford: Clarendon Press, 1913), 3. For a full discussion of Elizabethan and Jacobean vagrancy, see A. L. Beier, *Masterless Men: The Vagrancy Problem in England, 1560–1640* (London: Metheun, 1985). Among the causes for this increase in destitution were the dispossession of tenant farmers through enclosure, the demobilizing of military forces such as those raised against the Spanish Armada, and the dispersion of retainers from the breakup of feudal households: See Aydelotte, *Elizabethan Rogues and Vagabonds*, 5–17. For a more extensive list of causes and a somewhat different view of the scale and impact of sixteenth-century poverty, see John Pound, *Poverty and Vagrancy in Tudor England* (London: Longman, 1971), 3–24.

51. Aydelotte, *Elizabethan Rogues and Vagabonds*, 4; see also Pound, *Poverty and Vagrancy in Tudor England*, 25–30.

52. See Aydelotte, *Elizabethan Rogues and Vagabonds*, 56–75.

53. British Museum, MS. Landsdowne, 81, Nos. 62 and 64, reprinted in Aydelotte, *Elizabethan Rogues and Vagabonds*, Appendix A14, 167–74.

testifies that the common folk by no means fully cooperated with the law in its severe punishments.[54] Vagabonds were known to roam in groups, from two to sometimes forty or fifty (Pound, 29), and Hext advises the Council that the "able men that are abroade sekynge the spoyle and confusion of the land" could make up an army (Aydelotte, 171). The small band of outlaws and madmen braving the stormswept heath of *King Lear* had its dangerous analogue in sixteenth-century history. They may have aroused a mixed response in a Jacobean audience ("underdistancing" in Bullough's terms), ranging from aristocratic distaste to groundling sympathy.

That Edgar portrays not only a beggar but a Bedlamite builds a second layer of Jacobean realism into his disguise. A woodcut engraving of Elizabethan provenance, accompanying the ballad "New Mad Tom of Bedlam," and variously reproduced in the Stuart period,[55] depicts an Abraham Man much resembling Edgar's disguise. The beggar's hair is wild and matted; he is naked above the waist, with a blanket and skirt covering his loins and ragged leggings above his bare feet; he wears a large "Sharing-horn" on a string across his shoulder and carries a short staff. "New Mad Tom" of the ballad resembles Edgar's Poor Tom:

> Forth from my sad and darksome Cell,
> Or from the deep Abiss of Hell,
> Mad Tom is come to view the world again,
> To see if he can ease his distempered Brain:
> Fear and care doth pierce the Soul,
> Hark how the angry Furies howl;
> Pluto laughs and Prosperine is, glad,
> To see poor naked Tom of Bedlam mad.
>
> (1–8)

54. "In which default of Iustice manye wicked theves escape, for most comonly the simple Cuntryman and woman, lokynge no farther then ynto the losse of ther owne goods, are of opynyon that they wold not procure a mans death for all the goods yn the world, others vppon promyse to have ther goods agayne, wyll gyve faynt evidens yf they be not styctly loked ynto by the Iustyce," Aydelotte, *Elizabethan Rogues and Vagabonds*, 169.

55. The woodcut and the ballad are reproduced in W. G. Day, ed., *The Pepys Ballads*, facsimile vol. 1 in *Catalogue of the Pepys Library At Magdalene College, Cambridge* (Cambridge: Brewer, 1987), 502. The picture accompanies the ballad "Ragged, and Torne, and True" in the *Roxburghe Ballads*, 1:352, British Museum, Roxburghe Collection, and is reengraved from the woodcut, in W. H. Chappel, ed., *The Roxburghe Ballads*, vol. 2 (Herford: Printed for the Ballad Society, Stephen Austin and Sons, 1874), 409. "Ragged, and Torne, and True," with the Tom O' Bedlam woodcut, was "Printed by the Assignes of Thomas Symcock," a London printer of the 1620s and 30s.

These pictorial and verbal images of Mad Tom are both poignant and comic, the sadness and depredation of his circumstances distanced from his audience by conventionalizing the character—and, in such ballads as "Ragged, and Torne, and True," even sentimentalizing him. Tom of Bedlam was an Elizabethan and Jacobean "type," and Shakespeare shared with his contemporaries a "picture" of Tom available for stage adaptation.

Mad Tom's standard appearance, of course, has various literary sources, particularly Thomas Harman's *A caueat for commen cursetors vulgarely called vagabones* (1567).[56] While scholars have detailed the physical resemblances between Shakespeare's Poor Tom and the Abraham Men or Tom O'Bedlams of such underworld literature, I am more interested here in the distancing strategies that writers display toward Mad Tom. Harman's book is the grandfather of the genre, from which succeeding authors borrowed freely. His dedication sets out bluntly to convince Elizabeth, Countess of Shrewsbury of the hypocrisy of "these rowsey, ragged rabblement of rakehells" so as to discourage her charity.[57] Harman pictures Abraham men as tricksters claiming to have been beaten and abused in Bethlehem Hospital and gaining thereby the sympathy of almsgivers.[58] These creatures appear in Harman's work as glib, pre-Dickensian rogues dodging honest work: "Some of these be merry and very pleasant; they will dance and sing. Some others be as cold and reasonable to talk withal" (Judges, 83). Harman dehumanizes beggars with his crude taxonomy of them, a strategy followed by successive commentators on the Elizabethan underworld. His distancing attack, alternately angry and condescending toward its stereotypes, seeks to address strongly a public of divided engagement (as with the Countess's charity and that of the commoners referred to by Hext) and detachment regarding beggary. Harman views the lower social orders, those least capable of charity, as often the most "guilty" of it.

56. See also John Awdeley's *The Fraternitie of Vacabondes* (1565), Thomas Dekker's *The Belman of London* (1608), and the anonymous pamphlet *O Per Se O* (1612). These, with Thomas Harman's *A Caueat, or Warening, for Commen Cursetors Vulgarely Called Vagabones* and related publications, can be found in *The Elizabethan Underworld*, ed. A. V. Judges (London: George Routledge and Sons, 1930).

57. "I thought it good, necessary, and my bounden duty, to acquaint your goodness with the abominable, wicked, and detestable behaviour of all these rowsey, ragged rabblement of rakehells, that—under the pretence of great misery, diseases, and other innumerable calamities which they feign—through great hypocrisy do win and gain great alms in all places where they wilily wander, to the utter deluding of the good givers," Judges, ed., *The Elizabethan Underworld*, 61.

58. Harman takes particular pleasure in reciting how he unmasked a "Counterfeit Crank" named Nicholas Jennings who, bloody and rag-covered, begged around the Temple with enough profit that he actually kept a wife, fine clothes, and a well-appointed house in Newington: Judges, ed., *The Elizabethan Underworld*, 85–90.

The theatricality of Abraham men is a running theme of underworld literature, an image that sanctions spectatorial distance from them, as the pamphlet *O Per Se O* implies: "And to colour their villainy the better, every one of these abrams hath a several gesture in playing his part. Some make an horrid noise, hollowly sounding; some whoop, some hollow, some show only a kind of wild distracted ugly look, uttering a simple kind of maunding" (Judges, 372).[59] In Shakespeare's time madness was a source of public entertainment. Bethlehem Hospital was one of the premier sights of the city. O'Donoghue notes how in 1609 members of the house of Percy on a visit to London "saw the lions [at the Tower], the show of Bethlehem, the place where the prince was created, and the fireworks at the Artillery Gardens."[60] Visitors saw the "show of Bethlehem" by paying a fee to be guided by an official of the hospital along the ground-floor corridor housing the twenty-one cells of the insane.[61] Acknowledging the popularity of such entertainment, Thomas Dekker, in 1604, with *The Honest Whore, Part 1,* began something of a vogue for Bedlamites on the public stages.

Tom of Bedlam, then, was a complex figure deeply imprinted on the Elizabethan and Jacobean consciousness, toward whom his society demonstrated an ambivalent and incendiary engagement and detachment. In an economy of steadily worsening inflation, the fall into destitution was a frightening and heartrending plight with which many could easily identify. Nor did the citizenry wholly support the legal repressions against vagabonds of searches, whipping, branding, and hanging. Bethlehem Hospital, in addition, treated lunacy (particularly when diagnosed as demonic possession) with whipping, immersion, and manacled confinement in its dark, cold cells (Bethlehem was unheated). Bedlam beggars presumably enforced their charity by reciting the depredations of Bedlam itself. Against gestures of public sympathy, a derisive hostility also followed these specters of the Elizabethan underworld—fear for crime, outrage at sloth, suspicions of cozenage. Here psychic distance took also the opposite tack of sentimentalizing these merry beggars who only loved to sing, dance, and joy to the adventure of the road. Autolycuses, playactors all, just as the actual Bedlam inmates were objects of penny-entertainment.

---

59. Stephen Greenblatt investigates the similarly alleged "theatricality" of devil-possession and exorcism in his discussion of *King Lear,* "Shakespeare and the Exorcists," *Shakespearean Negotiations* (Berkeley: University of California Press, 1988), 94–128.

60. O'Donoghue, *The Story of Bethelehem Hospital,* 235 and 405; he cites from "Hist. MSS. Report VI, pt. i., appendix, p. 229b."

61. Robert Rentoul Reed, Jr., estimates that perhaps as many as seventy-five people a day might have visited Bedlam in the early 1600s, in *Bedlam on the Jacobean Stage* (Cambridge: Harvard University Press, 1952), 25–26.

Considering these divergent, uneasy attempts to deal with the horrors of poverty and insanity, it might not be overbold to suggest that Shakespeare's world had something in common with our modern engagement and detachment regarding the deinstitutionalized and indigent. The very figure of Tom invites a complex sympathy and denial.

In the storm scenes, a director may stress either a tragic Tom or a comic Tom, emphasizing our tears or our laughter, proximity or distance. Poor Tom is certainly comedic; he recites devils, details an unsettling Oswald-like past, displays his sheer inventiveness. Yet Poor Tom is also pitiful and hideous. Goldman argues that Edgar's physical appearance should reflect what is painful to watch in *King Lear*, the "indignities, tortures, and violations the actors' bodies suffer, and through them our own": "Edgar too is a horrible sight. . . . On stage Edgar must be filthy, grotesque, very nearly naked, and bear on his body evidence of horrible mutilation . . . so repellent, nasty, and noisy that you pay him to go away."[62] Such a presentation shocks with Elizabethan realism, reflecting the degradation of madness and penury and the reprisals against them. Edgar's frightening of the Fool out of the cave, then, does not merely exaggerate effects comically. Indeed, Poor Tom can explode on entrance with harried paranoia ("Away, the foul fiend follows me" [sc. 11.40]) and physical quivering ("Through the sharp hawthorn blows the cold wind" [40–41]), interweaving naturalism ambivalently with hyperbole. Lear's witnessing of Poor Tom's blighted and ragged body mirrors our own fascinated repulsion; conversely Tom's antiphonal allusions to coldness (e.g., sc. 11.41, 74, 134, 159), with whatever physical equivalents the Edgar-actor chooses, trumpet first his sympathetic realism and then, by the reductiveness of repetition, his fantasticality. Whether a director emphasizes the social verisimilitude of *King Lear*, and thus Edgar's wretchedness, or *Lear*'s existential absurdity, and thus Edgar's comedy, each of these two tones will become, in performance, the context of the other.

Edgar presents, and mimics, Tom of Bedlam, with several effects on the spectator. First, as we have suggested, Tom's realistic "typology" would have invited Renaissance audiences to recall their own attitudes toward the "thing itself" outside the theater gates. Likewise the modern playgoer. The ambivalences of spectatorial distance in the tragedy (the disturbing egotism of good, the seductiveness of evil, the ugliness of honest penury) can illuminate the ambivalences of social distance in life. Edgar's realism will also produce

---

62. Michael Goldman, *Shakespeare and the Energies of Drama* (Princeton: Princeton University Press, 1972), 94, 97.

enough spectatorial fascination with Tom to balance the disengaging effects of Lear's egocentrism as he, for example, tears off his lendings. Edgar privileges Lear. Next, Edgar's successful disguise, despite its humor and nascent sentimentality, hints at his heroic potential. The audience will always recognize the fact of Edgar's elaborate, assumed persona. Edgar never blurs into his disguise as do Lear and the Fool. The association of Poor Tom's history with Oswald, for example, distances such a past from Edgar. Edgar's lapses in "counterfeiting" also keep present for the spectator the difference between the Duke's son and the Bedlam beggar. Likewise Edgar's antic reaction to Gloucester's entrance ("This is the foul fiend Flibbertigibbet" [104]; "Poor Tom, that eats the swimming frog" [117]) reflects his fear of discovery, assuring the distanced spectator that Edgar is not Tom. Shakespeare reminds us of Edgar's disguise, and as long as we know that, oddly, we know too that the "worst" has not arrived and will not arrive. *Lear* would not seem to allow a tragic closure to Edgar's life as long as Edgar *pretended* to be Poor Tom. That Edgar always floats above "The low'st and most dejected thing of fortune" (sc. 15.3) buoys the audience surprisingly, too. We know the tragic danger of Lear's condition because he has passed beyond pranks and admiration; he has become madness. Similarly, the Fool can die because his wits, too, have turned as he has internalized into his own psyche the King's ruptured life. These characters are authentically desperate; Edgar is authentically in disguise. He stands apart. Shakespeare highlights the "esperance" of Edgar's counterfeiting when Edgar resolves, "Mark the high noises, and thyself bewray / When false opinion, whose wrong thoughts defile thee, / In thy just proof repeals and reconciles thee" (sc. 13.104–6). Edgar's moment of truth will come only when he can reveal himself to others. While critics have been quick to accuse Edgar of a basic fatuousness about worse and worst (e.g., sc. 15.1–6), playgoers nonetheless endure *Lear*'s spectacle of suffering partly through Edgar's inability to believe or become, quite, the "play" he is in.

Finally, the storm scenes give Edgar occasion for winningly "heroic" acting, like the Kent-actor's. Like him, the Edgar-actor has the chance to play three parts: the noble son, the Bedlam, and (Tom's history) "A servingman, proud in heart and mind" (sc. 11.76). Edgar, furthermore, must present arcane demonology, a detailed personal history, and a self-generated style and tone, as well as sudden changes of emotion and external focus, all with an improvisational immediacy (out-Edmunding Edmund) on which hinge the very success of his disguise. Edgar's own Brechtian "alienation," that is, his simultaneous projection of himself and of Mad Tom, displays the virtuosity to which *King Lear* can challenge an actor and a virtuosity that will win audience admiration for both actor and character. Edgar's performance demands energy, fortitude, invention, and control—theatrical valor.

V

Edgar's acting lies near the mysterious heart of perhaps the most affecting scene in Shakespeare (sc. 20): "Dover beach." Critics tax Edgar severely for withholding his identity from Gloucester, avoiding love, while he pursues a strange trick. Such readings condition how many now experience Edgar in the theater. I do not wish to oppose that view. Rather I would consider aspects of Edgar's performance that such a focus necessarily bypasses. At "Dover beach" Edgar's acting moves Gloucester and the audience. It works not because he maintains an elaborate fictional identity, mad Tom, but because he makes a sufficient personal commitment to what he enacts, however misguided. Edgar invites the spectator to coauthor the play's illusions, a triumph of communal truth. "Dover beach," too, becomes the "situation" through which Lear engages the audience beyond its conventional responses to character. Lear's interview with Gloucester uses "presence" to destabilize "situation," such that the audience comes to invest itself in a manner not unlike the Edgar-actor. The first two panels of the scene, Gloucester's attempted suicide and Lear's interlude, forge an experience of transformation, the sense that we have arrived at a place unforeseeable, a place where all that has happened until now, all the assigning of rights and wrongs, sinned-against and sinning, no longer matters. Before Lear has spoken a word, the audience knows that his mad entrance will not launch just another mad scene. Why so? Gloucester's suicide attempt makes possible Lear's transformation. While we could treat that connection as somehow internal to the action, we can also consider it as a product of acting and audience response.[63]

We begin the scene uncertain: "When shall we come to th' top of that same hill?," asks Gloucester; "You do climb up it now. Look how we labour," answers his son (sc. 20.1–2). Inside whose vision is the audience situated? Is the world steep or stage-flat? For a while, we do not know. Gloucester's impressions argue for the flatness we see. But only when Edgar insists that his voice is not altered, "You're much deceived. In nothing am I changed / But in

---

63. My understanding of the spectatorial effect of acting surrounding Gloucester's suicide attempt has profited greatly from conversations with Kathleen Campbell (April 1988).

my garments" (9–10), do we begin to grasp Edgar's game. Part of our initial confusion about situation arises because Edgar's voice and diction no longer imitate a Bedlam beggar, even though he claims to; the authority of his voice bespeaks some serious intent. Is he in disguise, as he says, or not, as we and Gloucester perceive him? The scene's success demands active interpreting from spectators, including accommodation of a different realism in Edgar's characterization. We have landed in a new "situation."

Before Gloucester's jump and afterwards, Edgar describes the fearful precipice, "th'extreme verge" (26) on which they stand. In staging these moments, most directors will send Gloucester and Edgar downstage, with Edgar moving forward of his father toward the edge of the platform: "Come on, sir, here's the place. Stand still. How fearful / And dizzy 'tis to cast one's eyes so low!" (11–12). Actors will instinctively marshal the physical resources of the stage, its extreme verge, to enhance the effect of the language.[64] At the Globe, Edgar might speak looking out into the audience (front), yet directing the lines, with some glances, behind him toward his father.[65] So conceived, the precipice speech requires great concentration from the Edgar-actor, for he must deliver it near the audience and facing it, the proximity for addressing an audience in soliloquy, but a proximity that now might be dangerously distracting. (This "situation" also subverts the commonly unlocalized stage *platea.*) Even more, Edgar's description (13–22) requires the actor imaginatively to locate objects in the middle and far distance: crows and choughs in the "midway air," samphire-gatherers "[h]alfway down," fishermen "upon the beach," and ship, cock, and buoy anchored at sea. The actor's gaze might focus on a shallow point in front of him, then lower and extend outward into the theater, further and further, until he himself appears dizzied (22–24). In so doing, the actor must isolate "spots" in the sea of people before him that he can fix on or play against. The precipice speech demands discipline, concentration, and intention. If it succeeds, this moment will engulf the audience, transforming the hazard

---

64. In discussing the staging of this scene, Alvin B. Kernan notes that the whole of it centers on "two opposing perspectives, looking down and looking up," "Formalism and Realism in Elizabethan Drama: The Miracles of *King Lear,*" *Renaissance Drama*, vol. 9, ed. S. Schoenbaum (Evanston: Northwestern University Press, 1966), 62. For the staging of the fall, see Alan C. Dessen, "Two Falls and a Trap: Shakespeare and the Spectacles of Realism," *English Literary Renaissance* 5 (Autumn 1975): 291–307.

65. Though I discuss the scene assuming such body placement, as well as the use of the stage edge, certainly different blockings are possible depending upon the strengths and preferences of the actors and the director. One recent and effective Edgar, as a colleague has informed me, delivered the precipice speech facing Gloucester, as if to shape him with his words. Nonetheless, an outward-looking Edgar standing on the stage's edge seems particularly congruous to the precipice speech.

of eye-to-eye contact into the spectator's emotional re-creation of Edgar's vision.

Edgar's description from the extreme verge, then, like his later images of the ten-mast height (53–54) and the "shrill-gorged lark" (58), enrolls the audience as much as (even more than) Gloucester. Unlike a soliloquy, where the actor becomes momentarily somewhat like the audience and steps partially into its world, here the actor, with technical focus and concrete imagery, gathers the audience into the world poetically imagined. The spectator participates actively. The scene invites the audience to invest in the fictional situation that Edgar creates, invest in the actor's triumph over limited physical resources and the distraction the audience itself represents. That the actor speaks in Edgar's voice, which we recognize better than does anyone on stage, further authenticates his description; Edgar's becoming more like himself, in turn, authenticates (makes "real") what he "sees." In a sense, Edgar's speech returns us to the initial condition of the scene: if a playgoer were to enter the arena at the moment of the precipice speech, that auditor would be unable to differentiate Edgar's deception from the narrative illusion. Edgar convinces solely from his commitment to what he utters. No wonder that spectators and critics have remembered this scene for centuries with the tag of "Dover cliff" or "Dover beach"! For to be touched by it is to entertain imaginatively that the cliff from which Gloucester plunges is real, even though we know differently with our sight—that lesser faculty in the play. The audience's emotional experience of the heights, an experience far greater than Gloucester's, has a reality separate from the quantum of the flat stage. We desire Gloucester's fall and rise, and we recognize our emotional affirmation in part because Gloucester tends to doubt Edgar's description: "But have I fallen, or no?" (56). Likewise, the audience may feel betrayed by Gloucester's later recidivisms into despair. He does reach some provisional acceptance: "Henceforth I'll bear / Affliction till it do cry out itself / 'Enough, enough,' and die" (75–77). But the audience has lived Gloucester's life as a miracle more than has he. At the center of *King Lear* lies the mystery of this scene: not only that Shakespeare would have a character jump off a cliff that is not there, but that he would bring the audience to believe the verity of the cliff at least as much as the unreality of the fall, the heart's truth so reaching beyond its empirical opposite.

Lear enters after the *felix culpa,* his "situation" transformed because the stage is now a different place. It is a place where the wondrous *can* happen, whether it did happen or not. Edgar, during Lear's fantastical interlude, has only four speeches: "O thou side-piercing sight!" (85); "Sweet marjoram" (92); "I would not take this from report; it is, / And my heart breaks at it"

(136–37); and "O, matter and impertinency mixed—/ Reason in madness!" (163–64). Edgar completes here his metamorphosis from ambivalent beggar-figure to audience-confidant, his intimacy with us now confirming his special relationship during the fall. Edgar addresses each speech entirely or in part to the audience, seeking to heighten the pathos of Lear by guiding spectatorial response: defining Lear, focusing emotional effect through images of the effect. Edgar's impressions detach the audience from Lear moment to moment. In the paradoxical reciprocity of engagement and detachment, the audience experiences the pathos of Lear, virtually inexpressible by Lear alone, through ideas about that pathos. Edgar's mediation leaves the audience contemplating as well as feeling Lear's pathos—"beholding" in its richest Shakespearean sense.

Edgar's incredulousness also magnifies a new process of characterization. For the audience, Lear develops toward opacity, strangeness, otherness. His "present" at Dover shatters the historical continuity of the play: It is a dialogue composed not only of the character we know but also of madness, of memories of the play misremembered, of fragments from a martial past unshared with the audience and floating downstream only now, and of dark images of law and sex outside the known circumference of his personality (and the play's historical period). Shakespeare disintegrates "Lear." As Gloucester's fall puts us emotionally at the bottom of a cliff, the matter-and-impertinency-mixed Lear puts us in a changed time, a continuous present where juxtaposed elements of character qualify each other: Lear's madness altering his memory of the storm, his bitterness toward Gonoril and Regan corrupting his idea of women and sex (the latent hint of incest newly recasting his relationship with his daughters), his allusion to his own soldiers, armies, and martial feats detailing a prowess by which to reexperience him retrospectively. The spectator's earlier witnessing (in the abdication scene, for example, or the Gonoril sequence) of events that both have already happened and are now happening for the first time translates now into the experience of character itself. The sense of "Lear" as a present creation increases as Lear speaks from his inner drama. He addresses the figures—soldiers, criminals, apothecaries, beadles—who populate his imagination. He conceives himself as general, king, justice, preacher and plays the parts. Lear's strange tangents possess the spontaneous moment-by-moment truth of theater. And as they are drama, as it were, reported within the drama, they have the authority of distance, reflection. Part of the "point" of this presentation, surely, is that Lear's character cannot be encompassed by referring to his psychology, history, politics, or even madness (for one thing, the play now introduces "facts" that have been heretofore beyond it). He is intensely real in the moment yet evanescent. And how this scene anchors the audience in the homely details of physical existence! Not only sexual smells, mortal hands, boots, or the weight of a purse, but how the physical body is coterminous with the vision: "Ay, every inch a king" (105), says Lear, with a voice or gesture or sudden pulling up of the torso that registers for the spectator the flesh and blood of kingliness. Lear's spatial "thereness" and his temporal "presentness" extend each other.

The logic of this second panel of the scene, then, is not supplied by the "logic" of Lear's character (the design underneath the ruined pieces of nature), for his "character" refutes logic. In performative terms, Lear is not dramatizing his character (something antecedent); rather the drama *is* his character. Further emphasizing Lear's "processual" character, the episode structures a twofold action of recognition. Shakespeare evokes psychic locale quickly and simply: "Give the word." / "Sweet marjoram." / "Pass." / "I know that voice" (91–94). The first segment constitutes Gloucester's recognition of Lear ("The trick of that voice I do well remember. / Is't not the King?" [104–5]), and Lear's new, sardonic enactment of his royalty ("When I do stare, see how the subject quakes!" [106]; "Here, wipe it first; it smells of mortality" [128]). This segment climaxes as Gloucester apprehends the wreckage: "O ruined piece of nature! This great world / Shall so wear out to naught" (129–30). The second segment starts with Gloucester's next breath: "Do you know me?" (130). The exposition follows "the case of eyes" (139), how "[a] man may see how the world goes with no eyes" (145–46), and culminates with Lear's reciprocal recognition of Gloucester: "I know thee well enough: thy name is Gloucester" (166). Gloucester and Lear recognize each other: That is the action of the interlude, and it includes the full acknowledging of their abject stations. Recognition, here arriving so slowly and with such pathos, is a quintessentially theatrical action and often creates a reflexive joy for characters and spectators. Part of the present release derives from simply identifying and naming, a rudimentary gesture that yet diminishes the remoteness and isolation of Gloucester and Lear. The audience cannot "understand" Lear in this scene, yet it can "recognize" him in all his ruin, incoherence, and majesty, a perspective of altogether different distance and power.

Much of this interlude comes in the form of oblique as opposed to interactive dialogue. Even such a line as, "The trick of that voice I do well remember. / Is't not the King?" (104–5), Gloucester addresses perhaps more to the audience than to anyone in the play. Likewise with his, "O ruined piece of nature!" (129). The Lear-actor will "spot" other characters for focus—"Ha, Gonoril! Ha, Regan!" (95)—while the content may zigzag into "impertinency": "They flattered me like a dog" (95–96). Part of the poignance of Lear's inner drama of madness is that he plays against the bodies, but not the identities, before him; part of the joy of recognition comes when he sees the characters for whom the bodies stand. Oblique dialogue surrenders to interactive dialogue.

The fascination of the episode rides upon the oscillations of extreme engagement and grotesque detachment. When Lear says, for example, "I remember thy eyes well enough. Dost thou squiny on me?" (131–32), one choice for the Lear-actor is to squint at Gloucester (as he will say later, "Mine eyes are not o' the best" [sc. 24.275]) creating a mirror-image that neither can recognize. Then Lear darts down his own path, yet inspired by the sight of blindness: "No, do thy worst, blind Cupid, I'll not love" (133). "Read thou that challenge" (134), says the king, returning to the person actually before him. Here the Lear-actor may pause for a response, bringing only silence from Gloucester, because the next request falls back from the first: "Mark but the penning of't" (134). Gloucester's reply, in the same dramatic rhythm, answers more than the question requires: "Were all the letters suns, I could not see one" (135), lines directed outwardly to the audience, or even inwardly, as much as to Lear. The entire interlude constantly scrambles "situation," the local and the abstract, the internal and the external, the story and the theater—a rhythm of engagement and detachment among characters and between them and the audience.

Recognition makes character whole simply by making it known, public. Shakespeare creates the logic and coherence of these characters, however fragmented like Lear, through each discovering the identity of the other. Mad Lear and desperate Gloucester give each other the world; each becomes the other's context. Identity arrives through mutuality. Understanding Lear for the audience requires no analysis. Certainly, we distance ourselves from these two old men: Lear's humor detaches us from Gloucester's point of view; Gloucester's interpretations (even "Alack, alack, the day!" [170]) keep us slightly on the outside of Lear. Yet a distance by which pathetic blindness, for example, can be a source of humor or insight confers value upon blindness (no matter whether we laugh at the humor or grow wise from the insight). Detachment running through this scene allows characters and spectators to embrace the given.

VI

King Lear's ending demonstrates how drama can create for the audience, even in the face of absence and loss, the wholeness of the present—the ultimate paradox of "situation" in the play. Kent and Edgar reappear, Kent echoing the play's falling and Edgar its rising action. Kent has often unexpectedly inspired spectatorial distance from Lear, sometimes mirroring his excesses. Edgar, on the other hand, has mediated the spectator's increasing engagement with the forces, however imperfect, that restore health. Now for a moment the two virtually collapse into one, undermining their separate "meanings." In a speech found only in the Quarto, Edgar tells Kent's story, prepares us for his entrance, the "dialogic" presentation—for Edgar now contains Kent—incorporating "the most piteous tale of Lear and him" (sc. 24.211) into Edgar's own comedic pattern. As Edgar abstracts Kent's history, he establishes spectatorial sympathy for the wandering earl, but at the distance of self-conscious narrative: "This would have seemed a period / To such as love not sorrow; but another / To amplify, too much would make much more, / And top extremity" (202-4). (Likewise, Albany has claimed himself "almost ready to dissolve" [200].) Shakespeare distances the spectator by calling attention to engagement. Edgar's lines even acknowledge the play's special theatrics: the actors' expressing of inexpressible grief and the sly characterization of the audience as such who *do* love sorrow.

Kent ripens from anger to pathos in *King Lear:* He turns from ineffectual attendant in the storm to part-reporter with the Gentleman (scene 17),[66] to the subject of report with Edgar. Edgar clarifies further the alternative dramatic directions he and Kent represent, and the one that the narrative chooses: "His grief grew puissant and the strings of life / Began to crack. Twice then the trumpets sounded, / And there I left him tranced" (213-15). Kent lingers, like others in this play, tranced in pain; Edgar proceeds. The Kent described here lacks, even surprisingly so, the energy and great purpose-

66. Scene 17, in which Kent quizes the Gentleman about Cordelia's responses to news of the indignities done her father and his sufferings on the heath, and in which the two also discuss Lear's shame concerning Cordelia and the state of military preparations, occurs in the Quarto but not in the Folio. That scene is largely reportage, and fairly saccharine stuff, at least from the ironic modernist perspective. Yet reportorial scenes recur in all drama and often succeed marvelously, as the opening (and many later) scenes of *Macbeth* illustrate. Scene 17 has certain functions. It charts the progressive marginalization of Kent, a dramatic feature of the Quarto with thematic intentions. It prepares spectators for Lear's entrance in scene 20 and influences the image of the war. It anticipates and intensifies Lear's reunion with Cordelia, but also underscores one of the Quarto's special considerations, the response to absence, loss, even failure. For comments upon this scene, see Michael Warren, "The Diminution of Kent," 65–67. Despite the interlude's thematic value, Richman notes that in his Quarto production audience attention flagged in scene 17 ("The *King Lear* Quarto In Rehearsal and Production," 381). Such episodes of reportage, along with those of sententiae (in which the Quarto also exceeds the Folio), seem to lose the modern spectators more easily than they lost their Renaissance counterparts.

fulness we have known in him before. Dramatically, however, Shakespeare transfers those qualities to Edgar, and Edgar's circumferencing of Kent's story completes that symbiosis. Shakespeare encloses the sadness of Kent within the hopefulness of Edgar, as Edgar's heroic role rises dialogically out of the *Lear*-community. We feel detached from Kent while we engage with Edgar as he tells Kent's story. The play will maintain this distance, for example, when Albany forgoes toward Kent the "compliment" that manners would urge but "time" deny (228–29).

The actorly challenges of "playing dead" in *King Lear*'s final moments create the tonic to resolve the tragic experience of the audience. Lear barely "knows" anything—like the spectator—and must navigate the world feelingly: "Howl, howl, howl, howl! O, you are men of stones" (253). His entrance with Cordelia's body demands (and communicates to the audience) enormous invention from both actors. "Howl" can be a virtual speech act, a stage direction, or a command. As a kind of speech act ("howl" works as a description of its own expression), it can show Lear extended almost to bestiality (a baying dog) in a pure, inarticulate reflex at pain. ("Howl" might also play as Lear's failing energy, his uttering the text or symbol of grief for the grief itself.) Viewed as a stage direction, "Howl" allows the actor to pick a sound appropriate for him in the immediate moment, the actor moving improvisationally into the experience of the character, a difficult challenge for an entrance-line. Finally, as a command, "Howl" would direct those characters on stage to share and express his agony, and their immediate inability to see his world feelingly will cue the charge, "O, you are men of stones. / Had I your tongues and eyes" (253–54). An actor, moreover, might use any or all of these possibilities to vary the quadruple "howl." I state them not simply to demonstrate that *King Lear* admits of many directorial interpretations, but rather to suggest that the ending is particularly rich in words and phrases that invite spontaneous discovery, invite the actor to recognize their vast possibilities even in the present moment of choice: "Is this the promised end?" (259); "So think I, too" (287); "O see, see!" (299); "And my poor fool is hanged!" (300); "Never, never, never" (303). The language here allows the actors to play with unusual force to what is in their visible, physical presence.

The central ambiguity of *King Lear*'s ending and its central physical object are the dead body of Cordelia. Lear enters carrying it, a feat of strength for an old man, whose difficulty the Lear-actor must represent. But the greater acting feat belongs to Cordelia, for the boy-player or actress must appear completely limp, surrendering his or her weight to the Lear-actor (and in such a way as to aid his balance). Altogether, Cordelia will be carried in, laid on the ground

("She's dead as earth" [257]), hovered over, and likely raised up and embraced. She must play dead for seventy lines, and weather at least four phases of scrutiny ("Lend me a looking-glass" [257], "This feather stirs" [261], "Ha? / What is't thou sayst?" [267–68], "No, no life" [300]). The Cordelia-performer must demonstrate steady concentration and imaginative focus, along with muscular and respiratory control. Playing dead provides a theatrical task in which even the Method actor must pretend more than "be" (the play has also celebrated a similar acting problem, playing mad). It calls for skilled acting.

The language of the ending drives the spectators' and actors' attention alike to Cordelia's body: Lear asserts alternately that she is dead and that she is alive; the audience gapes to see if it can observe the Cordelia-performer breathing, catch the slight rise and fall of the solar plexis. Watching a performer play dead fascinates in a definitively theatrical way. It gathers in one gesture the narrative fact, the exhilaration of acting peculiar to theater, and the audience's consciousness of its own interest, doubt, and delight. Playing dead illustrates simultaneously the truth and falsehood of theater. *King Lear,* more than any other of Shakespeare's plays, forces the audience and the actors on stage to linger in the question of a character's lifelikeness. Lear virtually investigates her acting: "Lend me a looking-glass. / If that her breath will mist or stain the stone, / Why, then she lives" (257–59). He floats a feather, or sees one floating: "This feather stirs. She lives" (261). His fleeting hopes draw power from our extradramatic knowledge that the Cordelia-actress only "pretends" and thus the character could come to life, and, behind that, our desire that Cordelia not die.[67] Here Shakespeare uses the special virtue of theater to tease our hope, even to suggest, since the Cordelia-actress must from moment to moment look as if she is breathing, that it is just happening—the feather stirs!

Of course, the audience needs Cordelia's death (even wishes it in part), and her performer's skill at playing dead will allow us to give up, separate ourself from, the character. Likewise, the semicircle around Lear conjures a distancing and finale-facilitating play-within-the-play. Lear addresses Cordelia, even thinks he hears her, speaking alternately to her and of her, in and out of the playlet: "Cordelia, Cordelia: stay a little. Ha? / What is't thou sayst?—Her voice was ever soft, / Gentle, and low, an excellent thing in women.—/ I killed the slave that was a-hanging thee" (267–70). Lear's memories of Cordelia create her reality out of her absence. He would make something out of nothing. His oscillating distance from her, as he continually slips out of his illusion that she

---

67. His hope may draw power from our dramatic memories, as well, since the apparently dead Desdemona does come alive momentarily in act V. See my comments in the Introduction, 1–3.

lives, also makes his play-within realistic; it forges his relationship to Cordelia as ours, including even the crystallizing of theatrical memory (her voice) and the tying up of narrative ends (the captain slain). Lear squinnies at Kent (echoing "Dover beach") and invites his great witness into the awful circle: "You're welcome hither" (284). Adds Kent, who climactically ties together his empathy and enervation: "Nor no man else. All's cheerless, dark, and deadly" (285). The play's acknowledgment of Kent, necessary to the spectator, "situates" *Lear*'s stage space, for the last time, as more emotional than physical. The Quarto Lear, unlike the Folio, dies with no delusions of Cordelia alive or as spirit, no bursting smilingly, no chance that redeems all sorrows: "Break, heart, I prithee break" (306). This version of Lear's death particularly honors what the stage provides: the material world in its whole, immediate present, with yet the aura, but not the pretense, of what is lost. Indeed, that Lear (who virtually wills his own death, every inch a king) has his own fate and not Gloucester's underscores that integrity of the present.

As Lear nears death, characters continue their choric roles: Kent sees, painfully, the narrative end that his "good intent" wished to avert or sees even Judgment Day itself—"Is this the promised end?" (259);[68] Edgar, who prefers the hopefulness of disguises, asks, "Or image of that horror?" (260). Later, Albany attempts a Malcolm-like ending (291–99). Edgar reprises Lear's theme over Cordelia's body, "Look up, my lord" (307), to which Kent calls a halt, "Vex not his ghost" (308). Even in this small exchange the two reenact their differences: continuance versus end. Edgar's foolish efforts to revive Lear may well annoy audiences, who wish no such detachment and willfully create, with Kent, the mysterious dignity Lear merits. Shakespeare sets such various responses before us, not so much, I think, to rock us between opinions of the same event, but finally to sink the always-partial interpretation under our respect for the thing itself, the immediate object, in *Lear* the actual present and its presence of loss: "Never, never, never" (303). Worth noting, the Quarto closes Edgar out of the last speeches, which go to Kent and Albany: no Folio equality here. If Kent becomes, in a sense, "left over" in the *Lear*-world, largely stripped of narrative function, a hint of that fate may now unexpectedly tinge Edgar—though less so if important stage action, such as carrying out Cordelia, otherwise occupies him. The distribution of the speeches, nonetheless, seems to project forward, rather than put at rest, the rhythms and surprises of character roles and spectatorial distance.

---

68. Robert Egan observes that at the close Kent, first through Lear's repulsion of him and then through the King's "contracting scope of awareness," "enacts and intensifies our own sense of loss and separation from Lear," in "Kent and the Audience: The Character as Spectator," 153.

That the quintessential experience in *King Lear* is the sensual appreciation of what is not there strikes me as highly theatrical.[69] Presence and absence, engagement and detachment, real actor and illusory character, our involvement with and our recognition of artifice all inhere simultaneously as we attend theater. Kent and Edgar stand, in their opposition, for that continuum of dramatic experience. They stand for the falling and rising rhythms of the narrative, and they help situate the spectator toward the protagonist, the *Lear*-world, and the play's moral dilemmas. Unlike those in *Othello, Lear's* secondary characters such as Kent and Edgar embody the contradictions of commenting upon a world that implicates them. Thus they invite early spectatorial interpretations, and then undermine those interpretations, keeping the audience always at risk. They lead us ultimately, as Edgar does in the "Dover beach" scene, to what may be most fascinating about *King Lear,* that the spectator's experience demonstrates what the story enacts, seeing the world feelingly: The theater proves the play.

69. Greenblatt describes theater as "an institution that calls forth what is not, that signifies absence, that transforms the literal into the metaphorical, that evacuates everything it represents. . . . The force of *King Lear* is to make us love the theater," *Shakespearean Negotiations,* 127.

5

The Audience In and Out of
Antony and Cleopatra

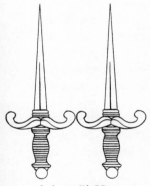

Noting *Antony and Cleopatra's* multiplicity of characters and perspectives, Janet Adelman argues that the hero and heroine, unlike those of other tragedies, fail to contain or embrace their tragic world: "In the major tragedies, the presentation of character and the structure generally function to focus our attention on the protagonists." But *Antony and Cleopatra,* Adelman continues, works to "diffuse and dissipate our attention through a wider universe" than that which the lovers know; "we see the universe as prior to and independent of them."[1] Yet we might argue that out of its multiplicity of voices, *Antony and Cleopatra* achieves, for the spectator, not dissipated but concentrated effects. The play proceeds according to a defining subtextual action, indeed, one most fully realized by Antony and Cleopatra themselves. Spectatorship, reciprocally with acting, stands as a dominant activity in *Antony and Cleopatra,* so much as to constitute the paradigm of its tragic action.[2] The play creates

1. *The Common Liar: An Essay on* Antony and Cleopatra (New Haven: Yale University Press, 1973), 44.
2. "Antony and Cleopatra are each other's best audiences. . . . If we may be said at all to identify with Antony and Cleopatra, it is their performances we identify with. . . . Even more,

a domain of action in the positionings of characters toward each other—their emotional distances, their maneuverings for psychological advantage—beyond the Aristotelean rise and fall of their fortunes. They play for legendry as much as for victory. *Antony and Cleopatra* engages audiences in the "double" of that action, characterized by the spectator's heightened self-awareness of "meaning" as contingent upon distance. The spectatorial paradigm does not resolve the uncertainties of *Antony and Cleopatra;* rather, it unveils, with criticism and delight, the mechanics by which characters make meaning—and playgoers too.

Other readers, with Adelman, have charged variously that *Antony and Cleopatra* refracts its action into commentary, manners, and spectacle that detach the audience from the essential tragic experience. Bradley threw up his hands at the tone of the first three acts: "People converse, discuss, accuse one another, excuse themselves, mock, describe, drink together, arrange a marriage, meet and part; but they do not kill, do not even tremble or weep."[3] *Antony and Cleopatra,* moreover, ranges famously among changing venues and diverse personages, boggling the audience's point of view and confounding its memory. Rather than deeply engaging us, so the thinking goes, the play offers opinions. John Danby argues that characters comment upon and judge each other in *Antony and Cleopatra* more than in any other Shakespearean play,[4] and Adelman sees in such multiplicity a rearrangement of tragic emotional emphasis: "[I]n *Antony and Cleopatra* we participate in the experience of the commentators more often than in the experience of the lovers" (40). The audience, accordingly, does "not partake of the tragedy so much as observe it as a spectacle."[5] In this line of argument, *Antony and Cleopatra*'s numerous voices diminish tragic concentration of power.

Yet, however centrifugal individual "judgments" are in the play, they fulfill a centripetal action: spectatorship or "beholding," the changeable perspective that commands how sensations, feelings, and thoughts become auditorial

---

perhaps, this is a play in which we identify with audiences, with Antony and Cleopatra as each other's audience, with ourselves as audience, and with the audience characters on stage," Michael Goldman, *Acting and Action in Shakespearean Tragedy* (Princeton: Princeton University Press, 1985), 138.

3. A. C. Bradley, "Shakespeare's Antony and Cleopatra," in *Oxford Lectures on Poetry* (London: Macmillan, 1909), 284. Though Bradley offers a profound appreciation of *Antony and Cleopatra,* he argues that its first three acts particularly neglect those events that "appeal most powerfully to the dramatic feelings—scenes of action or passion which agitate the audience with alarm, horror, painful expectation, or absorbing sympathies and antipathies" (283).

4. John F. Danby, *Poets on Fortune's Hill: Studies in Sidney, Shakespeare, Beaumont and Fletcher* (London: Faber and Faber, 1952), 131.

5. Mark Rose, Introduction, to *Twentieth Century Interpretations of* Antony and Cleopatra: *A Collection of Critical Essays,* ed. Mark Rose (Englewood Cliffs, N.J.: Prentice-Hall, 1977), 4.

perceptions. The governing "through-line" of *Antony and Cleopatra* emerges not merely in its story but in what the audience actually experiences, the *theatrical* imitation of a story, where the partiality of "distance" intrudes upon the story itself. Spectatorship—and the reciprocal dilemma of true and false acting—has its own Pirandellian fascination and poignancy. Thus can *Antony and Cleopatra* take us to the equivocal heart of drama: "For who," as J. Leeds Barroll asks, "can be trusted in a play?"[6] Because characters are always incomplete authorities about each other, "the paradox of dramatic form is its almost complete potential for redundancy" (58). *Antony and Cleopatra,* perhaps more than any other Shakespearean tragedy, translates this problem of aesthetics into dramatic action. Experiencing "authority" simultaneously with its "incompleteness" constitutes the spectatorial electricity of *Antony and Cleopatra.* The play highlights trust as an internal issue. Caesar's treachery is infinite; Enobarbus's infamous. Conflicts between the two great lovers are always about trust: They survive distrust rather than quell it. For each character, the process of the play is largely the Jamesian struggle to discover the truth about the others. All the major characters are watchers and interpreters, trusters and distrusters: "audiences" in themselves. Likewise, all are stage-actors, performing themselves before an audience, playing for trust.[7]

The action of spectatorship follows several lines in *Antony and Cleopatra.* Octavius presumes detachment, but the audience's distance from him exposes his strange obsession with the riotous lovers, beyond his Puritan and Lenten nature. Enobarbus, by contrast, mimics engagement. He stands, at least initially, as parodic and carnivalesque, the voice that keeps possibilities, alternate endings, open. But the more Octavius and Enobarbus struggle to escape the lovers, the more responsive they become, though each in different ways. Antony and Cleopatra star in this *theatrium mundi.* With one exception the two are never alone onstage together; their language aims at publicity. Antony and Cleopatra are always performing their relationship for supernumeraries. They are, moreover, both actor and audience to each other, a complete theater event. Partners, they yet contrast engagingly, each playing his or her love differently and to different audiences: Cleopatra's virtuosity is her dazzling abandon, her recklessness; Antony plays to "the story," binding "the world to weet / We stand up peerless"

---

6. *Shakespearean Tragedy: Genre, Tradition, and Change in* Antony and Cleopatra (Washington: Folger Books, 1984), 58.

7. The personae of *Antony and Cleopatra* self-create in a largely public arena, though often playing to different audiences: to the characters assembled on stage around them, to the public opinion of Rome, to history (the "story"), and to the theatrical audience (Goldman, *Acting and Action in Shakespearean Tragedy,* 113).

(I.i.39–40). Those of us surrounding the stage are that world. Witnessing this event is, in some sense, *the* event of the play. Our detachment becomes here a form of being exactly "present" to the tragedy. *Antony and Cleopatra* establishes a paradigmatic action that leaves the audience, like the characters, unusually touched yet creative and participatory in their spectatorship.[8]

I

Though Enobarbus plays the obvious audience-figure to Antony and Cleopatra, Octavius Caesar makes the more subtle and preeminent one, because throughout he induces the playgoer's participation in making meaning. The audience's detachment from Octavius reveals his engagements, as his attempts to reduce Antony and Cleopatra to spectators in his drama render him ever more the audience to theirs. The spectacle of the lovers fascinates him, not only because as a good Roman empiricist he is hungry for facts, but also because their voluptuousness engages him.[9] Examining Caesar from the perspective of character theory, Barroll suggests that Octavius is more an enigma, an intellectual puzzle, than a fully realized "character" (195). Here Caesar recalls the spectatorial paradigm: The audience must understand him not independently but only in relation to Antony and Cleopatra. Octavius validates the audience's attraction to the tawdry and meretricious glamor, the glitziness, of starlike characters such as Antony and Cleopatra.[10] Yet spectators may feel only

8. William E. Gruber discusses the play's relationship between actor and audience in "The Actor in the Script: Affective Strategies in Shakespeare's *Antony and Cleopatra,*" *Comparative Drama* 19 (Spring 1985): 30–48. Gruber contends that Renaissance audiences were less inclined than modern ones to separate their responses to actors from their responses to character, experiencing, rather, "an awareness simultaneously of the character *and* of the actor's degree of impersonation or metamorphosis" (33), so that, for example, perceiving the transvestitism of the boy-actor playing Cleopatra expands the character.

9. One might argue that Octavius, who evinces a Puritan sensibility, is to Egypt what the Puritan polemicists were to the Elizabethan theater. J. Leeds Barroll discusses the Puritan as a version of the material man; see his *Artificial Persons: The Formation of Character in the Tragedies of Shakespeare* (Columbia: University of South Carolina Press, 1974), 129–65. Similarly, Thomas McFarland calls Octavius a Machiavel, a "man who treats the world as if it were real" (208), "Antony and Octavius," *Yale Review* 48 (1958): 204–28.

10. "For Antony and Cleopatra are most actor-like in that they exhibit a magnetism that is culturally suspect. Paramount among the vile things they make becoming to the audience are the particular vices of glamorous actors. Cheapness and self-indulgence, narcissism and whoredom, hover about all their gestures," Goldman, *Acting and Action in Shakespearean Tragedy,* 123.

limited engagement with him.[11] He is too cold and prosaic, seldom emotionally at risk. Though Octavius is an audience-figure, the playgoer responds to him distrustfully, a paradox suggestive for the play. Spectatorial disengagement makes Octavius's critique of Antony and Cleopatra emotionally suspect; we evaluate his watching.

As audience to Antony and Cleopatra, Caesar progresses from presumed detachment to unwished empathy. He would dominate the two, yet his conquest embroils him more and more as their respondent. Indeed, Octavius becomes most alive when most like Antony. Similarly, Octavius enters most conspicuously into the dramatic action during his late interview with Cleopatra— where he plays Antony's part. Yet while he would make her a puppet in his triumph, he becomes a figure in hers, even as Egyptian paradox later touches his language.[12] Caesar's increasingly engaged spectatorship, exactly for its limitations, forwards the audience's self-conscious participation. He responds with pity (Antony's fate touches him) and wonder (Cleopatra's wins his admiration), a classic tragic spectator. Yet Caesar pities only the Roman suicide reported to him, not Antony's more erotically fulfilled death. (Caesar, for all his messengers, spies, and lieutenants, is always a little ignorant.) Similarly, his coroner's inquest at Cleopatra's tomb diverges emotionally from the spectacle before him. Half the point of Caesar's appreciation resides in its falling short. The audience repays Octavius's limitations with a more active response to Cleopatra's monumental figure in death. While he tracks the external mystery of the asp, the audience validates her greater mystery—our fancy's piece against Caesar's nature—because his tribute insufficiently measures what we feel. Caesar's empiricism activates the audience's imagination. Detachment from Caesar, then, becomes a condition of that spectatorial creativity that marks tragedy: We contemplate this scene by seeing even more than Caesar indicates, and that is the real action of tragic "beholding."

Octavius's brand of spectatorship arrives in Philo and Demetrius, the two characters who launch the play (I.i.1–13). They stand for Caesar's sensibility and define the audience's response to it. Philo soldiers in Antony's army. Demetrius, however, need not be a soldier at all, and his surprise marks him as newly arrived from Rome: "I am full sorry / That he approves the common liar, who / Thus speaks of him at Rome" (59–61). Philo's addressing of the

---

11. For a discussion of how Caesar's portrayal (like that of other characters) directs audience sympathy toward Antony and Cleopatra, see Philip J. Traci, *The Love Play of Antony and Cleopatra: A Critical Study of Shakespeare's Play* (The Hague: Mouton, 1970), 40–44.

12. Ralph Alan Cohen has observed to me (August 1988) that Octavius's "O noble weakness!" (V.ii.344) provides his first use of paradox in the play, a figure associated with Egypt.

audience in the guise of addressing Demetrius works best if his partner looks like an outsider (as we are outsiders). Yet the two share a point of view. Demetrius might even be played as Octavius's agent (his first concern is for Caesar's pride [56]), as we will learn later that the emperor has informants everywhere, news coming to him hourly (I.iv.34–35). These two, like Octavius, are not only in a play but at a play. Philo stresses their spectatorship in a call to the audience as much as to Demetrius: "Look where they come! / Take but good note, and you shall see. . . . Behold and see." "Behold" has a special resonance, capturing the thrust of the several lines, for it suggests "contemplation with the eyes," the perception of an image in such a way that it renders an idea, a dualistic seeing and thinking that suggest the engagement and detachment of spectatorship. "Behold" occurs more in *Antony and Cleopatra* than in any other of the tragedies; Shakespeare commonly associates "behold" with theatrical spectatorship.[13] "Behold and see," then, is an invitation to focus one's senses self-consciously, specifically as we do in the theater. But Philo makes a too-obvious gambit to dominate the spectators' impressions in advance: "Confirm my judgment with your viewing." The audience will temporize with Philo's instructions, as they will shortly with Caesar's similar instructions to Lepidus. The first thirteen lines are too early in a play for an audience to adopt any single perspective, particularly one, so insistently urged, that attempts to steal from the audience its theatrical pleasure in hypothesizing 'character' out of acting.[14] The conversation, as opposed to the opening ones of *King Lear,* lacks the ebb and flow of human doubts and feelings; it is polemical. Besides, Philo's image of Antony equivocates unintentionally, as will Caesar's. Philo likens Antony's dotage to his warcraft, through an unacknowledged pun: "O'erflows" and "o'er . . . glow'd" (2–4). The captain's heart bursting the buckles on his breast represents simply the approved military version of o'erflowing the measure. The Roman sensibility balks (unwittingly) more at the vehicle of excess, "lust," than at excess itself. Philo's overinsistence will establish unconsciously the audience's distance from the Roman view.

That Philo and Demetrius later close the scene tempts us to consider them as a "frame" to the action of *Antony and Cleopatra* (as Octavius ultimately "frames" the lovers). Alone, Philo and Demetrius will speak downstage; upon

13. For a discussion of Shakespeare's use of "behold," see the Introduction, 18–20.

14. Philo instructs us "to bend and turn our attention from the performance of character in order to lend a more privileged view to Philo's moralized emblem of 'dotage.' . . . [He] sidesteps the challenge of 'theatrical perception' that *Antony and Cleopatra* requires of its theatrical audience: to learn to see 'character' as an effect of acting": W. B. Worthen, "The Weight of Antony: Staging 'Character' in *Antony and Cleopatra,*" *Studies in English Literature 1500–1900* 26 (Spring 1986): 297–98.

the entrance of Antony and Cleopatra and their train, they might withdraw to one side of the front (near the audience) or retire toward the rear, these choices emphasizing to a greater or a lesser degree such "framing." Yet Philo and Demetrius are not Hamlet at Claudius's court, and a star such as Mark Antony (or Richard Burbage) would hardly allow himself to be upstaged by these two figures in the landscape.[15] The stage image, then, is fascinating and instructive for the relationship, ultimately, between Caesar and the lovers: Philo and Demetrius first occupy the privileged *platea*, the "no man's land," close to the audience (though we resist complete emotional identification); Philo points toward the physically and psychologically more distanced procession entering, the stage logistics further privileging his "position." Yet Rome and Egypt reverse geographic places (perhaps crossing on Cleopatra's "love" [14], the changeling for Philo's "lust" [10]). The lovers move downstage in brilliant costumes, their train following in pageantlike display, the flourish echoing in our ears.[16] That displacement of carping Rome by the spectacle, vitality, and capaciousness of Egypt is the true emotional progress of *Antony and Cleopatra*.[17] The opening moments enact, in stage geography as well as in dialogue, the audience's shifting "distance" toward the action in the paradigm of spectatorship. At the end of the scene, Philo and Demetrius regain the stage, only to reveal how empty it now is.

The audience's detachment from Octavius will undercut the detachment he presumes toward Antony and Cleopatra. With Octavius's entrance (I.iv), the play's rhythms change from the intimate to the formal, from the suddenly poignant leave-taking between Antony and Cleopatra (I.iii) to the stately display of the "Man of Destiny" (Bradley, 290). As the audience shifts locations it shifts distance, its engagement with love struggling for expression yield to the middle remove of exposition. Likewise, Octavius's immediate burden is to establish his own objective "distance" toward Antony in the eyes of his auditor: "You may see, Lepidus, and henceforth know, / It is not Caesar's natural vice to hate / Our great competitor" (I.iv.1–3). Octavius's seeing and knowing repeat exactly the double action of Philo's "behold." Caesar speaks like a moralizing drama critic. He summarizes Antony's plotline ("From Alexandria / This is the news" [3–4]), and concludes with the proper moral

15. I borrow this metaphor from J. Leeds Barroll, *Shakespearean Tragedy*, 61.

16. The stage direction reads, "*Flourish. Enter* Antony, Cleopatra, *her* Ladies, *the* Train, *with enuchs fanning her*" (at 10a).

17. The entrance of Antony and Cleopatra obviously calls for actorly or directorial choice: Antony can veer toward the noble or the libertine. It would take an extreme, even parodic, production, however, to validate Philo's "dotage," "gipsy's lust," and "strumpet's fool."

pill: Antony is "th' abstract of all faults / That all men follow" (9–10).[18] Yet this haughty judgment sounds slightly in excess of the facts (as Lepidus's demurral confirms), an early hint about Octavius: He appropriates a sententiousness that he has hardly earned. With the messenger's report (36–40) of the "discontents" who flock to Pompey (suggesting that Caesar is not universally beloved), Caesar solemnizes on the "vagabond" affections of the "common body" (44–47). If the Caesar-actor speaks these lines downstage to the spectators, directing the image into the audience as a subtle insult, Caesar's condescension toward them will further their distrust of him.[19]

Octavius stands for the third part of a triangle. The regal trains of Lepidus and Caesar parallel Antony and Cleopatra's entrance; the letter in Caesar's hand recalls the spurned messengers of the previous Egyptian scenes. Such spectacle invites the audience to behold Octavius positioned as Antony's alternative, the abandoned lover (Antony, he complains, "hardly . . . Vouchsaf'd to think he had partners" [7–8]).[20] Caesar's speeches intend to deny his emotional interest in Antony's voluptuousness, an invitation to the actor to present the character through the tension of self-deception. Octavius here and throughout the play expresses—as does "competitor" glossed as "partner" (3)—a vacillating love-hate for Antony. His language, which seldom rises to eloquence in the tragedy, becomes most charged and alive in talking of Antony: "[H]e fishes, drinks, and wastes / The lamps of night in revel" (4–5); "to tumble in the bed of Ptolomy, / To give a kingdom for a mirth, to sit / And keep the turn of tippling with a slave" (17–19). In the charged figure of transvestism, Antony's dotage disturbs Octavius: "is not more manlike / Than Cleopatra; nor the queen of Ptolomy / More womanly than he" (5–7). Sexual taboos rouse his attention, as does promiscuity: the bed of Ptolomy, the queen of Ptolomy. A knowing audience might register the transvestite reference with detachment, because it alludes to the theatrical event (for the Antony-actor and the Cleopatra-boy are more alike sexually than not). Octavius sounds like a Puritanical critic of acting.[21] Though the scene turns to the hostilities with

18. Cf. Hamlet's description of the players as "the abstract and brief chronicles of the time" (*Hamlet,* II.ii.524–25). The *Riverside* edition of *Antony and Cleopatra* reads "abstract" in place of the Folio's "abstracts."

19. This reading imagines the Caesar-actor choosing to play directly to the audience. Crowd-haters in Shakespeare's tragedies (Coriolanus, for example) often bear an uneasy relationship to the playgoer, a relationship that may justify blocking to underscore the dissonance. Caesar's lines are the kind that can also momentarily divide audience response, as some members of the audience might identify with the general populace and others with an aristocratic view of it.

20. This impression will be emphasized to the degree that Lepidus appears effete.

21. For one example, see John Rainolds, *The Overthrow of Stage-plays* (1599; repr. New

Pompey, the sexual undertones still call out: Menecrates and Menas "ear and wound" the sea with their "keels," making "hot inroads" in Italy.[22] Rather like fainting maidens, "the borders maritime / Lack blood to think on't, and flush youth revolt" (50–52). Finally Caesar, borrowing Antony's phrase for his relationship with Cleopatra ("such a twain" [I.i.38]), along with the lovers' presentational motif, wraps the scene in the vision of displacing his rival, "'Tis time we twain / Did show ourselves i' th' field" (73–74).

The winking allure of prodigal sexuality stands out exactly because Caesar's scene has so little other drama. Shakespeare chooses not to exploit the potential conflict in Octavius's relationship with Lepidus. Rather, theatrical interest and tension focus on Antony (the perils of his absence, his voluptuous riot, his heroism before culinary deprivations) and cumulatively on Octavius's emotional ambivalence toward him. The spectator's dramatic engagement is largely with Caesar's subtextual absorption over the figure absent. In some different scene, Caesar's apostrophe to Antony ("Antony, / Leave thy lascivious wassails" [55–71]) might disrupt stage illusion through its direction away from the characters present. Here the apostrophe fulfills the scene by confirming Octavius's great beholding of Antony and demoting any other scenic action. Indeed, the apostrophe is melodramatic, strange, and slightly parodic. Caesar condemns Antony's "lascivious wassails" in this speech, but approves his eating of "strange flesh" and drinking "The stale of horses" (62, 67). He works up an emotional outburst with his parenthesis, "(It wounds thine honor that I speak it now)" (69), and his address draws a tragic response from Lepidus: "'Tis pity of him" (71). Octavius betrays a love of extreme deprivation every bit the counterpart of Antony's extreme indulgence. Paradigmatically spectatorial, Octavius becomes interesting himself only in the eddies and ripples of the exotic rivers the lovers fish.

Indeed, for much of *Antony and Cleopatra,* Octavius drives the action but does not unfold in it. He stands for divine ambition puffed, but he says little, his dramatic distance from the audience echoing his coldness and detachment

---

York: Johnson Reprint, 1972). Rainolds, a great Puritan scholar, divine, and Oxfordian college president (some considered him the most learned man of his day), took as one of his main attacks against the stage the shamefulness of men dressing as women. Rainolds's treatise grew out of his refusal, July 1592, to attend a play by his colleague William Gager. *The Overthrow of Stage-plays* attracted enough interest to be reprinted in 1600, perhaps partly because the unwilling spectator Rainolds commanded, like Octavius, a position of historical and institutional authority.

22. "Ear" has a rich resonance in the play. Cleopatra uses it suggestively in the next scene: "Ram thou thy fruitful tidings in mine ears" (II.v.25). The word contributes to a running parallel between lovemaking and agriculture, as Enobarbus reports of Cleopatra, "She made great Caesar lay his sword to bed; / He ploughed her, and she cropp'd" (II.ii.227–28).

within the narrative. In the "concord" scene (II.ii) mediated by Lepidus, Caesar is Antony's straight man, and his accusations occasion only Antony's display of glibness, self-extenuation, and "honor." One moment of emotional individualization glimmers in his offended pride at Antony's treatment of his messenger (his proxy audience): "I wrote to you, / When rioting in Alexandria you / Did pocket up my letters; and with taunts / Did gibe my missive out of audience" (II.ii.71–74). Caesar expresses himself feelingly here, for his accusation thwarts the new tone of levity just introduced by Antony and Enobarbus over the unruliness of women.[23] At Agrippa's mention of Octavia, he manages a quip about Cleopatra's hot-bloodedness but then hangs back to study "how Antony is touch'd" (139). The quickly consummated wedding deal keeps Caesar still Antony's suitor.[24] Likewise, Octavius speaks few lines in the truce scene with Pompey (II.vi) and barely opens his mouth at the Roman drinking bout (II.vii), where he delivers only some fourteen of the 135 lines in the scene, mostly wishing he were gone. Octavius, cryptic and banal, supplies limited external dramatic interest.[25]

Into the vacuum of Caesar tumbles his relationship with Octavia; it stands out, because nothing stands out against it. Octavia's rebuff helps precipitate war in Plutarch, but in *Antony and Cleopatra* she functions as a well-wishing bystander, essentially a victim, to a mighty opposition already in motion. After Caesar peremptorily destroys Lepidus, Shakespeare shows us parallel scenes (III.iv and III.vi) of Antony and Caesar rehearsing separately their grievances toward the other, with Octavia entering each scene only after the fact, much in the way she comes after the fact as a "cause." Caesar, who has helped trap his half-sister, cherishes her as a bird in the cage. Shakespeare stresses, following Plutarch, Octavius's unusual fondness for Octavia: "A sister I bequeath you, / whom no brother / Did ever love so dearly" (II.ii.149–50). When the triumvirs disband, "Octavius weeps / To part from Rome; Caesar is sad" (III.ii.3–5), warning Antony, "You take from me a great part of myself; / Use me well in't"

23. For a discussion of the joke and Caesar's response, see J. Leeds Barroll, *Shakespearean Tragedy*, 198–99. Is Octavius behaving like an unruly woman?

24. Carol Thomas Neely suggests a homoeroticism in the marriage bargain—perhaps particularly revealing of its proposer, Caesar: "In Octavia's absence the two men enact an Elizabethan betrothal ceremony; parodying the customary form for spousals, they take hands, deny 'impediment,' and vow love and fidelity to each other," *Broken Nuptials in Shakespeare's Plays* (New Haven: Yale University Press, 1985), 143; as Caesar says, "Let her live / To join our kingdoms and our hearts, and never / Fly off our loves again" (150–52).

25. Worthen observes that "both Caesar and Octavia are so 'holy, cold, and still' . . . that actors may well be challenged to characterize these roles in enough detail to be credible," "The Weight of Antony: Staging 'Character' in *Antony and Cleopatra*," 300. The best Octavius I have seen projected a great physical tenseness into the role.

(24–25). These are strange words: Often in Shakespeare "part" carries genital connotations, furthered here by Caesar's "use" and "in't." The generally emotionless Caesar displays a suspiciously intense affection toward Octavia,[26] which Shakespeare showcases for the audience: The two even walk upstage so that Octavia might whisper mysteriously in his ear, at which Caesar nearly weeps, the half-siblings becoming for a moment a distanced spectacle within the play for others to muse over. The playgoer's overarching detachment toward Octavius invites curiosity for his singular emotional displays.

At such a spectatorial distance, Caesar's imagery reduces Octavia to object, possession, and "part": She is a "piece of virtue," the "cement" between building stones, who ought not become a battering "ram" to their love (III.ii.28–31). Later, juxtaposing his disgust for Antony and Cleopatra's ostentations in the public "market-place" (III.vi.3), Caesar criticizes Octavia's entering Rome unpompously: "But you are come / A market-maid to Rome, and have prevented / The ostentation of our love, which left unshown, / Is often left unlov'd" (50–53).[27] Octavius's apparently contradictory attacks disengage the audience and suggest that his anger at Antony and Cleopatra is in part jealousy and his annoyance at Octavia a further jealous reflex to the lover's display. Spectatorial detachment toward Caesar calls into doubt his intentions in trying to convince Octavia that she is the most betrayed of women: "You are abus'd / Beyond the mark of thought" (86–87). But the sister speaks little along that line other than "Is it so, sir?" (96), and is much more concerned about her divided love in the war brewing: "Ay me, most wretched, / That have my heart parted betwixt two friends / That does afflict each other!" (76–78). For these feelings Caesar has no ears, but rather manipulates her emotion to his own ends. He likes Octavia weak: "Pray you / Be ever known to patience. My dear'st sister!" (97–98). To the modern audience in particular, Octavius might appear less than attractive here. Nor has the play engaged us with him in a way that will bury this behavior under our goodwill; rather the opposite. In his voyeurism toward Antony and Cleopatra and his overbearing manipulation of his beloved half-sister, Octavius shows emotional frustration, even the hint of sexual sublimation. Our closeness to Antony and Cleopatra converts their gyves to graces; our remove from Octavius magnifies his faults and oddities. We see Antony's blemishes against the scenery of a vast character: "the spots

---

26. Irene G. Dash sees the possibility of "an incestuous bond between brother and sister," *Wooing, Wedding, and Power: Women in Shakespeare's Plays* (New York: Columbia University Press, 1981), 226.

27. The association of Antony and Cleopatra's "market-place" image with Octavia's "market-maid" likens her to the spectators at their enthronement.

of heaven, / More fiery by night's blackness" (I.iv.12–13). Not so with Octavius, whose singular acts of emotion, lacking context, invite suspicion. Theatrical distance creates meaning.

After Actium, Caesar continues to stand as audience to Antony and Cleopatra, but his role splits between the two: "For Antony, / I have no ears to his request. The Queen / Of audience nor desire shall fail" (III.xii.19–21). Caesar's defining obsession with Antony has not stopped; rather he has apotheosized Antony into the legend of Antony. Caesar instructs Thidias: "Observe how Antony becomes his flaw, / And what thou think'st his very action speaks / In every power that moves" (34–36). Here continues Octavius's dispassionate, Roman absorption in material facts. "[B]ecomes his flaw" suggests, ambiguously, images of Antony turning into his flawed fortune, or wearing his flawed fortune, or his fortune wearing him. As a spectator, Caesar allows Antony a complex relationship between personality and role. Caesar's further request to observe the eloquence of all Antony's motions and actions invites "beholding" Antony as a great actor.[28] Octavius becomes, if anything, a more passive and empathic audience to Antony here than before, capable now, with Antony's essential defeat, of being moved by him as by a figure on a stage. But if Caesar will study Antony, he will play with Cleopatra. "From Antony win Cleopatra" (27), he commands, suggesting a subtextual desire to unseat his great competitor even to the heart of loss. The closing action of the play concerns his efforts to deceive her and hers to elude him, his hypocrisy against her intuition. "[T]ry thy eloquence" (26), he says to Thidias, by which he means, "Try thy cunning" (31). Cleopatra will be the test for his bias against women: "Women are not / In their best fortunes strong, but want will perjure / The ne'er-touch'd vestal" (29–31).

Surprisingly, the victor will display a more winning humanity as he comes to resemble the vanquished. Caesar steps into the fourth act, as with the first, in his essential stage emblem: followers around, letter in hand, reacting to an absent Antony, his retainers an audience echoing his spectatorship. Antony has turned against Caesar the very words, "boy," "chides" (IV.i.1), by which Caesar had dismissed him in the beginning (I.iv.30–31). The language links the two even as their great competition speeds the destruction of one. Here, too,

28. W. B. Worthen notes how *Antony and Cleopatra* repeatedly focuses on its tension between 'character' and acting, the monumental Antony narrated by the figures around him and the difficulty of acting to rise to those conceptions, "The Weight of Antony: Staging 'Character' in *Antony and Cleopatra*," 295–308. In a remark apropos to Caesar's "becomes his flaw," Worthen states, "Antony alerts us to the more difficult kind of seeing that the theater entails, for he requires us to take good note of the relationship between theatrical 'becoming' and the 'great property' of character" (298).

Caesar, against his nature, calls for the army to "waste" some of its stores in "feast"—a gesture drawing him grudgingly toward Antony. Decretas's news of Antony's death (V.i) pulls the two triumvirs closest in kinship, with Caesar moved to his utmost in his spectatorship of Antony. So that Caesar might "behold" Antony's death, Decretas comes with a symbol, Antony's bloody sword, as well as words, the sword suggesting Antony's soldiership and his sexuality both. Decretas enters with an air of expectation, and ritualistically delays for a moment, heightening the tension theatrically. Caesar must twice ask Decretas's import. After "I say, O Caesar, Antony is dead" (13), the stage action might pause in silence, cuing Octavius's response: "The breaking of so great a thing should make / A greater crack" (14-15). Caesar feels Antony's death from his habitual sense of pageantry and spectacular effect,[29] like the theatrics of the fall of mightiest Julius: "The round world / Should have shook lions into civil streets, / And citizens to their dens" (15-17).[30] Caesar's choric retainers look "sad" (26); his own eyes wash with tears. As Agrippa and Maecenas vary Caesar's "contemplation" with sententious wisdom, Caesar, standing in the center, becomes the emblematic still life of spectatorial grief, the human nature up to which the dramatic mirror has been successfully held: "Caesar is touch'd" (33); "When such a spacious mirror's set before him, / He needs must see himself" (34-35). Indeed, the very word, "touch'd," links him with Antony (II.ii.139). On the stage, Octavius functions at this moment as an inset, dramatically distanced from the playgoer, a formalized figure contemplating with his (tearful) eyes, while we contemplate him with ours. To reduce this man of motion to utter stasis both signifies luminously and fulfills as an action Octavius's spectatorship of Antony: Octavius recognizes *himself* most clearly and passionately as audience to Antony, his emotional engagement (pity) bringing the reflex of detached self-awareness (fear).

Caesar attempts in his next speech to reverse the model, to make Antony a figure in Caesar's own "story" (as he will also with Cleopatra), while his dramatic position continues to render him a figure in Antony's. That is the paradox our own detachment reveals. Octavius once more pays Antony the tribute of apostrophe, just as he had done in act I. (If Caesar steps downstage on "I have followed thee to this," extracting himself slightly from his soldiers,

29. Earlier Caesar had chided Octavia for not entering Rome ostentatiously, hinting that his love for display activated best his love for her.

30. In *Julius Caesar*, Casca says before the murder: "Are not you mov'd, when all the sway of earth / Shakes like a thing unfirm? . . . Against the Capitol I met a lion, / Who gaz'd upon me, and went surly by" (I.iii.3-21).

he can move into the connotatively open *platea,* close to the audience, evoking a separate location that he now shares metaphorically with the absent Antony.) Octavius's praise of Antony echoes with "I," "me," "my," and "mine": "That thou, my brother, my competitor . . . my mate in empire . . . The arm of mine own body, and the heart / Where mine his thoughts did kindle" (43–47). That love-song would manipulate the audiences onstage and off; it seeks to appropriate Antony's glory, acts, and nobility to Caesar's cause.[31] If "competitor" and "mate" recall language from Caesar's first apostrophe ("competitor," "twain"), they hint further at the envy and desire that render him Antony's respondent. Shakespeare undercuts Caesar's "story" in yet another way, for Decretas's news is essentially a lie (though true in fact). Antony was not dead when Decretas "robb'd his wound" (25). Caesar, the great hypocrite and manipulator, is played upon, however slightly, by an insignificant soldier. Caesar suffers similar undiscovered trickery when his aide Dolabella betrays his intentions to Cleopatra, the Emperor's forever-ignorance later recalled by his play-closing trust, "Come, Dolabella, see / High order in this great solemnity" (V.ii.365–66). Such dramatic ploys continue to distance the audience from Octavius, because we know more than does he, lending a backwash of truth to Cleopatra's "ass unpolicied" (V.ii.307–8).

At Cleopatra's monument Caesar may be more active and engaged, more "in" the play, than anywhere else. Yet Cleopatra steals the scene from him, renders his patronizing of women ridiculous, and transforms his flattery into spectatorship before a theatrical art higher than his own. The episode begins with a double upstaging: Caesar's ignorance ("Which is the Queen of Egypt?" [V.ii.112]), possibly pretended, superseded by hers (so that Dolabella must prompt her, "It is the Emperor, madam" [113]). Caesar must sue her to rise. She turns his cynical assumptions of feminine weakness to her own advantage: "but do confess I have / Been laden with like frailties which before / Have often sham'd our sex" (122–24). When Caesar would leave, she holds his attention with virtuosic flattery—"And may, through all the world . . . Your scutcheons and your signs of conquest, shall / Hang in what place you please" (134–36)—and with what else this materialist loves: lists, letters, reports ("This is the brief: of money, plate, and jewels" [138]). Seleucus's embarrassing of Cleopatra is really her triumph. While the interlude raises doubts about Cleopatra's intentions, dramatically she thoroughly upstages Caesar. The narra-

---

31. I am indebted to Ralph Alan Cohen for his comments (July 1988) on Caesar's appropriation of Antony's story. Caesar's easy breaking of his formal and newly begun address to his followers (51) suggests that he has moved beyond sincerity to manipulation.

tive irresolution admits subtextual closure. Deliberately or not, Cleopatra's playlet with her treasurer reverses Caesar's playlet with her, and translates Caesar into a spectator and supporting actor in her dramatics (he acts to restrain her, perhaps even physically, with "Good Queen, let us entreat you" [158]). Indeed, Cleopatra condemns Caesar to his now-familiar role: "See, Caesar! O, behold, / How pomp is followed!" (150). Places reverse: He "entreats" her; she instructs him: "and when we fall / We answer others' merits in our name, / Are therefore to be pitied" (177–79). Caesar exits the scene believing that he has reduced Cleopatra to the dependency that he prefers in women: "Our care and pity is so much upon you" (188). Cleopatra takes over the stage, her spectatorship by intuition exposing his false acting: "He words me, girls, he words me" (191).

Although we hear of Caesar as a man of swift action, we see him instead as largely static: witnessing, listening, reacting. His dramatic "superobjective" is to rewrite the "story" of empire, so that Antony and Cleopatra are scutcheons in his gallery. He thinks he succeeds. Yet the dramatic distance Shakespeare establishes between Caesar and the audience reilluminates his actions as deeper and deeper surrender to his essential spectatorship. Caesar's relationship to the audience, then, differs from his role within the play; there he dominates Antony, but to the spectator he pays the tribute of constantly watching, abhoring, desiring, envying—Antony's audience. Rather than Cleopatra his scutcheon, he is hers. Bradley calls Octavius the "Man of Destiny." Caesar illustrates, if anything—just as Shakespearean tragedy argues—that fate and necessity in themselves are often not very interesting to watch. Our distance from Caesar steadily exposes the jealousy and sublimated desire in his haughtiness. As our theatrical distance defines Caesar by his relationship to the lovers, so too does he become most engaging not in his individualism but in his resemblances to Antony. Finally, in Cleopatra's suicide-tableau Caesar recognizes her strong toil of grace and busies himself with her manner of death. We require this inquest, for the audience will not fully acknowledge the greatness of her death until its external details are revealed to him. So Octavius stands for the spectator's recognition, but we also know far more than does he, and we appreciate Cleopatra's haunting monumental image beyond his words. The playgoers' uneasy relationship with Octavius—both accepting and suspecting him as audience—rebounds in our active re-creation of what he misses. Caesar invites the audience's consciousness of the action of beholding, yet deeply involves them with it, too.

II

Often considered the play's detached, "choric commentator,"[32] Enobarbus's spectatorship might rather be viewed as "dialogic" and processual. As audience, Enobarbus reverses the career of Octavius. The captain moves from carnivalesque spectator-participant to isolated, Romanized observer—from engagement to (attempted) detachment. That shift invites the audience to distance itself from Enobarbus. His detachment from Antony, commencing with the defeat at Actium (III.x), marks his change of "voice" in the tragedy and his corresponding dissolution. From representing a point of view "dialogic" in the Bakhtinian sense—that is, a voice that simultaneously parodies and yet honors the thing parodied[33]—Enobarbus changes into a unilingual, sententious, and lonely voice. To change voices is to change places. The more fixed in attitude he becomes, the less relevant and reliable for the audience Enobarbus becomes, too. He leaves Antony because he abhors his capricious generalship and recoils from the absorption of martial affairs into Egyptian emotionalism and subjectivism. But Enobarbus's disengagement from Antony provokes a parallel response toward him in the theater audience. We begin much engaged with Enobarbus because he stands metaphorically (and often physically) close to the audience. Yet later, as a detached critic, Enobarbus turns finally pathetic—pathos entailing the distanced superiority of the spectator. In Enobarbus, Shakespeare presents theatergoers with a model of loss of faith—preempting any need of the audience to invent the attitude for itself—and makes faithlessness self-abhorrent. Enobarbus, that is, demolishes the "choric" position. In one sense, Enobarbus's

32. Maurice Charney, *Shakespeare's Roman Plays: The Function of Imagery in Drama* (Cambridge: Harvard University Press, 1961), 117. Charney sees in Enobarbus an essential detachment: "Enobarbus is always the Roman in Egypt, fascinated, awed, enjoying, but never drawn from his basically Roman morality" (117). See also M. W. MacCallum's discussion of Enobarbus (349-59) in *Shakespeare's Roman Plays and Their Background* (London: Macmillan, 1967): "But with all his enthusiasm for Antony, [Enobarbus] is from the first critical of what he considers his weaknesses and mistakes, just as with all his enthusiasm for Cleopatra he has a keen eye for her affectations and interferences" (355).

33. Writing on *Eugene Onegin,* Mikhail Bakhtin defines the "zone of dialogic contact": "The author sees the limitations and insufficiency of the Oneginesque language and world view. . . . [H]e sees its absurd, atomized and artificial face. . . . [A]t the same time however the author can express some of his most basic ideas and observations only with the help of this 'language.' . . . The image of another's language and outlook on the world, simultaneously represented *and* representing. . . . They both illuminate the world and are themselves illuminated," in *The Dialogic Imagination: Four Essays by M. M. Bakhtin,* ed. Michael Holquist, trans. Caryl Emerson and Michael Holquist (Austin: University of Texas Press, 1981), 45.

death from thought is the parodic reduction of "commentary" as a response to this play.

Early, Enobarbus helps draw Antony to our affections. Essentially a carnivalesque figure (a mask, a voice[34]) characterized by drinking, eating, soldiership, and carnality—those projections of the physical body into its world—Enobarbus confirms Antony's heroism yet brings to it what Bakhtin might style the responses of folk life, of the marketplace. As a parodic figure, Enobarbus actually engages the audience with Antony, strengthens its identification. Enobarbus enters initially as a figure in the background supervising preparations for toasting healths and feasting (I.ii.13), his first self's role. His is not the Roman domain, governed by Octavius's goddess, Fortune, but the spontaneous domain of play: "Mine, and most of our fortunes to-night, shall be—drunk to bed" (46).

For the audience, Antony's emotional ebb and flow over whether to leave Egypt (I.ii) add up to a perfect stalemate. Enobarbus's satire, rather than clarifying perspectives as we might expect, will honor the ambivalence. Roman thought-struck, Antony converses (now) bluntly with messengers: "Speak to me home" (105). But Antony forestalls that speech himself by predicting the gossip of "the general tongue" and then erratically dismissing the messenger—unheard. His own engagement and detachment toward Fulvia reveal his torn consciousness: "There's a great spirit gone! Thus did I desire it" (122). Finally, Antony interrupts his ruminations on Fulvia with an apparent non sequitur, "I must from this enchanting queen break off" (128), and shouts for Enobarbus. On the level of psychology, that determination to "break off" looks like a decision. But, dramatically, the entrance of Enobarbus confirms the stalemate by replaying it in a comic key. Enobarbus does not function simply as a "chorus" or "commentator," because he arrives with a dramatic intention in the scene: to stay in Egypt. Antony and Enobarbus, as straight man and jokester, divide between them the yea and nay of action. Because the playgoers recognize that Enobarbus represents the clown's satiric viewpoint, they demand no exposition, no warming up of the character to his context: "*Antony*: I must with haste from hence. / *Enobarbus*: Why then we kill all our women" (132-33). Enobarbus parodies Cleopatra's "dying" as both melodramatic acting and sexual wantonness; he parodies her bodily responses as hemispheric storms and tempests; he parodies religion in the "consolation" to Fulvia's death; and he parodies Egypt's "business of state" as sex. The Rabelaisian body overruns the world. Subjects that are official, high, and serious Enobarbus

---

34. For a discussion of Enobarbus as a figure in the landscape, an "animated viewpoint," rather than a fully rounded character, see J. Leeds Barroll, *Shakespearean Tragedy,* 232-37.

inverts.[35] Particularly, Enobarbus lampoons the principals' various responses to adversities: their passions, moralisms, consolations. As respondent, Enobarbus is the satirist of response itself, of commentary. Yet Enobarbus's parody pays tribute to Cleopatra, engages the audience with her even as it exposes her (his misogyny simultaneously exposes him). His effect is not that of scorn, for Cleopatra emerges as virtuosic, grand, and winningly vulnerable—a great actress. Enobarbus's spectatorship does not so much comment upon Cleopatra as create her. He "presents" Cleopatra, caricatures her into a set of external gestures; yet simultaneously he "represents" her, invites the spectator to feel her celebratory larger-than-lifeness, such that our action of identifying becomes inseparably an action of identifying-with. Enobarbus praises Cleopatra in a manner available only through humor. Our laughter applauds.

As carnivalesque spectator, Enobarbus repeatedly inherits other characters' scenes. His presence in the position of "commentator," though not quite the "chorus" generally proposed, illustrates the paradigm of spectatorship infiltrating the action of the play. Though Enobarbus offers ironic contrasts and judgments, he will not exactly move the spectator to somber, cautionary reflection on events past or future (and his predictions are not always right). Rather, Enobarbus often expands the audience's engagement in the moment, the immediate evolving present. Though he surely "interprets" or "comments" upon preceding action, his prognostications never freeze into abstract spectatorial values. To the extent that it remains dialogic, his commentary remains also open-ended, partial, and contingent. Enobarbus's remark to Lepidus defines his auditorial position: "Every time / Serves for the matter that is born in't" (II.ii.9–10). He respects not propriety but spontaneity, and in that sense, Enobarbus stands close to the unhistoricized perspective of the audience. A leveling figure like a clown, Enobarbus has the privileges of the place; he is equally familiar with Egyptian ladies, triumvirs, pretenders, soldiers, or pirates. While Octavius is formal, cold, and removed, Enobarbus stands for accessibility and engagement.

Janet Adelman calls Enobarbus "that inveterate judge of others,"[36] but through the first part of the play, he participates in the actions he judges—a distinction with consequences. (After Actium, he distances himself—also with consequences.) In the theatrical "concord" scene (II.ii), when Maecenas

---

35. Enobarbus represents the carnivalesque mask as Bakhtin describes it. See, for example, "From the Prehistory of Novelistic Discourse," especially 167–206, in *The Dialogic Imagination;* and Mikhail Bakhtin, *Rabelais and His World,* trans. Helene Iswolsky (Bloomington: Indiana University Press, 1984).

36. *The Common Liar,* 25.

urges Antony and Caesar to forget their grievances, Lepidus utters his auditorial applause, "Worthily spoken, Maecenas" (102), and Enobarbus adds his sarcastic consolation that the two may return their loves back again after they finish with Pompey (103–5). Enobarbus's judgments here participate in the drama, his comment prompting both Caesar's wish for a hoop to hold him and Antony staunch and Agrippa's suggestion of marriage. As Adelman observes, the concord scene is a "formal spectacle," with major characters functioning as actors and minor characters as "their interpretive audience," a typical scenic pattern in the play (31) that underscores the paradigm of spectatorship. In that scene, Lepidus and Enobarbus also constitute a prologue shaping audience expectation, the first eager to avoid explosion, the latter ripe for it. When his fellow triumvirs arrive, Lepidus stage-manages the formally arrayed meeting, urging, in Hamlet-like advice to the players, soft and modulated voices (19–25). Antony and Caesar parlay ceremoniously, playing to their audiences: "Tis spoken well" (25), says Antony; they out-courtesy each other in sitting; Caesar fears being "laugh'd at" (30). Here, as elsewhere, Enobarbus, Maecenas, Agrippa, and others assume the image and action of audience, distancing the theatrical spectator from the inset.

Critics of *Antony and Cleopatra* frequently discuss such "framing" of a scene, and Adelman finds the device particularly rife in *Antony and Cleopatra*,[37] not surprising in a play where spectatorship becomes action. In the schematics of "framing," secondary characters at the beginning of a scene introduce an action and secondary characters left onstage "comment" upon what has just passed—the choric function. By that line of reasoning, "commentary" disengages the spectators emotionally from the principals and substitutes the chorus's evaluations. I would argue, however, that in *Antony and Cleopatra* such scenes do not detach the audience so much as "framing" conventionally suggests. Rather, they engage the audience in the ongoing, joyful ambivalence of spectatorship as participation. Here the observer resonates dialogically with the thing observed, making commentary creative and contingent—a creature of the moment. Certainly Enobarbus comments and predicts knowingly, as he insists that Antony will leave Octavia for Cleopatra (II.ii.233, II.vi.116–17), resulting in war (II.vi.126–30), just as Menas predicts that Pompey has ruined his chances (II.vii.81–84). But Enobarbus and his end-scene companions speak of cabbages as well as kings. Their talk expresses a structure and a voice that qualify "commentary" (just as

37. "This pattern appears with astonishing consistency throughout the play. . . . Either partial or complete framing of this sort occurs in no less than twelve scenes; significant elements of this process occur in many more scenes" (31); see *The Common Liar,* 30–34.

the Enobarbus-actor might become "moved" himself as he describes Cleopatra at Cydnus [II.ii.190–226]).

Enobarbus's exchange with Menas concluding the truce scene between Antony, Octavius, and Pompey (II.vi) displays his voice in such "framing" scenes during the first half of the play. Enobarbus's and Menas's subtextual mimicking of the generals prevents the audience from receiving them solely as choric commentators or cautionary "frames" (no would-be Philos and Demetriuses here). Instead of disengaged doomsaying, the audience hears the structural parody, rivalry, humor, and desire of the "commentators." Enobarbus and Menas lack the detachment that would ensure our parallel detachment. Their conversation unconsciously imitates their superiors, and the two function far more engagingly as carnivalesque participants than as juries. "You and I have known, sir" (83), greets Menas, echoing his boss Pompey's earlier words to Enobarbus, "I know thee now" (71). Enobarbus's "I will praise any man that will praise me" (88) likewise repeats his exchange of praise with Pompey (73–78). Enobarbus has "done well" (86) by land and Menas by water—just as the triumvirs outweigh Pompey at land and he them at sea. Menas's jest that Enobarbus has been a land thief echoes Pompey's charge against Antony that he has essentially stolen his father's house. They shake hands, as did Antony and Pompey, Pompey and Enobarbus. Menas's "All men's faces are true, whatsome'er their hands are" (97–98) touches Pompey's reply to Caesar, "Well, I know not / What counts harsh Fortune casts upon my face" (53–54). Menas's image of Pompey laughing away his fortune (104–5) harkens back to Caesar's "give a kingdom for a mirth" (I.iv.18). The two fighters finally turn to Octavia and Cleopatra, and Enobarbus repeats his predictions from the concord scene that Mark Antony "will to his Egyptian dish again. Then shall the sighs of Octavia blow the fire up in Caesar" (126–27). Menas invites Enobarbus aboard his galley for drinking, the same exiting image that Pompey uses with the triumvirs.

Enobarbus and Menas redeploy words, images, and actions of the earlier segment and from earlier scenes in a humorous key. They dramatize their rivalry as a comedy routine: First they praise each other for prowess at land and sea, then each claims that he deserves great praise, next they accuse each other of being land-thieves and water-thieves, and Enobarbus concludes, full-circle, by denying the praise of his "land service" (86–96). Their allusion to true faces (97) winks at their own false hands. "Commentary" about Antony, Octavius, and Pompey comes in the form of self-incriminating parody (Enobarbus and Menas hardly mention the preceding action) that obliterates the distinctions between high and low. Their criticism cannot be sorted from their enthusiasm.

Enobarbus and Menas certainly predict the consequences of erratic choices, but the audience engages not with doomsaying but with the carnivalesque parody, creative humor, and self-evident pleasure these two discover in the unpredictable moment, as they spin out commentary upon jest and jest upon commentary: "*Menas*: Pray you, is he not married to Cleopatra? *Enobarbus*: Caesar's sister is call'd Octavia" (108–9). They predict, in fact, exactly what they hope, for the two would rather fight than make peace (102–4). Enobarbus and Menas can hardly function chorically or dispassionately in this epilogue, for they bring their own intentions—what the exchange reveals comically—their wish for war.

The "framing" of Enobarbus and Menas reveals itself as engaged participation, spoken out of their own desires, predilections, and resemblances to those whom they discuss. Enobarbus's estimations may be true (that is one of their functions) but far more important, they are pleasurable. They arise out of his pleasure in Antony, his pleasure in rivalry, his pleasure in "land service," his pleasure in humor—and our pleasure in the two lieutenants' mimicry of their bosses. Enobarbus and Menas stand for spectatorship as a delighted, self-incriminating, re-creative action in the play. They are of the world they "interpret." We may have a sense, ultimately, not so much of "commentary" (something finished, decisive—alarmingly so) as of the same chaotic elements of this play-world reassembling into form after carnivalesque form. For Enobarbus, "beholding" becomes hilariously self-involving, just as his irony toward Cleopatra is always, too, a form of praise. In a different tone or key, Enobarbus's predictions might incite the spectatorial anxiety common to doomsaying and foreboding. But here their impact—their "truth"—emerges as much in their delight.

While the truce scene shows Enobarbus as epilogue, the departure scene between Caesar, Octavia, and Antony (III.ii) shows Enobarbus and Agrippa as prologue and running "commentators." The opening exchange between the two soldiers is surely sarcastic, summary, and predictive. Agrippa enters calling Caesar and Antony "brothers" (III.ii.1); Enobarbus encodes Pompey's fate, "They have dispatch'd with Pompey, he is gone" (2), and parodies Lepidus's future in his epicene vulnerability: "Lepidus, / . . . is troubled / With the green-sickness" (4–6). The two then engage in an extended series of satiric imitations of Lepidus's praise for Caesar and Antony. As an inset of mockery, the exchange distances the audience, "presenting" the lapdog essence of this Polonian triumvir for our contemplation. Such is one surface level of "commentary." But the exchange engages us on another, multivalent level that more readily justifies its length and its presence here (Lepidus himself is not important to our story). The exchange is a competition in which Enobarbus and Agrippa essay to outdo one another, each mimicking Lepidus's fulsome praise of the other's master, and mocking, too, Lepidus's attempt to balance hyperbole in one direction with hyperbole in another. While the interlude could be played as straight comedy, actors might also find a subtextual tension in this exchange; Enobarbus subtly accuses Caesar of being the more honored, and Agrippa counters that Antony and Caesar are admired equally. "Indeed he plied them both with excellent praises" (14), says Agrippa, perhaps wishing to end the "revue." But Enobarbus keeps at it: "he loves Caesar best, yet he loves Antony" (15); "But as for Caesar, / Kneel down, kneel down, and wonder" (18–19). Such a caricature of Caesar's self-glorying may strike too close to the bone, for Agrippa attempts more sharply and perhaps more irritably to close off the joke: "Both he loves" (19). Beneath the humor, insults brew: accusations of pomposity, hints of wounded honor. As lieutenants to Caesar and Antony, Agrippa and Enobarbus suggest the nascent discord under the concord that we are about to witness in the generals ("*Antony*: Make me not offended / in your distrust. *Caesar*: I have said" [33–34]). If Enobarbus and Agrippa reveal indirectly the egotism behind the competition for empire, must the spectator behold the emperors with a freshly wry sense of distance? Yes—and no, for the mockery between Enobarbus and Agrippa engages us with its pleasure and play. Hyperbolic praise, hyperbolic glory, and hyperbolic wonder at human presumption are as much fun for the audience as for the characters. Enobarbus and Agrippa participate in what they ridicule. The same self-incriminating joking repeats exactly when Enobarbus recoils, "Will Caesar weep?" (50). Agrippa humorously accuses Antony of weeping earlier, "When at Philippi he found Brutus slain" (56), and Enobarbus replies parodically, "I weep too" (59). As in previous scenes, Enobarbus's spectatorship engages the audience dialogically—seriously and mockingly at the same time.

When Enobarbus moves from parodist to critic—from dialogic to univocal, from embedded to exclusive—he detaches himself from Antony's "story" and from the audience's empathy as well. In this second panel of Enobarbus's narrative diptych, the audience experiences him more as seasoned and serious soldier than as festive comedian. He opposes Antony's decision to fight at sea (III.vii); afterwards, alone on stage, he reels, appalled, eyes "blasted," at Antony's flight at Actium. Whereas before Enobarbus has inherited scenes in conversation with another character, in his second action he will finish them alone in soliloquy. His isolation on stage parallels his withdrawal from Antony's world. Likewise he will speak directly to the audience, without a supporting dramatic context, with mere arguments vulnerable to our "judgment" and their own limitations. Enobarbus's detachment from Antony places him naked before the audience, so that our "beholding" of him weighs toward evaluation rather than empathy, as his does of Antony. Enobarbus's betrayal turns on the classic struggle of intellect against heart, detachment against engagement. "I'll yet follow / The wounded chance of Antony, though my reason / Sits in the wind against me" (III.x.34–36), he says after Actium. Likewise, he determines that Antony has made "his will / Lord of his reason" (III.xiii.3–4) and impugns all such postlapsarian judgment: "I see men's judgments are / A parcel of their fortunes, and things outward / Do draw the inward quality after them, / To suffer all alike" (31–34). An interesting judgment itself (how Roman and sententious Enobarbus has turned), with much truth for this play—Enobarbus included! Enobarbus's judgments against Antony, that is, work against him as well—as do most efforts to distinguish the world from oneself in *Antony and Cleopatra*. The spectatorial effect is of eavesdropping. The audience does not here join in participatory, self-aware, communal laughter, but witnesses a self-deception that distances Enobarbus from himself ("Mine honesty and I begin to square" [41][38]). Accumulatively Enobarbus's self-distancing will distance the audience from his criticisms, no matter their truth.

"Mock not, Enobarbus" (IV.vi.24), says the soldier reporting that Antony has sent his treasure after him with bounty overplus. Enobarbus has forfeited his right to "mock," and gained his isolation: "I am alone the villain of the earth, / And feel I am so most" (29–30). His final speeches will dwell upon the superior value of feeling to thought: "This blows my heart" (33); "but thought will do't, I feel" (35). Enobarbus feels himself a finished object in the "story" more than an evolving participant. In his last scene, alone, he calls upon night to be his "witness" (IV.ix.5, 7), his audience, and speaks of the "record" (8), "memory" (9), the "register" (21), and his own infamy (19). Here Enobarbus, who has served as "frame" and audience to so many scenes, is himself audited by the soldiers without his knowledge. He has forfeited, in his treachery to Antony, his dramatic position in the play, his privileged spectatorship. His death makes an object lesson of too much judgment and demonstrates that he cannot so easily withdraw his deeply engaged emotions from Antony as his "commentary" suggests. The knowledge that Enobarbus discovers and dies from is that the heart's truth, that domain of communal engagement and

---

38. In this speech Enobarbus starts out toward defection yet ends with renewed allegiance. In modern editions the whole speech is marked as an "aside," though not so in the Folio. One way to play the speech is to allow Cleopatra, who might be moving downstage from the exiting servant, to enter Enobarbus's voice range, so that her hearing him and his sympathy for her state might prompt the midline turn (43). Such a reading would merely support the interpretation that Enobarbus's interaction with others keeps his feelings and thoughts in balance, while his isolation warps the one by the other.

participatory humor, is deeper and more compelling by far than any Romanized judgments. His corruption as an audience to Antony and Cleopatra affirms the level of response at which to value them most truly. Both Octavius and Enobarbus, the one formal and detached, the other comedic and engaged, arrive at spectatorship as an irreducible form of conspiracy with the thing observed, so that they, even unconsciously, yield to its influence, take its part, enter its domain.

III

Distance surrenders to tribute in *Antony and Cleopatra*. Enobarbus's betrayal of Antony uncovers his greater love; Caesar's cold detachment only draws him into the precincts of Egypt. While these two figures stand for the action of spectatorship in the play, Antony and Cleopatra complete the pattern; in a formal sense, they are performers as well as audience.[39] As performers, they reciprocate the attention of the secondary characters and supernumeraries who constantly "behold" them, for a special dimension of the twain is that they incessantly "play to the audience." Except for some ten lines at the height of Antony's anguish, they are never onstage alone together. They perform, imitate their relationship always before others, "in the public eye," even "I' th' market-place" (III.vi.11, 3). Antony threatens, as publicist, to punish the world unless it recognize "[w]e stand up peerless" (I.i.40). "Playing to the audience" is the subtextual through-line of all that Antony and Cleopatra do. Their playing always manipulates, overtly and sometimes crudely. If they play only to a single character, they yet conceive that character as standing for a public that can confer reputation, renown, even nobleness. Just as Octavius loves reports, Antony and Cleopatra take pains to behave in a reportable manner. An audience represents "history," that cultural shaping which transforms a life into a "story." While the good opinion of a character-as-individual is not necessarily worth having, the good opinion of a character-as-audience is always worth having. Audiences have valorizing power: Their groupness valorizes the experi-

39. In modern theater, of course, spectatorship does not include the practice of verbal response or reply, as it does with Shakespeare's internal audiences in such plays as *Love's Labors Lost, A Midsummer Night's Dream,* or *Hamlet* or as it apparently sometimes did with Shakespeare's own spectators. Antony and Cleopatra reveal their spectatorship to each other mostly in *how* they respond, in the way their replies invoke spectatorial language and a theatrical model of action.

ence of the individual member; their creative participation in the play valorizes what they see; and their assent to the performance valorizes and stimulates the performer. Antony and Cleopatra in playing to the audience seek their own image in the eyes of their beholders, as both identification (we are such a mutual pair and such a twain) and estimation (we stand up peerless). Playing to the audience has a corollary: The approval it manipulates for is immediate, not a matter of winning abstract arguments but of affirming the present gesture. Thus playing to the audience is optimistic, even antideterministic, for it assumes the spectators susceptible, persuadable by thought and emotion well displayed—even when they see through the very act of persuasion.

The theatrical spectator will experience Antony and Cleopatra as "acting" their love. Love will look, as a histrionic style, "presentational": "The nobleness of life / Is to do thus" (I.i.36–37). Such presentational acting, such telling-about rather than being, will necessarily distance the spectator, by differentiating implicitly the character from the gesture. We become conscious of imitation as an action. Presentational acting even constitutes a form of spectatorship, because it implies a character's observation of himself or herself, a detachment in the moment of action. Imitation and presentational acting typify Antony and Cleopatra. Caesar's concern that Antony use Octavia well, for example, echoes what we know, that Antony can pretend. Cleopatra, of course, "becomes" everything; she is mutability itself. Cleopatra displays herself, moreover, as an accomplished and inveterate mimic (like Enobarbus). She imitates Octavius, she imitates Fulvia, she imitates Eros, she imitates Venus and Isis and Thetis, she mimics Antony out of countenance. This characterizing activity, we might add, bestows a brilliant gift on the boy-actor, for it allows him to be all the more convincing as Cleopatra, first in mimicking his own real gender, and second by defining her essence through the very virtuosic labor that he as an actor must undertake.[40]

As characters and actors bridge the distance between presenting and representing, the audience will find its detached purchase incorporating the

---

40. Goldman analyzes how the increasing challenge of the Cleopatra-role can win the audience by demonstrating the virtuosity of the boy-actor, who must move progressively "beyond the limits of his art," in Michael Goldman, *The Actor's Freedom: Toward a Theory of Drama* (New York: Viking, 1975), 141–45. See also Honigmann's discussion of the range and display of physical action which the Cleopatra-role invites, in E. A. J. Honigmann, *Shakespeare: Seven Tragedies: The Dramatist's Manipulation of Response* (London: Macmillan, 1976), 155–58. William E. Gruber takes exception to Goldman and others by arguing that the boy-actor's transvestism enters the audience's perception of Cleopatra, which "oscillates continually between various interdependent contradictions: person-role, male-female, self-other. . . . '[B]oying' Cleopatra becomes a formula through which masculinity is redefined or even reinvented," "The Actor in the Script: Affective Strategies in Shakespeare's *Antony and Cleopatra*," 42–43.

acceptance associated with engagement.[41] Spectators discover that qualities merge, that imitation is the play's only action, that we are capable of loving the showiness of the public marketplace, and that the thing imagined, at a high virtuosic level, is actually the thing itself. The audience's response to Antony and Cleopatra moves from bedazzlement, through puzzled concern (even distress), to a liberating sympathy that embraces realism and affectation alike. The mutual pair "charm" us with their manipulative self-dramatizing, act upon us, "impress" us. Yet in the second and third acts the audience moves away from Antony in particular: In Rome he looks smaller than in Egypt. (Cleopatra with the messenger marks time hilariously in creative self-deception.) But though their fortunes collapse before Caesar, though Antony makes shallow and stupid choices and Cleopatra's mutability invites disaster, our engagement with the lovers finally deepens. Earlier they "acted" upon us; now we take their part. We learn how willing we are to be moved by affectation. Our engagement grows even after Antony's posturings toward Thidias and his sentimentality before his servants; it grows as Antony distrusts Cleopatra's faith but never renounces his love; it grows with the access of inexplicable joy that these two discover. By the end, our engagement embraces the self-dramatizations of Antony and Cleopatra as much as their "representations." We accept mimesis as selfhood. In this deliquescent play, the acting of the stage players mirrors the imitation by the characters, mirrored further by the audience's self-conscious and imaginative engagement with actors and acted.

The first scene of *Antony and Cleopatra* pairs with the third to reveal the glory and the quicksand of the presentational style, even as the second scene will parody Egyptian preoccupations and the fourth scene will extend Roman concerns.[42] The opening fairly bludgeons the playgoer with the paradigm of spectatorship and playing to the audience: the prologue and epilogue of Philo and Demetrius, the pageantic entrance, the stage configuration of centered stars and ringed supernumeraries, the grandiose language, the successive one-upping, the imitative acting and the acting of imitations. Philo prompts us

---

41. On Shakespeare's uses of self-conscious theatricality in *Antony and Cleopatra,* Michael Shapiro writes, "Once the stage illusion expanded to include presentational elements, the audience's attitude towards theatricality was subtly altered, so that it could respond more favorably to Cleopatra's histrionic behavior. Shakespeare made his audience see Cleopatra as an actor playing an actress, and then encouraged them to judge the Queen's performance as they would the boy's, by aesthetic not moral criteria" (13), Michael Shapiro, "Boying Her Greatness: Shakespeare's Use of Coterie Drama in *Antony and Cleopatra,*" *Modern Language Review* 77 (January 1982): 1–15.

42. Granville-Barker captures the second scene memorably: "Next, we have a taste of the chattering, shiftless, sensual, credulous Court, with its trulls and wizards and effeminates," Harley Granville-Barker, *Prefaces to Shakespeare,* vol. 3, *Antony and Cleopatra, Coriolanus* (Princeton: Princeton University Press, 1946), 6.

(too much) to dislike Antony and Cleopatra; Philo and Demetrius stand, for the spectator, as the obstacle that Antony and Cleopatra's magic surmounts. The lovers are flamboyant; they quarrel; Cleopatra turns bitchy, Antony red-faced; they sweep away derisively. Yet even here, as we shall see, the essential spectatorial structure of the play emerges, and the audience, rather than alienated by their vanities, falls under their charm.

Antony and Cleopatra each play with a different style, a different actorly intention, and to different audiences. They argue the definition of love: "If it be love indeed," challenges Cleopatra, "tell me how much" (I.i.14). Cleopatra's utter immediacy and directness can be, for the audience, slightly breathtaking; nothing can embarrass her. She "angles" for Antony, in public, deftly and recklessly; he is her audience; we are her voyeurs. They enter engaged, already at play, and the audience hurries to catch up; Cleopatra would goad Antony into an outrageous quantification, a definition to hold against him, an advantage. Love in Egypt is physical, immediate. Antony, equally at play, dodges: "There's beggary in the love that can be reckon'd" (15). While Cleopatra's challenge is concrete, Antony's response is abstract, more "presentational" and contrived, harder for the audience to grasp (we must first calculate how reckoning, oxymoronically, can be beggarly). He shifts ground, will not answer her on her terms. Love is Romanesque, an empyrean empire: "Then must thou needs find out new heaven, new earth" (17). His audience is first Cleopatra, but secondarily history, the "story"; he speaks not only to elude Cleopatra's hook but also to say something quotable "for the record." The lovers use definitions merely as staging ground; the audience "learns," if anything, that they shall defy and subvert the "bourne" of definitions. These two overripe voluptuaries do not charm us in that we wish to be them; rather, they awe with the sheer egotism of their play (as on the stage gleeful egotism always charms), the outsized scale of self-dramatization.

Antony self-dramatizes experimentally. His response to the messenger, "Grates me, the sum" (18), takes him momentarily out of his part, revealing its artificiality by contrast. Cleopatra, on the other hand, mimics instinctively: She parodies the message: "Fulvia perchance is angry" (20); she boys Caesar's greatness: " 'Do this, or this; / Take in that kingdom, and enfranchise that; / Peform't, or else we damn thee' " (22–24). These moments allow the boy-actor (or actress) a choice of manners and voices, lending to the impersonations an air of spontaneity that will further engage the spectator. Cleopatra self-consciously pursues her own game, ignoring Antony's rising anger and then (evidence that she was not ignoring him) turning it to his disadvantage: "Where's Fulvia's process?—Caesar's, I would say—both? / . . . Thou blushest, Antony" (28–30).

Cleopatra thrills us with her recklessness. Her accusation that Antony turns shame-faced because "shrill-tongu'd Fulvia scolds" (32) finesses what she knows, that Antony reddens at *her* shrill-tongued scolding.[43] She cites Fulvia on her own behalf. Like Enobarbus, Cleopatra parodies within the game that she herself plays. She scores manipulatively with the Fulvia card, yet Cleopatra can also touch the audience; Antony's faithfulness to Fulvia represents the principle of fidelity she wants, but not the object.

Antony responds with flamboyance fanned: "Let Rome in Tiber melt" (33). "Here is my space" (34) likens Egypt to a stage (just as he now occupies a stage within the theatrical stage), and he completes the metaphor with one of the stagiest gestures in the play: "the nobleness of life / Is to do thus" (36–37). Most editors add a direction here, in which Antony kisses or embraces Cleopatra (although some other movement is possible). The gesture is so fraudulent that it coopts the spectator by mere cheek. Self-consciously dramatized, doing "thus" will characterize Antony. Later his highly theatricalized and botched suicide will repeat the first scene: "to do thus / I learnt of thee" (IV.xiv.102–3; cf. II.ii.26–27 and III.ii.63). Though Antony condemns Rome to liquefaction, he is contradictorily concerned for public opinion (which Rome epitomizes), binding the world to know the peerlessness of the two. Cleopatra deflates this version of the *miles gloriosus* with her accusation of transparent acting: "Excellent falsehood!" (40). She exposes the disingenuous self-dramatizing that the audience suspects, but only to turn the acting metaphor to her own advantage: "I'll seem the fool I am not. Antony / Will be himself" (42–43). He attempts to upstage her with "But stirr'd by Cleopatra" (43), loses his poise with "Fie, wrangling queen!" (48), and recovers theatrically with "Whom everything becomes" (49). The two exit turning the tables on (and underlining) the actor-spectator model: "we'll wander through the streets and note / The qualities of people" (53–54). Antony and Cleopatra, in their own ways, each "play to the audience" and become spectator to the other. First Cleopatra does impersonations and psychodrama; then she criticizes Antony's acting and appeals to the onstage audience (41). Antony blinkers in and out of character, recomposing himself by upstaging her. It is all play, and all the same game, for Cleopatra (like any actress) wishes to hold Antony's attention as much as he wishes to have his attention held. The messenger debate, like a play-within-a-play, enacts the answer to Cleopatra's question: "If it be love indeed, tell me how much."

Antony's leave-taking (I.iii) reverses the effect on the audience of the first

43. That Cleopatra sounds herself "shrill-tongued" emerges later when she hears of Octavia's voice (III.iii.12–14).

scene: there the triumph of acting, here its quicksand. This scene disengages the spectator far more than the other, for Cleopatra's constant interruptions and the Fulvia joke break the flow. The staging and upstaging, auditing and playing to the audience, become more overt: Antony launches on a set speech; she preempts him by acting sick and mimicking his endearments: "Eternity was in our lips and eyes, / Bliss in our brows' bent" (I.iii.35–36). The scene momentarily reflects upon itself with "Can Fulvia die?" (58), a humorous double-take pointing out that the characters are fashioning themselves in one dramatic genre while history might give them another. Cleopatra cranks up the metaphor of spectatorship and acting: "Good now, play one scene / Of excellent dissembling, and let it look / Like perfect honor" (78–80) praises his performance ironically (81), and even overruns Antony's line to ridicule his oaths as more acting: "And target. Still he mends" (82). Half-sarcastically she admires Antony's fitting the action to the word: "Look . . . / How this Herculean Roman does become / The carriage of his chafe" (83–85). Then in successive clauses of false starts and stops, Cleopatra brilliantly improvises upon acting/not-acting, the contrived speech that fails the emotion: "Sir, you and I must part, but that's not it; / Sir, you and I have lov'd, but there's not it" (87–88). She ends forgetting her lines: "O, my oblivion is a very Antony, / And I am all forgotten" (90–91). Now the sardonic critic, Antony accuses her of impersonating "idleness" (91–93) almost convincingly. They end tensely, Cleopatra essaying the "right" speech ("Upon your sword / Sit laurel victory" [99–100]), Antony a forced and hollow poetic closure ("And I hence fleeting, here remain with thee" [104]).[44]

The great tension of this scene rises out of the ruling metaphor of performance and spectatorship. What was play in the first scene becomes earnest in the third, for Cleopatra really doubts Antony's sincerity, and her acting begins to irritate him. What bonded them together there, the creation of a private space, produces strife here. What they disbelieved only in play there (because they both had the same desire) they truly disbelieve here (because they have different desires). If in the first scene the presentational style matched the grandiloquent fashioning of love, here that style, taken as dishonest, duplicitous, deceptive, separates the two. These are dangerous waters. The accusation of "acting" appears infinite; it has no bottom. The style by which Antony and

---

44. Linda Bamber observes that "We are not really sorry to see him leave; we are pleased to see him recover his decisiveness and resist Cleopatra's wiles. But we should be troubled, I think, to notice that Antony's language as he leaves for Rome becomes transparently rhetorical," *Comic Women, Tragic Men: A Study of Gender and Genre in Shakespeare* (Stanford: Stanford University Press, 1982), 51.

Cleopatra communicate their love to each other and declare themselves to the world contains its own no-exit, as inherently susceptible to the charge of lying as to applause for art. That represents, of course, the great paradox of theater. The paradigm of acting and spectatorship holds Antony and Cleopatra—the more relentlessly the more uneasily. Their manner is both great and at issue.

Shakespeare continues to detach the audience, particularly from Antony during his Roman scenes (II.ii–III.iv) and through the battle of Actium (III.vii–III.x); while individual members might respond to separate scenes with different degrees of distance, the action accumulatively moves the beholders in the same direction. Antony's flamboyance, which in Cleopatra's presence charms the spectator, looks off-key before Octavius. In the Roman sequence, we see Antony almost always in the company of Caesar (five scenes). With the effect of disengagement, the play "contextualizes" Antony at Rome. He appears here frequently in conference, not simply with Octavius but with others who are conferees, advisers, participants in the scene: the concord scene where Lepidus, Enobarbus, Maecenas, and Agrippa all play a part; the truce scene with Pompey; the Roman drinking bout; the farewell scene with Caesar and Octavia and with the soldiers who take the foreground to parody and observe. In Egypt Antony and Cleopatra played downstage ("Here is my space"), the two relatively alone on an implied inner stage, behind them the onstage audience. In the Roman scenes, while Antony and Caesar will often take the foreground or center of an ensemble, the characters will also mix-and-match, and the two triumvirs will occupy less often a special locus, downstage and apart. Rather than creating a magical inner world that becomes the measure of all things, the central characters will mingle into a larger, encircling world that measures them.

The concord scene with Caesar (II.ii) communicates not through its specific issues but through its tidal shift in momentum, the spectator grasping first-hand what the Soothsayer will tell Antony later: "Thy lustre thickens / When he shines by" (II.iii.28–29). Caesar is brief, relentless, implacable; Antony sounds eloquent, witty, and finally, from sheer volume of talk, glib. The momentum of the scene reverses course. Antony starts out accusatorily ("I learn you take things ill which are not so—/ Or being, concern you not" [II.ii.28–29]), even implies that Caesar lies ("And have my learning from some true reports / That drew their swords with you" [47–48]). But midway Antony surrenders the initiative, turns defensive. To his direct question, "How intend you, practic'd?" (40), Caesar makes an Antonian deferral, "You may be pleas'd to catch at mine intent / By what did here befall me" (41–42). From there on, from Fulvia's garboils (twice explained, once with attempted humor) down to his rudeness to messengers, Antony will explain and explain himself. For the audience, such a fall into self-extenuation must compromise the speaker. On the stage, a steely and motionless quiet from Caesar, like Hamlet's toward Claudius in the court scene, can compromise a more peripatetic and agile-tongued Antony.[45]

For the audience, Antony's luster continues to thicken as he meets Pompey (II.vi). Unlike Caesar, Pompey acts agitated, excitable; unlike Caesar, too, he has grounds of personal honor. Antony's wrongful dispossession of his father's house goes unanswered (merely lamented), though for Pompey's good offices to his mother, Antony comes prepared to make "liberal thanks" (47). If, for the spectator, Antony falters in style with Caesar, he falters in substance with Pompey. After the truce an unresolved tension lingers between the two, Antony now touchy about his personal life and ready to take offense (64–66). That edginess frets not only at Pompey but later at Caesar. In their leave-taking (III.ii), as he has in the concord scene, Caesar warns Antony to take care toward Octavia, which irritates Antony (27–34). His response disengages the spectator—"You shall not find, / . . . the least cause / For what you seem to fear" (34–36)—who knows long since that he has thought of escaping to Egypt where his pleasure lies (II.iii.39–41).

The Soothsayer advises Antony's return to Egypt, Enobarbus predicts it, Caesar fears it—and the audience desires it. Our expectation that Antony will desert Octavia and retreat to Cleopatra actually requires little affirmation from him, though we have that too. Shakespeare's dramatic technique places us largely outside Antony's thoughts about Octavia, while we are already convinced of what he will do. Our expectations make us observers, detached analysts toward Antony rather than empathic partners to his considerations about Octavia. We wonder: Is Antony insincere in this declaration to Caesar (and in the marriage altogether) or is he well-intentioned but changeable?[46] The audience's overwhelming confidence that he will return calls forth doubts according to alternatives, vacillation or dishonesty, which no explaining can remove. Here

---

45. For a contrasting view of Antony, see Granville-Barker, *Prefaces to Shakespeare*, 61–62. I picture an impassively strong Octavius, but a stage production could also make Caesar look priggishly stiff before Antony's easy manner. In either case, the advantage shifts in midscene from Antony to Caesar, forcing a new spectatorial perspective regarding Antony.

46. Ernest Schanzer, viewing our response from the point of view of character analysis, argues against ever seeing Antony as a conscious deceiver to Caesar, Octavia, or Cleopatra and for viewing him in terms of the extreme oscillations of feeling that underlie the play's structure: "Rather should we see him as sincere in all his protestations, believing each to be true at the moment it is uttered, until he is suddenly drawn into a contrary allegiance," *The Problem Plays of Shakespeare: A Study of* Julius Caesar, Measure for Measure, Antony and Cleopatra (London: Routledge and Kegan Paul, 1963), 145.

Shakespeare succeeds in making Antony's protestation sound hollow and his silence like guilt. Between the concord scene and the marriage settlement, the audience will suspect Antony's verbosity and his reticence both. What spectators know and what they do not know disengage them from Antony.

Such ignorance frustrates, for we also wish to believe well of Antony. Shakespeare not only leaves us in our ignorance but compounds it. The play o'erleaps entirely his actual decision to return to Cleopatra, even the reunion itself: In one brief scene (III.v) we hear of him in his garden brooding over Lepidus's fall; in the next Caesar damns his public disports in Alexandria with Cleopatra. This surprise instances wonderfully a patented Shakespearean ploy: unexpected bulges of information about a character, unexpected hollows. If Antony's specific decision to return to Egypt might be taken as a tragic error (like, for example, Romeo's decision to fight Mercutio), then the narrative lacuna also keeps the audience utterly blank to what it might have expected to see firsthand. Shakespeare makes a similar move moments later with Antony's almost preoccupied decision to fight Caesar at sea.[47] Everyone (except his Thetis)—Enobarbus, Canidius, even a telepathic soldier—opposes it. Antony's reason: "For that he dares us to't" (III.vii.29). Likewise we never learn exactly why the *Antoniad* follows Cleopatra. Yet in Aristotelean terms, these choices all call out, "tragic error, tragic error."

The situation disturbs, detaches, the audience to the degree that we demand "more" or to the degree that we distrust the information characters give us. The play having touched such niceties as those concerning Antony's mother or Caesar's messenger, we might well expect more than cryptic news of Antony in the public marketplace or "By sea, by sea" (40). No hero of a tragedy, we say, behaves that simply! Such frustrations call to mind Janet Adelman's observation that *Antony and Cleopatra* prevents us from seeing the universe fully through the eyes of the protagonists or entirely in relation to them, a profound difference from the other tragedies. Yet these frustrations take place within the audience's larger perception of the exciting onrush of short, varied, episodic scenes that won Dr. Johnson's delight and Granville-Barker's praise. Thus we rumble merrily along—dragging one foot. Shakespeare engages us satisfyingly

---

47. Peter Erickson offers an interesting perspective on Shakespeare's omissions: "Paradoxically, Antony's essential destiny is not to recover his military identity but to lose it. It is important to formulate the dramatic action in this way because it frees us from an inappropriate concentration on the moral that Antony should not have made the mistake of committing himself to Cleopatra, *Patriarchal Structures in Shakespeare's Drama* (Berkeley: University of California Press, 1985), 132.

in the heady pulse of tragic events, and at the same time confronts us with the perception of how ungenerically Antony and Cleopatra behave as tragic heroes. Lacking their moral exploration, the play lacks a moral center in the consciousness of either protagonist. To borrow from Gertrude Stein, there is no "there" there.

And that may be exactly the point. Shakespeare forces the spectator to recognize a new experience of tragedy, and makes it succeed. Antony and Cleopatra live on the surface of events, within the ebb and flow of their own passions, in the spontaneity of their actions. Shakespeare explores not the process of tragic deciding, as in *Romeo and Juliet, Hamlet,* or *Othello,* but the life on the other side of choice. Not decisions but responses.[48] We see Antony and Cleopatra often when nothing is to be done or when what to be done is obvious: "Think, and die" (III.xiii.1), says Enobarbus to Cleopatra's question, "What shall we do" (1). We explore responses, not reasons, for "reasons" —retrospective, rational—may never explain choices. Shakespeare's interest in aftermath, indeed, studies self-presentation and self-observation exactly, rather than the authenticating moment of choice, as grist for tragedy. Shakespeare leaves characters with their own inability to explain or comprehend themselves, leaves them only to "present" themselves, and invites the audience to engage with presentation as the thing itself.

IV

Against the distancing strategies of *Antony and Cleopatra* Shakespeare begins, after the disaster of Actium, to build a new spectatorial engagement. This engagement arises variously: not only in the course of Antony's shame and his magnanimity, well explored by critics, but most strongly through the theatrical engagement between the two, even in the face of Antony's pathos and his distrust of Cleopatra. Here the lovers discover, deeper than all their garboils, a

---

48. "It is characteristic of the handling of events in *Antony and Cleopatra* that we do not see Antony's failure of nerve at Actium; we see Canidius', Scarus', and Enobarbus' response to it, and following that, we see Antony's reaction. . . . [T]his is a play of reaction rather than of action," Robert Ornstein, "The Ethic of the Imagination: Love and Art in *Antony and Cleopatra,*" in *Stratford-upon-Avon Studies 8: Later Shakespeare,* ed. John Russell Brown and Bernard Harris (London: Edward Arnold, 1966), 40.

new access of joy.[49] In the whipping of Thidias and the accusing of Cleopatra, and in his address to his servitors (III.xi–IV.ii), Antony moves repeatedly from desperate posturings to calmness and even renewal. Throughout these scenes, Shakespeare continues to stress the actor-audience paradigm in the play: Enobarbus, of course, speaks of beholding Antony's desertion (III.x.1,15), and Octavius orders Thidias to "Observe how Antony becomes his flaw" (III.xii.34); Enobarbus scorns to think that "high-battled Caesar will / Unstate his happiness, and be stag'd to th' show / Against a sworder!" (III.xiii.29–31); Antony recognizes his decline in language of Macbethian theatrics: "while we strut / To our confusion" (III.xiii.114–15), envisions Thidias's humiliation in Caesar's triumphal procession (135–37), and terms Thidias's whipping as "thy entertainment" (140); after winning the second day, Antony calls for the pomp of trumpets and tamborines before the city, so that heaven and earth might "applaud" their approach.

The spectatorial metaphor also defines the action. When Cleopatra encounters Antony in his despair after his sea-flight (III.xi), the audience's attention shifts from Antony's remorse to the (up-)staging of remorse. We are first engaged watching Antony attempt to disengage his onstage audience: "Pray you look not sad, / Nor make replies of loathness . . . let that be left / Which leaves itself" (17–20). The mournful steadfastness of those supernumeraries cues the offstage spectators' response. Cleopatra enters, led by Charmian, Eros, and Iras. And with her theatrics of grief, the entire scene pivots; we become conscious of the two not as grief-stricken characters only, but as actorly presenters of grief, Cleopatra, as always, bettering another's cause for passion with her more attention-demanding performance of passion. Antony sits on the ground, talking to himself, his retainers still gathered about, enacting like a storyteller his own inset drama: "he at Philippi kept / His sword e'en like a dancer, while I strook / The lean and wrinkled Cassius" (35–37). (Antony's lines, "No, no, no, no, no" [29] and "O fie, fie, fie!" [31], could be played as recognition of Cleopatra's presence on stage or as grief addressed inwardly about his "story.") Cleopatra sits or attempts to sit, too, and must be prompted by her attendants to move toward Antony. The drama of the attendant's verbal and physical ushering and her resistance and yielding displaces the static Antony in the audience's engagement (he regresses into memory), so that the

---

49. Carol Thomas Neely describes the change in terms of gender roles: "No longer fixed in the comic roles of romantic soldier-servant and worshiped beloved (as Antony imagined) or of mocking heroine and exasperated hero (as Cleopatra contrived), Antony and Cleopatra now play more mutual roles. Loving and fighting together, their union is political, erotic, dynastic," *Broken Nuptials in Shakespeare's Plays*, 145.

dynamics of the pair in the present moment—how will they be reconciled? —becomes of far greater dramatic weight than that which their folly has forfeited. Here staging is "meaning."

A similar shift happens in the Thidias scene (III.xiii). Antony, struggling affectedly to refurbish his honor, would "stage" Caesar to the "show" of a personal duel. With the whipping of Thidias, such pomposity grows embarrassing and grotesque for the spectator. Antony makes a production of his anger ("Have you no ears?—I am / Antony yet" [92–93]) and overreacts to the trifle of hand-kissing. He proceeds to vent his true anger against Cleopatra. She acts as audience to Antony, in steps that establish the playgoer's detachment from his outburst: first, "Good my lord—" (109); "O, is't come to this?" (115); "Wherefore is this?" (122); then differently, "Have you done yet?" (153); "I must stay his time" (155); and, finally, "Not know me yet?" (157). These brief but beautifully modulated spectatorial responses move from annoyance and intervention to patience to, at last, illumination. "Not know me yet," partly because of the process that brings it forth, rings for the audience with a truth deeper than any boggling. Cleopatra's interjections suggest that Antony, besides his real rage and frustration toward her, is also performing himself in a tragedy, full of Senecan "sentence"—"But when we in our viciousness grow hard / (O misery on't!), the wise gods seel our eyes" (111–12)—and Senecan doom— "Alack, our terrene moon / Is now eclips'd, and it portends alone / The fall of Antony!" (153–55). Indeed, his performance aims not at unconcealing the truth but at manipulating Cleopatra ("Cold-hearted toward me?" [158]), and the oath he prompts from her overthrows all that is spoken ("I am satisfied" [167]). Issues of morality and tragic self-recognition transpose into the dramatic maneuverings and upstagings between these two consummate actor-spectators.

That scene ends yet on a self-presentational note, "I'll make death love me; for I will contend / Even with his pestilent scythe" (192–93), that Enobarbus sharpens, "Now he'll outstare the lightning" (194), as Antony goes off to address his captains for one more "gaudy night" (182). There Antony embraces his servitors, again in self-dramatics: "I look on you / As one that takes his leave. . . . / I turn you not away, but like a master / Married to your good service, stay till death" (IV.ii.28–31). Such theatrics puzzle Cleopatra ("What does he mean?" [23]) and move his audience to tears—the classic tragic response—until Enobarbus intervenes. Antony, we might say, has been watching his own prospective "ending" (beholding the beholders). Once more Antony is caught up in his own performance, and once more an interruption shifts his very mode of enactment (from presented self toward represented self), as he

suddenly recognizes, abashed, the effect that he has wished, perhaps unconsciously, to extract.

In each of these scenes, I would argue, the audience moves (though different
members might move at different paces) from watching to feeling, from
detachment to involvement and emotional proximity, as we experience Antony's
access to a truer self realized in dramatic relationship with those around him.
The power in these scenes is not in the pathos of the dying lion, though that is
present, but in the self-centeredness of that pathos used to arrive at the
magnanimity underneath. We are aware not only, or so much, of what is
"shown" (the tragedy of what is lost) but of the manner of showing, so that we
become engaged with Antony essentially beyond the tragedy, toward which we
are distanced, engaged with his present struggle to discover himself as the self
seems to be crumbling ("Have you no ears?—I am Antony yet"). Our change
in focus, moreover, comes through the mediation of others' responses to him.
Antony arrives at his magnanimity in these scenes by overacting, thus exorcising,
unburdening himself of, his tragic persona. Shakespeare engages the playgoer
with the tension, the onstage conflict of this process, and each struggle
produces a moment of release for character and spectator. Here the very
dynamics of the play concern not ruin but posturing and pathos, not Actium
so much as acting.

Antony will "present" himself once more as he approaches suicide, but in
such a way that the audience becomes engaged with the person inside the
persona, the poignant, mutable teller of the tale. That experience epitomizes
the audience's engagement with the character-as-actor; we accept Antony's
acting as the reagent for his essential authenticity. Shocked by the yielded fleet,
Antony's mood, in contrast to, say, the restless striving of a soldier such as
Macbeth, is noticeably composed, detached, even gentlemanly: "O sun, thy
uprise shall I see no more, / Fortune and Antony part here, even here / Do we
shake hands" (IV.xii.18–20). In anger, he accuses Cleopatra of playing "fast
and loose" with him, of having beguiled him to "the very heart of loss"
(28–29), but when she appears (their only moment alone together on stage),
he first threatens to murder her, then consigns her to Caesar's triumph—in
essence, does nothing. The love between Antony and Cleopatra, the audience
sees once more, is deeper than her wavering and his rage, and such emotional
storms as Antony's merely expose that irreducible union.

"Eros, thou yet behold'st me?" (IV.xiv.1), asks Antony, and that question
establishes for the audience his own "beholding" of his end. He arrives at
suicide in a manner so abstract—the imagery of the cloud—as to sound
impersonal. Antony may enter the scene looking past the stage, lost in contem-

plation of sky and space. The cynosure of all eyes, he feels now invisible. The images of dragon, lion, towered citadel, mountain, and stately trees form and reform his metaphor of colossus, until Antony discovers the essence we too behold: "black vesper's pageants" (8). Against his static stage presence, the extended metaphor of ever-dislimning rack functions as a metaphysical conceit, leaving the playgoer perhaps momentarily baffled, distanced, as is Eros, over the direction of Antony's thought. Antony completes the metaphor in a paradox: "[N]ow thy captain is / Even such a body. Here I am Antony, / Yet cannot hold this visible shape" (12-14). Here the presented self and the represented self contrast, for what Antony directs the audience to see is his solid and compact form. Within a score of lines Antony will merge the tenor and vehicle of this metaphysical conceit ("Unarm, Eros. . . . Bruised pieces, go" [35-42]). The essential Antony exists not in one self or another, the figurative or the solid, the spirit or the flesh, the Egyptian or the Roman, but in the relationship between the two. The scene, as does the play, halves Antony, to reveal what is truest of him in the dialects of the parts. Here Eros stands dramatically for a share of Antony's consciousness, so that their talk is always a dialogue of self and soul: "[S]he, Eros, has / Pack'd cards with Caesar. . . . Nay, weep not, gentle Eros, there is left us / Ourselves to end ourselves" (18-22). The "us" who will end ourselves and the "we" who must sleep (36) refer ambiguously to both Antony and Eros. The scene demands audience attention and finally absorption. To be engaged in the interaction between stoic captain and his tearful beholder is to be engaged with the essential Antony himself, his authentic dialogism externalized, at once dramatically "presented" and deeply involving.

That the audience knows Cleopatra lives does not make the scene ironic in the sense that we discount Antony's emotional sincerity. Yet our knowledge of Cleopatra's trick contributes to a quality that can distance the spectator toward the scene as a whole: the comic subtext of death as sex. The very presence of a character named "Eros" (a fortunate inheritance from Plutarch) emphasizes the sexual metaphor, just as Seyton in *Macbeth* may evoke the satanic. Each step in the scene rings with sexual imagery. "O, thy vild lady! / She has robb'd me of my sword" (22-23), says Antony, the line playing upon the idea of emasculation (the bloody sword will be carried to Caesar). Cleopatra's reported suicide is intensely erotic: "Then in the midst a tearing groan did break / . . . . She rend'red life, / Thy name buried in her" (31-34). Antony goes toward death, as toward bed—"we must sleep" (36); "Lie down and stray no farther" (47)—by taking off his clothes. Language such as "battery" (39), "cleave my sides" (39), and "Crack thy frail case" (41) hints distantly at sexuality. Indeed, if spectators were to start listening intently for sexual allusions, such lines as "Eros!—I come, my queen!—Eros!—Stay for me!" (50) could provoke a titter of laughter. Antony again emphasizes his emasculation, "I, that with my sword / Quarter'd the world, . . . lack / The courage of a woman" (57–60). The dialogue between Antony and Eros uses imagery of sexual coupling (with Antony now as woman) and prolongs the stage action in a manner reminiscent of intercourse: "Come then; for with a wound I must be cur'd. / Draw thy sword . . . Draw, and come. . . . My sword is drawn. . . . Then let it do at once / The thing why thou has drawn it. . . . Shall I strike now? . . . Now, Eros" (78–93). Eros "dies" on a "thus" (94), just as Antony will "do thus" (101), the words that "presented" his first embrace to Cleopatra. Lest the subtextual metaphor is still lost upon us, Antony's own suicidal gesture is explicit: "I will be / A bridegroom in my death, and run into't / As to a lover's bed" (99–101).

On the stage this scene could be performed at either extreme, as erotic parody or as suicides both noble (Eros) and pathetic (Antony), with obvious differences in the spectators' detachment or engagement toward the action (just as the sexual hints around Octavius could be played up or down). But we might expect even a comedic interpretation to leave a residue of empathy for Antony and for his double, Eros. On the other hand, a more austere version cannot wholly submerge the sexual metaphor, which, at least momentarily, will distance the wondering playgoer. Indeed, with this scene so volatile, so inherently unstable and cloudlike, even a restrained production might evoke divergent responses on any given night, for once some element of an audience begins to track its emotions by a sexual metaphor laughter becomes infectious. Thus the scene inserts some tension in the audience's relationship to action and characters; indeed, like everything else in *Antony and Cleopatra* the audience becomes here a Janus-faced, "deliquescent," Enobarbian observer-participant.

V

Ambivalent connotations buried in Antony's suicide turn overt in Cleopatra's closing scenes; what was self-compromising and parodic there is self-enhancing and even noble here; what detached us then engages us now. Cleopatra does not so much change in the course of *Antony and Cleopatra* as that the audience changes toward her. The play unconceals Cleopatra, by situations that call forth her qualities and by her contrasts to Antony.[50] When Antony says of her "Whom every thing becomes," the most obvious meaning is "who wears all things (attitudes, emotions) well." That primary meaning implicitly distinguishes between Cleopatra and the garment of her moods. The buried meaning that the play progressively exposes, of course, is "who transforms into all attitudes—and who does so becomingly." Indeed, Cleopatra in the first and third scenes of the play not only mimics Fulvia, scolding shrill-tongued, but becomes her, sees her own position as identical to Fulvia's, and affords Fulvia a greater and more sympathetic humanity than does any other character in the play. What strikes the audience at first as pretended and affected appears progressively as realistically protean and representational.[51] In the closing scenes of the play Cleopatra stages herself and her dreaming so effectively that her "imitations" dominate, control, and rearrange the "real" world. If her performed world so successfully displaces her onstage audience's, if Cleopatra's

50. Recent feminist criticism has greatly enriched our understanding of the Cleopatra whom the play unconceals. Although, as Irene Dash argues, the play's male characters overlook Cleopatra's considerable political skills much as critics have historically done, "In *Antony and Cleopatra,* Shakespeare suggests that a woman of power has the unusual opportunity of combining her sexual and political selves" (209), *Wooing, Wedding, and Power,* 209–47. Similarly, Linda Bamber discusses Cleopatra as a female "Other" with a special wholeness, integrity, and intention (to "make herself matter" [64]): "Antony struggles with Nature by struggling with himself; Cleopatra has no quarrel with herself and struggles exclusively with the outside world. . . . She is aware of no gap between what she is and what she ought to be, only of the gap between what she wants and what she has. Even when we put Cleopatra in the position of the striving Self, we must notice that she struggles as an Other, as a fixed identity. She is not self-divided, like the tragic heroes; she is at work on her destiny but not, like them, on herself" (59), *Comic Women, Tragic Men,* 45–70. Peter Erickson, on the other hand, sees the play experimenting with a new "heterosexual androgyny," in which "Antony and Cleopatra engage in a gender-role exchange that enlarges but does not erase the original and primary sexual identity of each" (133), *Patriarchal Structures in Shakespeare's Drama,* 123–47. Carol Thomas Neely argues, instead, that in *Antony and Cleopatra,* "gender roles are not exchanged or transcended, but are played out in more variety than in the other tragedies," so that Antony "returns to Cleopatra and achieves with her the synthesis of love and heroism, authority and sexuality, autonomy and mutuality sought in the problem plays and early tragedies" (137), *Broken Nuptials in Shakespeare's Plays,* 136–65. In a recent politically oriented discussion sharing affinities with both Dash and Erickson, Theodora Jankowski argues that, "Like Elizabeth I—whom Shakespeare seems to have had in mind when he created her—Cleopatra is shown to work against existing patriarchal stereotypes to create a strategy for rule that works within the conditions of her society. . . . [L]ike Elizabeth, Cleopatra manages to counter the threats caused by the fear of female power by creating a more positive, more androgynous kind of power" (105), " 'As I Am Egypt's Queen': Cleopatra, Elizabeth I, and the Female Body Politic," in *Assays: Critical Approaches to Medieval and Renaissance Texts,* vol. 5, ed. Peggy A. Knapp (Pittsburgh: University of Pittsburgh Press, 1989), 91–110.

51. As Bamber observes, "Antony aims for constancy, of identity and of Fortune; Cleopatra reveals the constancy of her identity through her extravagant feigning and controls her Fortune by changing roles faster than it requires her to do," *Comic Women, Tragic Men,* 60–61.

spectators (Proculeius, Dolabella, Caesar) change heart, align themselves to her theatrics, then the "real" Roman world transfers some of its reality to her art.

The theatrical metaphor dominates Cleopatra's action at her monument. The monument itself, no matter how a particular production might construct it, will always suggest an elevated stage—a stage within the stage—for Cleopatra's greatest performance.[52] Antony's botched suicide has ended with his enjoinder to his guards to defeat suffering by bearing it lightly (IV.xiv.135–38). He is stoic; but Cleopatra, following almost immediately, rejects solace, expands into grief: "our size of sorrow, / Proportion'd to our cause, must be as great / As that which makes it" (IV.xv.4–6). She claims her full dramatic expressiveness. Cleopatra memorializes Antony—and steals his death scene—and finally "becomes" him, too. For the audience, taking her part moves from empathy to a parallel imaginative activity—the culmination of spectatorship in the tragedies. Antony enters the scene in order to die upon a kiss (19–21)—the relentless sexual metaphor—and Cleopatra, in the first of several reversals, refuses him entrance.[53] Her preoccupation is with staging, with the "imperious show / Of full-fortun'd Caesar" (23–24) that Antony has taught her earlier to fear (IV.xii.32–38). Cleopatra's refusal momentarily disrupts the audience's expectation that the romantic hero will die, by rights, with his heroine. Just as quickly, however, Cleopatra agrees to draw him up, and then, according to Margaret Lamb, halts her "sport" in midair, the boy-actor pausing (perhaps even twice) to catch his breath.[54] These interruptions engage with anticipation and conversely detach with grotesqueness; our responses, too, suspend in midair. The lifting of Antony makes the theatrical subtext apparent, for—besides referring to Cleopatra's "angling" or to phallic elevation—it places Antony upon her stage, offers him apotheosis by devising a deus ex machina in reverse. Aloft, Antony begs leave to speak "a little" (42) before he dies, but Cleopatra disrupts famously the pattern of tragedy ("No, let me speak" [43]), again distancing the spectator with a betrayal of the genre we are in.

Cleopatra even dismisses Antony's dying advice (48); her wrecking of the audience's tragic expectations steals his death scene from Antony. We become

52. If a "gallery" area such as the musician's room of the Swan Drawing were used for the monument, that adaptable site might further underscore the blending of perspectives of actor and audience in the play.

53. I am tempted to write "entrance" in quotation marks, for the monument suggests a vast visual pun on womb-tomb. The mind reels.

54. Antony and Cleopatra *on the English Stage* (Rutherford, N.J.: Fairleigh Dickinson University Press, 1980), 180–85. Lamb suggests that the hoisting manifests Cleopatra's great sexual metaphor: fishing.

interested, instead, in her *staging* of his demise. Even a line such as "the soldier's pole is fall'n" (65), with its sudden sexual connotation, draws our attention toward the speaker rather than her object. "Young boys and girls / Are level now with men" (65–66) refers extratheatrically as well as narratively, for on the Jacobean stage at that moment boys playing girls replace the lone adult male actor. Paradoxically, the audience's awareness of theatricality here serves Cleopatra's character. Shakespeare identifies Cleopatra with the audience by evoking her ordinary womanhood:[55] "No more but e'en a woman, and commanded / By such poor passion as the maid that milks" (73–74). But Cleopatra starts to "become" Antony, performing his role, and to "take his part" in a humorously literalistic way. Her fainting is a mock death, a reflexive version of his expiration; here the upstaging becomes a restaging (and "fainting" has its own sexual resonance in the play). She echoes Antony's suicide language in her imagery of maddened impatience (79–80), rushing into death (81), and the spent lamp of life (85; for these images, cf. IV.xiv.41; 100–101; 35–36, 46). More dramatically, she now masculinizes and Romanizes herself and her women: "Good sirs, take heart, / . . . what's brave, what's noble, / Let's do't after the high Roman fashion" (85–87). Antony's audience before, Cleopatra now assumes his role.

In the play's finale, Cleopatra, so far from being an "outcast" (Holloway, 119–20), turns a series of scenes-within-the-scene into her own dramatic triumphs when the "story" would rightfully belong to Caesar. She does so by consistently reversing the actor-audience alignment that circumstances predict and the theatrical audience would expect. What ultimately matters most to characters in *Antony and Cleopatra* is chronicle, record, history, memory, reputation: how they will be viewed—the "impression" they leave upon a current or imagined audience. (The characters know they are alive when they know that others know their history: They exist, almost self-consciously, as phenomenological objects.) What Cleopatra "plays" for, then, is the play. Cleopatra's Roman visitors are a rising tide of magnificence—Proculeius, Dolabella, Caesar himself—that she overwhelms. Each of these would-be actors upon Cleopatra leaves not only changed into an audience but also changed himself—"impressed." They cue our "development" toward Cleopatra.

Proculeius attempts to disarm Cleopatra psychologically, but only succeeds physically. His mission is to demonstrate Caesar's overflowing generosity (as vast a lie as any in the play), and he begins by verbally restoring her title as "Queen of Egypt" and requesting her "fair demands" (V.ii.9–11). Caesar, true

55. John Holloway, *The Story of the Night: Studies in Shakespeare's Major Tragedies* (London: Routledge and Kegan Paul, 1961), 117–19.

to what he desires from women, wishes to hear "report" of her "sweet dependancy" (25–26) upon him. Proculeius's capture of Cleopatra clarifies Caesar's grace, of course, as his words reveal Caesar's essential game: to "[l]et the world see / His nobleness well acted" (44–45). Cleopatra responds to the stage mastery hinted there as the true issue: "Shall they hoist me up, / And show me to the shouting varlotry / Of censuring Rome?" (55–57). Perhaps because Proculeius knows that Cleopatra's forebodings are true, perhaps because he is touched by her passionate resolve, he expresses "content" that Dolabella relieve him, urges gentleness toward her, and offers to speak to Caesar on her behalf (67–70). Proculeius fails to subdue Cleopatra's spirit or to convince her of anything; instead her vision overwhelms his actions and leaves him her intercessor.

Dolabella collapses even more spectacularly. Not only does Cleopatra deflate his smug sense of fame, demurring from having "heard of" (71) him, she also immediately substitutes her vision for his, and wins his emotional allegiance to her. Cleopatra first sets up Dolabella as a carping audience to her acting ("You laugh when boys or women tell their dreams" [74]), overruns his efforts to regain the scene, and convinces him to take her part. The Antony she conjures forth is almost Rabelaisian in his gargantuanness: "His legs bestrid the ocean . . . " (82–92). This description has struck some critics as marginal to the play's motion.[56] Indeed, Cleopatra's "size of dreaming" speech (96–100) is so cryptic and difficult (starting with the peculiar syntax of "But if there be, nor ever were one such") as to demand at least the "pointing" of slow and self-conscious delivery. The lines may be slightly out of character for Cleopatra; they echo with Roman sententiae. Since Dolabella is hardly her real audience, the actress or boy-actor would deliver the lines as much to the auditors across the stage threshold as to the one at hand. These speeches sound "stagey" because oratorical and declamatory, "theatrical" because they transgress the audience's sense of the theater it is watching. At such decontextualizing moments, the performer becomes more like himself or herself. If the speech is marginal, it is marginal for sounding authorial. Cleopatra re-creates Antony powerfully and memorably, overwhelming both Dolabella and the audience, in part because her lines replace one kind of theater with another. For the spectators what is "presentational" here wears the garb of "truth." Cleopatra steps "out" of the play and into a kinship with the audience making the imagined real. Her effect on Dolabella outstrips that on Proculeius. Struck with tragic pity, he turns not only audience but vassal, completing the theatrical subtext of the interlude as he admits Caesar's intention to lead Cleopatra in triumph (110). Like a spectator, Dolabella validates Cleopatra by "taking her part": "but I do feel, / By the rebound of yours, a grief that smites / My very heart at root" (103–5).

These dramatic rhythms continue through the appearance of Caesar; Cleopatra not only steals the scene from him, but makes him an actor in her own play-within and even instructs him (as audience) on the foibles of kingship, as we have already seen. In the course of these three episodes Cleopatra increases the engagement of the theatrical spectator with her by upstaging the Romans against our expectations (with the Seleucus segment the greatest triumph of all because it converts embarrassment to martyrdom). Cleopatra's byplay with the Clown, a character from Elizabethan folk life, completes the audience's sense of affinity with her and, because the Clown tends to steal the scene, underscores the shifting dynamics of the spectatorial paradigm. Cleopatra's most triumphant self-dramatization is, of course, her own death: The "lass unparalleled" finishes reducing Caesar to "ass unpolicied" and reenacts her masterpiece at Cydnus. She also makes a success out of the kind of suicide Antony has botched, consciously uniting its comically sexual and its tragically heroic elements and making self-presentation into representation. Her death recalls Antony's by likeness and contrast.[57] Cleopatra, like Antony, meets death erotically ("The stroke of death is as a lover's pinch / Which hurts, and is desir'd" [295–96]). In addition, she dresses for her part ("Give me my robe, put on my crown" [280]), as Antony has undressed; while he has imagined invisibility, she would be "marble-constant" (240); she feels upbraided that Iras dies sooner, as he had that Eros preceded him (Iras becomes a virtual pun upon Eros); she goes to meet Antony as he had to meet her; each is "discovered" and carried to the other. For the spectator, death and sex are comically discontinuous in Antony's suicide; with Cleopatra they are knowingly the same act. What might have been nervous laughter-at in the earlier scene converts to laughter-with in the last scene. The audience remains deeply engaged with Cleopatra even as she creates an artistic object out of herself.[58] The presentational in Cleopatra unites completely and perfectly with the representational.[59]

57. As a general pattern, Ernest Schanzer argues that "The lovers' echoes of each other's words and sentiments, though found scattered throughout the play, increase greatly in the last two acts," *The Problem Plays of Shakespeare,* 134; see 134–38.

58. For a rich discussion of this aspect of the play, see Ornstein, "The Ethic of the Imagination: Love and Art in *Antony and Cleopatra,* " 31–46.

59. Carol Thomas Neely likens Cleopatra's death to Antony's: "Like his, it is partly a mockery, partly an expansion, partly a transformation of the roles she has played all along," *Broken Nuptials in Shakespeare's Plays,* 160.

The audience "beholds" Cleopatra at the end in a way that leaps the differences between engagement and detachment in the play. We see her as tableau, seated in a chair of state, yet Charmian must adjust her crown, an imperfection in the creation that humanizes her.[60] Onstage, adjusting the crown will really mean that Charmian must touch and straighten Cleopatra's head, an intimate and potentially unnerving gesture for the audience. Touching, adjusting a corpse: The audience can experience acting (playing dead) with a shock at its realism. Caesar, too, surrenders to the compelling imitation, not of death, but of life: "she looks like sleep" (346). The Cleopatra-performer makes presentation realistic and the Cleopatra-character makes reality presentational. Caesar's words set up another distancing tension: His coroner's inquest into the logistics of death demonstrates cool Roman empiricism at the same time that it must, for the audience, drawn magnetically by Cleopatra's image, miss the point. This Roman fussing leaves Cleopatra all the more mysterious and opaque, essentially inaccessible to them. Spectatorship is action. The theatrical audience "completes" Cleopatra—recognizes her vastness—with the aid and the misfirings of Caesar's beholding. The playgoers' creative intercession, making up what the play calls for but leaves out, validates their experience of Cleopatra differently than might a richer tribute from Caesar. Our completing of Cleopatra recapitulates the spectatorial action of the play; the wonder of Antony and Cleopatra depends upon the audience's action in co-creating, through the play's self-conscious theatricality, its life as art. The spectators rather than the characters develop in *Antony and Cleopatra.* Yet all's one: As Cleopatra has created herself, so has the player boyed her greatness successfully, so have the King's Men created the "story," so has the audience completed the play's actions with its thoughts. At the end, all actors turn audience: Not only has Cleopatra forced her Roman visitors to be spectators when they came as actors, but now dead in her chair Cleopatra gives final audience, just as the actors will in a moment bow before the applause of the performing playgoers.

60. John Styan, *Drama, Stage and Audience* (Cambridge: Cambridge University Press, 1975), 33.

Selected Bibliography

Adamson, Jane. *Othello as Tragedy: Some Problems in Judgment and Feeling.* Cambridge: Cambridge University Press, 1980.

Adelman, Janet. *The Common Liar: An Essay on* Antony and Cleopatra. New Haven: Yale University Press, 1973.

Artaud, Antonin. *The Theater and Its Double.* 1938. Translated by Mary Caroline Richards. New York: Grove, 1958.

Awdeley, John. *The Fraternitie of Vacabondes.* 1565. Reprint. *The Elizabethan Underworld,* edited by A. V. Judges, 51–60.

Aydelotte, Frank. *Oxford Historical and Literary Studies.* Vol. 1, *Elizabethan Rogues and Vagabonds.* Oxford: Clarendon, 1913.

Bakhtin, Mikhail. *The Dialogic Imagination: Four Essays by M. M. Bakhtin.* Edited by Michael Holquist. Translated by Caryl Emerson and Michael Holquist. Austin: University of Texas Press, 1981.

——. *Rabelais and His World.* Translated by Helene Iswolsky. Bloomington: Indiana University Press, 1984.

Bamber, Linda. *Comic Women, Tragic Men: A Study of Gender and Genre in Shakespeare.* Stanford: Stanford University Press, 1982.

Barber, C. L. *Shakespeare's Festive Comedy: A Study of Form and its Relation to Social Custom.* Princeton: Princeton University Press, 1959.

Barroll, J. Leeds. *Artificial Persons: The Formation of Character in the Tragedies of Shakespeare.* Columbia: University of South Carolina Press, 1974.

——. *Shakespearean Tragedy: Genre, Tradition, and Change In* Antony and Cleopatra. Washington: Folger Books, 1984.

Bayley, John. *Shakespeare and Tragedy.* London: Routledge and Kegan Paul, 1981.

Beaumont, Francis, and John Fletcher. *Comedies and Tragedies.* 1647.

Beckerman, Bernard. *Dynamics of Drama: Theory and Method of Analysis.* 1970. Reprint. New York: Drama Book Specialists, 1979.

——. *Shakespeare at the Globe: 1599–1609.* 1962. Reprint. New York: Collier Books, 1966.

——. "Shakespeare's Dramatic Method." In *William Shakespeare: His World, His Work, His Influence.* Vol. 2, edited by John F. Andrews, 397–416. New York: Charles Scribner's Sons, 1985.

Beier, A. L. *Masterless Men: The Vagrancy Problem in England, 1560–1640.* London: Methuen, 1985.

Belsey, Catherine. *The Subject of Tragedy: Identity and Difference in Renaissance Drama.* London: Methuen, 1985.

Bentley, Eric. *The Life of the Drama.* 1964. Reprint. New York: Atheneum, 1983.

Berger, Harry, Jr. "Text Against Performance in Shakespeare: The Example of *Macbeth.*" *Genre* 15 (Spring–Summer 1982), edited by Stephen Greenblatt: 49–79.

Berry, Ralph. "*Richard III:* Bonding the Audience." In *Mirror up to Shakespeare: Essays in Honour of G. R. Hibbard,* edited by J. C. Gray, 114–27. Toronto: University of Toronto Press, 1984.

——. *Shakespeare and the Awareness of the Audience.* London: Macmillan, 1985.

Bethell, S. L. *Shakespeare and the Popular Dramatic Tradition.* London: Staples, 1944.

Bevington, David. *Action Is Eloquence: Shakespeare's Language of Gesture.* Cambridge: Harvard University Press, 1984.

Blayney, Peter W. M. "The Folio's Major Alterations." Unpublished chapter for *The Texts of King Lear and their Origins.* Vol. 2.

Booth, Stephen. King Lear, Macbeth, *Indefinition, and Tragedy.* New Haven: Yale University Press, 1983.

——. "On the Value of *Hamlet.*" In *Reinterpretations of Elizabethan Drama: Selected Papers from the English Institute,* edited by Norman Rabkin, 137–76.

Bradbrook, M. C. *Shakespeare The Craftsman.* New York: Barnes and Noble, 1969.

Bradley, A. C. "Shakespeare's *Antony and Cleopatra.*" In his *Oxford Lectures on Poetry,* 279–308. London: Macmillan, 1909.

——. *Shakespearean Tragedy: Lectures on* Hamlet, Othello, King Lear, Macbeth. London: Macmillan, 1904.

Brecht, Bertolt. *A Short Organum for the Theatre.* In *Brecht on Theatre: The Development of an Aesthetic,* edited by John Willet, 179–205. New York: Hill and Wang, 1964.

Brook, Peter. *The Empty Space.* 1968. Reprint. New York: Atheneum, 1978.

Brooke, Nicholas. *Shakespeare's Early Tragedies.* London: Methuen, 1968.

Brown, John Russell. *Discovering Shakespeare.* New York: Columbia University Press, 1981.

Bullough, Edward. " 'Psychical Distance' as a Factor in Art and an Aesthetic Principle." In his *Aesthetics: Lectures and Essays,* edited by Elizabethan M. Wilkinson, 91–130. Westport, Conn.: Greenwood Press, 1977. Originally published in *British Journal of Psychology* 5 (1912): 87–118.

Calderwood, James L. "Speech and Self in *Othello.*" *Shakespeare Quarterly* 38 (Autumn 1987): 293–303.

Carroll, William C. " 'The Base Shall Top Th'Legitimate': The Bedlam Beggar and the Role of Edgar in *King Lear.*" *Shakespeare Quarterly* 38 (Winter 1987): 426–41.

Cartwright, Kent, and Mary McElroy. "Expectation, True Play, and the Duel in *Hamlet.*" *Arete: The Journal of Sport and Literature* 1 (Fall 1983): 39–56.

Cavell, Stanley. "The Avoidance of Love: A Reading of *King Lear.*" In his *Must We Mean What We Say?: A Book of Essays,* 267-353. New York: Charles Scribner's Sons, 1969.

Chaim, Daphna Ben. *Distance in the Theatre: The Aesthetics of Audience Response.* Ann Arbor, Mich.: UMI Research Press, 1984.

Champion, Larry S. *Shakespeare's Tragic Perspective.* Athens: University of Georgia Press, 1976.

Chappel, W. H. *The Roxburghe Ballads.* Vol. 2. Herford: Printed for the Ballad Society, Stephen Austin and Sons, 1874.

Charlton, H. B. *Shakespearean Tragedy.* Cambridge: Cambridge University Press, 1961.

Charney, Maurice. *Shakespeare's Roman Plays: The Function of Imagery in Drama.* Cambridge: Harvard University Press, 1961.

Cole, David. *The Theatrical Event.* Middletown, Conn.: Wesleyan University Press, 1975.

Cole, Toby, and Helen Krich Chinoy. *Actors on Acting.* Rev. ed. New York: Crown, 1970.

Cook, Ann Jennalie. *The Privileged Playgoers of Shakespeare's London: 1576-1642.* Princeton: Princeton University Press, 1981.

Craik, T. W., Clifford Leech, and Lois Potter, gen. eds. *The Revels History of Drama in English.* 8 vols. London: Methuen, 1975-83.

Cullum, Graham. " 'Condemning Shadows Quite': *Antony and Cleopatra.*" *Philosophy and Literature* 5 (Fall 1981): 186-203.

Cunningham, J. V. *Woe or Wonder: The Emotional Effect of Shakespearean Tragedy.* Denver: University of Denver Press, 1951.

Danby, John F. *Poets on Fortune's Hill: Studies in Sidney, Shakespeare, Beaumont and Fletcher.* London: Faber and Faber, 1952.

Danson, Lawrence. "*King Lear* and the Two Abysses." In *On* King Lear, edited by Lawrence Danson, 119-35. Princeton: Princeton University Press, 1981.

Dash, Irene G. *Wooing, Wedding, and Power: Women in Shakespeare's Plays.* New York: Columbia University Press, 1981.

Day, W. G. *Catalogue of the Pepys Library At Magdalene College, Cambridge: The Pepys Ballads.* Facsimile Vols. 1-2. Cambridge: Brewer, 1987.

Dekker, Thomas. *The Belman of London.* 1608. Reprint. In *The Elizabethan Underworld,* edited by A. V. Judges, 303-11.

——. *O Per Se O.* 1612. Reprint. In *The Elizabethan Underworld,* edited by A. V. Judges, 366-82.

Dessen, Alan C. "Two Falls and a Trap: Shakespeare and the Spectacles of Realism." *English Literary Renaissance* 5 (Autumn 1975): 291-307.

di Grassi, Giacomo. *Giacomo di Grassi His True Arte of Defence.* 1594.

Dollimore, Jonathan. *Radical Tragedy: Religion, Ideology and Power in the Drama of Shakespeare and his Contemporaries.* Chicago: University of Chicago Press, 1984.

Downes, John. *Roscius Anglicanus, or an Historical Review of the Stage.* 1708.

Dusinberre, Juliet. *Shakespeare and the Nature of Women.* London: Macmillan, 1975.

Egan, Robert. "Kent and the Audience: The Character as Spectator." *Shakespeare Quarterly* 32 (Summer 1981): 146-54.

Eliot, T. S. *On Poetry and Poets.* London: Faber and Faber, 1957.

——. *Selected Essays 1917-1932.* London: Faber and Faber, 1932.

Elliott, Martin. *Shakespeare's Invention of Othello: A Study in Early Modern English.* London: Macmillan, 1988.

Erickson, Peter. *Patriarchal Structures in Shakespeare's Drama.* Berkeley: University of California Press, 1985.

Evans, Bertrand. *Shakespeare's Tragic Practice.* New York: Clarendon, 1979.

Evans, Robert O. *The Osier Cage: Rhetorical Devices in* Romeo and Juliet. Lexington: University of Kentucky Press, 1966.

Fass, Ekbert. *Shakespeare's Poetics.* Cambridge: Cambridge University Press, 1986.

Felperin, Howard. *Shakespearean Representation: Mimesis and Modernity in Elizabethan Tragedy.* Princeton: Princeton University Press, 1977.

Fergusson, Francis. "*Hamlet, Prince of Denmark:* The Analogy of Action." In his *The Idea of a Theater: A Study of Ten Plays: The Art of Drama in Changing Perspective,* 109–54. Garden City, N.J.: Doubleday, 1949.

——. *Shakespeare: The Pattern in His Carpet.* New York: Delacorte Press, 1970.

Fraser, Russell. *Shakespeare's Poetics in Relation to* King Lear. London: Routledge and Kegan Paul, 1962.

Freud, Sigmund. "The Uncanny." 1919. Translated under the supervision of Joan Riviere, 1925. In *On Creativity and the Unconscious: Papers on the Psychology of Art, Literature, Love, Religion,* edited by Benjamin Nelson, 122–53. New York: Harper and Row, 1958.

Frost, William. "Shakespeare's Rituals and the Opening of *King Lear.*" *Hudson Review* 10 (Winter 1957–58): 577–85. Reprint. *Shakespeare: The Tragedies: A Collection of Critical Essays,* edited by Clifford Leech, 190–200. Chicago: University of Chicago Press, 1965.

Fuegi, John. *The Essential Brecht.* Los Angeles, Calif.: Hennessey and Ingalls, 1972.

Garber, Marjorie. *Coming of Age in Shakespeare.* New York: Methuen, 1981.

——. *Shakespeare's Ghost Writers: Literature as Uncanny Causality.* New York: Methuen, 1987.

——. " 'Vassal Actors': The Role of the Audience in Shakespearean Tragedy." In *Renaissance Drama,* n.s. 9, edited by Leonard Barkan, 71–89. Evanston, Ill.: Northwestern University Press, 1978.

Gielgud, John. *Early Stages.* New York: Macmillan, 1939.

Girard, René. "Hamlet's Dull Revenge." In *Literary Theory / Renaissance Texts,* edited by Patricia Parker and David Quint, 280–302. Baltimore, Md.: Johns Hopkins University Press, 1986.

——. "The Politics of Desire in *Troilus and Cressida.* " In *Shakespeare and the Question of Theory,* edited by Patricia Parker and Geoffrey Hartman, 188–209.

——. *Violence and the Sacred.* Translated by Patrick Gregory. Baltimore, Md.: Johns Hopkins University Press, 1977.

Goldberg, S. L. *An Essay on* King Lear. Cambridge: Cambridge University Press, 1974.

Goldman, Michael. *Acting and Action in Shakespearean Tragedy.* Princeton: Princeton University Press, 1985.

——. *The Actor's Freedom: Toward a Theory of Drama.* New York: Viking, 1975.

——. *Shakespeare and the Energies of the Drama.* Princeton: Princeton University Press, 1972.

Granville-Barker, Harley. *Prefaces to Shakespeare.* Vol. 3, *Antony and Cleopatra, Coriolanus.* Princeton: Princeton University Press, 1946.

——. *Prefaces to Shakespeare.* Vol. 4, *Love's Labour's Lost, Romeo and Juliet, The Merchant of Venice, Othello.* Princeton: Princeton University Press, 1946.

Greenblatt, Stephen. *Renaissance Self-Fashioning: From More to Shakespeare.* Chicago: University of Chicago Press, 1980.

——. *Shakespearean Negotiations: The Circulation of Social Energy in Renaissance England.* Berkeley: University of California Press, 1988.

Grennan, Eamon. "The Women's Voices in *Othello:* Speech, Song, Silence." *Shakespeare Quarterly* 38 (Autumn 1987): 275–92.

Gruber, William E. "The Actor in the Script: Affective Strategies in Shakespeare's *Antony and Cleopatra.*" *Comparative Drama* 19 (Spring 1985): 30–48.

Gurr, Andrew. *Playgoing in Shakespeare's London.* Cambridge: Cambridge University Press, 1987.

Hapgood, Robert. "Shakespeare and the Included Spectator." In *Reinterpretations of Elizabethan Drama: Selected Papers from the English Institute,* edited by Norman Rabkin, 117–36.

———. *Shakespeare the Theatre-Poet.* Oxford: Clarendon Press, 1988.

———. "The Trials of Othello." In *Pacific Coast Studies in Shakespeare,* edited by Waldo F. McNeir and Thelma N. Greenfield, 134–47.

Harbage, Alfred. *Shakespeare's Audience.* New York: Columbia University Press, 1941.

Harman, Thomas. *A Caueat, or Warening, for Commen Cursetors Vulgarely Called Vagabones.* 1567. Reprint. In *The Elizabethan Underworld,* edited by A. V. Judges, 61–118.

Harrison, G. B. *Shakespeare's Tragedies.* London: Routledge and Kegan Paul, 1951.

Hartwig, Joan. *Shakespeare's Analogical Scene.* Lincoln: University of Nebraska Press, 1983.

Hattaway, Michael. *Elizabethan Popular Theatre: Plays in Performance.* London: Routledge and Kegan Paul, 1982.

Hawkes, Terrence. *"Telmah."* In *Shakespeare and the Question of Theory,* edited by Patricia Parker and Geoffrey Hartman, 310–32.

———. *That Shakespeherian Rag: Essays on a Critical Process.* London: Methuen, 1986.

Heinemann, Margot. "How Brecht Read Shakespeare." In *Political Shakespeare: New Essays in Cultural Materialism,* edited by Jonathan Dollimore and Alan Sinfield, 202–30. Ithaca, N.Y.: Cornell University Press, 1985.

Helgerson, Richard. "What Hamlet Remembers." In *Shakespeare Studies,* vol. 10, edited by J. Leeds Barroll III, 67–97. New York: Burt Franklin, 1977.

Heywood, Thomas. *An Apology for Actors.* 1612.

Hirsh, James. *"Othello* and Perception." In Othello: *New Perspectives,* edited by Virginia Mason Vaughan and Kent Cartwright.

———. *The Structure of Shakespearean Scenes.* New Haven: Yale University Press, 1981.

Holloway, John. *The Story of the Night: Studies in Shakespeare's Major Tragedies.* London: Routledge and Kegan Paul, 1961.

Honigmann, E. A. J. *Shakespeare: Seven Tragedies: The Dramatist's Manipulation of Response.* London: Macmillan, 1976.

Howard, Jean E. "Crossdressing, The Theatre, and Gender Struggle in Early Modern England." *Shakespeare Quarterly* 39 (Winter 1988): 418–40.

———. *Shakespeare's Art of Orchestration: Stage Technique and Audience Response.* Urbana: University of Illinois Press, 1984.

Hosley, Richard. "The Staging of Desdemona's Bed." *Shakespeare Quarterly* 14 (Winter 1963): 57–65.

Hunt, John. "A Thing of Nothing: The Catastrophic Body in *Hamlet.*" *Shakespeare Quarterly* 39 (Spring 1988): 27–44.

Jacobi, Derek. "Hamlet." In *Shakespeare in Perspective,* vol. 1, edited by Roger Sales, 186–92. London: Ariel Books, 1982.

Jankowski, Theodora A. " 'As I Am Egypt's Queen': Cleopatra, Elizabeth I, and the Female Body Politic." In *Assays: Critical Approaches to Medieval and Renaissance Texts,* vol. 5, edited by Peggy A. Knapp, 91–110. Pittsburgh: University of Pittsburgh Press, 1989.

Jardine, Lisa. *Still Harping on Daughters: Women and Drama in the Age of Shakespeare.* Totowa, N.J.: Barnes and Noble, 1983.

Johnson, Samuel. *Johnson on Shakespeare: The Yale Edition of the Works of Samuel Johnson.* Vol. 8, edited by Arthur Sherbo. New Haven: Yale University Press, 1968.

Jones, Emrys. *Scenic Form in Shakespeare.* Oxford: Clarendon Press, 1971.

Jones, Robert C. *Engagement With Knavery: Point of View in* Richard III, The Jew of Malta, Volpone, *and* The Revenger's Tragedy. Durham, N.C.: Duke University Press, 1986.

Judges, A. V., ed. *The Elizabethan Underworld.* London: George Routledge and Sons, 1930.

Kahn, Coppélia. "Coming of Age in Verona." *Modern Language Studies* 8 (Winter 1977–78): 5–22.

Kernan, Alvin B. "Formalism and Realism in Elizabethan Drama: The Miracles of *King Lear.*" In *Renaissance Drama,* vol. 9, edited by S. Schoenbaum, 59–66. Evanston, Ill.: Northwestern University Press, 1966.

Kliman, Bernice. Hamlet: *Film, Television, and Audio Performance.* Rutherford, N.J.: Fairleigh Dickinson University Press, 1988.

Knight, G. Wilson. *The Wheel of Fire: Interpretations of Shakespearian Tragedy with Three New Essays.* 1930. Reprint. London: Methuen, 1961.

Krook, Dorothea. *Elements of Tragedy.* New Haven: Yale University Press, 1968.

Lamb, Margaret. Antony and Cleopatra *on the English Stage.* Rutherford, N.J.: Fairleigh Dickinson University Press, 1980.

Leavis, F. R. "Diabolical Intellect and the Noble Hero." In his *The Common Pursuit.* 1952. Reprint. New York: New York University Press, 1964.

Lenz, Carolyn Ruth Swift, Gayle Greene, and Carol Thomas Neely, eds. *The Women's Part: Feminist Criticism of Shakespeare.* Urbana: University of Illinois Press, 1980.

Levin, Harry. "Form and Formality in *Romeo and Juliet.*" In *Shakespeare and the Revolution of the Times.* New York: Oxford University Press, 1976.

Levin, Richard. "The Two-Audience Theory of English Renaissance Drama." In *Shakespeare Studies,* vol. 18, edited by J. Leeds Barroll, 251–75. New York: Burt Franklin, 1986.

———. "Women in the Renaissance Theatre Audience." *Shakespeare Quarterly* 40 (Summer 1989): 165–74.

Lower, Charles B. "*Romeo and Juliet,* IV.v.: A Stage Direction and Purposeful Comedy." In *Shakespeare Studies,* vol. 8, edited by J. Leeds Barroll III, 177–94. New York: Burt Franklin, 1975.

MacCallum, M. W. *Shakespeare's Roman Plays and Their Background.* London: Macmillan, 1967.

Mack, Maynard. "Engagement and Detachment in Shakespeare's Plays." In *Essays on Shakespeare and Elizabethan Drama in Honor of Hardin Craig,* edited by Richard Hosely, 275–96. Columbia: University of Missouri Press, 1962.

———. King Lear *in Our Time.* Berkeley: University of California Press, 1972.

Martin, John. *The Modern Dance.* 1933. Reprint. New York: Dance Horizons, 1965.

Mason, Edward Tuckerman. *The Othello of Tommaso Salvini.* New York: Putnam's, 1890.

Maus, Katherine Eisaman. "Horns of Dilemma: Jealousy, Gender, and Spectatorship in English Renaissance Drama." *ELH* 54 (Fall 1987): 561–83.

McElroy, Mary, and Kent Cartwright. "Public Fencing Contests on the Elizabethan Stage." *Journal of Sport History* 13 (Winter 1986): 193–211.

McFarland, Thomas. "Antony and Octavius." *Yale Review* 48 (1958): 204–28.

McGuire, Philip C. *Speechless Dialect: Shakespeare's Open Silences.* Berkeley: University of California Press, 1985.

McNeir, Waldo F., and Thelma N. Greenfield, eds. *Pacific Coast Studies in Shakespeare.* Eugene: University of Oregon Press, 1966.

Moisan, Thomas. "Rhetoric and the Rehearsal of Death: The 'Lamentations' Scene in *Romeo and Juliet.*" *Shakespeare Quarterly* 34 (Winter 1983): 389–404.

Molinari, Cesare. *Theatre Through the Ages.* Translated by Colin Hammer. London: Cassell, 1975.

Montrose, Louis A. "The Purpose of Playing: Reflections on a Shakespearean Anthropology." *Helios,* n.s. 7 (1979–80): 51–74.

Mooney, Michael E. "Location and Idiom in *Othello.*" In Othello: *New Perspectives,* edited by Virginia Mason Vaughan and Kent Cartwright.

Morrell, Roy. "The Psychology of Tragic Pleasure." *Essays in Criticism* 6 (January 1956): 22–37.

Mowat, Barbara A. *The Dramaturgy of Shakespeare's Romances.* Athens: University of Georgia Press, 1976.

Murray, Timothy. "*Othello's* Foul Generic Thoughts and Methods." In *Persons in Groups: Social Behavior as Identity Formation in Medieval and Renaissance Europe,* edited by Richard C. Trexler, 67–77. Binghamton, N.Y.: Medieval and Renaissance Texts and Studies, 1985.

Nasser, Eugene Paul. *The Rape of Cinderella: Essays in Literary Continuity.* Bloomington: Indiana University Press, 1970.

Neely, Carol Thomas. *Broken Nuptials in Shakespeare's Plays.* New Haven: Yale University Press, 1985.

Nevo, Ruth. *Tragic Form in Shakespeare.* Princeton: Princeton University Press, 1972.

Newman, Paula, and George Walton Williams. "Paris: The Mirror of Romeo." In *Renaissance Papers 1981,* edited by A. Leigh Deneef and M. Thomas Hester, 13–19. Raleigh, N.C.: Southeastern Renaissance Conference, 1982.

Novy, Marianne. *Love's Argument: Gender Relations in Shakespeare.* Chapel Hill: University of North Carolina Press, 1984.

Nungezer, Edwin. *A Dictionary of Actors and of Other Persons Associated with the Public Representation of Plays in England before 1642.* New Haven: Yale University Press, 1929.

Odell, George C. D. *Shakespeare from Betterton to Irving.* 2 vols. New York: Charles Scribner's Sons, 1920.

O'Donoghue, Edward Geoffrey. *The Story of Bethlehem Hospital: From Its Foundation in 1247.* London: T. Fisher Unwin, 1914.

Ong, Walter J. "The Writer's Audience Is Always a Fiction." *PMLA* 90 (January 1975): 9–21.

Ornstein, Robert. "The Ethic of the Imagination: Love and Art in *Antony and Cleopatra.*" In *Later Shakespeare.* Vol. 8 of *Stratford-upon-Avon Studies,* edited by John Russell Brown, 31–46. London: Edward Arnold, 1966.

——. *The Moral Vision of Jacobean Tragedy.* Madison: University of Wisconsin Press, 1965.

Parker, Patricia. "Shakespeare and Rhetoric: 'dilation' and 'delation' in *Othello.*" In *Shakespeare and the Question of Theory,* edited by Patricia Parker and Geoffrey Hartman, 54–74.

Parker, Patricia, and Geoffrey Hartman, eds. *Shakespeare and the Question of Theory.* New York: Methuen, 1985.

Pechter, Edward. "Remembering *Hamlet:* Or, How it Feels to Go like a Crab Backwards." In *Shakespeare Survey,* vol. 39, edited by Stanley Wells, 135–47. Cambridge: Cambridge University Press, 1987.

Perelman, Ch. and L. Olbrechts-Tyteca. *The New Rhetoric: A Treatise on Argumentation.* Translated by John Wilkinson and Purcell Weaver. Notre Dame, Ind.: University of Notre Dame Press, 1969.

Peterson, Douglas L. "*Romeo and Juliet* and the Art of Moral Navigation." In *Pacific Coast*

   Studies in Shakespeare, edited by Waldo F. McNeir and Thelma N. Greenfield, 33–46.
Pirie, David. "*Hamlet* without the Prince." *Critical Quarterly* 14 (Winter 1972): 293–314. Reprint. *Shakespeare's Wide and Universal Stage,* edited by C. B. Cox and D. J. Palmer, 164–84. Manchester: Manchester University Press, 1984.
Porter, Joseph A. *Shakespeare's Mercutio: His History and Drama.* Chapel Hill: University of North Carolina Press, 1988.
Pound, John. *Poverty and Vagrancy in Tudor England.* London: Longman, 1971.
Rabkin, Norman. *Shakespeare and the Common Understanding.* Chicago: University of Chicago Press, 1967.
———, ed. *Reinterpretations of Elizabethan Drama: Selected Papers from the English Institute.* New York: Columbia University Press, 1969.
Rainolds, John. *The Overthrow of Stage-plays.* 1599. Reprint. New York: Johnson Reprint, 1972.
Reed, Robert Rentoul, Jr. *Bedlam on the Jacobean Stage.* Cambridge: Harvard University Press, 1952.
Ribner, Irving. *Patterns in Shakespearean Tragedy.* 1960. Reprint. London: Methuen, 1971.
Richman, David. "The *King Lear* Quarto In Rehearsal and Performance." *Shakespeare Quarterly* 37 (Autumn 1986): 374–82.
Rose, Mark. *Shakespearean Design.* Cambridge: Belknap Press of Harvard University Press, 1972.
Rose, Mark, ed. *Twentieth Century Interpretations of* Antony and Cleopatra: *A Collection of Critical Essays.* Englewood Cliffs, N.J.: Prentice-Hall, 1977.
Rosenberg, Marvin. *The Masks of* King Lear. Berkeley: University of California Press, 1972.
Rozett, Martha Tuck. "The Comic Structures of Tragic Endings: The Suicide Scenes in *Romeo and Juliet* and *Antony and Cleopatra.*" *Shakespeare Quarterly* 36 (Summer 1985): 152–64.
———. *The Doctrine of Election and the Emergence of Elizabethan Tragedy.* Princeton: Princeton University Press, 1984.
Rymer, Thomas. *A Short View of Tragedy.* 1693. Reprint. *The Critical Works of Thomas Rymer,* edited by Curt Zimansky, 132–64. New Haven: Yale University Press, 1956.
Salgado, Gamini. *Eyewitnesses to Shakespeare: First Hand Accounts of Performance 1590–1890.* London: Sussex University Press, 1975.
Saviolo, Vincentio. *Vincentio Saviolo His Practise.* 1595.
Schanzer, Ernest. *The Problem Plays of Shakespeare: A Study of* Julius Caesar, Measure for Measure, Antony and Cleopatra. London: Routledge and Kegan Paul. 1963.
Schmitt, Natalie Crohn. "John Cage, Nature, and Theater." In *A John Cage Reader,* edited by Peter Gena and Jonathan Brent, 17–37. New York: C. F. Peters, 1987.
Segar, Sir William. *The Booke of Honor and Armes.* 1590.
Seltzer, Daniel. "The Actors and Staging." In *A New Companion to Shakespeare Studies,* edited by Kenneth Muir and S. Schoenbaum, 35–54. Cambridge: Cambridge University Press, 1971.
———. "Elizabethan Acting in *Othello.*" *Shakespeare Quarterly* 10 (Spring 1959): 201–10.
Serpieri, Alessandro. "Reading the Signs: Towards a Semiotics of Shakespearean Drama." Translated by Kier Elam. In *Alternative Shakespeares,* edited by John Drakakis, 119–43. London: Methuen, 1985.
Shakespeare, William. *Hamlet.* Edited by Philip Edwards. Cambridge: Cambridge University Press, 1985.
———. *Hamlet.* Edited by Harold Jenkins. London: Methuen, 1982.

——. *King Lear.* Edited by Russell Fraser. New York: New American Library, 1963.

——. *The Most Excellent and Lamentable Tragedie of Romeo and Juliet: A Critical Edition.* Edited by George Walton Williams. Durham, N.C.: Duke University Press, 1964.

——. *A New Variorum Edition of Shakespeare.* Vol. 3, *Hamlet.* Vol. 1, *Text,* edited by Horace Howard Furness. London: J. B. Lippincott, 1877.

——. *Othello.* Film. Directed by Stuart Burge, starring Laurence Olivier, Maggie Smith, and Frank Finlay. Britain: B.H.E., 1965.

——. *Othello.* Edited by Alvin Kernan. 1963. Reprint. New York: New American Library, 1987.

——. *Othello.* Edited by M. R. Ridley. London: Methuen, 1958.

——. *Othello.* Edited by Norman Sanders. Cambridge: Cambridge University Press, 1984.

——. *The Riverside Shakespeare.* Edited by G. Blakemore Evans. Boston: Houghton Mifflin, 1974.

——. *Romeo and Juliet.* Edited by G. Blakemore Evans. New York: Cambridge University Press, 1984.

——. *Romeo and Juliet.* Edited by Brian Gibbons. New York: Methuen, 1980.

——. *Shakespeare's Plays in Quarto: A Facsimile Edition of Copies Primarily from the Henry E. Huntington Library.* Edited by Michael J. B. Allen and Kenneth Muir. Berkeley: University of California Press, 1981.

——. *William Shakespeare: The Complete King Lear, Texts and Parallel Texts in Photographic Facsimile.* Prepared by Michael Warren. Berkeley: University of California Press, 1989.

——. *William Shakespeare: The Complete Works.* General editors, Stanley Wells and Gary Taylor. Oxford: Clarendon Press, 1986.

Shank, Theodore. *American Alternative Theater.* New York: Grove, 1982.

Shapiro, Michael. "Boying Her Greatness: Shakespeare's Use of Coterie Drama in *Antony and Cleopatra.*" *Modern Language Review* 77 (January 1982): 1–15.

——. "Role-Playing, Reflexivity, and Metadrama in Recent Shakespearean Criticism." In *Renaissance Drama,* n.s. 12, edited by Alan C. Dessen, 145–61. Evanston, Ill.: Northwestern University Press, 1981.

Sidney, Sir Philip. *An Apology for Poetry.* Edited by Forrest G. Robinson. Indianapolis, Ind.: Bobbs-Merrill, 1970.

Siemon, James R. "'Nay, that's not next': *Othello,* V.ii in Performance, 1760–1900." *Shakespeare Quarterly* 37 (Spring 1986): 38–51.

Silver, George. *Paradoxes of Defence.* 1599.

Smith, Bruce R. *Ancient Scripts and Modern Experience on the English Stage: 1500–1700.* Princeton: Princeton University Press, 1988.

Snow, Edward. "Language and Sexual Difference in *Romeo and Juliet.*" In *Shakespeare's "Rough Magic": Renaissance Essays in Honor of C. L. Barber,* edited by Peter Erickson and Coppélia Kahn, 168–92. Newark: University of Delaware Press, 1985.

Snyder, Susan. *The Comic Matrix of Shakespeare's Tragedies.* Princeton: Princeton University Press, 1979.

Soens, Adolph L. "Tybalt's Spanish Fencing in *Romeo and Juliet.*" *Shakespeare Quarterly* 20 (Spring 1969): 121–27.

Speaight, Robert. *Shakespeare on the Stage: An Illustrated History of Shakespearean Performance.* London: William Collins, 1973.

Sprague, Arthur Colby. *Shakespeare and the Actors: The Stage Business of His Plays (1660–1905).* Cambridge: Harvard University Press, 1945.

——. *Shakespearian Players and Performances.* Cambridge: Harvard University Press, 1953.

States, Bert O. *Great Reckonings in Little Rooms: On the Phenomenology of Theater.* Berkeley: University of California Press, 1985.

Stewart, Stanley. "Romeo and Necessity." In *Pacific Coast Studies in Shakespeare,* edited by Waldo F. McNeir and Thelma N. Greenfield, 47–67.

Stoll, Elmer Edgar. *Art and Artifice in Shakespeare: A Study in Dramatic Contrast and Illusion.* Cambridge: Cambridge University Press, 1933.

Stone, Lawrence. *The Crisis of the Aristocracy: 1558–1641.* Abridged Edition. Oxford: Oxford University Press, 1967.

Styan, John. *Drama, Stage and Audience.* Cambridge: University of Cambridge Press, 1975.

Sutherland, James. "How Characters Talk." In *Shakespeare's World,* edited by James Sutherland and Joel Hurstfield, 116–35. New York: St. Martin's, 1964.

Taylor, Gary. *Reinventing Shakespeare: A Cultural History from the Restoration to the Present.* New York: Weidenfeld and Nicolson, 1989.

———. *To Analyze Delight: A Hedonist Criticism of Shakespeare.* Newark: University of Delaware Press, 1985.

———, and Michael Warren, eds. *The Division of the Kingdoms: Shakespeare's Two Versions of* King Lear. Oxford: Clarendon, 1983.

Traci, Philip J. *The Love Play of Antony and Cleopatra: A Critical Study of Shakespeare's Play.* The Hague: Mouton, 1970.

Turner, Victor. *From Ritual to Theatre: The Human Seriousness of Play.* New York: Performing Arts Journal Publications, 1982.

Urkowitz, Steven. *Shakespeare's Revision of* King Lear. Princeton: Princeton University Press, 1980.

Van Laan, Thomas F. *Role-playing in Shakespeare.* Toronto: University of Toronto Press, 1978.

Vaughan, Virginia Mason, and Kent Cartwright. Othello: *New Perspectives.* Rutherford, N.J.: Fairleigh Dickinson University Press, 1991.

Verhoeven, Cornelis. *The Philosophy of Wonder.* 1967. Translated by Mary Foran. New York: Macmillan, 1972.

Warren, Michael. "The Diminution of Kent." In *The Division of the Kingdoms: Shakespeare's Two Versions of* King Lear, edited by Gary Taylor and Michael Warren, 59–73.

———. "Quarto and Folio *King Lear* and the Interpretation of Albany and Edgar." In *Shakespeare: Pattern of Excelling Nature,* edited by David Bevington and Jay L. Halio, 95–107. Newark: University of Delaware Press, 1978.

Weimann, Robert. *Shakespeare and the Popular Tradition of the Theater: Studies in the Social Dimension of Dramatic Form and Function.* Edited by Robert Schwartz. Baltimore, Md.: Johns Hopkins University Press, 1978.

Whitaker, Virgil K. *The Mirror Up to Nature.* San Marino, Calif.: Huntington Library, 1965.

Wickham, Glynne. *A History of the Theatre.* Cambridge: Cambridge University Press, 1985.

Williamson, Marilyn L. "Romeo and Death." In *Shakespeare Studies,* vol. 14, edited by J. Leeds Barroll, 129–37. New York: Burt Franklin, 1981.

Wilshire, Bruce. *Role Playing and Identity: The Limits of Theatre as a Metaphor.* Bloomington: Indiana University Press, 1982.

Wine, Martin L. Othello: *Text and Performance.* London: Macmillan, 1984.

Worthen, W. B. "The Weight of Antony: Staging 'Character' in *Antony and Cleopatra.*" *Studies in English Literature 1500–1900* 26 (Spring 1986): 295–308.

Index